F. C. Armstrong

**The Cruise of the Daring**

A Tale of the Sea

F. C. Armstrong

**The Cruise of the Daring**
*A Tale of the Sea*

ISBN/EAN: 9783337122140

Printed in Europe, USA, Canada, Australia, Japan

Cover: Foto ©ninafisch / pixelio.de

More available books at **www.hansebooks.com**

# THE
# CRUISE OF THE DARING.

A Tale of the Sea.

BY

CAPTAIN C. F. ARMSTRONG,

AUTHOR OF "FRIGATE AND LUGGER," "THE TWO MIDSHIPMEN,"
"THE WARHAWK," "THE YOUNG COMMANDER," &C., &C.

LONDON:
WARD, LOCK AND TYLER,
WARWICK HOUSE, PATERNOSTER ROW.

# THE CRUISE OF THE DARING.

## CHAPTER I.

ABOUT four-and-twenty miles from Waterford, stood, in the year 179—, scattered over half a square mile, in anything but picturesque confusion, the insignificant and little frequented town of Dungarvon, consisting of a number of small houses, small tenements, and innumerable mud hovels.

There is an old saying in those parts of Ireland, when anything unusual is likely to occur, "Oh, it will make jolly Dungarvon shake;" but we presume nothing unusual did happen at the period of our story, or jolly Dungarvon would have shaken itself into ship-shape, or some other kind of shape, and thereby improved its appearance.

Within a mile or so of this said town, and close to the sea-beach, was a remarkably pretty cottage, its front facing a white estuary of the sea, protected from the waves by a long spit of land or barrow. At high tide this estuary resembled a beautiful lake; but at low water it was a vast bed of slime and mud, neither picturesque, nor very pleasant to the olfactory nerves. The view was bounded by a range of high hills to the south and west, while the open sea lay to the southward and eastward. The cottage had a large garden at the back, enclosed by high stone walls, and the scenery without the walls was rather pretty than otherwise. This cottage had one very great advantage: there was neither cabin nor hovel nearer to it than the town.

In this pleasant residence, consisting of eight rooms—comfortably, if not elegantly, furnished—lived a gentleman named De Burgh, a widower, and his only son, four years of age; one female, of about two or three-and-thirty years of age, very honest, very thrifty, but rather deaf, who acted in the capacity of housekeeper, cook, and housemaid; these were the only inmates, if we except divers persons hired at times for gardening and other purposes.

Mr. De Burgh was a remarkably fine and handsome man, and at the period of his selecting Dungarvon as a residence, was not more than two-and-thirty years of age. Though his manner was reserved and stately, and his features always bore a sad and serious expression, his liberality to all he employed, and his exceeding kindness to the poor or indigent—and they abounded in jolly Dungarvon—made him much loved and respected; he received no visitors, except at rare intervals, when he conversed for an hour or so with either the curate or the parish priest.

His selection of this retired residence, in so remote and thinly populated a town, with scarcely a resident gentleman in the immediate vicinity; his retired mode of life, and his serious, sad, but very handsome features, created, as usual, a considerable amount of guesses and surmises as to whom he could be; and why so handsome a gentleman, and one so young in years, should bury himself even in "jolly Dungarvon."

There are gossips everywhere, and why should there not be some in Dungarvon? But all their thoughts, guesses, and inuendos were mere "bosh," for they came to no other conclusion than that it was very strange, very extraordinary, and there must be a reason for it—who knows, and so forth. After a time, the gossipping died a natural death, and Mr. De Burgh lived in peace.

His little boy's name was Francis; every one that saw admired him, for he was in truth a most lovely child, and his father seemed to idolize him. The boy grew rapidly, and at seven years old was a remarkably fine, intelligent little fellow; but so fond of the sea, boats, &c., that he kept both his father and their attendant, Jane, in continual hot water, and oftentimes salt water, watching him.

Dungarvon at that period possessed a great number of fishing hookers, remarkably fine boats, ranging from ten to twenty tons burden; their crews were hardy, venturesome seamen—pilots when wanted—would face any weather, but, like most sailors, singularly superstitious.

The entrance to Dungarvon harbour, which is only a natural one, is up a long, tortuous channel, with sand banks, and shoals, and rocks intersecting it, requiring skill and seamanship to bring a boat or vessel safely up to the town. At the time of our story there was a ford across the river, which divided the town into two unequal parts, over which there is now a stone bridge. The river was shallow, except during floods and high tides, and emptied itself into the sea, running past Mr. De Burgh's cottage. It was customary with the pilot boats and fishing hookers to anchor opposite the cottage, to wait for tide, and sometimes to land their fish.

Francis De Burgh was well-known to all the fishermen, for he delighted in getting into their punts, to rock himself about in them, whenever he could escape from the vigilance of Jane.

Mr. De Burgh possessed a fine and rather large library, purchased in London, and forwarded in boxes to Dungarvon. He passed most of his time reading, and instructing his son; he spoke several languages, and was well learned in navigation. His only recreation was either working in the garden, of which exercise he seemed fond, or walking out with his little boy.

One morning young Francis was in the front of the cottage, when a fine hooker anchored before it, and the crew came ashore in the punt, and walked up to the town, leaving their boat on the beach, held by a small grapnel. Francis got into the boat, and pushed out the length of the rope with a boot-hook, to amuse himself rocking her; but, from carelessness, the rope was ill-fastened, and slipped through the ring, and the boat, caught by the strong tide, drifted rapidly out. Frank, not at all frightened, tried to lift one of the oars to scull back; but being too heavy for him, it slipped out of his hand, and making a grasp at it, he overbalanced himself, and fell over the side.

Completely bewildered by this sudden immersion, he sunk, but coming up, and being a stout-hearted boy, he made a vigorous attempt to keep himself up. When nearly exhausted, he suddenly felt himself grasped by the collar, and heard a voice say, "Don't be frightened, and don't catch hold of I, and I'll take 'ce ashore;" and accordingly ashore the bold swimmer took him, just as Mr. De Burgh—without a coat, for he had been working in the garden at the time of the accident—and Jane, both alarmed by the screams of some fisherwomen who beheld the accident, rushed to the water's edge.

The youth who had saved Francis was a stout, open-featured, fine lad, not more than four years older than the little boy.

"You are a brave lad," said Mr. De Burgh to Francis's preserver, taking up his son in his arms, and telling the boy to follow him into the cottage.

"Faix, your honour," replied the lad, "I must cotch the boat, or father will be mad."

And quite coolly he jumped into the water, feeling as comfortable in the said element as a Newfoundland dog, and swam after the boat, scrambled in, and then sculled after the oar which had caused the accident, and having picked it up, returned on board the hooker.

Young De Burgh took the matter quite as coolly as his preserver, told his father he must let Bill Mullaghan—the name of the lad, he knew him very well, as Bill had often rowed him out about the lake, while keeping watch over the hooker—he must let Bill Mullaghan teach him to swim.

Mr. De Burgh with great difficulty prevailed upon Bill to take even a couple of guineas for a reward; but he eagerly accepted the office of swimming tutor to Master Frank, always at first under the eyes of his father, who took a great fancy to Bill, and taught him to read and write, and some useful knowledge besides.

Old Bill Mullaghan, the father, was a man tolerably well-to-do in the world; he owned the pilot boat, the St. Patrick, the finest hooker in the port. He had two sons, so Bill was often spared to boat and play with Master Frank, to whom he became most singularly and firmly devoted, When Francis De Burgh reached his sixteenth year, and Bill his twentieth, they became noted for their daring exploits in boats. They often took the hooker out by themselves, and performed several singular achievements in boarding ships, and piloting them in under the Helwick Head.

Notwithstanding these exploits, and destroying large numbers of wild ducks, Francis De Burgh devoted many hours of the day to study. His father, like the admirable Crichton, seemed to excel in all accomplishments. At sixteen, Frank spoke French and Italian fluently, studied hard at Latin and Greek, could fence exceedingly well, and had a singularly correct ear for music; and before he was eighteen, became well grounded in navigation, &c., &c.

Frank idolized his father, whose health seemed considerably impaired of late; he suffered, without complaining, a disease of the heart, but did not consider it dangerous. At that period this disease was not much understood.

Francis thought his father intended him for the sea, and being passionately fond of the water he would gladly have become a midshipman; he could reef, steer, splice a rope, or serve a block with any man in or out of Dungarvon; knew the dangers of the harbour, and the bay without, as well as the oldest pilot, and such confidence had the men in his courage, skill, and good fortune, that they would go to sea with him, no matter what the weather, provided he expressed a wish to go. As to Bill Mullaghan he swore there was not such another youth from Waterford to Cape Clear, the only two extremities of his native land that Bill was acquainted with.

And Francis De Burgh merited Bill's encomiums, for at the age of twenty it was impossible to behold a finer or more athletic youth, full six feet in height, uniting id his person a singular and natural gracefulness, with great muscular strength. His features were extremely pleasing and fascinating in their bland expression; to so pleasing an exterior he added a bold, high-spirited temper, excessive good nature, and a most prepossessing frankness.

Bill Mullaghan had grown into a fine muscular man, with a fist capable of felling an ox, an open cheerful face and an inexhaustible stock of good humour. In his own mind he was fully determimed to follow his young master to the end of the world, but where that was Bill did not inquire; he always declared he would go whenever Master Francis should leave Dungarvon.

At twenty years of age young De Burgh thought it was time that he should see a little more of the world than Dungarvon, Waterford, and the wild sea coast east and west of them. His father's library afforded him works relating to all parts of the world, and being fond of reading, of a social and cheerful nature, the uncommon retirement in which his father lived, was in fact becoming too serious a trial for so young and high spirited a youth.

Latterly Mr. De Burgh went oftener to Waterford, and generally remained absent three or four days; once he was actually a week away, and young De Burgh became alarmed, though his father always told him not to be under any apprehension should he be detained longer than he anticipated.

Francis had never heard his father mention his mother. There were neither portraits nor pictures in the cottage; the only remarkable article of furniture was a very beautifully inlaid cabinet, about three feet high and two broad. This stood in his father's bedroom. Latterly his father wrote much, and always locked up what he wrote in this cabinet, as well as all the letters he received. Francis was neither of a curious nor prying disposition; he would not for worlds let his beloved father suppose that he wished to inquire into any circumstances that his parent did not think fit to make him acquainted with. Such, then, was the posture of affairs in the month of January, in the year 1798.

We have not remarked upon the unhappy state of Ireland at this memorable period, because we do not intend to meddle or express our opinion upon the political, religious, or social state of the Emerald Isle, then on the eve of a great rebellion; we intend simply to state events as they became connected with the future fate of our hero; therefore our readers will not be detained by observations, remarks, or opinions upon the many parties that troubled unhappy Ireland at that most miserable period. As yet Dungarvon remained tolerably tranquil, though the surrounding country was considerably disturbed. Just at this time an event occurred that eventually turned the current of our hero's life into another and widely different channel.

## CHAPTER II.

WE have remarked in our preceding pages that the fishing population of Dungarvon, as indeed that of any other fishing town in Ireland, was remarkably superstitious, and singularly given to regarding omens, some of them highly ludicrous. On no account, if it were possible to avoid it, would the men go to sea to fish or pilot on a Friday. If on their way to their boats their path was crossed by an old woman or a pig, they would either make a circuit of a mile or stay at home. Two straws crossed lying in their way was awful. There were numerous other omens to be regarded, but these are sufficient for our purpose. Oftentimes the bay swarmed with herrings or mackerel, but from having encountered one or other of these signs, the fish were left to take their departure. The case is something altered now in Ireland, but we speak of sixty years ago—a long time in this galloping and scientific age.

Within half a mile of Mr. De Burgh's cottage was the residence of the parish priest, Father O'Flagherty; a merry, good-hearted and attentive pastor was the priest: he looked after not only the souls of his numerous and indigent parishioners, but attended to their worldly welfare. Father O'Flagherty was not one of those worthy fathers who kept a brace of greyhounds and a very smart niece to look after their establishment. His housekeeper was an ancient dame, and the only quadrupeds belonging to his establishment were a well-fed pony and a remarkably sagacious tom cat.

Nothing annoyed the priest more than to see the crews of the fishing boats staying at home, and the bay full of herrings. In vain their pastor lectured them, told them they were a parcel of "omadawns."

All the answer he could get was—

"True for you, Father, so we are; but it's unlucky to go out on a Friday, and faix I myself," said a huge broad-shouldered pilot, "met this morning ould Nancy Sticks and her pig, right in my path, and, be gorree, the next moment the wind blowed one straw right over another making a big cross. Sure, your reverence, after that, and the wind howling like a wild baste, who'd go out?"

"You're a disgrace to your sex, Tom Murphy," angrily

exclaimed the priest, "the Almighty sends you plenty of fish, right before your noses, and because a harmless old woman and a pig—oh, my conscience! You'd eat the pig fast enough if it was salted and hanging up in your cabins."

"Oh, by the powers, your reverence," exclaimed many of the group the priest was talking to, "it wouldn't be a pig then, it would be bacon; and for the matter of that, faix, it's not very often the likes of us gets bacon."

"Ye don't deserve it, ye pack of idle hulks; but I'll manage you next Easter; wait, a bit, since you won't get me a dish of good fresh herrings when they are just ready to jump into the frying pan for the asking. I'll know how to manage ye."

This little scene happened after coming out of chapel one Friday morning. It had blown hard the previous three or four days, and none of the boats had put to sea. Bill Mullaghan, who was much less given to minding omens, thanks to Mr. De Burgh's instructions in his boyhood, said to three or four of his comrades, as they sauntered idly down to the beach—

"Be gor, I have a great mind to go out with the hooker for a run as far as Helwick Head. Mister Frank wanted sadly this morning to have a cruise."

"Be jabers, I don't care if I go!" said one of the best hands, which was responded to by two others, "if Master Francis will go. We won't take our nets, but we can stand off, and see if any ships want pilots."

Mr. De Burgh was accustomed to witness his son take those trips in the hooker, and as Francis had studied hard the last week, and had but little exercise, he made no other remark than telling him to take a couple of bottles of wine with him, and some cold provisions, as it would be impossible to return with that night's tide.

Mr. De Burgh was very busy writing, so Francis filling a basket gave it to Bill to carry aboard, and half an hour after the St. Patrick was standing out with a stiff breeze from the southward and westward to the great surprise of some of the old hands, who shook their heads, predicting that no good could come of a cruise on such a day, and after so many bad omens.

"But Mister Francis is a Protestant," said one, "and more's the pity; he laughs at us, but it's good humouredly. Tare-and-'ouns, after all, he's as fine a lad as any in ould Ireland."

The channel out from Dungarvon into the open waters of the bay is an extremely intricate one, and can only be attempted by vessels with a leading wind, a good pilot, and three quarters flood. About three miles out is a safe anchorage called the Pool, where vessels may lie afloat, protected from the surges by the land to the northward and east, and the Deadman Sands to the south-west. Two miles further lies the reef of the Helwick, a long range of rocks, lying off Prehan point, with a passage, but a dangerous one, between the reef and the land, while to the westward lies the bold headland called Helwick Head. Under this Head large ships, if piloted in, may lie in safety in storms, from the nor'-west to sou'-sou'-west. A gale from the east or south-east, would be sure to drive any vessel at anchor under the Head ashore.

Francis De Burgh, as he steered through the intricate channel, observed to Bill Mullaghan that it looked very like a return of the old gale from the southward and eastward. It was so thick and hazy seaward, and the ground-swell ran in, breaking on the Helwick sands with tremendous violence.

"Faix, there's no doubt in the world of it," said Bill, "my ould father said as much this morning, and that he would not wonder but we would fall in with some of the homeward bound Liverpool ships; it has been so thick this week back. Let us stretch well out on the next tack, Mister Frank; be gor, now we open the sea, clear of the Head, we begin to feel the chop. There's been a very heavy gale to the southward which does not always blow home in our bay."

The St. Patrick was a remarkably fine boat, of some nineteen or twenty tons burden, cutter rigged, and with a very comfortable forecastle, fitted with a brass stove, a present to old Mullaghan from Mr. De Burgh. It was now necessary to take in a couple of reefs, both wind and sea increasing rapidly. Still the hooker stood seaward, the crew keeping a keen look out, at least as far around them as they could, for the weather was exceedingly thick and foggy, though blowing hard.

"Did you set the Head, Master Frank?" observed one of the men, an old man-of-war's man, "it's getting so dirty; we shall have a job making it out."

"All right," returned Frank. "I think we may stand in again; it's impossible to make any vessel out a quarter of a mile distant. If any large vessel was near the coast, and tried her soundings, she would fire a gun for a pilot, so let us stand in, and come to under the Head."

"Faix, if there's a vessel within a league of the land she will be sucked into Tramore Bay. Do you remember last winter the 'John Browne.' The captain abused us for offering our services, said we were a pack of sharks! but, be gor! she left her ribs to bleach in the sun on Tramore Sands for all that."

As the hooker ran in for the Head it grew rapidly dark, having every appearance of a tremendous night; thick drizzling rain and sleet, and the gusts heavy and frequent, and occasionally shifting a point or so.

But the St. Patrick was run in safely, and rounding the Head, stood into water as smooth as a mill-pond, though the squalls roared over the Head and over them like thunder. Though completely sheltered where they lay they were not more than a mile from the Helwick Sands, upon which the sea broke with a tremendous din. Having secured the hooker, and fastened everything that the storm was likely to make free with, Francis De Burgh and his four comrades entered the forecastle, and lighting their lamp, stirred up the fire in the stove, and taking out the cold provisions and the rum, made themselves as comfortable as possible, little heeding the roaring of the gale overhead, or the thunder of the surf under their lee.

We have said that one of the crew of the St. Patrick was an old man-of-war's man; he was a native of Dungarvon, by name Edward Maloney. Ned, as he was always styled, was a hale old fellow of sixty-four; thirty of the sixty-four years had been passed in a man-of-war, but getting a severe wound, he had retired on a pension, and returned to his native town; but recovering tolerably well—limping a little it is true—though otherwise quite hearty, he took to fishing and piloting. Ned was a favourite, for he could spin no end of yarns, scenes of his past life. A glass of grog would set him off, till there was no stopping him.

Francis, being seated in the place of honour, served out the rum. He loved this wild life; it was a kind of excitement breaking in upon the solitary and sedentary life he at other times led.

"This is just the kind of night, Ned, for a good tough yarn," said Francis, who was very partial to Maloney's stories. "Let us have one now."

"Aigh, aigh, Master Francis," returned the old salt, smacking his lips after a stiff horn of grog, "I'll spin you a yarn about a Friday, as this is a Friday, and we old sailors still stick to it, that it's better to remain at anchor on a Friday than make sail. Let you say what you will, Mister Francis, though for the matter of that every man has a right to please himself as far as thinking goes. Our good priest, though, pitches it into us rather roughly at times, as well as your honour, and says God made all the days of the week, and therefore Friday is as good a day as any other. I don't say nothing whatsumdever against that, but howsumdever I can't help saying Friday's Friday."

"That is quite true, Ned," returned our hero, "but freshen your nip, as you say, and let us hear what happened to you on a Friday."

"Thunder and turf, Mister Francis! Plenty of things happened to me on a Friday. I chalked 'em all down. First, I was pressed on a Friday, and just as I was going to get spliced to as neat and tidy a craft as ever went in stays, or put one leg before the other. On a Friday I was hit in the hip, and, be the powers, I was discharged from the sarvice on a Friday, and when I got back to ould Dungarvon I axed after my little Judy. Be gor! she was spliced to Jem Collins, the carpenter, and was the mother of nine children. Well, I had the curiosity to go see on what day she was spliced, and, be the powers, it was on a Friday."

"Be jabers, Ned! that was a lucky Friday for you," said Bill Mullaghan, laughing, "for poor Jem Collins swears he darn't call his life his own. Your little Judy bates him to shavings with his own chips."

"Sarve him right," returned old Ned, laughing, "he shouldn't have got spliced on a Friday."

"Well, at all events, Ned," said Bill, "you escaped being the father of nine children."

"Be gorra, there's something in that," muttered Ned, "but here goes for my yarn; a tough one it is, but you must know it's a true one, tough as it is."

But Ned was not destined to spin his yarn that night, at all events, as our readers will discover in our next chapter.

## CHAPTER III.

Ned Maloney, after taking another stiff horn of grog, had made sundry preparations for commencing his story, and his auditors (notwithstanding the roaring of the gusts as they swept down the cliffs, and whirled over the little hooker, making her reel under their power) settled themselves comfortably to hear him, when the loud boom of a heavy gun from seaward caused all assembled in the cuddy to spring to their feet with an exclamation of "A ship's gun, and close in shore by the sound!" As they stood for an instant irresolute, a second and even louder report followed, and then every one, without a word, hurried upon deck.

Our hero, as he gained the fore deck of the hooker, gazed eagerly seaward. The night was not perhaps quite so dark as it it had been; but the wind blew tremendously, and right into Dungarvon Bay. It was, however, too dark to enable him to see far to seaward, and the Head blocked the view; so turning to the men, he said:

"Well, my lads, what do you say? Shall we up anchor and stand out clear of the Head? No doubt there is some large craft too close in with the land. We may be able to save life."

"Aigh, aigh, sir," cheerfully exclaimed the men, "we are always ready to risk ours."

And away flew the hardy crew to close reef their mainsail, run in their short bowsprit, and make the hooker as snug as possible to encounter such a gale as was then blowing. It requires but a spark to kindle a flame. In fifteen minutes the anchor was up, and the St. Patrick standing out into the storm-tossed sea, with young De Burgh at the helm, feeling as confident in her powers of endurance as the captain of a three-decker would, walking the quarter-deck of his magnificent ship.

It certainly required stout hearts to stand out from the shelter of the Head on such a night, and in so small a craft as the little hooker. Without the Head, the sea was in a sheet of foam, as the wild gusts tore the tops from the seas, and hurled them, as if in mockery, over the deck of the St. Patrick, drenching her hardy crew to the skin. Just as they cleared the Head, which required great skill and nerve, for the breaking seas rolled in extremely heavy as they felt the land, a bright flash was seen seaward. Then came the loud boom of the gun over the troubled sea.

nine children. Well, I had the curiosity to go see on what day she was spliced, and, be the powers, it was on a Friday."

"Be jabers, Ned! that was a lucky Friday for you," said Bill Mullaghan, laughing, "for poor Jem Collins swears he darn't call his life his own. Your little Judy bates him to shavings with his own chips."

"Sarve him right," returned old Ned, laughing, "he shouldn't have got spliced on a Friday."

"Well, at all events, Ned," said Bill, "you escaped being the father of nine children."

"Be gorra, there's something in that," muttered Ned, "but here goes for my yarn; a tough one it is, but you must know it's a true one, tough as it is."

But Ned was not destined to spin his yarn that night, at all events, as our readers will discover in our next chapter.

## CHAPTER III.

Ned Maloney, after taking another stiff horn of grog, had made sundry preparations for commencing his story, and his auditors (notwithstanding the roaring of the gusts as they swept down the cliffs, and whirled over the little hooker, making her reel under their power) settled themselves comfortably to hear him, when the loud boom of a heavy gun from seaward caused all assembled in the cuddy to spring to their feet with an exclamation of "A ship's gun, and close in shore by the sound!" As they stood for an instant irresolute, a second and even louder report followed, and then every one, without a word, hurried upon deck.

Our hero, as he gained the fore deck of the hooker, gazed eagerly seaward. The night was not perhaps quite so dark as it had been; but the wind blew tremendously, and right into Dungarvon Bay. It was, however, too dark to enable him to see far to seaward, and the Head blocked the view; so turning to the men, he said:

"Well, my lads, what do you say? Shall we up anchor and stand out clear of the Head? No doubt there is some large craft too close in with the land. We may be able to save life."

"Aigh, aigh, sir," cheerfully exclaimed the men, "we are always ready to risk ours."

And away flew the hardy crew to close reef their mainsail, run in their short bowsprit, and make the hooker as snug as possible to encounter such a gale as was then blowing. It requires but a spark to kindle a flame. In fifteen minutes the anchor was up, and the St. Patrick standing out into the storm-tossed sea, with young De Burgh at the helm, feeling as confident in her powers of endurance as the captain of a three-decker would, walking the quarter-deck of his magnificent ship.

It certainly required stout hearts to stand out from the shelter of the Head on such a night, and in so small a craft as the little hooker. Without the Head, the sea was in a sheet of foam, as the wild gusts tore the tops from the seas, and hurled them, as if in mockery, over the deck of the St. Patrick, drenching her hardy crew to the skin. Just as they cleared the Head, which required great skill and nerve, for the breaking seas rolled in extremely heavy as they felt the land, a bright flash was seen seaward. Then came the loud boom of the gun over the troubled sea.

"Keep her away! keep her away, Master Francis!" exclaimed Bill. "Hard a-starboard! I can make her out."

As Bill spoke, a brilliant blue flame burst into a volume, and then they beheld, not a mile from them, a very large ship, with her foremast gone, but still carrying canvas on her main and mizen, and evidently making vain efforts to keep off shore. Young De Burgh gazed anxiously at the ship, and ran over in his active mind her small chance of safety in the perilous position she was placed in. In half-an-hour she would be on the Helwick reefs, for weather them without her foremast she could not.

"Be the immortals, Mister Frank," said Bill, "she'll be in splinters on the reef if we don't get close to her, and then what can she do without head sail?"

"Burn a pitch torch, Bill," said Francis, altering the course of the hooker so as to pass close under her stern.

The pitch torch threw a wild bright glare over the foaming waters, into which the boat plunged at times fearfully, trembling from stem to stern as she rose upon the following sea, and casting the spray over her like a snow-drift. The crew felt the utmost confidence in their young helmsman. With him it was a passion; his heart beat, not for himself or his companions, for on that subject he bestowed not a thought; but the noble disabled ship before him—doubtless containing many human beings trembling at their fearful position—occupied and absorbed all his thoughts as to how to rescue her from the terrible doom menacing her.

"Stand by, my lads," shouted Francis, as they rapidly neared the ship; the crew evidently perceiving them, kept burning blue lights, by the glare of which numerous faces could be seen gazing over her lofty bulwarks.

"Steady men, steady!" exclaimed the clear voice of Francis; "they will heave a rope. Make it fast round your waist, Bill, and get on board. Let them up helm, and follow us under the Head. She can bring up in four-fathom dead low water; it's her only chance. See, we are within half-a-mile of the reef."

They were now close by the ship, which was over one thousand tons. She rolled heavily, and made tremendous leeway.

"Stand by with a rope!" shouted the trumpet voice of Bill Mullaghan.

A cheer pealed over the broken surges from the eager crew of the ship.

The next moment a coil of rope flew over the hooker. Whether from haste, over eagerness, or the rapid movement of both ship and hooker, the crew of the latter, as each grasped at the rope, missed it. The rope was rapidly vanishing, when, as it whirled by Francis De Burgh, he seized it. The next moment he was overboard, struggling in the furious surges! It was but for a moment, for the crew of the ship hauled him rapidly and cautiously up over the side. The moment he gained his feet, Francis gave himself a shake, and cast off the rope.

"You are a gallant fellow!" exclaimed a stout, well-built man, with a speaking trumpet in his hand, addressing our hero.

Numbers gathered round, holding lanterns; but pushing his way through the press, Francis De Burgh ran towards the wheel.

"Where are we? For God's sake be quick, my lad, let us know," exclaimed the stout man, following.

"In five minutes you will be on the Helwick reef," exclaimed De Burgh, seizing the spokes of the wheel, and in a clear, steady voice saying, "brail or furl your after sail, and square your yards, so that we may follow the boat before you. I will take you, please God, to a safe anchorage."

As he spoke, the ship wore slowly round, and then, indeed, the captain and crew beheld their awful peril; for as her head went about they could see plainly enough the tremendous seas breaking upon the Helwick reef, upon which they would have been in a few minutes more.

"Good God!" exclaimed the captain, "the Helwick reef, in Dungarvon Bay. As yet, you have saved the ship," he continued, turning to our hero, who, with another man, was calmly steering, keeping right after the hooker, the crew of which kept lighting pitch torches; "in what water can you bring the ship to?"

"Nearly four fathoms, dead low water, and tolerably smooth, and in good holding ground."

"That will do," said the captain, gazing by the light of the ship's lanterns into the handsome and striking features of young De Burgh with great surprise.

"When the hooker extinguishes the lights," exclaimed Francis, eagerly watching her movements, "be prepared to let go."

The captain breathed hard, and then gave the necessary orders. Francis had now time to look round him, for he was confident of the safety of the ship as the wind then stood. Close alongside of him, holding by a rope, was the tall figure of a man, and with her arm through his, though protected by a large military mantle, was a young female. De Burgh could see that she was young, and though very pale, exceedingly lovely, the strong light from the binnacle falling full upon her features; he could also hear her say, looking up into the tall man's face:

"Oh, father, shall we indeed be saved? Can so young a man as he who guides us, save us?"

"With God's help, Mary, I trust he can. The pilots on this coast are able and skilful seamen."

"But he is no pilot, father; I am sure of that," she added, in a low, tremulous, sweet voice; and casting an anxious, timid look into the flushed features of De Burgh, who heard the words, and with a smile said:

"Pardon me, lady, for overhearing your words. It is true, I

am not a pilot, except on this occasion; but have no fear, in half-an-hour you will be riding as smoothly at anchor as in harbour."

The gentleman was about to say something, but the captain's first mate came up, the latter saying:

"All is ready. I trust the ground is good; if it is, you have saved this ship, and the lives of sixty-seven human beings, young gentleman, for I see plainly enough you are neither pilot nor fisherman."

"And yet I am sometimes both," returned Francis, with a smile; but as to the ground, have no fear. You may part your cable, but you will never drag your anchor. Steady men, for the Head looms before us."

Already the water grew less agitated as the ship brought the bold headland between her and the storm; everything was in readiness for letting go two anchors, and when the word was given, the vessel was rounded to, and then the anchors were let go, and the men flew aloft to furl the sails and make everything as snug as possible. The ship swung to her anchors steadily and easily; and though the gale roared through her rigging, and the thunder of the surf was heard close at hand upon the Helwick Sands, yet all on board felt secure and transported with joy at their happy deliverance from shipwreck.

"Thank God!" fervently exclaimed the captain, as he came aft, and the sweet voice of the young girl echoed the words, but so gently and so reverently, that Francis de Burgh thought the accents music itself.

The gentleman on whose arm the young lady was leaning approached our hero, and offering his hand, said:

"To you, sir, we all, under Providence, owe our lives; allow me now, not to offer you thanks, for no thanks can repay the service you have performed, but come to my cabin, and permit me to offer you a change of apparel; it is piercingly cold, and you are soaked through, perhaps bruised."

"Not in the least, sir," returned Francis; "our little hooker will drop alongside directly, I can then get a change of garments without inconveniencing you. I have only done what all the brave fellows on board the hooker were eager to do; they missed catching the warp thrown, but knowing the terrible danger of further delay, for you were running on a fatal reef, I let go the helm and seized the rope as it flew by."

"You are a noble youth," said the stranger; "but come with me, I pray you. Mary, my child, tell this young gentleman he must come, for I feel sure he is dear to some one, and he must not suffer for his noble daring."

"I pray you, sir, do as my father wishes," pleaded the sweet girl beside him; "you will make us both unhappy if you do not, for indeed, indeed, we never expected to see to-morrow's light again."

That musical voice seemed to have a strange effect upon young

De Burgh. He knew but little, in truth, of the fairer portion of the creation, little beyond the rough specimens he daily beheld, and the few fair dames and maidens he encountered during casual visits to Waterford. This was, perhaps, the first time the kind, sweet tones, of one in the higher class were ever directly addressed to him, and they penetrated to his heart.

As Francis was following the stranger, the captain of the ship came up, and laying his hand on our hero's shoulder, said, in a kind tone of voice:

"You have saved this noble ship from leaving her ribs on yonder terrible rocks; but come below, you shall command all that is on board."

"He is coming with me," observed the stranger; "my garments will fit him better than yours, captain."

"You are quite right, General," returned the captain, with a laugh; "I am too fat, and not tall enough. But do not stand talking, he is dripping wet, and the wind is as keen as a razor. The hooker is dropping down alongside us; I wish to get the brave fellows amongst us; it was a terrible night for such a craft to live in."

"Oh," observed De Burgh, as he began descending the cabin stairs, "you do not know our hookers; they will live as long in a sea as this fine ship, and suffer less."

On descending the stairs the steward showed the young lady into the saloon, while the gentleman, styled General, taking a light, led our hero into his private cabin. As young De Burgh passed the state saloon, he perceived that it contained several ladies and three or four gentlemen; but just as he followed the General into his special cabin, the steward ran down the stairs from the deck with a bundle in his hand. Placing it in a chair, he said:

"The hooker has just dropped alongside, sir; and one of the men requested that Mr. De Burgh might get this bundle."

"Thank you," replied our hero; "this is just what I wanted."

At the name of De Burgh, the General turned round with a start, exclaiming:

"Excuse me, sir, I am not quite certain if I heard your name correctly; is it De Burgh?"

The door was open, and the distance from the main cabin trifling. As the General pronounced the word De Burgh rather loudly, a gentleman, apparently about thirty years of age, came out into the passage, saying:

"General, I thought I heard you call me."

Francis De Burgh looked with some surprise at the speaker; he was a tall, dark-complexioned young man, wearing a military undress frock-coat; his eyes, hair, and moustache were black, and his features were tolerably handsome.

In reply to his question, the General said:

"No, Captain, I did not summon you; it is, however, a somewhat strange coincidence that this young gentleman, who has so gallantly saved this ship and our lives, bears, it seems, the same name as yourself."

The person addressed started, and looked with a singular, and, as our hero thought, a fierce expression, into his face; but the instant after, with an apology to the General, he turned away and re-entered the saloon.

The General poured out a glass of cordial he took from a spirit case, and lighting a lamp, said:

"Drink that, and then change your garments, my dear sir, as quickly as possible. I will return and introduce you to our party. We have not yet supped, and were not likely to do so, but for your providential appearance."

This was quite an adventure to our hero. As yet he knew nothing of where the ship came from, or where bound to; she appeared splendidly fitted up, and full of passengers. He rapidly changed his garments, but his thoughts were very busy; he longed again to behold the face of the young girl, the General's daughter; he also thought how singular it was finding a gentleman bearing his own name, far from a common one, also on board. To his surprise, on looking at a watch hanging from a pin, he perceived it was nearly two o'clock in the morning. He soon finished his toilet, and was again joined by the General.

"All our fair voyagers have retired," said the General, "worn out with the anxieties of the last twenty-hours, deferring till to-morrow at breakfast the pleasure of thanking their deliverer; but an old friend of mine is in the cabin, and will join me in drinking your health." So saying, he led the way into the saloon.

Supper was laid, with wine and glasses, on one end of a long table, at which sat an elderly gentleman.

"Allow me," said General Grey—such was his name, "to introduce you, Mr. De Burgh, to my old friend, Lord Delamaine."

His lordship rose, and with a fixed and earnest look at our hero, offered his hand. For a second he stood gazing into the features of the young man with a troubled, perplexed look, but the instant after he shook him warmly by the hand, and in a few but well chosen words, he declared how deeply he, as well as others, felt the obligation conferred upon them. They then took their seats at the table, and General Grey set the example, late as it was, in doing justice to the refreshment before them, observing:

"We have suffered so much from the weather these last few days, that we have not enjoyed a peaceful meal. The old ship rides now as quiet as if in a mill-pond."

Francis De Burgh had no objection to either the food or the wine, and willingly partook of the former. He could perceive the fine, thoughtful eyes of Lord Delamaine fixed at times earnestly upon him; but there was neither rudeness nor harshness in the expression of his features.

"It is somewhat singular, is it not, my lord," remarked General Grey, "that our preserver should bear the same name as your nephew?"

"Perhaps," said his lordship, seriously, but in a friendly tone, "perhaps this young gentleman may be an offshoot of the same family; at all events, we owe him not only our most grateful thanks, but a debt of gratitude we can never repay. The brave crew of the pilot boat no doubt will be entitled to a reward in proportion to the service they have rendered."

"Captain Scott is a very liberal man," returned the General, "and they will find that they have not risked their lives without hopes of reward."

"But, pray, Mr. De Burgh," observed his Lordship, "what on earth brought you out on such a night, and in such a craft? Most providentially, it is true, for us. Pray excuse the question, but do you belong to any king's ship; a seaman you surely are, for none but an experienced sailor would have displayed such singular presence of mind, nor have exhibited such great skill in bringing this large ship to a safe anchorage. I was on deck the whole time, and it excited my admiration to see such daring and coolness in one so young."

"Indeed, my lord," returned our hero with a flush on his cheek, "you overrate my services. From childhood I have been passionately fond of the sea, and am, in reality, only a seaman from love of the element. What I know of navigation was taught me by my good father. As to our being out last night, your guns induced us to put to sea; we were here at anchor under this Head, having during the day stood out some leagues to sea thinking we might find some ship wanting a pilot, as this coast is particularly dangerous with such a gale as the one now blowing. But, may I request to know where this ship is from, and where bound to?"

"Certainly, my dear sir," said General Grey; "this vessel belongs to the firm of Miller, Bright, and Hopkins, of Liverpool. She is called the British Queen, and sailed from Ceylon; but Lord Delamaine, Captain De Burgh, his lordship's nephew, and myself and daughter, and governess, embarked at the Cape. We had a very prosperous voyage till we made the Irish coast, near Kenmare Head; a dense fog then set in with calms for several days, after which we had heavy gales from the south-east and south. The foggy weather continuing, we never sighted the land, and in a tremendous gale of last Tuesday and Wednesday we lost our foremast. Captain Scott was still in hopes of keeping off the land till the weather moderated, and a jurymast could be got up; but last night he was confounded at finding himself so close in to the land, and fired several guns; anchoring in such a sea was out of the question.

There is no doubt had you not reached us at the precise moment you did, we had all perished either on the Helwicks, or on the coast."

"Well, General," observed Lord Delamaime, after some few observations concerning their situation, and rising from his chair, "the best thing we can now do is to seek a few hours' repose, not having had much these last three nights." To Francis De Burgh he spoke many kind and friendly words, and pressing his hand wished him good night, adding, "we shall all meet refreshed, I trust, at breakfast," his lordship then retired.

"I think his lordship is right, Mr. De Burgh," said the General, ringing the bell for the steward, who answered the summons.

"You will please accommodate this gentleman with a berth, Mr. Saunders."

"It is all ready, sir; the captain gave orders long ago. He has turned in for an hour or so himself."

"Well, I wish you good night, my young friend, for such I trust you will permit me to call you, I confess to being tired;" and pressing his hand, added, "now mind, send to me for any thing you may want in the morning."

"Will you follow me, sir," said the steward, leading the way. "It would have been all up with the ship, sir, but for you."

"It was a very close shave, I confess, Steward," replied our hero, entering a very handsome state cabin. "What has been done with the hooker and her crew?"

"Oh, she's all right, sir; the men have supped; she is now close alongside; they are fine hearty fellows, sir."

Francis, satisfied that his boat's crew were all comfortable, took the light from the steward, who retired, uttering some homely but kindly remarks concerning his and all the crew's gratitude for the assistance afforded them.

## CHAPTER IV.

At this period of his life, young De Burgh cared as little about the loss of a night's rest as he would have done for the loss of a breakfast; indeed, the latter would have been the greater deprivation of the two. Though he undressed and tumbled into a very comfortable berth, he felt not the slightest chance of sleep; the stirring events of the last few hours were of too exciting a nature to let him rest as he usually did. His thoughts were fully occupied; but above all rose the memory of the sweet voice of General Grey's daughter; the slight glimpse he had of her countenance charmed him, and he longed for a more perfect view of her fair young face. There is an inexpressible fascination in a sweet musical voice, it rivets at once the attention, and leaves an impression after it, perhaps more lasting than beauty of feature.

Francis longed to hear that voice again, and pictured to himself a face charming in its youth and beauty. The father too, he thought, was a noble-looking gentleman, and in his youth must have been very handsome, he was apparently about fifty-six or seven. Lord Delamaine, he thought, was older, shorter in stature, but his whole bearing was that of a perfect English aristocrat. For a moment his thoughts rested on his namesake, Captain De Burgh, and he wondered could there be any tie of relationship between them, for De Burgh was by no means a common name; but Francis knew nothing of kith or kin, no name of relation ever passed his father's lips.

The impression left on our hero's mind by the short glance he had of Captain De Burgh's features was an unpleasant one.

As he lay thus restless he could hear the roar of the gale through the rigging of the ship, and then the heavy pattering of rain upon the deck; he muttered to himself:

"This will bring the wind into the nor'-west; but a gale from that quarter will not hurt, and this is first-rate holding ground." Thus communing with his thoughts muttering half aloud various ideas and reflections, till at last as daylight broke in through the skylight, he fell into a slumber.

But his imagination was quite as active, though his body appeared at rest; a thousand fantastic visions floated before his excited brain. One more vivid than the rest, was a vision of Captain De Burgh carrying a female in his arms, and struggling to put her on the deck of a ship on fire. The female shrieked violently, and called out loudly, "Francis! oh! Francis, save me!"

He had no idea what part he was performing himself in his dream, or whether he was the Francis called upon; but at the sound of the voice calling for help, he started up from his slumber so suddenly and violently, that his head struck with force against the ceiling of his berth and knocked him back wide awake, and with a very considerable addition to the size of his head.

Finding it broad daylight and hearing much trampling of feet overhead, as if the crew of the ship were exceedingly busy, he jumped out of his berth and commenced his toilet.

He was soon dressed, and opening his cabin door proceeded at once on deck. The first person he encountered was Captain Scott, who, after shaking him warmly by the hand, and asking him how he had rested, looked into his face, saying:

"God bless me! what a young man you are; and so you have served neither in the navy nor merchant service; it is very extraordinary your knowledge and skill."

Francis smiled, saying:

"Practice makes perfect; I ought to know how to come into this place blindfold; it is not a bad place of refuge, Captain Scott."

"Far from it, Mr. De Burgh, but it required great nerve to run in here. We are not, I see, more than three hundred yards from yonder bank, and the sea breaks on it tremendously; you must have shaved that bank last night."

"It's the tail of the Helwicks," said Francis, "the hooker I knew would lead clear, and I followed her strictly. It was Hobson's choice, for so large a ship with such a draught of water; I confess it was nice work. I see you are preparing a jury-mast."

"Yes," returned Captain Scott, "I am, and we must be quick, for to be caught here with an easterly gale would be no joke."

"There is no likelihood of an easterly wind, Captain, now it has got well into the west and north-west; you may be sure of a week or two at least, and most likely northerly breezes and frost, for we have had no frost yet."

"We have been preparing our mast since daylight, and with more help we should have it in its place by to-morrow night."

"Oh, you will have plenty of help," said our hero, pointing towards Dungarvon, "see, our boats are all running out with this fine clear nor'-westerly breeze."

"Ah, I am glad to see them, just the kind of lads I want; your crew are capital fellows, and will make a good thing of this I can tell you. Here comes his Lordship and General Grey; they are always early risers, though they certainly had a right to an extra allowance of sleep after last night."

Francis de Burgh could not complain of his reception, either by his Lordship or General Grey; their greeting was warm and friendly in the extreme.

"I hope you rested well, my young friend," said the General, "for I am sure you earned a sound sleep."

"And yet, General, as is often the case, when well earned, the balmy restorer deserts you."

"That was my case, at all events," said Lord Delamaine, "I was thinking about your name, my dear sir, it is a very old name, and I almost fancy there must be some tie of relationship between us."

"I should feel very proud, my lord," replied Francis, "to be able to establish such a supposition, but I fear I shall not be so fortunate."

"You will, however," exclaimed Lord Delamaine, "excuse my asking you a few questions; the desire does not arise from idle curiosity, but strange memories of the past come over me, and your features recall those long gone. Your father, of course, was a De Burgh; may I request your mother's name."

A flush came over the fine features of De Burgh as his lordship spoke, certainly not a flush of shame, but he replied:

"Alas! my lord, I am quite ignorant of my mother's name, I never beheld her, neither have I heard my father mention her. I always considered, as far as I could judge, that the loss of my mother has affected my father's whole life; from my earliest infancy he has always lived in deep seclusion from the world."

Lord Delamaine, while Francis spoke, looked seriously and anxiously in the young man's face; when he ceased, he laid his hand on his arm, saying:

"I fear I have touched upon a painful subject, we will say no more now, for I perceive we are summoned to breakfast; but believe me, if ever you require it, count upon me as a sincere friend, who will forward your views should you hereafter entertain any, to the utmost of his abilities and power."

Francis was forcibly struck by his lordship's tone and manner; it was more than kind, it was affectionate and fatherly.

As they proceeded across the deck, General Grey observed, "We may expect the presence of our fair friends this morning to breakfast, which has not been the case this week past; they have been sadly knocked about, poor things!"

"I have a great mind," observed Lord Delamaine, "to land here, and proceed to Dublin, and then cross over to Holyhead; this groping our way up Channel is anything but pleasant. What say you, General?"

"Well, my good lord, for several reasons I must stick to the old ship: a couple of days with this fine breeze will make our port; besides, this is a bad time of year for land travelling, and particularly in Ireland. Suppose, Mr. De Burgh, that you were to take a trip to Liverpool with us, and see the old ship safe to her destination. My daughter says she should feel quite confident if we kept our pilot with us."

The young man felt a thrill of delight pervade his heart at these words. His cheek flushed, and his heart beat, as he eagerly replied:

"If my good father will spare me, I shall feel rejoiced; not that my services beyond this coast would be of any use."

Just as they entered the cabin, Lord Delamaine said:

"We must get up a round robin to your good father. We must positively have you with us."

Our hero did not reply, for they were now in the saloon of the British Queen. It was an exceedingly handsome cabin, more than fifty feet long, and the principal private state rooms opening into it, the doors and panels being of beautiful mahogany, divided by imitation white marble pillars. There was a blazing fire in the stove, and the long table in the centre was covered with the various edibles for a most substantial breakfast, to which had been added fresh milk, eggs, and butter, procured from the little hamlet under the Head.

Seated on the sofas, here and there, were five ladies and four gentlemen; and at the head of the table was an elderly lady, with a very pleasing expression of countenance, occupied in superintending the tea and coffee.

The tall, graceful figure and handsome features of Francis De Burgh, his cheek flushed with the excitement of the moment, attracted all eyes as he was introduced, and had to reply to the many kind things said by all present, save and except Captain De Burgh, who merely bowed, as he was seating himself beside one of the loveliest young girls De Burgh had ever beheld, or his imagination pictured; but that beautiful girl rose up, with a slight addition of colour on her cheek, and holding out her hand to our hero, said in that never-to-be-forgotten voice:

"I am rejoiced, Mr. De Burgh, to see that you are not a sufferer from your exertions and terrible immersion. I shall never forget the horror I felt when I beheld you dragged through the boiling surges."

Our hero scarcely knew what he said in reply, but he took the fair hand held out to him, and said something that made the young girl's cheek flush like his own. She smiled, however, and taking a chair, he sat down beside her, and immediately recovered his presence of mind and usual easy, graceful manner. Had he looked up at that moment, into Captain De Burgh's face, he would have felt astonished at the malignant glance that shot from his dark and meaning eyes.

The sole topic naturally for some time turned upon the perils of the previous evening: and from the ladies Francis De Burgh had to stand a torrent of inquiries as to the reasons that could have induced him to be at sea on such a night. After all their questions had been answered, the conversation naturally took another direction, and our hero had an opportunity of casting a look round upon the party assembled at the breakfast table.

The beautiful girl by his side was of course the first to be minutely noticed. Miss Grey did not appear more than seventeen; rather above the middle height, her figure was eminently graceful, and, for her years, fully developed; her features were perfect, but derived their principal charm from their ever-varying expression; brilliant dark hazel eyes, with jet black hair in glossy ringlets, set off a face altogether of exceeding loveliness.

Opposite Miss Grey sat a Miss Probert, a remarkably handsome and very lively girl of some two-and-twenty years of age. She was the eldest of five children, her mother returning to England with the younger branches of the family for the benefits of education.

The elderly lady at the head of the table was the widow of an officer who had been killed at the Cape; she had for the last four years superintended the education of Mary Grey. It is needless going over a description of the remainder of the passengers, as they do not figure in our future pages.

"Pray, Mr. De Burgh," observed Lord Delamaine, who appeared very thoughtful and serious during breakfast, "how long would it take to sail up to Dungarvon in one of your hookers? I have a great fancy to have a look at the place, if we could get back before night."

"If you start at once, my Lord," replied Francis, "you will have plenty of time, as this is a soldier's wind, fair to and fro, and the tide serves nicely—up with the last of the flow, and back with the last of the ebb."

"Very good," returned his Lordship; "then, if you will permit me, as I heard you say you were going, I will accompany you in your hooker. Does anybody else feel inclined to go?" he added. "I do not mean this question for any one of our fair friends to answer, as I dare say they would think the hooker, after this huge ship, little better than a cockle-shell."

"Oh, I do not know that, my Lord," said Mary Gray, with a smile; "the little cockle-shell was quite as safe last night, tossing on the great seas, as our leviathan ship. If papa will go, I for one should like to put my foot upon land after our long voyage. What do you say, Miss Probert?"

"Well, indeed," replied that young lady, who was listening to something Captain De Burgh was whispering, "I should like it amazingly."

"Very good," said the General; "I must go, of course. What do you say, Captain?"

"Of course," returned the soldier, with a half sneer, "we are bound to follow, though I fancy those boats are rather fishy in their accommodation, and the ladies may require a double allowance of eau de Cologne."

"You will not find that the case, Miss Grey," said Francis De Burgh, quietly; "though of course a pilot-boat is not so trim as a yacht."

"You may depend, Mr. De Burgh," said Miss Grey, rising, "that I shall look upon her with much more admiration and pleasure than the finest yacht in England; for without her it is more than probable we should not be here. So now, father, I will go and get ready; ten minutes will do, so you shall not have it to say the ladies detained you."

Francis followed with an intense look of admiration her graceful, youthful figure, as she and Miss Probert left the cabin, with a feeling he could scarcely define. He jumped up, and, full of thought, went on deck and hailed the St. Patrick. She was close alongside, and her crew were already on deck, actively helping the crew of the British Queen in getting ready the jury foremast.

Altogether, the scene around was lively, and not unpicturesque, though Dungarvon Bay is not remarkable for any great beauty; but the weather had cleared, and the sun shone out dazzlingly, and was, for the time of the year, a remarkable contrast to the previous day.

"Well, Mister Francis," said Bill Mullaghan, coming up, "this Friday, be gor, has turned out well. Faix! Ned and his tough yarn of Fridays, for he tould us it afterwards, is beat all to tatters."

"I shall not forget this last Friday, at all events, Bill; but I want you to get the little craft ready at once, and make her as neat as possible, as a few of the passengers wish to go to see Dungarvon; there are two or three ladies, a real Lord, and a General," added Francis, with a laugh, "so make yourselves smart."

"Oh, by the powers, Mister Francis, won't we make ould Dungarvon shake for once, anyhow? A Lord! and a General! Now won't the people stare! Bide a bit; I'll have some cushions, and I'll make the craft as tidy as Moll Flanigan's parlour at the 'Red Cow.'"

And off went Bill in great glee, to make, as he said, a yacht of he hooker.

## CHAPTER V.

In less than half an hour, the whole party intending to visit Dungarvon were seated in the open part of the hooker. Bill was as good as his word: he had borrowed chairs and red cushions, and sundry other articles from the steward, and one or two flags, so that the long open space of the hooker, to the mast, looked both gay and comfortable.

Hookers round-in, in their build, very much at the sides; consequently, their great breadth of beam is not seen, looking from gunwale to gunwale. The St. Patrick was a very roomy boat, and her flooring quite new and extremely neat; there was no fishing gear on board; in fact, the vessel was mostly employed piloting.

Miss Grey, with her sweet voice, quite won Bill Mullaghan's heart by expressing her pleasure at being on board the boat that had so providentially saved her and the other passengers from a watery grave. She declared, too, that it was as neat and tidy as a yacht, and she would not be afraid to cross over to England in her.

"Long life and glory to you, miss," said Bill, doffing his tarpaulin hat, and smoothing down his front locks, with his best bow. "The St. Patrick is proud of having such a beautiful freight. Be gorra, your ladyship, she'd take you to the end of the world entirely, without wetting a hair of your precious head, with my young master at the helm."

Francis heard Captain De Burgh say in rather an audible tone to Miss Probert:

"What an uncouth monster."

"Dear me," replied the young lady, laughing, "do you think so? Well, really, I think him a very fine specimen of a sailor, and a very handsome man."

Bill Mullaghan, who was taking a pull at the main sheet, while Francis was steering, heard every word that was said; there was a droll smile on his face, as he gave a kind of nod towards Captain De Burgh, which Francis understood, and he thought to himself:

"If my worthy comrade had an opportunity, Captain De Burgh would soon find out, unpleasantly perhaps, whether Bill Mullaghan was an uncouth monster or not."

"How very smoothly and well these boats sail," observed Lord Delamaine. "Pray what do you call this long spit of land we are running past? Even now the sea breaks heavily on its outward edge."

"These are terrible sands, my Lord," returned our hero. "That bank is known as the Deadman Sands, and this sheet of water we are running through is called the Pool; you see it is sheltered from all winds. I thought last night of bringing the ship in here; but the risk, owing to the curve in that bank, would have been very great; moreover, the channel is so very narrow, and close to those rocks on our right hand."

"It does appear a most intricate and narrow channel. Surely you do not attempt it at night?"

"Oh, we are quite at home here night or day," replied Francis. "With the first of the tide the banks are all bare and the water smooth; if the hookers touch, they get off with the flow of tide. By daylight the marks are easy to distinguish, and rarely a boat meets with an accident."

In pointing out to Miss Grey and Miss Probert various picturesque spots, and explaining the different objects presenting themselves as they sailed rapidly up the harbour, the time passed too quickly for Francis. He never felt so elated or so happy at any period of his life; he did not for a moment contemplate that in a few hours he might be left again to a life of solitude, and the events of the last few hours might pass like a dream.

"Dear me, what a pretty cottage, and how charmingly situated," exclaimed Miss Grey, getting a full view as they rounded the point of Mr. De Burgh's residence; and what a placid beautiful sheet of water; it is more like a great lake."

"In that cottage, Miss Grey," remarked Francis to his fair companion, "I have lived from the earliest period of my recollection, with my beloved father for my sole companion and instructor."

Mary Grey looked up into the young speaker's face, and for an instant her sweet expressive eyes rested upon his. She appeared serious, but looking down she said:

"Then, indeed, you have passed your life in great retirement. Your father, nevertheless, must be a man of great acquirements, and one who must have seen a great deal of the world."

"I should say so too, Miss Grey; but of his previous life, his sorrows or his joys, I really know nothing."

The hooker was now brought to an anchor directly opposite the cottage, and in a few minutes the whole party were landed.

Both Lord Delamaine and General Grey appeared somewhat thoughtful, and during the short voyage conversed frequently in a low serious tone. As soon as the party had landed, Francis, addressing his Lordship, expressed a hope "that he would with the rest of the party honour his father's cottage with a visit."

"Do you not think," said his Lordship, "that we are too formidable a party to storm your good father's castle?"

"I feel quite sure he will not think so," returned our hero, offering his arm to Miss Grey, just as Captain De Burgh was stepping forward to offer his; but Miss Grey placed her arm within that of Francis, saying:

"How strange is the feeling of treading on British ground after a long voyage, and years of absence from your native land. You see, Mr. De Burgh, I make no distinction between our two countries."

"How long have you been absent from England?" questioned Francis of his fair companion, as they walked up the beach towards the cottage.

"Four years," she replied, with a slight sigh. "I left my native land with a beloved fond mother, and in one short year I lost her. My dear father from that period has longed to return to England; he held a high military appointment at the Cape, but after that deplorable event he could not bear his residence. At length he was enabled to resign his command; a year before that event his old friend Lord Delamaine touched at the Cape, and owing to a severe illness was forced to remain. He was returning from Ceylon, where he was Governor. His nephew, Captain De Burgh, who holds a commission in the —— Dragoons, was already there, so that when we embarked they embarked with us. Captain De Burgh either resigns or exchanges, so I have heard."

Before Francis could make any remark, the party entered the little garden in front of the cottage. Mr. de Burgh's attendant, Jane, was standing at the door, looking with exceeding surprise.

"Is my father within, Jane?" demanded our hero.

"No, sir," replied the old dame, with a low salutation to Miss Grey, "he went away to Waterford early this morning by the Cork mail, but there is a letter for you, Mr. Francis, on the parlour table."

Francis looked somewhat annoyed at this *contre temps*, and so, evidently, did Lord Delamaine. Still the young gentleman, seeing there was no help for it, ushered the party into their only sitting apartment, which was, however, a good-sized room extending from front to rear, and opening out with glass doors into the tolerably extensive garden at the back. The furniture, though not rich or very expensive, was extremely good and appropriate, the bookcase containing a choice collection of books, and on the walls hung several very fine pictures by old masters, among which were three fine landscapes by Claude.

"I regret exceedingly, Mr. De Burgh," said Lord Delamaine, "your father's absence; do you think he will return to-day?"

"He most frequently returns by the night mail," replied Francis, "and I trust, for several reasons, he will do so to-night. If you will excuse me I will look at his letter; it may inform me how long he will remain absent."

Francis then perceived, for the first time, that Captain De Burgh had not entered the cottage, and Miss Grey taking Miss Probert by the arm, said:

"Will you permit us to stroll through your pretty garden, though in truth it is not a time of year either to judge of its beauty or its merits?"

Our hero threw open the glass doors, observing:

"You will find, Miss Grey, some rare plants, though few in number, in the greenhouse."

He then opened his father's letter, while his Lordship and General Grey were admiring two of Claude's landscapes, which Francis had often heard his father say were gems.

The letter was short, though it gave the reader much pain and vexation, so much so that his face flushed with excitement. It contained the following lines:—

"MY BELOVED BOY,

"I heard very early this morning of your adventure, and all about those on board. Till that vessel takes her departure, for certain reasons, I must remain absent. You have acted with great courage and skill, at which I sincerely rejoice. God bless you, my son; pay the passengers all the attention in your power, and make use of the cottage in any way you please, and its contents if needful to their comfort; Jane has the keys.

"Your affectionate father,

"G. H. DE BURGH."

"Well, Mr. De Burgh," remarked Lord Delamaine, "when do you expect your father's return?"

Francis coloured to the temples as he replied, "Indeed, my lord, I am sorry to say his absence may extend to several days; this gives me great concern and vexation, for I find, in consequence of his protracted visit, I shall have to forego the pleasure I anticipated in accompanying you all to Liverpool."

"I really do not see why you should not," remarked General Grey, turning round, "for recollect there may arise a question or salvage on the British Queen, whose cargo alone is above sixty thousand pounds; at all events, the pecuniary remuneration will, Captain Scott says, be very large, and you in particular will be entitled to a share, which you should feel proud to accept. Excuse me, my young friend, in giving you advice; in my mind, we always do wrong in refusing a recompense honorably gained, and at the hazard of life; unless indeed in a position of life to enable us to bestow the gold elsewhere. Cannot you write a line to your good father, state the particulars, and say you are going for a few days to Liverpool to look after the interests of the crew of the hooker; you can take one of the crew with you."

Francis eagerly caught at this proposal, which too well accorded with the secret promptings of his heart; he did not analyze his feelings, perhaps he could not; he was very young, just twenty, and though for his years much given to thought, yet of love he knew nothing, it was a passion as yet new to his breast; but that absorbing feeling was fast creeping over his heart with a might that threatened soon to overpower all other thoughts and sensations.

Jane had by this time placed on the table whatever refreshments the cottage afforded; in truth, the old dame was an excellent housekeeper, and Mr. De Burgh kept, though small, a most liberal establishment, and the very best wines.

In a few minutes Miss Grey and Miss Probert returned from the garden, the former with a large blossom of the beautiful odoriferous plant, the daphne of which there were two in the green-house.

"You see, Mr. De Burgh," said Mary Grey, holding up the blossom and with her sweet voice and smile a thousand times more fascinating, "You see I am not content with only looking, I have robbed you of this magnificent blossom; it scents the air all round the green-house."

Francis might have said she was much more likely to rob him of his heart, with her musical voice, and her lovely innocent face so touching in its youth, and exquisite softness of expression.

Our hero made neither excuse nor remark on the simple refreshment laid before his distinguished guests, neither did they require pressing to partake of it.

Lord Delamaine merely observing with a smile, "Upon my word, Mr. De Burgh, one would imagine you had anticipated our visit to your cottage and provided accordingly; at all events you are determined to be the good Samaritan in all respects."

The young ladies appeared in great spirits, and enjoyed the refreshment of ham and fowl exceedingly, as fresh meat was getting very scarce abroad, though Captain Scott carried a good stock packed in lead.

Just then Lord Delamaine, for the first time, observed:

"What has become of my nephew? I did not miss him till now; I suppose he has gone in quest of antiquities, or any other lions the place may contain."

"He did not enter the cottage at all, my lord," returned Francis, "and if he expects curiosities or antiquities in Dungarvon I fear he will be disappointed."

We will, however, in our next chapter follow the Captain in his rambles.

## CHAPTER VI.

Captain Herbert De Burgh, as Miss Grey, leaning on the arm of Francis, proceeded towards the cottage, stood gazing after the party with a smile of bitter malice on his lip. Even Miss Probert did not turn round and remark that the gallant Captain did not follow. As soon as he beheld them enter the cottage, he turned away with a smothered execration against his young rival, for such he considered our hero.

"I will baulk and defeat him yet," he muttered, "a mere boy—an unpolished cub—who flatters himself, and prides himself on the paltry achievement of steering a dismasted ship into a place of security, a feat any dolt of a pilot would do for a few pounds; but I will baffle him and find out who he is too. He does not bear the name of De Burgh with a right, I swear; it is suspicious."

The Captain kept muttering these sentences to himself as he proceeded towards the town, on reaching which he inquired if there was a decent inn.

"Aigh, sure, as good a one as any in ould Ireland," replied the woman of whom he made the inquiry, "sure, there's Mrs. Flanagan's, the 'Red Cow,' as tidy a house as any in Dublin, and then there's the 'Bell,' where the Waterford mail stops, right forenent you, if you think it looks better; faix, may be ye will pay more for the looks, and get worse treatment."

The Captain, with a look of disgust, hastened away from his loquacious informer, and went at once to the "Bell," a tolerably large, neat-looking house; and entering the parlour, where there was a good fire, he rang the bell. A waiter answered the summons, who looked with surprise at his aristocratic guest, for Captain De Burgh was a tall and handsome man, well dressed in an undress military frock; and wearing moustachios, and having a soldier-like bearing, he struck the waiter with great reverence; at the same time exciting his curiosity as to where he could have come from, as no vehicle of any kind had passed, and the Waterford mail was still due.

"Can I have a well-dressed chop and a bottle of sherry?" demanded Captain De Burgh.

"Be dad, you can, sir," returned the waiter, rubbing his hands, "and the best of sherry, too."

"Well, get it quickly."

"Yes, sir; in less than no time."

"Stay," said the Captain; "is this a private room?"

"Certainly, sir; the coach-room is opposite."

"Is there an attorney in this village?"

"Village, sir!" returned the waiter, rubbing the corner of his eyes with a dubious coloured apron; "be gor, your honour, we calls Dungarvon a town, with a mayor and corporation, and—"

"D—— your corporation!" interrupted the testy Captain; "a drunken lot, I dare say, who every night smoke bad tobacco and drink execrable whisky."

Dennis McGrath, for years the waiter at the "Bell," and who was accustomed to consider the mayor and corporation of Dungarvon as almost sacred objects, was astounded. He shut one eye, and looked up, for he was very short, into the Captain's face, with a bewildered expression.

"Bad tobacco and ex— Oh!" he suddenly exclaimed, "he must have meant it. Double X whisky—that's the word."

"Well, sir!" exclaimed the Captain, "what are you staring at me for? I asked you was there an attorney in the town?"

"Be gorra! maybe he wants somebody to drink the bottle of wine with. I hate's drinking alone myself," muttered the waiter; "I'll give him a broth of a boy at all events. Yes, sir; thanks be, we have two attorneys. It's always the cheapest to have two of that sort, sir; if we had only one, we'd be ruined. Shall I send Mr. Green to you, sir? He can stand thirteen tumblers without winking, and only charge six and eightpence for taking them."

"Ah!" muttered the Captain, thinking of something else, "that's just the man for me. Send some one for Mr. Green, and say there is a gentleman here who wishes to see him."

"Be dad, I hit the right nail on the head this time," said Dennis McGrath in great glee, giving a sweep with his apron to the table, a furious poke at the fire with a broken shovel, and hurrying out of the room, muttering half aloud, "Mutton chop, bottle of sherry, and an attorney. Be gor! there'll be a blow out."

In less than twenty minutes, Captain De Burgh was served with his chop and his bottle of sherry; and just as he finished his lunch, the waiter, with a very knowing look, introduced Mr. Green, who advanced into the room with a low bow, a furtive glance at the tall figure of the Captain, and a side glance at the decanter of sherry, detecting at once that there were two wine glasses on the table.

Mr. Green was in years about fifty, middle height, dressed in shabby black; thin in figure, with a sharp, intelligent, cunning face; no whiskers, and a thin crop of sandy-coloured hair.

Captain De Burgh politely requested the attorney to be seated; observed that it was a cold day, and hoped he would take a glass of wine. Mr. Green bowed, said it was a cold day, and helped himself to a glass of sherry, which holding up, he said with a smirk :

"Pleasure of drinking your health, Mr. ——"

Captain De Burgh bowed, returned the compliment, but paid no attention to the attorney's fishing for his name.

"I wish to ask you a few questions, Mr. Green—professionally, of course. You may be able to do me a service here, and I can afford to pay liberally for any information I may receive."

"Most happy to be of service professionally," said Mr. Green, finishing his glass, and inadvertently filling it again.

"There is a gentleman living in this neighbourhood, I believe, who goes by the name of De Burgh, is there not?"

"Dear me," exclaimed Mr. Green, "how singular! He is a tenant of mine, sir—rents my cottage by the sea shore—fine, handsome man—has only one son—pays liberally for everything—does not appear to want for money—never sees anybody, and leads a life of total seclusion."

"How long, Mr. Green, has this Mr. De Burgh lived in this part of the world?"

"Let me see!"

And Mr. Green lifted his glass, and looking through the clear wine as if calculating its age, he swallowed it, and then said:

"Just sixteen years; his son was then four years old."

"Sixteen years," repeated Captain De Burgh, as he helped himself to a glass of wine, perceiving that if he did not, the decanter would be emptied without his assistance. "He was a widower then, I suppose, Mr. Green?"

"I should say no, sir," returned the attorney, "though perhaps he might only be separated from his wife."

"Did you ever hear anything of his previous life, Mr. Green? People will, you know, try and find out anything that looks mysterious, and a gentleman living so many years in deep retirement is a mystery."

"Never could make out a word about him, sir," said Mr. Green emphatically, and filling his glass systematically, the decanter showing symptoms of an ebb tide within.

Captain De Burgh paused a moment, and then said:

"This country, Mr. Green, I hear, is on the eve of a great rebellion. Report speaks of French spies; and persons connected with the French government are known to be residing in this neighbourhood. Could this gentleman—whose name I have every reason to know is assumed—could this person not be connected secretly with the political disturbers of this country?"

Mr. Green started, and looked perfectly electrified, exclaiming:

"The thought never struck me, it's more than probable; his strange mode of living, his knowledge of several languages, his frequent absences—"

Mr. Green looked important with the ideas crowding into his brain, to dissipate which he filled the last glass in the decanter and drank it, as if it was required to relieve him.

"You know the reward, Mr. Green, the Government would give for the discovery of those detestable political offenders, who are setting your unfortunate countrymen on fire with imaginary wrongs. Now I tell you what you can do, a clever discerning man like you."

Mr. Green looked at the empty decanter and sighed, while Captain De Burgh continued:

"Set some one to watch this Mr. De Burgh and his son, drop a line to one of your most energetic magistrates, point him out as a suspicious person, and depend on it you will soon find out who he is."

"Yes," said Mr. Green slowly, "and lose sixty pounds a year rent for my cottage, well paid, and in advance."

"And most likely gain five thousand pounds for positive information, if you play your cards well, Mr. Green; I know what I am about. But I will not detain you now, your time is valuable, and must be paid for," and Captain De Burgh placed a guinea on the table near Mr. Green, which that gentleman pocketed with a dry cough, and got up. "I give you the hint, Mr. Green, and in less than a fortnight I will pay you another visit; till then it will do no harm for you to keep your eyes upon that gentleman's movements; depend on it he is a concealed spy."

Mr. Green looked startled and troubled, stood a moment irresolute, and then said:

"I will go cautiously to work, and will let you know the result when we meet again," and with a low bow and a look of regret at the empty decanter, he slided out of the room.

Captain De Burgh curled his lip and laughed, saying:

"That fellow would be a rogue for a very small amount, I never knew a drunkard that would not."

He was just going to ring the bell to pay his reckoning, when the sound of a horn induced him to go to the window, he then perceived the Waterford mail coming rapidly up the street, and draw up at the door. There were two passengers outside, evidently tradesmen; and the waiter throwing open the coach door, a tall, dark-whiskered, powerful man, in a military mantle, descended. He looked up for a moment, and then Captain De Burgh fell back with a flushed face, exclaiming:

"Good heavens! how extraordinary!"

The gentleman in the mantle entered the house, for the mail stopped twenty minutes for passengers to dine. Ringing the bell violently, Captain De Burgh tore a leaf out of a memorandum book, wrote with a pencil some words in French, and when the waiter entered he said:

"Give this slip of paper to the gentleman who just now got out of the mail, the only inside passenger I believe."

"The only one, sir; he's eating a slice of ham and fowl. Not much time to lose, sir."

"Give him the paper, sir, that's all you have to do."

The waiter vanished, and the next instant the inside passenger hastily entered the room, his face flushed and his manner agitated, and closing the door, he exclaimed:

"Is it possible, Herbert, that I see you, and in Dungarvon," and he embraced the Captain with considerable emotion.

"By Jove, sir, it's a fact, strange as it is; but I fear you are compelled to go on with the mail, we shall have short time for explanation. I expected to find you in either Dublin or Liverpool, but certainly not in Dungarvon."

"I must go on in the mail, Herbert; why cannot you go to?"

"For the best of all possible reasons," returned the Captain, "I am here with my uncle, Lord Delamaine."

"Good God!" exclaimed the stranger, turning very pale, "Lord Delamaine in this house!"

"No, not exactly," returned the Captain, "but not very far off, in a cottage belonging to a person who calls himself De Burgh."

"By heavens! you bewilder me, Herbert," exclaimed the stranger vehemently, "what De Burgh? I know of no De Burgh out of our family."

"Nevertheless, there is a gentleman with an only son just twenty years of age residing here, calling himself De Burgh; and, moreover, Lord Delamaine seems to have taken a strange liking to the said son. I returned with my uncle, who wished me to resign my commission and come back to England with him. We embarked at the Cape, fell in with a storm off this coast, and this young De Burgh was it seems out in a pilot boat, and guided us in here. We lost our foremast in the storm, and consequently the ship is detained to enable the captain to get up a jury-mast; but as soon as that is accomplished we sail for Liverpool, so now you know all in a few words."

"A very confused all it is, Herbert," said the stranger, hardly breathing from anxiety, "but I can make something out of it. I begin to see that what I suspected to be the case is actually the fact, but it is not past remedy; I would not have Lord Delamaine see me, or know that I was in Ireland for five thousands pounds. Hark! there's the horn, the horses are to! Now mark me, Herbert, be cautious, I shall return here after you sail, and will afterwards meet you in Liverpool; look for me at the Crown, Spellman Street, ask for Mr. Curtis. Remember now, not a word about our meeting; I'll find out about this De Burgh; as sure as fate it is the very man."

Again the horn sounded, and the waiter showed his face at the door.

"Should you want help here," whispered Captain De Burgh, "ask for Green, the attorney. Make him drunk, and he'll cut his own throat if you wish it."

"Good," exclaimed the stranger; "just the man I shall require."

"Now, sir," said the guard, thrusting his jolly face into the room.

"Dinner, three and sixpence, sir; no punch," said the waiter, with an air of regret.

"There," said the stranger, tossing him a crown piece, "drink the rest."

Dennis McGrath bowed to the ground, saying:

"Be dad, he's a nobleman, anyhow."

Cheerily blew the horn; the heavy coachman gathered up the ribbons, and picked a fly off the near leader's ear, which set the team cantering, and away went the Waterford mail, with the tall stranger inside, waving his hand to Captain De Burgh in the parlour.

The Captain rang the bell, and having ascertained what he had to pay, discharged the demand, gave the astounded waiter half-a-crown, and then sallied forth to meet the party he had left, and of whom he caught a glimpse coming over the bridge.

While these scenes were taking place at the "Bell," the party at the cottage, having finished their lunch, agreed to a stroll through the town till the tide turned.

Before leaving the cottage, Francis De Burgh wrote a letter to his father, stating his intention of going to Liverpool, and his reasons for doing so, requesting his father to write to him there, and that he intended taking Bill Mullaghan with him. He left the letter with Jane, who was utterly astounded at his taking such a prodigious voyage; nevertheless, the good dame set about packing up requisite linen, &c. Having walked through the town, and encountered Captain De Burgh, who merely said he had taken a long walk to stretch his legs after so much confinement on shipboard, the party returned towards the cottage.

The tide was on the turn, and evening setting in rapidly, when the whole party embarked. Francis said a few words to Jane, who accompanied the ladies to the water's edge, telling her he did not expect to be more than a fortnight absent. He thought there was a glad smile on Mary Grey's sweet face when his little portmanteau was handed in; whether it was so, or whether it was mere fancy, it nevertheless made him supremely happy, and in most exuberant spirits.

As they sailed down the Channel, Captain De Burgh, with a sneer, observed, that he thought Dungarvon one of the most miserable and filthy towns he ever visited; indeed, he wondered that any one, with the pretensions to be a gentleman, could dwell in such a hole. Francis felt his cheek flush, and was about to reply somewhat sharply; but Bill Mullaghan, who stood close behind for the purpose of lifting the boom clear over the ladies, when it required shifting, said, with one of his sly, good-humoured laughs:

"Be gorra, your honour, if you only thought a moment, you ought to think jolly ould Dungarvon a paradise of a place, in comparison with the place your honour might be in, if we hadn't picked you up. Faix! all Father Flaherty's prayers, and he always prays for the souls of shipwrecked sinners, wouldn't have saved ye."

Captain De Burgh was turning savagely upon Bill, when Lord Delamaine, with a good-humoured laugh, said:

"Upon my word, my good fellow, you are quite right. It is bad taste abusing the native place of those who risked their lives to save us."

Miss Grey looked at Francis De Burgh with an anxious expression of countenance, but he said not a word; and then she observed, there were several pretty picturesque spots about and in the vicinity of Dungarvon, and that she thought the place remarkably quiet, and the people singularly civil and clean.

"Dungarvon has a very large population," observed General Grey, " and I believe sends two members to parliament; it will be a considerable place some of these days. Ha! there's our ship, and the jury-mast up, so we may expect to sail to-morrow. What do you think of the weather, Mr. De Burgh; it looks fine, eh?"

To a landsman it certainly did look fine; the sun was setting, and the sky appeared of a golden tint, and the sea also.

Still Francis De Burgh did not like the appearance of the heavens; there were long, tiny streaks in the sky, the horizon seaward was thick, and an imperceptible ground-swell rolled gently in from the south-east. However, he replied:

"I hope it will keep up, and we shall make a short run of it to the mouth of the Mersey."

The next moment the hooker shot up alongside of the British Queen, just as the sun dipped behind the high hills to the westward of Dungarvon.

## CHAPTER VII.

WHEN Francis de Burgh retired to his berth, after spending the first evening on board the British Queen, he confessed to himself that he had never before enjoyed so agreeable an evening in his life. It had passed chiefly in conversing with Mary Grey. Young as she was, she knew infinitely more of the world than her youthful admirer; his knowledge was gained chiefly, indeed altogether, from books; Mary Grey's from actual intercourse with society.

During a residence of four years at the Cape, where a constant and intimate intercourse is kept up by the British residents, and where a large circle of military is always located, Mary Grey mingled much in society. Her father, holding a high military appointment, was, to a certain degree, bound to assemble around him the best society in the settlement; but the loss of a beloved and accomplished mother was a terrible blow to her young and affectionate heart.

General Grey was known to be very wealthy, and of a high family. His daughter—young, beautiful, accomplished, and an heiress—was the flower of the Cape beauties; but Mary Grey was not to be won by either a glittering uniform or an insinuating tongue. Young as she was, and early as she had been deprived of a mother's fostering care, she had imbibed feelings and principles, too firmly grafted in her heart to be erased in after years. Her heart, at her departure from the Cape, was still in her own possession, notwithstanding the determined assiduities and attentions of the gallant and persuasive Captain Herbert De Burgh. In fact, she disliked the Captain, though her father rather approved of him, since he knew he was next heir to the Delamaine title and estates, and on several occasions had shown courage and skill when brought into action with the fierce Caffirs of the Cape. The arrival of Lord Delamaine at the Cape rendered his nephew, Captain De Burgh, a person of much consideration. Several young ladies would most willingly have felt proud of the Captain's attentions, the eldest Miss Probert particularly, and she was at one time considered engaged to him; but his attentions to Miss Grey became, notwithstanding all her efforts to avoid them, so evident, that all attempts upon the Captain's heart were abandoned by the other belles of the Cape.

During Mary Grey's conversation with Francis De Burgh the previous evening, the latter, with all the candour of youth, and inspired by the new-born feeling pervading his heart, made her fully acquainted both with his situation and his prospects; the latter he could only imagine.

"We must only enjoy the present, Miss Grey," observed Francis, with a somewhat serious smile, "and leave the future to Providence, always, however, putting our own shoulder to the wheel."

"Perhaps you are right," returned Mary Grey, in a thoughtful voice, "especially in your case, as you cannot by any possibility see or foretel what is in store for you. I wonder your father, after taking such pains with your education, did not permit you to enter either the army or navy: for I am sure," she added, with her sweet smile, "no other profession would suit you. I fear you will think that I am taking a very great liberty with you."

"I shall never forget either your kindness or the hours I have spent in your society, Miss Grey," returned Francis, with a voice tremulous with emotion; "it will be a period to look back to, with a feeling of happiness, during my future struggles—perhaps in adversity."

"Always look forward with hope, not despondingly," said Miss Grey, in a low, soft tone, for at that moment Miss Probert, who was engaged in a game of chess, said, laughing to her antagonist, Captain De Burgh:

"Well, upon my word, Captain, you are taking off my poor queen very unceremoniously. Do not you see she is guarded by the castle and knight?"

Francis De Burgh looked across the table as the Captain said, with a sneering laugh:

"If all ladies were as well guarded as your queen, Miss Probert, knaves would not be able to assail them on their weak sides."

"But we have no knaves on a chess board," returned Miss Probert markedly, "so I suppose you must mean yourself for walking off with my poor queen so cavalierly."

"Mr. De Burgh," said Lord Delamaine, entering the cabin, for his Lordship and the General had left the saloon for a turn on deck, the other parties being engaged either reading or writing letters, "Mr. De Burgh, Captain Scott wishes to ask you a question or two; there is a shift of wind, but very light flaws, and it looks calm and beautiful."

Francis arose, and with an unmistakable look at Captain De Burgh, went on deck; but not before Miss Grey had risen, saying:

"I must bid you good-night; it is late, and before your return I shall be dreaming. The exercise I have taken to-day has been a great luxury."

Francis bade the dear girl, so kind, so gentle, if not affectionate in manner, good-night, praying in his heart of hearts that he might be mingled in her dreams, as she was sure to be in his.

On reaching the deck, our hero found Captain Scott pacing backwards and forwards, conversing with the first mate. All was still and in repose aboard the ship, except the usual watch on deck; but the sky was not clear; though there were no clouds apparently to the eye, a thin hazy atmosphere lay upon the sleeping waters, while the low and not unpleasant sound of a slight ground-swell was distinctly heard upon the banks astern of them.

"Here is a change of weather, Mr. De Burgh," said Captain Scott; "I don't half like it. You see what little wind there is, is from the old point. Is there much sea here with an east wind?"

"Not unless it has a considerable southing in it, Captain."

"We shall be all ready by twelve o'clock to-morrow, I suppose," and Captain Scott looked up and on every side, adding, "No fear for to-night, I should think."

"Well, I do not like the appearance of the weather, Captain Scott, tranquil as it looks. We are very far in under the Head; your situation the other night, and the great sea running, forced me to bring you far in; in fact, with a strong south-east wind and any sea up, you could neither weather the Head on one tack, nor the Helwick reef on the other, and would be forced, even with a southerly wind, to remain at anchor."

"Then what would you, who know this coast and bay so well, advise?" asked Captain Scott.

"In truth," returned our hero, "it seems presumptuous for me to offer an opinion to one who has had so much experience."

At that moment the ship was hailed, and on looking over the side, they perceived the small boat of the St. Patrick, with Bill Mullaghan and Ned Mahony in her.

"Well, Bill, what's the matter?" demanded Francis. Are you doubtful about the weather?"

"Be gor, Mister Francis, that's just what brought us here!" exclaimed Bill, catching a rope, and coming up over the side. "My father bade us pull aboard and tell the captain the ould wind will be back before daylight, more southerly, perhaps, and that it would be better to warp the ship, while it is dead calm, further out, so that she may weather the Helwick reef on the starboard tack, and thus make a fair run past the Saltee's."

"You are right, quite right, my man," said the Captain. "Make fast your boat; I will rouse all hands. Mr. Turner, will you turn the hands up? A couple of hours' work will give us a good berth in ease of need. It won't do to be caught napping,

Mr. De Burgh; you see your opinion is backed by one of the oldest pilots on the coast."

"I will just go below, Captain Scott," said our hero, "and let your passengers know you are merely shifting your berth. It will prevent them being alarmed by the sudden clamour you must unavoidably make."

"You are very thoughtful for one so young," observed Captain Scott, looking after the young man as he disappeared down the cabin stairs. "A thousand pities he was not put into the navy."

On entering the cabin, he found General Grey reading, and Captain De Burgh with a decanter of wine before him, with a stern expression on his features, his gaze steadily fixed upon the wine.

The General looked up, saying:

"Well, my young friend, what do you think of the night? We have arrived at a period of the year when rapid changes occur."

"The weather is quiet enough at present General, but the Captain is rousing all hands to work the ship further out, so as to make a good start to-morrow, should the wind continue southerly, and I thought it desirable that our fair passengers should know that the noise they will hear is merely changing our berth."

"Thank you, thank you, my friend, for your forethought," said the General, rising. "I will tap at their doors, and let them know what the crew are about."

Francis De Burgh turned and left the cabin. Just as he gained the top of the stairs, Captain De Burgh touched his arm. Francis paused, while the Captain said in a low but stern voice:

"I saw you look, sir, awhile ago as you left the saloon; you must explain that look, sir, or give me satisfaction."

"I shall never explain my looks to Captain De Burgh," said our hero quite calmly; "therefore you may demand what satisfaction you think fit," and without another word, he walked on; but he heard the Captain say in a fierce tone:

"My satisfaction, mind, boy, will cost you your heart's blood."

Francis De Burgh felt his face flush, but he crushed the feeling that burned his cheek, and joined Captain Scott by the capstan.

The first mate, who was a clever able seaman, clearly saw their position, and the necessity for changing it. In less than ten minutes the whole crew were on deck, and the main brace being spliced each man went cheerfully to work. The St. Patrick dropped down alongside, and a heavy kedge or stream anchor was put aboard; the wind had freshened a little from the southward, which added zest to the men working, for they themselves felt the necessity of getting a good starting berth.

In less than two hours the ship was quite a mile out, and to windward, and then anchored, for the foretopsail and other sails were yet to be bent, and some of the cargo replaced. But all hands worked cheerfully and well.

"By Jove, there is no playing with this anchorage, Mr. De Burgh," said Captain Scott.

"Oh! there is no danger," returned our hero, "for we can, with this wind, if you are not ready, take you into the Pool, where you may ride out all weathers."

"Yes, yes," returned the Captain, "but I might not get out of the Pool, if the wind held southerly for a month, now I shall be ready in four hours."

"Very good, Captain; in three or four hours it will blow hard, but you are in a good berth."

Bill Mullaghan had remained aboard, and was one of the most active in bending the topsails, and setting up the rigging of the new foremast.

Francis did not retire to rest, for the wind rapidly increased, and the sea, as usual on that coast, was as rapidly getting up, so that by daylight the ship was rolling somewhat heavily, and the Captain became so anxious, that though the vessel was rather out of trim from the shifting of some of the cargo, he resolved to up anchor, and make sail.

It was past eight o'clock in the morning as the hands began manning the capstan; the wind came in from the southward in heavy squalls, thick mizzling rain, and a rapidly-increasing sea.

Francis felt anxious, and frequently looked at the compass, and then at the Helwick reef upon which the sea already beat furiously.

Every sailor acquainted with the climate and the coast of Ireland must know how rapid in the winter seasons are the changes in a few hours from a gale to a calm, and a calm to a hurricane. Such was the case at present.

The topsails were double reefed, and all made as snug as possible. The St. Patrick was under weigh under her double-reefed mainsail, riding over the seas like a wild sea-bird sporting on its element, tossing the white spray over her bows as if in sport.

Bill only remained on board the ship, and he stood for a moment beside his young master, whose countenance bore a serious expression.

"The ship looks by the head, Bill," said Francis, "she does not rise so buoyantly out of the seas as one could wish."

"They shifted a lot of heavy goods forehead, sir," said Bill, "in getting at the stump of the ould foremast, and the Captain is too anxious."

"She will scarcely weather the reef, Bill; it's all well if she stays."

"Be gor, sir, she's à fine ship! but there's no fear, sir. If the worst comes to the worst, we have the Pool. Be the powers, how the St. Patrick walks through it!"

Just then, the anchor broke ground, the ship paid off, her yards were braced sharp, and then gracefully bending to the gale, for gale it had become, the good ship looked up well to windward of the reef.

"Hurrah!" said Bill, going forward, "she looks up in the wind's eye."

But Francis De Burgh's youthful features did not change; he watched anxiously the wild gusts as they swept by. It had ceased to rain, but the scud flew over head with lightning speed, and the sea roared on the reef and banks like thunder. The Captain and first mate came aft, the latter putting his hand on the wheel, helping the seaman steering.

"She looks up well, Mr. De Burgh," said Captain Scott, "and yet," he added as a furious gust beat the ship off a couple of points, "and yet the wind is not true, it baffles in the squalls."

Our hero did not reply; he waved his hat to the crew of the St. Patrick, who, hauling their foresheet to windward, lay like a duck taking its rest on the troubled waters.

The squall came frequent and violent, and unsteady, still the ship looked up clear of the reef. A shift of wind just abreast of it would have been awful. Just then the tops of the seas were lifted off by a furious squall from the south-east, which tore along the deep, and roared through the rigging like thunder, forcing the ship right off her course; for an instant they were buried in mist, the next Captain Scott exclaimed:

"Good God, she will not weather the reef; we must 'bout ship."

Francis De Burgh stood close by the wheel; he understood well the apparently fatal position the ship was placed in, by the wind shifting two or three points; if she missed stays her position was perilous. Again, if she did go about she could not weather the Head, and the indraught of the bay and the set of the sea were driving her rapidly in. However, he said not a word, but watched her movements with intense anxiety, so much so that he did not at first perceive that several of the passengers, amongst them General Grey, his daughter, and Miss Probert had come upon deck.

Everything being in readiness the ship was put about, but so baffling and violent were the squalls, and so troubled the sea, the strong tide acting against the wind, and being out of trim, that she went up to the wind but slowly. Our hero saw at once she would not pay off on the other tack, for an instant she shivered in the wind, and then fell rapidly off on the same tack. The Captain and mate were quite cool, though the former looked a little startled.

"We must wear ship and anchor," said the Captain.

"Pardon me, Captain Scott," said Francis De Burgh in a calm steady voice, "if you do so you will, I am almost certain, strike on the tail end of the Deadman. Will you trust me, and I will take you into the open sea through the channel, between the Helwick reef and Preharven point; but be quick in your decision,"

"Be the toe of St. Peter," said Bill Mullaghan in an excited voice running up, "if you don't give him the helm, Captain, you'll lose the ship; he'll take you through the gut, if any man in the barony can do it."

"It is all broken water across," said the Captain hesitating, "my chart gives only two fathoms water."

"Be gorrie the chart tells a lie," said Bill, "take the wheel, Mister Francis, or be St. Patrick she's on the Helwicks, and the women will perish."

Francis sprang to the wheel with Bill Mullaghan to aid him, the Captain pressed his lips hard, he looked at the surf thundering on the Helwicks. Another glance aft at the broken water on the end of the Deadman, and then said:

"Be it so, Mr. De Burgh, but for God's sake recollect the lives."

"There are those aboard dearer to me than five thousand lives," said the young man in a firm stern tone, as he rapidly turned the spokes of the wheel to port, adding, "leave the yards as they are."

Mary Grey heard the words uttered by our hero, and they went to her heart—they were never forgotten.

The entire crew of the vessel stood breathlessly watching the course of the ship as she stood off from the wind, passing within less than a stone's throw of the reef, and not twenty yards from a sunken rock at its western point. But the ship payed off well, and having passed the reef, Francis and his ally Bill allowed her to run along the inside of the reef, and then they opened the narrow channel between the reef and the eastern point of Dungarvon Bay.

"By heavens! it is one sheet of broken water," exclaimed the Captain in a tone highly excited, and looking into the calm features of De Burgh.

"There are four fathoms water in the part I shall take you through," said our hero, in a calm clear tone, "I will stake my salvation on her safety. The broken water you see is the strong spring ebb, making out through the narrow channel. Order a pull at the braces, Captain, I wish her to look up as near as possible."

There was perfect silence aboard the ship as she plunged heavily into the breaking seas, and yet there was not a man on the deck of the British Queen that did not feel the greatest confidence in the skill of the young helmsman.

"Steady Bill, steady," said Francis to his assistant, "we have her now, and room to spare."

"Aigh! aigh! sir," returned Bill triumphantly with a look of pride into the flushed cheeks of his master. "Be the bright eyes of Judy Maloney, you could take her through the eye of a needle."

"There's not fifty yards of channel; if she touches," said the Captain to the first mate, "it's all over."

"If she never touches the bottom till she touches it here," said our hero emphatically, "the good ship will have a long life."

The same instant with a fierce gust and a heavy plunge, the vessel surged through the broken water, throwing a cloud of spray over her bows, and forcing every one on deck to grasp a rope or some support. The Captain and mate hardly breathed, but the ship rose again with her broad bows to the seas, and going a point or two off her course, she gathered way instantly, and in ten minutes more the British Queen was breasting the blue waters of the open sea, her head looking well to windward of all dangers.

Captain Scott stood for a moment immovable, but Francis, as he called a seaman to take his place, felt a hand upon his shoulder, and turning round his eyes met those of Mary Grey; she was leaning on her father's arm.

From that moment Mary Grey and Francis De Burgh knew they loved, and that that love was never to be shaken.

"You were born to be our preserver, my young friend," said the General with much emotion, as he pressed his hand.

Captain Scott, in his blunt but true-hearted manner, with rather a startling oath, swore as he shook him repeatedly by the hand, that he was fit to command a frigate.

Lord Delamaine was leaning against the capstan, which was on the quarter-deck, looking fixedly at young De Burgh; the next instant he was beside him, saying:

"You are a noble fellow, Francis; count upon me, next to your father, as a protector through life;" and taking a purse full of gold from his pocket, to the amazement of Bill Mullaghan, he thrust it into his hand, saying: "You are as brave and cool a seaman as your master, and that's saying a great deal; spend the gold, and keep the purse in memory of this day."

Bill pulled off his hat, smoothed down his curly locks, and looking at his lordship, as he thrust the purse into his pocket, and gave his waistband a hitch, saying:

"Long life and glory to your lordship. Faix! ther's no doubt about my spending the money, and drinking your honour's health.

But the purse I'll keep, till I can persuade Judy Malouey to take charge of it, which, please St. Patrick, she will some of these days, when she becomes Mrs. Mullaghan."

Lord Delamaine smiled, saying:

"When that happy event takes place, I hope to be within visiting distance, to give something more substantial in the keeping of the future Mrs. Mullaghan."

The good ship was now heading out into the open sea, and holding a good course, and caring little for the heavy squalls and seas breaking around her. The next day she was off the Tuscar, for the wind veered more to the eastward, and then blew steadily with clear, cold weather. Having got the ship into good trim, she worked well to windward, and working up channel, with a fine, steady breeze, the time passed delightfully with Francis De Burgh, for Miss Grey loved the sea, and never suffered illness of any kind during the voyage. Five days passed like magic; the sixth a north-west wind brought them off the mouth of the Mersey.

Francis De Burgh had many long conversations with Lord Delamaine, who evinced exceeding interest in his welfare, and gave him a most pressing invitation to visit him at his seat in Hampshire.

"I have observed," said his Lordship, "the coldness between you and my nephew. I will make no remark on the cause. I spoke to him, and he confesses he was hasty, and that he was in the wrong; therefore I pray you think no more of what passed between you; he promises he will not."

"Then you may depend, my lord, I will not," returned Francis De Burgh; and thus the matter apparently ended.

When the vessel anchored in the Mersey, off the dock she was to enter, our hero for the first time felt a depression of spirits; he looked at Mary Grey, and then whispered to himself:—"Here ends the dream!"

No word of love had passed his lips to the fair young girl; but Mary required no words; she knew she was loved, and she had a hopeful, trustful heart.

General Grey was equally kind and affectionate to our hero. As yet he had no settled residence in England, but said if he was not obliged again to go abroad, he intended, if possible, to purchase a place near his friend, Lord Delamaine's, in Hampshire.

"When you come to London, which of course you will do," continued the General, "when you visit his Lordship, if you inquire at the banking establishment of Messrs. Gordon and Joyce, you will hear of our residence, wherever it may be. Believe me, you will always be a welcome guest."

Lord Delamaine and General Grey put up at the Imperial, in Liverpool, and there Francis De Burgh spent the evening before their departure for London. Both Francis and Mary Grey were very serious; whether the General perceived what was passing in the hearts of the young people or not, we cannot say. There were bright tears in Mary's eyes, as she held out her fair small hand to Francis to bid him farewell that night; his heart beat, and his hand trembled as he took hers. For the first time he raised it to his lips, and in a low, tremulous voice he said:

"God bless you! Mary. May you be as happy as my heart wishes you to be."

The tears ran down Mary's cheek; she looked into the face of her lover, but no word could pass her lips, but there was a world of meaning in her look : and thus they parted.

## CHAPTER VIII.

We shall not detain our readers, or retard our story, by details of the various meetings and consultations between the wealthy owners of the British Queen and the owners of the cargo in her. Before their departure, both Lord Delamaine and General Grey had an interview with both parties, giving their opinions candidly with respect to the services rendered the ship by the cool courage and skill of Francis De Burgh. Captain Scott, with his usual bluntness, fairly stated he should have lost the ship the first night, had it not been for the assistance afforded him by Mr. De Burgh, who boarded the vessel at the imminent hazard of his life. These examinations and consultations did not take place from any desire to lessen or depreciate the service rendered; but as Francis De Burgh positively declined demanding any remuneration beyond what the owners considered the services rendered deserved, they became desirous to do the thing handsomely, and satisfy all parties. During the time they were arranging matters, Francis De Burgh received numerous invitations from some of the wealthiest Liverpool merchants. His distinguished appearance, simple but elegant manners, and cheerful disposition, won him the esteem and admiration of the society he mingled in for the three weeks he remained in Liverpool, and had his heart been free, he would have found it difficult to escape from the bright smiles and handsome persons of the merchant princes' fair daughters.

To his great relief, he received a letter from his father, though the tone and substance of the letter both surprised and pained him. His father stated that he had suffered from his old disease of the heart more than usual; that events had occurred that would change the current of his life materially, but he refrained from stating anything particular in a letter that might never reach him; that the country was terribly disturbed, and that he was anxious to quit Ireland, which he would do the moment he (Francis) returned; and that a splendid career was before him.

Francis De Burgh's heart beat wildly as he read those last words, "A splendid career was before him!" Would it enable him to aspire to the hand of Mary Grey? was the first thought that rushed with electric speed through his brain. Would the mystery of the past, and his father's previous life, be revealed? He became intensely anxious to return to Dungarvon, and, fortunately, the following day the owners of the British Queen came to their final settlement.

It was determined that the sum of three thousand pounds should be presented to Francis De Burgh, and a sum of two thousand pounds to the crew of the pilot boat, to be equally divided. Francis De Burgh was surprised at the liberality of the merchants; but he requested the sums should be reversed, that is, three thousand pounds to the pilot boat, and two thousand to himself, and after a little discussion, it was so settled. Though the sum was liberal, it was not more than would be awarded at the present day. The cargo was worth sixty thousand pounds, and the ship twelve thousand pounds, and all would have been lost but for the assistance rendered.

Lord Delamaine and General Grey had left one hundred pounds each, to be divided amongst the crew of the pilot boat. They both knew that the high spirit and disposition of Francis De Burgh would be pained by any attempt on their part to show their gratitude by any pecuniary gift; but they agreed to purchase a very handsome cup, with appropriate inscriptions and devices, and send it to their young preserver.

Francis, before his departure, having received the money and lodged it in a Liverpool bank, to be transferred to the Bank of Ireland, proceeded aboard the British Queen to take leave of the mates and crew; with Captain Scott he had previously taken leave. He was a prodigious favourite, and they all heartily wished him joy of his good fortune; but our hero came aboard with the determination that they should enjoy some of it. He therefore, to their great surprise and gratitude, distributed one hundred pounds amongst them, which elicited a cheer on his departure which might have been heard on the Cheshire shore.

That night he departed for Holyhead, there being no packets from Liverpool at that period. The Holyhead packets of those days were small, cutter-rigged crafts, of about seventy or eighty tons burden, some of them commanded by half-pay navy lieutenants. They were first-rate sea-going vessels, but with very limited accommodation, consisting of one small cabin for male and female passengers, with berths that resembled ill-made wooden boxes; remarkably little space between the sleeper's head and the ceiling, requiring considerable caution in getting up suddenly. These vessels had to encounter, during the winter months, almost perpetual gales of wind, and a cross tumbling sea.

Francis De Burgh went on board, with his attendant Bill, who was now fully determined that nothing henceforth should separate him from his young master. Bill took it into his head, while in Liverpool, to dress in what a sailor calls long togs, *i. e.* a shore-going coat, &c. Bill saw no earthly reason why, as his master was nearly six feet high, and he himself was not much less, he should not make a valet when occasion required it. When on land, therefore, Bill doused his sea-going garments, and, when he could, his sea phrases; but he made a most amusing medley of it, though his great good humour, athletic frame, and handsome open countenance made him a favourite with all he came in contact.

It was early in the morning when they embarked aboard the Medusa packet, the wind blowing strong from the west. There were no less than twenty-seven passengers, sixteen of them first cabin. It appeared to our hero that some of the children must have been borrowed for that especial occasion, for there was one each for every passenger, and two over for himself! It rained hard, which drove them all into the small cabin. Every passenger in those days, when steam and electricity were unknown as modes of propulsion, carried his own provisions, the packets only furnishing a remarkably thin mattress, and blankets cut to the minutest possible dimensions, so that when you contrived to cover one side you exposed the other. The steward furnished an unlimited number of basins, which article, Francis De Burgh, to his dismay, found were continually required. It struck him that if a steward was provided for every basin, he would have quite enough to do, for unfortunately the wind was dead on end, and a cross tumbling sea, which set every one in the cabin, not provided with sea legs, tumbling one over the other.

Many of the passengers had arrived by late coaches, and had had no breakfast, but sanguinely thought they could pick a bit of cold fowl and tongue; but the first pitch of the merciless Medusa into the race outside, alas! settled the chicken and tongue, and a vociferous cry for steward and basin replaced the much-desired refreshments.

Our hero remarked a singularly stout lady, who, having abandoned her two children to a poor girl, an attendant, infinitely more sick than herself, contrived, after several violent efforts, with a total disregard to the drapery over her unfortunate legs, to get into an upper berth, after bestowing sundry kicks and thumps to a most patient sufferer underneath.

"Oh, steward, oh dear! a glass of brandy and water, quick."

"Coming, ma'am," exclaimed that much-prized individual, bringing a glass full, not very high coloured; the lady sipped it.

"Oh dear, steward, too much brandy, or too much—"

"Oh! I see, ma'am," exclaimed the steward, "I'll suit you," and throwing out half the water he filled it up with brandy.

"Ah! dear me, quite nice now, I don't like it too strong; always make it like this."

"Humph!" muttered the steward as he ran to another summons, "I thought by your nose you liked it stiff."

Notwithstanding the rain, and the sea at times beating over the vessel, our hero preferred the deck; what with the cries of the poor children, the moans of the suffering parents, the heat, &c., the cabin was rendered anything but a pleasing place of shelter.

At the expiration of thirty-three hours the Medusa ran into Howth harbour, and landed her miserable passengers.

Being anxious to reach home, Francis De Burgh took the first machine he could get, which was a conveyance called a "Jingle," now extinct, a species of inside car with one horse, on four wheels, holding six persons inside and the driver out. Much as he wished to see Dublin, he resolved not to delay longer than that night, and then depart by the Waterford mail. It was nearly four o'clock when he reached the hotel in Dawson Street, so after eating an excellent dinner, and finishing a pint of wine, he set out for the mail coach office, to take a place for himself and Bill Mullaghan.

It was a wild stormy night, and piercingly cold; the mail coach office was down a side street off College Green. On entering the office he perceived a counter and desk, and a clerk writing in a ledger behind it, and standing with their backs to him two men wrapped in the long grey frieze coats, worn generally by the Irish peasantry.

They were conversing earnestly, and warming themselves before a very poor sea-coal fire. Francis noticed these men particularly, they were such broad shouldered, powerful looking fellows, and conversed in Irish. Though one of them turned round he could see nothing of his face, as a huge red handkerchief was tied round the neck and hid all but the nose, and the hat was far down over the face. These were serious times, for Ireland was heaving like a turbulent sea, shaken about by conflicting parties, and just on the eve of explosion.

"Can I have two inside places for Waterford?" said our hero to the clerk.

"No, sir," returned the clerk, "I have but one inside, and you are fortunate to get that, for I expected it to have been taken long before."

"Very well," said Francis, "book me an inside and an outside."

"Very good, sir; what name?"

"De Burgh," returned Francis.

As he uttered the name the two men turned round with an exclamation, and our hero distinctly caught the word, "Diowl!" and then without a word more they left the office.

Francis did not bestow much thought on the circumstance, for as he received his change a female covered with a long grey mantle and hood hastily entered the office, and in a hurried agitated tone said:

"Oh, Mr. Gilmore, I hope I am in time; I had such trouble to make up the money, and to lose the inside place now would be dreadful."

Our hero paused, for he was leaving the office when the plaintive tones of the female voice struck him.

"Indeed, indeed, ma'am," said the clerk in a compassionate tone, "I kept the place as long as I dared."

"Oh, my God! what will my poor child do, for I must go outside, and such a night. But it's God's will—I must see my husband."

Francis De Burgh turned back with a flush on his cheek, and approaching the female said:

"Excuse me, ma'am, is it an inside place to Waterford you require?"

The female turned round throwing back the hood of her cloak, and by the light of the lamp Francis saw a very pale but youthful countenance; she could not be more than eighteen years of age, and her dark expressive eyes met his as she replied:

"Yes, sir, I did wish for an inside place on my poor baby's account; God knows not for myself, I can bear much."

As she spoke the mantle fell back, and showed to our hero an infant scarcely seven months old, warmly wrapped up in her arms.

"Will you be so kind, Mr. Gilmore," said Francis, "to transfer the place I took to the young woman."

"Certainly, sir, certainly," eagerly exclaimed the clerk; "yes, he's a strong powerful youth," continued the clerk, muttering to himself, "he can stand the weather; she, poor thing, is a crock, a mere crock."

"Ah! sir," said the young woman, her voice tremulous with emotion, "God will bless you; but you will suffer dreadfully outside."

"No, my poor girl," said Francis De Burgh kindly, and placing an outside fare on the counter.

"Sir," exclaimed the clerk, "I have to give you the difference."

"No," said our hero, "I pray you to accept it from me, madam, who can well afford it. Excuse me, but I heard you say you had a difficulty in getting the money."

The young mother burst into tears, but before she could utter a word he hurried out of the office, and went back to his hotel.

Wrapped in their heavy pilot coats, and a thick shawl round their necks, Francis De Burgh and Bill Mullaghan, carrying a small portmanteau, set out for the Post Office, College Green, where the mail coach finally started at that period. It was certainly anything but an agreeable night for outside travelling, but the cold had increased, and a keen east wind was sweeping up College Green with a wild wailing sound, as if its every breath were razors, at times accompanied by a shower of sleet.

"Upon my conscience, sir," said Bill, casting a look at what he called the upper deck of the mail coach, "we'll have to grin and bear it to-night. Be gor, there's no more bulwarks to shelter a fellow on this here craft than a sand barge. Well, we shan't sleep on our watch anyhow."

"Now, my man, take your place," said one of the guards coming out from the Post Office, followed by another with a formidable brass blunderbuss, and a large pair of pistols that might on an emergency serve as swivels in a gun-boat.

The passengers were all up, as well as Francis De Burgh could see, so he and Bill mounted in front, behind the coachman: there was some kind of an individual seated beside the driver, at least there was a vast pile of coats and mufflings, as to the coachman himself, how he got into his seat puzzled our hero: he appeared of immense bulk, cape upon cape, and wrapper upon wrapper. Bill sat on one side of Francis, and a tall fellow in a frieze coat, like one of the countrymen he had seen at the Coach-Office, on the side next Bill. This individual attempted to keep up an umbrella. At the back were two persons and the two guards.

"All right, Bill," said a low smothered voice, coming, as it seemed, out of the coachman's chest.

Bill Mullaghan, thinking he was the individual addressed, sung out, "Aye, aye, my hearty, slack your sheet and go a-head!"

The coachman tried hard to turn round, giving Francis De Burgh a slight glimpse of a remarkably large and red proboscis. Just then one of the guards called out:

"All right, James, all right," and a blast of a horn followed, and away went the four half-bloods at a canter up College Green, and down a side street to the Quay, along the Liffey. The gusts of wind were here extremely violent, the sleet driving in their faces caused by the eddies.

"I say, my hearty," sung out Bill Mullaghan to his neighbour with the umbrella, "if you keep poking your gib-boom into my bows, I'll have to spoil your figure-head. Douse your top-sail: what lubber would keep a sail bent on this here craft."

At that moment the man shifted the umbrella, and a violent gust turned it inside out, and finally tore it out of the man's hands, and the next minute it was in the Liffey.

Bill burst into a loud laugh, saying, "My eyes, there goes your sky-raker; now you will be snug under bare poles!"

"Tare-and-'ouns, man, what are you talking about?" said the loser of the umbrella, in a fierce tone: "Your cursed nonsense has cost me three-and-sixpence."

"Sarve you right," said Bill, "who'd think of carrying canvas on a craft with no more beams than a bean cod!"

"Carry your grandmother," said the man in a towering passion, "diowl!"

"Carry my ould grandmother!" repeated Bill with his good-humoured laugh, "Och, be me sowl, if you were alive when my ould grandmother slipped her cable, you'd be in hot quarters to-night, anyhow, my beauty!"

"Hold your jaw!" said the man savagely: "if I had you on Ballyhack, I'd teach you something you haven't *larnt* yet."

"Be gorra, I'm obliged to you entirely," said Bill, "but hawl in the slack of your cable, or may be I'll teach *you* something, without going to Ballyhack for a school-room."

"Come, come, Bill," said Francis De Burgh to his attendant, knowing his pugnacious propensities when roused, "let your neighbour enjoy himself in his own way; it's not exactly a night for conversation."

"By the powers, it's not, sir," said Bill, "in our little hooker there's always a corner for shelter, but faix, the wind is all round the compass here."

On went the four horses, splashing through the muddy roads, the lamps throwing but an indifferent light ahead from the violence of the wind. Not a word was spoken by the coachman to the mass of garments beside him, and thus they continued without changing horses till they drew up before the snug little inn at Naas, where the mail passengers supped.

A great crowd of people were gathered about the front of the inn, and there seemed to be a great deal of excitement amongst them, all eagerly inquiring the news from the metropolis.

"Come, Bill," said Francis to his attendant, "let us into the house, and get something warm; a tumbler of punch is rather an agreeable mixture for an outside passenger."

"Be the powers it is, Mister Francis, or even two of them."

Francis jumped down, and making his way through the crowd, who looked at his tall figure as he passed on, very earnestly, he entered the parlour of the inn.

There was a blazing coal fire, and the table was covered with eatables of all kinds, with tea and coffee, muffins, and toast. Immediately after him came in the young female with the baby in her arms, for whom Francis placed a chair by the fire. She sat down, and uncovering the baby to let it feel the heat, she said:

"Ah, sir, I fear you have suffered by your kindness."

"Not at all," said Francis, "but I should have suffered had you been outside, and I in."

Just then a remarkably fat woman, in a most showy gaudy gown and shawl, entered the room, followed by a very thin, sallow-faced man, in a bright-blue coat, carrying sundry mufflings and a basket: he was followed by a rosy-faced, buxom-looking girl, about eighteen, and three other inside passengers. Francis had mixed himself a tumbler of punch, and was attacking a plate of ham and fowl, when the two just-mentioned sat down to take supper.

Seeing the young woman still at the fire, he went to her and asked her if she would not take something for supper.

"Nothing for me, thank you," she replied, "but I should like a little milk for the baby."

Francis at once proceeded to the table, and, taking up the jug, brought it to the young mother, who proceeded to fill a bottle with it. As he replaced the jug upon the table, the fat lady cast her eye into the vessel, saying:

"Upon my word, young gentleman, you seem to think there is no one who takes milk but your baby."

Francis laughed heartily, saying, "Pardon me, ma'am, I will ring for more; but you mistake the matter, I have not the happiness yet of being either a husband or father."

As Francis turned to pull the bell, the fat lady's daughter—for such the rosy-cheeked damsel was—said:

"Laws, ma, what a thing to say! That is a gentleman, and quite a boy almost."

"A very big boy then," returned the mother, as the waiter placed more milk on the table, "the biggest boy I ever saw: if he isn't the husband or father of the young woman, he oughtn't to have taken the milk. Milk is milk in these here inns, and we pays for it too."

"We do," said the thin man in a meek voice, helping himself to some, "and this is but milk and water."

In the meantime Francis insisted on the young mother taking a cup of tea, after which he went out to see what Bill was doing, for fear that he might get into an argument with the man in the frieze coat. But Bill was remarkably comfortable in the large room opposite, in which was a roaring fire, with a plate of beef on the table, and a hot mixture beside it. He was filling up the pauses in his occupation by making sundry speeches to a very comely housemaid, to the infinite disgust of the waiter. But amongst the bystanders, who were laughing at Bill's sea-phrases, and who were partaking of whisky punch at his expense, the two men in the frieze coats were not to be seen.

The horn of the guard summoned the passengers, and Francis hastened to help the young female and the baby into the coach, having first paid for his supper and her cup of tea before she could interfere. He then resumed his place, and found their frieze-coated neighbour also seated.

The coachman having ascended to his place by means of a ladder, off they went to the tune of "The girl I left behind me," played tolerably well by one of the guards; albeit it was not exactly a night for sweet sounds.

## CHAPTER IX.

On dashed the four spirited horses through the gloom of night, the wind still blowing in fitful gusts, but the sleet and rain had ceased; it was intensely dark. After the first change of horses, they seemed to Francis De Burgh to be driving through a wild dreary country: it was too dark to distinguish objects, but they were evidently in a mountainous district.

The mail was just commencing the ascent of a steep hill, when the coach was suddenly surrounded by a body of armed men, the horses' heads seized, and the reins and traces were cut like magic. The two guards behind were knocked over the side, by the two powerful men seated on the back of the mail, before they could fire a shot, though both men carried their fire-arms on their knees.

Our hero started to his feet, but at the same instant the man in the frieze coat levelled a pistol towards Bill Mullaghan's breast, and was pulling the trigger when Bill struck him a tremendous blow in the face, knocking him over the side. The pistol exploded nevertheless, narrowly missing its intended victim.

A dozen voices from below called out in savage tones and curses in Irish, for them to come down off the roof, or they would blow their brains out.

"The curse of Cromwell on ye," shouted Bill, "what do you take us for?"

"Jump down, Bill, jump down," said Francis, springing to the ground, when several men seized him by the collar; the first two went to the ground; but a dozen hands dragged him on, saying: "Diowl, bring the lantern, till we see if this is the right man."

The individual who occupied the coach-box, having cast off his wrappers, now came up with the lamp and held it full in our hero's face. Seeing that he was mistaken for somebody else, he remained quiet; he could see all the unfortunate females standing shivering in the wind and cold a few paces off.

"Why d——n," savagely exclaimed the tall man holding the lamp, "this is not him: by heaven! he has baffled us again."

"If it's not him," exclaimed the ruffian who fired the pistol, and who came limping up, "it's one of his spies—a Sasanach spy, sent to betray us. Shoot him, boys; shoot him, diowl curse him."

"Villain, you lie," passionately exclaimed Francis, struggling to release himself, while a dozen men could hardly hold Bill Mullaghan, in his rage to get loose.

Half a dozen pistols were raised, and it is very probable that his doom would have been sealed, had not the young woman in the grey mantle, with a wild cry, rushed forward, saying:

"Stop! no murder; I am Holt's daughter."

"Diowl, take that at all events," savagely exclaimed the fellow that fired his pistol; and taking the heavy weapon by the muzzle, he dealt our hero a blow on the back of the head with such force that he fell forward perfectly senseless.

How long he remained unconscious Francis could not conjecture. On opened his eyes, and looking around him, he perceived to his surprise that he was lying on a peasant's pallet, in a small chamber of a poor cabin. There was a turf fire in the chimney, a deal table near the bed, and a bottle with a tallow candle stuck in it. The room had one small window in it with one pane of glass, the others were filled with pieces of wood.

In attempting to turn round, he felt an acute pain under his left arm; and on examination he found he had received a pistol shot, but fortunately a mere flesh wound. He had bled much, but the wound had been washed and bandaged, so also had been the cut at the back of his head, which gave him considerable pain. As he lay quiet, a recollection of the recent event came vividly across his mind; the door opened, and an old and rather decrepid woman of the peasant-class entered the room. She carried a bowl of something hot in her hands, and looking up she perceived that our hero had recovered his recollection. Coming close beside the bed, she said something in Irish, which Francis De Burgh did not understand. He made some remark to her in English, but she shook her head, and offered him the contents of the bowl.

Francis looked at the mixture with a doubtful look; but being very thirsty, and thinking it whey, or something like it, he drank, and found it far from unpleasant, with a strong taste of herbs in it. He had scarcely finished it, when the young female in the grey cloak entered the room.

"Ah, sir!" she exclaimed, with a tremulous voice, "you have come to your recollection. Thank God! If they had killed you, what misery I should have undergone. Do you feel much pain?"

"No, ma'am," returned Francis De Burgh, "I do not. But for you, I should doubtless have lost my life. Why my life was attempted I cannot imagine."

The young woman's pale face flushed as she replied:

"I can only say, sir, the men who stopped the mail would not have harmed you when they found out their mistake. Who the ruffians were who wounded you, I know not, nor their motive. The men who surrounded the mail are not robbers: they are—" she hesitated, and then said, "they are United Irishmen. You are too weak to talk, sir, for you have lost a great deal of blood. I am happy to say you are quite safe now, so rest easy."

And then wishing our hero good night, she left the room, leaving him greatly astonished and perplexed, and enraged with himself for not asking after Bill Mullaghan.

As for sleep, it was impossible; he was exceedingly feverish, and his brain full of a thousand strange ideas and visions, and especially tormented with the thought, that it might require several days to get well enough to move, and wondering who on earth Holt's daughter could be, and in what part of the country he then was. He also felt much uneasiness about his father; he had written to him two days before he left Liverpool, stating the day he intended departing; and now he might be detained by the wound in his side several days. The attempt on his life he imputed to nothing but savage malice in the man seated next Bill on the mail; but why he should vent his passion on him was puzzling, and beyond his comprehension.

As Francis lay thinking over these matters, and watching the candle in the bottle, his eye was attracted by something white, pressed against the pane of glass in the cabin window. He raised himself on his elbow, and stared at the object; it was a human face. The next moment it was withdrawn, and then one of the wooden panes was thrust in, and then, with pleasure and astonishment, Francis De Burgh beheld the countenance of worthy Bill Mullaghan.

"Hist! your honour," said Bill, in a low voice: "don't speak out. Be gor, I've found you; that's something."

"Thank God!" exclaimed our hero, speaking within his breath, "that I see you alive and well. But I do not think there's any danger here; there are only two females, who are both very kind."

"Oh, faix, there's no fear but the women will take care of your honour; but, be jabers, there's over thirty of the villains cooking supper in a large barn a few yards off. Are you much hurt, sir?"

"No, Bill; a pistol ball, it seems, went through the flesh under my left arm. As to the knock on my head, we Irishmen count them as nothing. I am, however, too weak to move for a day or so. But how did you get here? You must be perished."

"Not a bit of it, sir. Faix, I was even with the raparees. Be gor, they are all rebels. We'll put the military upon them—"

"No, no," interrupted Francis anxiously, "on no account—the young woman here saved my life. I suspect that her husband is one of those misguided 'United Irishmen.' In a day or two I shall, I think, be able to leave this place. What became of our portmanteau and the mail ?"

"Hush !" said Bill ; and suddenly his face disappeared from the pane, and a dead silence ensued.

Francis listened painfully, and then he caught the murmur of men's voices outside, and after awhile all became silent again.

He could feel his heart beat violently, so anxiously did he feel for Bill's safety, fearing a scuffle. So inveterate was the feeling experienced by the rebels against all whom they believed to be spies or informers, that there was scarce a doubt in his mind but that Bill would be shot if detected lurking about their retreat. However, all remained perfectly quiet; therefore he supposed Bill had escaped detection. An hour afterwards he was fast asleep. When he awoke it was broad daylight; some person had been in the room, for the bottle with the candle was gone, the fire had been made up, and the piece of wood replaced in the window.

Francis felt so much better and stronger, that he got out of bed and dressed himself, feeling only a little stiffness and soreness under the arm. His head was nearly well, though he could feel there was a considerable cut down the back of it. He then looked out through the pane of glass. The cabin, he judged, was situated on a considerable elevation, and was built in the midst of a vast heap of barren, craggy rocks, some of immense size; here and there green fern and furze, but not a tree or even bush was to be seen. He looked up at the sky, and saw it was overcast with heavy clouds, driving with great velocity before a violent wind.

A noise at the door caused him to turn round. On doing so, he was greatly surprised at seeing a tall and well-built man, with very agreeable features, enter the room. He was attired in a kind of uniform, of very dark green, wore a brace of pistols in a broad black belt, and had a short carbine in his hand, which he laid down on entering the room. He stopped a moment, and regarded our hero with a look of great surprise. He was a young man, certainly not more than six-and-twenty.

"Well, upon my word, sir," said the stranger, in a careless but good-humoured tone of voice, "you have had a marvellously good elixir, or your wounds were very trifling."

"Trifling they were," replied Francis De Burgh, in a rather stern tone ; "nevertheless, I might have been spared the infliction, especially as they were made in a dastardly and cowardly manner, upon an unarmed man, and against whom even a 'United Irishman,' which I presume you are, could have no cause of complaint."

"All I can say is," returned the stranger, with a flushed cheek, and in a serious tone, "that if I knew who the ruffian was that held the pistol that wounded you, I would blow his brains out myself. He did not belong to the party that attacked the mail last night. You, sir," he added, in a very mild tone, "were kind and generous to my poor young wife and child, who were unavoidably left in great destitution in Dublin. Intelligence was conveyed to her that I was mortally wounded, and lying in Waterford gaol. I was certainly wounded slightly, and made prisoner; but was enabled to escape, and get into these mountains. Last night a party of my father-in-law's men surprised the Waterford mail, expecting to capture a most important personage; but it seems he was aware of it, for he went by the Limerick mail, and you were supposed to be he. Who the villain was that declared you were a spy, and knocked you on the head, I have not been able to find out. My wife had you carried here, for my men spared your life at her intercession, for they insisted you were a Sasanach spy. I only arrived this morning, and promised to examine you myself. I am quite satisfied, and will stake my life upon it, that you are neither Sasanach nor spy. I deeply regret the injuries you have received; but to-morrow night you shall be conducted to a place where you may be taken up by the night-mail to Waterford."

There was a frankness, and kind gentlemanly tone in the words and manner of the stranger, that pleased Francis De Burgh; he therefore replied that he thought little of his wounds, his only anxiety was to reach Waterford, and he believed he should be quite well enough to proceed that night.

"Well, we will see about that," said the rebel leader; "at present, I think some breakfast would do you no harm. My wife and child are gone on to her father's retreat; she will be s' there, and she begged me to express her deep gratitude to you the generous assistance and kindness you shewed her."

So saying, the stranger retired, promising that he would send in breakfast.

Shortly after, the old woman made her appearance, with some tea, coffee, and cold meat; and, adding more turf to the fire, retired without uttering a word.

Considering his situation, and the uneasiness of mind he experienced, Francis De Burgh made a tolerable breakfast, and then sat down at the little window, to endeavour to while away the time by looking out on the dreary prospect before him. While doing so, his thoughts naturally reverted to his late adventure. In thinking it over in his mind, he recollected that in the mail-coach-office in Dublin he first noticed the two men in the frieze coats, and remembered the start they gave when they heard the name of De Burgh. Though it did not make an impression at the time, it now, as he turned the circumstance over in his thoughts, looked suspicious.

He felt almost positive that the man who fired at him on the roof of the mail was was one of those two men; the other was, doubtless, behind. Though they did not, as the stranger said, belong to either his men or the rebel leader, Holt, yet they were evidently rebels also, for they joined the others at once, savagely exciting them to shoot him as a Sasanach spy. It appears, therefore, on reflection, to our hero, somewhat extraordinary that two men, allowing them to be rebels, should have imbibed without cause so deadly an animosity against him. But as he could make nothing but perplexing suppositions out of it, he banished the circumstance from his mind, and turned his thoughts on fair Mary Grey.

Thus a good portion of the day psased, during which the old woman brought in some dressings for his wounds, and forced him to submit to have them attended to, though he assured her he felt little inconvenience from them. She shook her head, examined the hurts, and certainly her dressings eased the pain considerably.

During the day several men passed the window, all in a kind of green uniform and sash of the same colour and all well armed He observed that they climbed to the top of some rock, and looked down, as if into the valley below, or watching something.

It was getting dusk, when the old dame brought in a cold fowl and some hot potatoes, and placed them before our hero. Not many minutes had elapsed, ere Holt's son-in-law entered the room, and taking a chair, sat down, looking serious and seemingly sad or fatigued.

"I am sorry, Mr. De Burgh," he said, breaking the silence, "to keep you thus confined; but situated as we are, it is unavoidable. The country below is overrun with cavalry, but they cannot ascend these hills."

"I should be sorry," observed Francis, "that you should incur any risk on my account. Surely I can descend the hills without putting you to inconvenience or danger."

"It may appear so to you, sir," returned the 'United Irishman,' "and I would most willingly trust you; but if you were seen or met by any of the military, they would insist on your stating where you came from; and if you refused, you would be taken before a magistrate and detained till you did. You are not aware how perilous the times are, even to those most innocent of aught against the government. However, in a few hours it will be dark, and I will attempt your descent."

There was so much candour and sincerity in the tone and manner of the "United Irishman," that Francis De Burgh, after a moment's consideration, thought it best to tell him how his attendant had discovered his abode. The "United Irishman" started and looked serious, and not a little confounded, saying:

"Good God! he might have been shot, or he may betray our retreat."

Francis assured him that there was not the slightest probability of Bill Mullaghan doing so; he had been attached to him from boyhood, and he was aware how deeply grateful he was to Holt's daughter for her interference, and probably for saving his life.

"It is very surprising," remarked the rebel leader, "how he could have found his way here; there is but one path, and it is most intricate."

"Probably," remarked our hero, "he followed our track the first night."

"It is possible," returned the 'United Irishman;' "but he incurred a terrible risk. If discovered, he would unquestionably have been shot. Do you know we are nearly three hundred men in these mountains?"

"Yours is a perilous career," observed Francis De Burgh, looking into the thoughtful and expressive features of his companion. "I will not attempt to analyse your reasons for embracing it, for great and good men have embarked life and fortune in the same career; but I feel satisfied it is a bootless struggle, and a fearful penalty will have to be paid in the end."

The "United Irishman's" features were much agitated, and he appeared greatly moved, as Francis spoke in a kind and well-meaning tone. He bent his eyes on the ground, then suddenly looking up, said:

"I never dreamed, Mr. De Burgh, from the very first, that we should succeed; still, believe me, there are many hundreds of us who have taken up arms, and have done so with the honest hope of serving our beautiful, but, alas! unhappy land. I am not a Roman Catholic, neither am I biassed by religious feelings in the struggle. I had much to lose, and nothing but the hope of benefiting my country to gain. I know not how it is, but you interest me much, and I would wish that when you leave this, you would pity, and not condemn us as mere rebels. A few words will explain my situation, and it will help to pass the time. My poor Kate spoke of you in such high terms, that you were so gentle, and so kind, and compassionate to her, that you won my heart before I saw you."

Francis held out his hand, feeling kindly towards the brave but mistaken man before him.

"I respect your motives and feelings," he said, "and though I cannot agree with you either in opinion or feeling, yet it is not for me to dare to condemn your motives. I am too young, and know too little of my native land—for I suppose by birth I am an Irishman—to attempt to judge of the feeling that have caused this outbreak, but I will listen to you with attention, and shall always remember your kindness with gratitude."

The "United Irishman" pressed our hero's hand with fervour, and then gave him the following short sketch of his career, which our readers will find in our next chapter.

## CHAPTER X.

"You are aware, Mr. De Burgh," began the 'United Irishman,' "that my father-in-law's name is Holt, a name now well-known in Ireland, though perhaps quite unknown to you. A very few words will explain how he became a leader of 'United Irishmen.' He is the son of a highly respectable landholder in the county of Wicklow; as he advanced in life, he held several public situations, and it was he who captured the notorious robber, Patrick Rogers. That rascal and his band were long the terror of the County Wicklow."

"In the year '97, Mr. Holt was in Dublin, with his wife and favourite daughter. I was then pursuing my career at the Dublin bar, as a barrister, with every prospect of success, but entirely dependent on my own exertions. I became acquainted with Miss Katherine Holt; and though my finances were limited, Mr. Holt gave his consent to our marriage, and we were united.

"At this period Mr. Holt joined with another person, and became road-observer for the repairs of roads. Mr. Holt found all the money, and paid those employed every Saturday night. On applying, after some time, to the treasurer for repayment, my father-in-law found that his coadjutor had contrived to receive all the money, and had absconded. For a length of time he remained unpaid, but by unceasing application and perseverance he received his money. At this period, I can safely say, Mr. Holt was quite unaffected by the political opinions rapidly gaining ground all over Ireland. I unfortunately was not, and frequently attended the meetings, neglected my affairs, and got into great distress.

"The villain who had absconded with Mr. Holt's money became his most bitter and unrelenting enemy; for he was forced to surrender the sum he had absconded with, and condemned to three months' imprisonment. This man contrived to raise against my father-in-law the cry of 'United Irishman.' These are terrible times to have suspicion attached to you; and merely upon the bare word of this scoundrel, he, with a party of soldiers, surrounded Mr. Holt's house at night, and set fire to it, his wife and son escaping with difficulty. Mr. Holt was from home. I will not detain you with all the particulars; suffice it to say, branded as a 'United Irishman,' he became one; soon raised a formidable band, and took up his quarters in the mountains near Luggalau. Shortly after he joined the army under General Roche. This leader was cruel and brutal to his men, whilst Holt became extremely popular. In the bloody affair of Ballyellis he gained considerable military reputation, having had the command for the day. After this he was received by the Wexford gentry with acclamation, and soon had a band of sixteen hundred men under his own individual command.

"At this period in Dublin there existed a numerous gang of infamous spies and informers. My letters to my father-in-law were intercepted; I was declared a 'United Irishman,' and I had just time to escape and save my life. I joined my father-in-law, leaving my poor wife and baby in Dublin. [Holt's life is a matter of history; his career, &c., form a part of the history of the Irish Rebellion; we merely give a brief sketch, as it is necessary to the interests of our tale.] This brief sketch is quite sufficient to give you, although it is a mere outline. I was planning how to get my wife from Dublin, when she heard the false rumour of my being mortally wounded and in prison; she was in deep distress; your kindness probably preserved my child's life. How all this will end God alone knows."

For more than an hour Francis continued to converse with Holt's son-in-law upon his career and the unhappy state of Ireland; but, as we said before, we will not mix up politics in our story.

As it grew dark, Mr. W—— rose up, saying he would go and put two confidential men to keep a keen look-out for Bill Mullaghan, to protect him from injury, and conduct him to the cottage.

Francis found out that the old woman was quite right in dressing his wounds, for towards night they became sore and irritable, not sufficiently so, however, to prevent his leaving the cottage when the time came.

It was nearly ten o'clock when Mr. W——, with Bill Mullaghan, entered Francis De Burgh's room in the cabin. Bill was rejoiced to see our hero, but Mr. W—— cut short his expressions of joy, by saying:

"Now, Mr. De Burgh, you must be moving; we have no time to lose, as the Waterford mail will pass through Bally——s in two hours, and we have five miles of bad ground to go over. You were quite right about your attendant, he tracked or followed you here; but in truth it was a dangerous experiment."

"It was not so difficult, your honour," said Bill, "for faix, the poor young woman had to walk the whole way with the baby in her arms. Be gor! I had a great wish to step forward and offer to carry them both."

The insurgent leader looked kindly at the broad-shouldered, good-humoured Hibernian, saying:

"You are a kind-hearted fellow. I should not like to have heard you had been shot for a spy."

"Oh, by the immortals! nor I either," muttered Bill, but he must be a queer omadawn of a chap that would venture to say Bill Mullaghan was a spy."

"In the dark, my friend," returned Mr. W——, "if you had met any of our scouts, and had not the word of the night, you would have fared badly. I see your master is ready, so let us be moving."

The three now left the cottage; it was extremely dark, but guided by Mr. W—— they commenced descending the rugged face of a very steep hill, so covered with great masses of boulders and fragments of rock, as to be impassable to a stranger.

After descending about a mile, they passed through a species of cavern, or a passage under a monstrous pile of rocks, heaped one over the other by some convulsion of nature. Mr. W—— informed our hero, that the rocky barrier he saw extended for nearly three miles on each side, so that any one, looking up from the vale below, would fancy those rocks the summit of the mountain.

In three quarters of an hour they reached the bottom, and a mile further they came out on a kind of lane or by-road. Here their guide paused, saying:

"You are now, Mr. De' Burgh, out of our district, and will not encounter any of our scouts. We have passed many, but have not been challenged, as I sent on a man before us to explain matters. It appears that your attendant passed through our retreat last night unseen, in consequence of the scouts having left their posts to come up to the cottage to attend a meeting there, most important to us, and they were absent three hours.

"I must now bid you farewell. Follow this road till you come into the Waterford road, which you will do after walking half a mile or so; turn to the left and you will reach Bally——s before the mail, which changes horses there. A party of dragoons will be there attending the mail, you had better therefore go to the public inn close to the mail-stables, and send the ostler to inquire for places, and excite as little attention or suspicion as possible; not that you incur any risk, but to avoid any kind of delay."

Francis De Burgh held out his hand, which was pressed by the unfortunate Mr. W—— with much emotion. Our hero could not wish him success in his mistaken career; but truly and sincerely wished that his poor wife and child, and himself, might escape the fatal penalty of his rash enterprise. After a few more simple instructions they parted, and Francis De Burgh and his attendant pursued their way along the muddy and narrow road.

"Well, sir, thank God you are well out of this scrape," said Bill Mullaghan; "bad luck anyhow to the villain that hurt you Do you feel much pain, sir?"

"No, Bill, I do not; my left arm is stiffish and sore, but

otherwise I am all right. Did you sleep at Bally——s last night?"

"Faix, I had no such luck, sir. I got out of my course coming back, and wandered about these confounded rocks till daylight."

"You had a cold berth of it, my poor fellow; but look around you, that is as far as you can. Is this the main road?"

"Bother the road," muttered Bill, getting out of a muddy ditch he had stumbled into; "it was only the other day I was wishing to see the world, but faix this is not a pleasant part of it."

They soon discovered that they were on the main road, and in half an hour more they entered the little town of Bally——s, splashed and covered with mud to their knees. The town consisted of an interminable row of mud cabins, several slated houses, and an immense barn and stables belonging to the proprietor of the mail-coach-horses. They had not much difficulty in finding the public-house; and, entering the kitchen, caused infinite surprise to the host and hostess and half a dozen countrymen, drinking whisky in its native state, and very much occupied in spelling a printed handbill.

The whole party turned round, and surveyed the tall and powful forms of the new comers with evident surprise.

Francis called for some whisky and hot water, and then inquired when the Waterford mail would arrive.

"She ought to be here very soon," said one of the men, "anyhow, if she ain't stopped by the boys."

"Be jabers, there's a troop of dragoons to be with them now, a-cause of the stoppage the other night," said the grim-looking, unshaved host of the ale-house, handing our hero a tumbler of smoking whisky punch, and Bill another.

"Will you send some one to take two places to Waterford?" said Francis De Burgh.

"Oh, by this and by that, you needn't fear; there's no one from this place will go in the mail. May I make bould to ax your honour where ye come from, for, faix, you look as if ye'd been cruising over a bog," and a grim grin sat on the man's face.

"Mind your own business," said Bill, staring the host in the face, "and, be gor, keep better whisky than this; faix, it's poor stuff."

"Ax your pardon, sir," said the host, in a cringing tone, "but as to the whisky, perhaps you don't know what good whisky is."

"Oh, botheration!" muttered Bill.

Just then the sound of a horn was heard, and, with a shout, off started all the countrymen to see the mail and dragoons come in.

Francis De Burgh having paid for the two glasses of whisky, which he merely called for to avoid attracting attention, walked out, followed by Bill Mullaghan, and arrived in time to see the mail dash up to the stables, followed by half a dozen mounted troopers.

Francis, accosting the coachman as soon as he got down from his box, inquired if he could have an inside and outside seat to Waterford.

As soon as the man heard his voice, he started back with an exclamation of surprise, the moment after calling out:

"Bill, I say Bill, come here with the lamp; as sure as a gun here's the gemman that was on the mail, when we was attacked by those bloody rebels."

The guard came running up with the lamp as Francis De Burgh said:

"You are quite right, coachman: I think I remember *you:* you drove the mail that night."

"The very same, sir; I drives the mail every second night from Dublin to Carlow."

The guard had come up, and so did every one present, staring, by the rays of the lamp and one or two lanterns, at our hero and his attendant, as if they had risen from the dead.

"Well, sir," said the guard, "I'm blowed if I ain't glad to see you bain't murdered; we all thought you was killed and buried somewhere here. There's Mr. McCarthy, the magistrate, in the mail. Now, he will be glad to take down your deposition; he lives near Athy, and yesterday with a party of dragoons he scoured the whole country round."

"Hallo, guard!" said a clear manly voice from the mail-coach window, "what is the matter? What are you waiting for?"

"Why, sir," returned the guard, "here's the gemman as was murdered the night before last."

"He, the deuce he is!" exclaimed the same voice, in a laughing tone, "pray open the door, and let the murdered gentleman in, if he's going our way; if not, let me out."

"There's only two inside, sir;" and throwing open the coach door, Francis De Burgh sprung in, the guard saying, as he threw the light of the lamp upon our hero's face:

"This is the gentleman, your worship."

"Upon my word, sir," said the magistrate, looking with surprise Francis De Burgh, "for a person that was murdered and buried the night before last, you look remarkably well; I am rejoiced to see you, however, and we can talk the matter over as we proceed."

In a few minutes the dragoons were mounted, the coachman and guards and Bill on their seats, the horn sounded, and off went the mail at a canter, followed by the troopers, to the great admiration of those assembled, and leaving them besides an abundance of matter to puzzle their brains about.

Francis De Burgh began to consider his position none of the pleasantest, for he made no doubt of being asked sundry and various questions, which he made no doubt he would find extremely difficult to answer or evade.

He could see there were two gentlemen in the coach, but he could not distinguish their features.

"Well, sir," began the magistrate, as soon as they were well on the road, "you may count yourself a remarkably fortunate person; here you are sound and well, and printed hand-bills dispersed about the country, stating your supposed murder by the rebels, and a reward for the recovery of your body, and apprehension of your assassins."

"Good God, sir!" exclaimed our hero, exceedingly annoyed, for he thought if such a report should reach his father before his arrival the consequences might be serious.

"Why, what's the matter, Mr. De Burgh?" said Mr. McCarthy; "you seem agitated: do you object to not being murdered?"

"No, sir," returned our hero, but such a report reaching a father's ears might be serious."

"True, true, so it might," replied the magistrate, in a more serious tone; "pray excuse my levity, I really spoke without consideration; but I trust you will get home before any such report arrives there, and, thanks to me, I think you will."

"I hope so, sir," returned our hero, "but may I ask you why you say thanks to me?"

Mr. McCarthy laughed, saying, "Why you see I am not very particular, and not at all fond of hanging people, even supposing them to be rebels. Now, the night you were supposed to be murdered, Sir W—— was expected to be a passenger in the Waterford mail; the baronet is a tall powerful man. Now, Sir W—— is notorious through the county as the hanging magistrate; and the rebels, if they could catch him, would, I do verily believe, have given him a dance of the same kind. But Sir W—— was too cute to be caught napping; his name was put down in the Waterford mail way-bill, while he started in the Limerick. You were evidently mistaken for him. Now, if any of my brother magistrates stumbled on you, as I have, they would have sent you back under escort to Athy; there you would have been examined, cross-examined, and very likely delayed a day or two. It was fortunate for you that it was my turn to make this journey; I cannot see, for the life of me, the use of tormenting a person who must be anxious to get home. So all you have to do is to favour me with a brief account of what happened to you after the stopping of the mail up to this period. I will take it all down in the three quarters of an hour the coach stops at Carlow; you will sign it with your place of abode, and then you can go on by this mail to Waterford."

"You are very kind, sir," said Francis, much pleased with the tone and amiable manner of the Athy magistrate, "and I shall of course be ready to give you all the information you may require; though, in truth, I have little to say, for I was senseless for a considerable period, both from the blow on the head and a pistol-shot under the arm."

"Good God! then you were wounded? They did, then, attempt to murder you?" exclaimed Mr. McCarthy, in an anxious and interested tone. "Will you pardon me for my careless, thoughtless manner? I imagined, seeing you so apparently well, that the whole affair was a mistake, and that you had been merely confined in some barn for a night. You are not seriously hurt, I hope.— That gentleman in the corner," added the magistrate, "sleeps very soundly; he has not stirred."

"No, sir," said the gentleman in the corner, in rather an unpleasant, sharp tone, "I do not sleep; it would be devilish hard to sleep, with such incessant chatter about nothing."

"Well," said the magistrate drily, "I am glad to hear you have a tongue, although not the politest in the world. But I beg pardon, Mr. De Burgh, I was requesting to know if you felt pain or uneasiness from your wounds."

"None, Mr. McCarthy, worth naming," returned Francis, rather surprised at the tone and words of the man in the mantle in the corner.

"Pray, when you recovered your senses," said the magistrate, "what did you see, or where did you find yourself?"

"In a chamber in a very poor cabin, attended by an old woman, who spoke only Irish, and who had dressed my wounds. My servant found me out the next day; and some hours ago, finding myself able to leave, I set out for Bally——s."

"A most extraordinary adventure," said Mr. McCarthy, thoughtfully. "They first try to shoot you, and then nurse you to recover you. The coachman reports that the daughter of the rebel leader, Holt, was a passenger in the mail that night, and that she called out, 'Don't murder him;' but that he heard the pistol-shot, and saw you fall dead, as he thought, and then they all went off, taking your body with them, and also Holt's daughter."

"Rather a curious story," said the stranger in the corner, in a sneering voice. "I was in Bally——s when the mail arrived after being attacked, and I heard a fat lady who was passenger—I believe her name is Figgins, and she keeps a bacon store in Waterford—I heard her say that the goung gentleman shot by the rebels was extremely intimate with that young woman, calling herself Holt's daughter; and she also heard one of the rebels say they would carry the body to the mountains till their leader saw it."

"Pray, sir," said Mr. McCarthy sharply, and before Francis De Burgh could utter a word, "pray, sir, who are you?"

"I am an Englishman, sir, at your service," returned the speaker. "My name is Brown."

"And what may be your business in this part of the country, and especially in such a place as Bally——s?"

"Upon my word, sir," returned the stranger, with his sneering laugh, "you seem to regard my desire to give you information rather curiously. As my business is of a private nature, you must excuse my informing you. However, if you insist, you shall have ample proof of my identity when we reach Carlow."

"It is certainly a very bad specimen of the human heart," said Francis De Burgh, "that the simple attention I showed to a delicate female, scarcely eighteen years of age, with a young baby in her arms, should be so perverted by one of her own sex."

Our hero then explained to the really worthy, kind-hearted magistrate, the simple facts relating to his meeting with Holt's daughter.

"Your conduct, sir," said the magistrate, feelingly, "does you credit, and I doubly respect you. But here we are."

And the mail dashed up to the door of the principal hotel in Carlow.

## CHAPTER XI.

As the mail drove up to the hotel door, and the waiters and some others came out with lights, Francis De Burgh felt exceedingly anxious to have a look at the stranger calling himself Brown, which name he set down in his own mind as a *nomme de guerre*. He fancied there was a great deal of malice in the stranger's observations. Mr. McCarthy got out first; he was a man of middle stature, about forty, with an extremely gentlemanly exterior, and agreeable expression of countenance. As he leaped out, he laid his hand on our hero's arm, saying:

"Come, Mr. De Burgh, we have not a great deal of time to spare. I will take down your deposition; you can put your name to it, and then resume your journey."

Young De Burgh followed Mr. McCarthy, the stranger walking up the steps after them, into a large room, where supper was laid, and a blazing fire threw its cheerful light over the comforts before them.

Francis cast a glance at the gentleman calling himself Brown. He was a tall, athletic man, decidedly a gentleman in appearance and manner, in age about fifty-two or three. He was remarkably well dressed; rather elaborately for stage coach travelling. His dark hair and moustachios were but very slightly grizzled; and although his features were decidedly handsome, their expression was stern and forbidding. Having approached the fire, he desired the waiter to bring him a bottle of sherry, and order a bed, as he intended sleeping there.

Mr. McCarthy looked fixedly at the Englishman, then taking a chair, opened a very neat and compact travelling writing-case, and taking out pens, ink, and paper, requested Francis De Burgh to sit down beside him, and repeat briefly his previous statement. This our hero did. Mr. McCarthy wrote rapidly, and the matter was soon terminated; when our hero, happening to look up, caught the Englishman's eyes fixed upon him, with a most sinister and ferocious expression. Francis, with a flushed cheek, started up, and looking him steadily in the face, said, calmly enough:

"Sir, you regard me in a most strange and repugnant manner; as far as my memory serves, I have never seen you before, therefore I feel forced to notice your behaviour."

"You are quite welcome, young gentleman," returned the

stranger, haughtily and sneeringly, "to put what construction you please on the expression of my features. I did not make them, sir, therefore am not accountable for the effect they appear to have upon you."

"Ha! by-the-bye, Mr. Brown—1 think you said that was your name," interrupted Mr. McCarthy, stepping in between our hero and the stranger, "you said you would afford me information respecting your appearance two nights consecutively in the same locality, that locality bearing a very bad name. Pray, may I ask you what brought you to Bally——s?"

"Well, sir," returned the Englishman, in his cold, sarcastic tone, "I presume the license of the times permits magistrates to ask what at any other period would be considered impertinent questions."

Mr. McCarthy coloured to the temples, but he kept his temper, not even making a reply. Mr. Brown took a pocket-book from his vest, and opening it, selected two letters from it, looked them over a moment, and then handed them to Mr. McCarthy, saying:

"Those papers will, I presume, satisfy you as to my motives for being in this miserable, rebellious country; but at the same time I must insist, as you have put me to the disagreeable necessity of exposing my private business to you, that the disclosure may be strictly confined to yourself."

The magistrate hesitated a moment, but the next instant took the letters.

As he ran his eyes over the contents, Francis De Burgh saw him slightly change colour; however, he refolded the letters, and returned them, saying coldly, but politely:

"I am quite satisfied, sir; the state of this country, and my private instructions from government, authorize me to act as I have done;" and then with a slight salutation to the stranger, Mr. McCarthy said: "There's the horn, Mr. De Burgh; pray put your name to this paper, also your residence. Of course you will hereafter ready to answer any questions it might be necessary to be put to you respecting this deposition of yours."

"Certainly, sir," returned Francis, putting his name and residence on the paper, finishing just as the guard came in, saying:

"Now, gentlemen, if you please."

Our hero shook the worthy and good natured magistrate heartily by the hand, and, without further notice of the stranger, left the room. Five minutes after, the mail was going full speed out of Carlow, with an addition of two inside passengers and one out.

As they proceeded, Francis, finding his fellow-travellers settling themselves for a nap, passed his time thinking over the late scene at the inn, and conjecturing who the stranger could possibly be. There was no mistaking the look of malice and hatred he had detected in the Englishman's features, but he could not assign any possible reason for such an expression; he, however, congratulated himself on escaping any further questions relating to Holt's daughter, and his residence in the secret haunt of a large body of insurgents.

Early in the morning the mail reached Waterford, and having breakfasted, Bill was despatched to hire a car, as no coach would start till night. The four-and-twenty long miles to Dungarvon took our hero nearly as much time to get over, as it had taken him to get from Carlow to Waterford. He was all anxiety to reach home; still he felt no unusual depression of spirits, no promptings, as they are termed, of fate. To get home quickly was all the anxiety he experienced.

On reaching the bridge, Francis paid for and dismissed the car, leaving Bill on it, as he lived the other side of the river, and was anxious also to see his old father.

Striking across the fields, our hero took a short cut to the cottage, and walked on rapidly. On reaching the front door, over which there was a verandah, covered with creeping plants, he was struck by the door being closed, and the blinds down in his father's room. Both these circumstances were unusual; for Jane being deaf, and the kitchen on the left hand of the door, it was usually left open during the day, and he knew his father kept his window wide open from the time of rising to the hour of retiring to rest. On knocking for admittance, which he did with rather an uneasy feeling, the door was opened by a young girl, who sometimes assisted Jane in household affairs.

"Where is Jane? Is my father in the house, Kate?" inquired Francis, as he walked into the hall.

"Jane, sir," said the girl, timidly, and with her apron to her eyes, "is with the master, who was took bad last night."

Francis De Burgh, without waiting to make further inquiry, with a bound sprang up the stairs, his heart beating painfully, his hand trembling with agitation. The idea of his father being dangerously ill came over his mind with a terrible chill. Opening the door softly, he beheld, by the subdued light coming through the blind, Jane warming something at the fire. There were no curtains to the bed, which stood facing the windows, and on this Francis cast his glance with great anxiety. He beheld his father, but how strangely, fearfully altered! He was lying on his back, the eyes sunken and closed, and the fine, noble features wasted and thin, and fearfully pale.

Francis remained rooted to the spot; he could not have stirred if his life depended on the movement, the tears were in his eyes blinding him; he had never stood by the sick couch of friend or foe. He knew nothing of the grim enemy of mankind, except when his hand was laid upon those dying a violent death. But yet, as he gazed upon the wan features of his beloved father, his heart smote him, for he saw at a glance that death was not far off

—he was appalled! When the old dame turning round, and beheld him, devoutly crossing herself, she said:

"The Lord be praised, Mr. Francis, you are come; the poor master was taken sudden last night, Dr. Creigh was sent for instantly, and now it's not ten minutes since he left."

"My God!" exclaimed Francis trembling, and the perspiration falling from his forehead, "tell me, Jane, did my father hear that any accident had happened to me?"

"No, dear, nothing of the kind," said the old dame affectionately, the tears rolling down her cheeks as she took him by the hand; "Oh! Mr. Francis, don't take on so—oh don't; it's God's will, dear, and it may be He may cure him, acushla!"

Still gazing into his father's face, and watching him as he breathed like a sleeping child without change of feature or movement of the body,

"Tell me, Jane," he said, "when and how this happened, and what Doctor Creigh thinks?"

"Three days ago, darling, he came home from Waterford not very well, indeed, a little pale, but nothing to frighten one. When I asked him if he felt tired or ill, he said, 'Oh, no, only the old palpitation of the heart a little more troublesome, perhaps.' Yesterday evening—God save us! he was busy writing a letter in the parlour, and all at once I heard the bell ring quick like and sudden, so I ran in. Lord save us! he was lying back on the sofa gasping for breath. I thought I should have died, such an all-overness came about me; but as luck would have it, Kate came in with some linen, and I sent her off for the doctor, while I raised the master and did all I could; but his breath seemed to go faster and faster, till the doctor came. What he did I don't know, further than that he bled him, and then came some of the neighbours, who carried him upstairs; and old Dame Wilkinson, and Kate, and I, got him to bed. But the Lord save us, he has never rallied since; but he's just as you see him, breathing like an infant.

Francis De Burgh was overwhelmed with grief, and told Jane to send for Doctor Creigh, to say that he had come home and wished to see him immediately.

As Jane left the room Francis threw himself on his knees beside the bed, he took his beloved father's hand, which was cold and clammy, and the pulsation scarcely perceptible. But, as he held the hand, he thought the pulsation became somewhat quicker; and looking up he drew in his breath, for his father's eyes opened, and instantly were fixed on those of Francis, whom he knew at once. A smile of intense happiness came over his pale features, a slight pressure of his hand, and all was over!

We must not dwell on this part of our narrative, upon that moment of bereavement and agony to our young hero. During his life he had often braved death, and in various ways suffered privations and hardships; but all those were nought compared with that one hour of deep and silent suffering.

What between the agony of his mind and the neglected state of his wounds, the day after he followed his father's remains to their last resting place, a severe fever ensued; and for several days he remained quite unconscious of all around him. But by Doctor Creigh's kind and skilful attention, at the expiration of a month he was able to leave his bed, a mere shadow of his former self. But his youth and a good constitution befriended him; and he made rapid progress in bodily health, though saddened in feeling.

During his illness his faithful follower, Bill Mullaghan, scarcely ever left his side; he was a huge nurse it is true, but yet his movements and his manner were as gentle as those of a child. In vain the doctor assured him that the fever was infectious; Bill growled, and told the doctor to mind his own business, the fever knew better than to board him. He'd watch his master night and day, if he had the plague; and if the doctor didn't cure him, be gor, he wouldn't leave a whole bone in his skin.

The doctor and Bill got on badly at first, but before a week was out they became the best friends in the world. When Francis De Burgh first recovered a full recollection and perception of things and persons around him, he beheld Bill, holding a small saucepan over a spirit lamp, and scientifically stirring the mixture with a spoon.

Francis called him by name, which gave Bill such a start, that he dropped the saucepan and extinguished the lamp, upsetting the spirits over himself, so that he appeared in a blue flame.

"Be gor! he's come to himself," exclaimed Bill, swearing at himself for his awkwardness, and trying to extinguish the flame before he approached the bed. "The Lord be praised, sir, but I'm a great baste; I've spilled the mixture ould Creigh was so particular about, and sorrow a drop more is there. But now you're come round, the less you take of this stuff the better," and the poor fellow repeatedly kissed his master's hand, uttering all kinds of strange sentences.

"In a few days, sir, you'll be all right," resumed Bill.

"Yes, Bill, my body may get well, but it will take time to heal the wound the mind has received. My home is gone for ever."

"It's the Lord's will, sir," said Bill soothingly, "and sure Father Flaherty says we must glory when the Lord takes the good; and sure there never was a better man than the master— rest his soul in glory!"

And Bill crossed himself devoutly and seriously.

A few days more, and Francis De Burgh was able to move down stairs. Old Jane was the kindest of nurses. The curate of the parish called often; he was a curate of the olden time, fond of his glass, of a good horse, and could cross the country with the best fox-hunter in it. With old Father Flaherty Francis was a prodigious favourite; he would pass an hour with him, chatting cheerfully on all subjects, but never intruded his religious opinions. Francis always liked the worthy priest, and his conversation was often a great consolation to him.

Jane said to her young master one evening:

"There are two or three letters for you, dear; and may be now you would like to see the last letter the poor dear master—glory to him!—was writing the evening he was took."

"No, Jane," returned Francis, with a slight shudder, "not yet —not yet; I must gain strength."

A few days more passed, and he rapidly approached convalescence.

On the twenty-first of January—the day our hero completed his twentieth birthday—the morning had been ushered in by one of the heaviest snow storms that had been known for years, with a furious gale from the eastward. In the morning, Bill Mullaghan had gone to sea with the St. Patrick, his father not being well; and great anxiety was experienced towards evening, as neither the hooker or three others had returned. Francis De Burgh was seated in the parlour, where, for so many years, he had been accustomed to see his beloved father, and to hear his kind soft voice, as he taught him many things; and now he sat, on his twentieth birthday, with the howling of a winter's storm, rocking the cottage during the furious gusts as they swept by. He was alone, for Jane, two hours before the storm began, had gone as far as the town bridge to a neighbour, and she had not come back; for after her departure the storm commenced and the heavy snow began to fall, and the night set in with intense darkness, notwithstanding the white covering of the ground. Jane had attempted to return, but found it impossible; the storm forced her back to the nearest cabin for assistance; but there she only found a widow and her three young children, and there she was compelled to remain.

Before Francis De Burgh lay a pocket-book, given him by Jane that morning; it contained the half-finished letter of his lamented father, and two others.

For several minutes he allowed the letters to lie unopened on the table, for memory was very busy with the past. It was certainly not a night to soothe or allay excited feelings, for the squalls of wind roared round the house like thunder, and the seas broke loud and heavily upon the outward sands. The two letters lying before him bore the English post-mark—one had an earl's coronet on the seal. At length he took up his father's unfinished letter, and unfolding it, read as follows:—

"My beloved Son,

"The time has arrived, when the past may be unfolded, and the events of bygone years laid before you. It is true I have deposited in the cabinet, in my chamber, a full history of my life; have also stated my motives for passing so many years in seclusion. You will find many important and valuable papers, necessary to you, should anything happen to me before your return. I trust in God there will be no harm befall you; still we are in the hands of God, and we know not what an hour of time may bring forth.

"I find it important and necessary that I should leave here to-morrow for London, though I expect you in a day or two; still I cannot delay, for fear of any untoward event or accident. I will here set down a few particulars necessary for you to know, and to show you how to act, so that you may obtain the rank and station you are entitled to."

Francis De Burgh paused, surprised by the last words he had read. It was not that he felt elated at such a prospect as his lamented father stated was before him; but many conflicting thoughts agitated him at that moment. As he was about to resume the reading, a violent blow, struck against the door leading out into the garden, caused him to rise from his chair and listen; another violent rush, as if some heavy body had fallen against the door, and the instant after it gave way with a crash. Laying down the letter, Francis De Burgh seized the poker, the only defensive weapon in the room, and hurried towards the door, satisfied that the back kitchen door had been burst open, and not by the storm, for the gale was at the other side of the house.

He had scarcely thrown open the parlour door, when several men rushed through the narrow passage, and, with a variety of fierce oaths, made an effort to seize him; but the first that approached he struck to the ground. In the scuffle, the candle he held in his other hand was extinguished, just as two powerful men threw themselves upon him, dragging him violently into the parlour.

Though weak and exhausted by his late illness, Francis De Burgh was not easily overcome; by a desperate effort he freed himself from one of the ruffians, and rolled over on the floor with the other, upsetting the table and all on it. Two other men now fell on him and held him down, while one of the others getting up, said, with a savage oath:

"This is too bad; curse his impudence! Hold him there till I re-light the candles. We need not be afraid of interruption."

"Do you want a knife in your ribs," said one of the men, holding our exhausted hero on the floor; "if you do, you shall get it, unless you take my advice, and keep quiet."

"Diowl!" said a savage voice, with a strong Irish brogue, "let him go, Dick; be my soul, if he stirs, I'll blow his brains out."

By this time the candles were lighted, and the men holding Francis let him go; and placing their backs to the door, stood with cocked pistols extended towards him.

Trembling with passion and excitement, Francis rose to his feet, and gazed sternly and steadily at the fierce men then in the room. They were covered with snow flakes from head to foot, but they were rapidly melting; three of them had their faces blackened, and handkerchiefs tied across their hats, and around the throat.

One of the four, the one that was lighting the candles, was a man rather above the middle height, but singularly robust and powerful in frame; he spoke with an English accent, and had neither crape nor other disguise over his features. He wore a dark-grey great coat buttoned to his chin, with a black silk handkerchief round his neck. His features had nothing remarkable in them, but his dark eyes and extremely heavy brows, gave a savage expression to his countenance; in years, he could not yet have reached forty.

Stooping down, he deliberately picked up the three letters lying on the carpet, and thrust them into his pocket; as he did so, Francis with difficulty curbing his passion, said:

"Stay, those letters can be of no use or utility to you; give them back, and take what else you please."

"Oh!" returned the Englishman, drawing a pistol from the breast pocket of his coat, and coolly cocking it, "so you give us leave to help ourselves; well, that's consoling." The men at the door burst into a laugh. "But," continued the man with a mocking tone, "we came here to help ourselves, without asking leave. If you do not want your brains blown out keep quiet, for I have a way of my own in transacting business of this sort; or the first thing I should have done, would have been to have put you out of the way of doing any further mischief. Now take warning, your life hangs by a hair."

Turning to his three associates, he said:

"You, Will, come with me, and carry one of the candles; there's only a deaf old woman in the house, in bed I suppose. If she makes a noise cut her throat, it will be an act of mercy; and you two stand at this door, and if this young madman attempts to move towards you, only one step, use your pistols, it will save all further trouble. Do you understand me?"

"Oh, be jabers, Captain Dove, the instructions are simple and easy, and be sure it shall be done."

Turning round, the Englishman **and his comrade** left the room, closing the door after them.

## CHAPTER XII.

Francis De Burgh, after the door closed, stood absolutely astonished, and for the moment bewildered. Had he had his usual strength and nerve, there is scarcely a doubt but he would have rushed recklessly upon the two ruffians before him, who were conversing in a low voice in Irish, but never taking their eyes off him, or their fingers from the triggers of their pistols. It was by this time very evident to him that this outrage was not for plunder; the tone and manner of the Englishman, though fierce and savage, were evidently those of a man of a superior position in society to those of the other men, who were of the lowest class of Irishmen.

The snow had melted from their garments, disclosing the long grey coats worn by the peasantry. After a moment's thought Francis De Burgh threw himself into a chair; he heard the heavy tramp of the two men overhead, and his mind was tortured with the knowledge that they would, without doubt, plunder his father's cabinet of all the valuable papers and documents it contained, and he knew not what besides. He felt ready to sink with weakness and rage, and twenty times was on the point of braving death from the pistols of the two watchful ruffians before him.

In less than twenty minutes he heard the two men descending the stairs, and immediately after they entered the room. The Englishman at once advanced close up to our hero, who could see that his companion carried a large bundle of something under his coat. He held his cocked pistol in his hand, and when close beside our hero, he said calmly and deliberately, holding the pistol within a foot of young De Burgh's head:

"Now tell me the truth, or die—did you, or did you not open your father's cabinet since his death?"

"Villain!" exclaimed De Burgh, losing all command over his temper, caring for nothing but to grapple with the robber before him, and with a sudden spring he displaced the muzzle of the pistol, striking his persecutor with something of his former strength right in the face. The man staggered back several paces from the blow, but with a frightful execration he pulled the trigger of his pistol, but strange to say missed his victim. A wild cry was heard at the same moment without the cottage, and a violent blow was struck at the door; the table and candle were fortunately again upset by the fall of the Englishman, for one of the villains at the door fired hastily at our hero, wounding him very slightly on the right shoulder; but as the shouts without increased, and the violent blows against the hall door redoubled, the three men turned and fled. With a spring Francis would have closed upon the Englishman, but cursing the cowardice of his men, he rushed through the door, pulling it after him; and the key being on the outside, he turned it in the lock.

Francis rushed to the window, and bursting open the shutters threw it up, calling out, "Who is there?"

"The Lord be praised!" said the voice of Jane, "it's the master's voice. Blessed Mary! what has happened? Are there robbers in the house?"

"There were," bitterly exclaimed our hero, "but they have escaped by the back."

"Musha, the Lord be good to us!" said a man's voice, "can you open the door, sir?"

Francis retired from the window with bitterness and vexation in his heart, and then for the first time he recollected the glass doors leading out into the garden; it is true there were shutters up outside, but they were easier to force than the parlour door.

Opening the glass doors, he forced back the shutters; for though fastened inside, yet to prevent heavy winds shaking them, a wooden bar was stretched across them outside.

Entering the garden the snow lay a foot deep on the ground, the bitter eastern blast cutting like a razor; but he felt it not, for his blood was at fever heat. He passed on, and coming to the back door leading into the kitchen, he saw by the faint light the snow trampled all round, and the door lock smashed by a great stone. Groping his way in he passed on to the hall door, and unhooking the chain, he allowed Jane and an elderly looking peasant to enter.

"Holy Virgin, sir, what has happened?" asked the man, shaking with cold and fear, while poor Jane trembled in every limb as she looked up into her young master's flushed cheek, and saw his dress all torn and disordered. She could do naught but clasp her hands and utter unceasing lamentations.

Closing the door De Burgh proceeded into the kitchen and lighted a lantern, and, turning to the man, whose name was Murphy, and who was accustomed to work in the garden, he said:

"The villains that have plundered me of valuable papers came in through the back door leading into the garden; follow me, and let us see how they entered."

"Lord love ye, sir!" said Jane anxiously, "don't go out without hat and coat; think how weak and poorly you have been."

Francis took his hat from the kind-hearted old dame, and then passed out through the back door.

G

"Musha, my God!" exclaimed the labourer, "the villains smashed the door: here be the tracks of many feet."

Our hero did not utter a word, but silently followed the track of the feet through the snow, which was falling thick and fast at that moment. They traced the steps to the small garden gate in the high wall, and which led out into a by-lane. Here, again, they found the lock smashed to pieces, and the door open, and the wind rushing through with violence. Without, the snow was driving furiously before the blast; therefore, it was utterly out of the power of our hero to trace them further, however much he was inclined to do so.

Sick at heart, and trembling with intense vexation, Francis returned into the house, and fastened up the door with bolts. Telling Jane to give Jim Murphy a glass of warm spirits and water, he unlocked the parlour door, and entering the room, lighted the candles, and then sat down for an instant to collect his scattered thoughts. Feeling a smarting pain in his right shoulder, he stripped off his coat, and on investigation found that the ball had merely raised the skin, and that a piece of sticking plaster was all the hurt required.

As he sat, half stupified by the late events, Jane entered the room, her face pale as a ghost, and shaking as if in an ague.

"Oh, sir! oh, dear heart! the wretches have broken the master's beautiful cabinet, and taken everything it contained with them. Oh, wirra strew! wirra strew! was there ever the like? Acushla machree, the villains tried to murder you too," she anxiously exclaimed, gazing in terror at the blood on his arm.

"The ruffians did their best, Jane," said our hero bitterly, "but as to this hurt, it is nothing;" and putting on his coat he proceeded upstairs to ascertain the mischief the robbers had perpetrated.

It was too true; he found his father's Indian cabinet broken in a brutal fashion; the four drawers and two compartments completely divested of their contents, whatever they were. There was not a part of it that was not broken by a heavy hammer, to ascertain if there were any secret drawers. Francis knew there was a considerable sum of money in it; for, before his departure to the wreck, his father had received a very large sum, and there it must have been deposited. On the floor lay a heavy blacksmith's hammer; two presses and two trunks had been burst open, and their contents ransacked and thrown about the room.

Francis sat down, pressing his lips hard, with a feeling of intense vexation and rage. It was, in truth, very evident to him that this cruel outrage was the work of some secret enemy, who had at last discovered his father's residence. The loss of his father's letters and papers left him destitute, and hopeless of ever unravelling the mystery of the past. The real desolation of his situation struck him with a terrible distinctness: he stood apparently alone in the world, without tie of kindred, or friend. He thought of Mary Grey, and a chill came over his heart, for there now seemed an insurmountable barrier raised between them.

His faithful attendant, Jane, finding him stay so long alone, and brooding over his misfortunes, came up, and with the privilege of long and faithful services, she implored him to take something warm and retire to bed, to regain strength, saying, "Please God, the next day he might be able to trace the robbers."

With a sigh, he rose up, followed her instructions, and then threw himself, weary and dispirited, into his bed, hoping to bury in sleep the memory of his misfortune; for as to discovering any trace of the depredators, after the heavy fall of snow, he had little hope.

The following day, strange to say, Francis De Burgh felt himself, as far as his bodily health was concerned, little the worse for the exertion of the past night. As he suspected, though the gale of wind had ceased, the fall of snow had covered every foot-mark with an impenetrable cover. Several of the neighbours, and worthy Father Flaherty, called early in the morning. The priest was shocked, and really most unhappy at the daring robbery committed upon his favourite; and vowed he would discover the depredators if they were any of his parishioners, and that confession should not save them.

A great deal of uneasiness existed about the absence of Bill Mullaghan's pilot boat and the two fishing smacks. Many of the male relatives of the absent fishermen had gone, despite the storm, to Ardmore and Youghal to try and gain tidings of the boats.

Late in the day, Doctor Creigh called. He had heard a rumour of the robbery, and came to offer every assistance in his power; he was rejoiced to see that Francis was nothing the worse, looked at his shoulder, said he had had a narrow escape, but that the wound, as our hero said, was of no consequence. The doctor agreed with his patient, that in the distracted and disturbed state of the country, any attempt to discover the miscreants would, he feared, be abortive.

Towards the latter part of the day the sky cleared, and the weather moderated altogether. Francis passed a gloomy evening; he was alone with his thoughts, and for one so young they were desponding enough; but this was not to last; the natural energy and vigour of his constitution and disposition were sure to return with his renewed health. He did not for a moment think or dwell on the pecuniary loss he had sustained, neither did he trouble himself how he was to obtain funds for the future; his principal thought was the terribly sudden deprivation he had experienced, in the loss of a parent he was so fondly and devotedly attached to. He regretted also the loss of the two letters, which he conjectured were from Lord Delamaine and General Grey.

The following morning, while dressing, he was overjoyed to see the St. Patrick pilot-boat running up the harbour; crowds of women and children were on the beach, waving their hands to the crew. The St. Patrick had carried away a bout four feet of her mast-head, and was under reefed canvas, but all the crew appeared on board.

The people on the beach were extremely anxious for the St. Patrick to anchor, as they hoped that tidings of the two missing fishing-boats might be obtained. Francis, after the pilot-boat anchored, beheld Bill and another man pull ashore in the punt; he then descended to breakfast, knowing that Bill would soon be up at the cottage. As he anticipated, Bill Mullaghan very shortly afterwards entered the room, with a most anxious expression of countenance.

"Thank God, Bill, that you are safe and well," said our hero, holding out his hand to the faithful fellow, who gave it a squeeze that would have troubled some to have borne.

"Well, it was a mercy of Providence, your honour, for it was bad enough in all conscience; it was nearly up with us, when we carried away our mast-head off Ardmore—five minutes sooner and we should all have had a berth in ould Davey's locker. But weathering the Head, we went dead before it, without a stitch of canvas, working for our lives; and, in a lull of the gale, we got got up a block, and ran in under Ballycotton Island."

"And what became of the other two hookers, Bill?"

"The Lord save us, sir! I'm afraid they must either have foundered or gone ashore; the last we saw of them was four leagues off Ardmore Head, when the snow-storm hid everything from us. We began working to windward this morning before daylight from our anchorage, and never sighted a single craft. But what about the robbers, sir? The villains! och! murder! if I had stayed at home, and kept my post here, be gor! I'd a spoiled some of their faces, and so would your honour, but in by reason the sickness; but the two of us together would have beat a dozen of them."

"I wish to Heaven you had been here, Bill," said De Burgh, with a sigh, "for they have robbed me of all my dear father's documents and papers, a thousand times more valuable to me than the gold they deprived me of."

"But sure, sir, they must have come purposely for those papers—robbers or thieves would never think of those sort of things."

"I am quite aware of that, Bill; but I refrained from saying much about this affair, because I do not wish to call the attention of our neighbours to my private affairs or present situation. I feel satisfied also, that no effort of mine at this moment will lead to the detection of the author of this cruel outrage."

"Who knows, Master Francis, who knows? You say some of the villains were Irish peasants; who knows but a word here and a word there, when the whisky begins to work, may betray them; for some of them must belong to these parts, and know all about the ways of the place: be the powers, sir, we may catch them yet."

"Well, I will not discourage your hopes, Bill. However, now you are returned, and I am well enough, we may as well settle this salvage of the British Queen. Luckily, the money was lodged in the Bank of Ireland. So let us fix to-morrow; perhaps you had better have Green, the attorney, to settle it."

"Tare and ages, your honour, don't let us have one of those land pirates amongst us. True, the thing was settled in Liverpool, and your honour cut away part of your own share to add to ours; and if we had our will it should be given back again, for, only for you, sir, we should not have gone to sea that night; and all of us missed the rope but you, sir, and you ran the greatest risk."

Francis smiled at Bill's arguments, saying:—"Well, as you say you are all satisfied as it now stands, all we have to do is to divide the sum as already arranged, so tell your father I am ready to hand him over the order on the bank to-morrow."

This business was most satisfactorily arranged the following day, and created, as Bill said, such a sensation in Dungarvon, that if ever the old town shook it surely did then, for such a windfall never before fell to the lot of the pilots of that port. Francis himself considered it a most fortunate event in his own life; had he not obtained this money he would have been absolutely penniless, neither had he the slightest idea where to procure any funds. He was thus enabled to pay all expenses and debts due, which he did immediately, erecting at the same time a simple but elegant monument over his lamented father's grave.

As he rapidly regained his former strength, the energy and buoyancy of his disposition returned: to forget his beloved father was impossible, but he looked upon his bereavement with more resignation.

One morning Jane ushered in Mr. Green, the attorney, the owner of the cottage. This gentleman, with his usual bland smile, after some trivial observations on the weather, said:

"It is with deep regret, Mr. De Burgh, that I hear rumours of your having lost valuable papers, besides money, by the robbers who so daringly entered this cottage. I trust this is but rumour."

"You must expect, Mr. Green," said Francis De Burgh coldly, "that such an event as a house broken into would lead to all kinds of reports, and surmises, and embellishments."

"Oh, certainly, certainly," returned Mr. Green, "it is always the case in small communities. I am happy to hear that the rumour is false. Have you gained any clue to the perpetrators, Mr. De Burgh?"

"I have not exerted myself to do so, sir," returned our hero. Wishing to change the subject, he added, "As you are here, Mr. Green, it is a good opportunity to let you know that I intend giving up the cottage next March."

"I sincerely regret to hear you say so, Mr. De Burgh," said the attorney, with a side glance into our hero's features. "Tired of this certainly lonely part of the world—going to Dublin most likely."

"I have not the slightest idea, Mr. Green, where my rambles may lead me."

"Oh, I beg pardon; but not to detain you," continued the man of law, "I will state the reason I have intruded on your time. Your lamented father was, as I suppose you know, a yearly tenant at sixty-four pounds, payable in advance. The year expired according to agreement, the twenty-fifth of March; but there is a year's rent due, the present year not being paid as usual, in advance."

Francis De Burgh looked at the speaker with some surprise, saying: "That is very singular, Mr. Green, after sixteen years' residence, that the last year's rent should be unpaid; however, it is of no consequence, it shall be paid."

"My dear sir," returned Mr. Green with a bland smile, "your late father's papers, for he was very regular, will settle the matter: it is quite possible it may have been paid, but I have no memorandum of it. Indeed, thinking it must be so, I have for several days back been hunting over old papers, and into all my ledgers and account books, but can find no such entry; however, take time, we may find it yet, or you may stumble on the receipt I must have given if it was paid. I will now wish you good morning, expressing my great regret at losing so estimable a tenant."

"Now," thought Francis De Burgh, looking after the worthy attorney, "that man is a rogue; he has heard I have lost all my father's papers, and he thinks the attempt at obtaining a second year's rent from me worth trying. I shall have to pay him, no doubt; still, the man is a rogue, and Bill was quite right in calling him a land-pirate."

On seeing his old attendant he said to her, "Pray, Jane, have you any remembrance of my poor father having paid this year's rent for the cottage to Mr. Green, for he says it was not paid."

"Bless me, my dear, what a falsehood!" said the old dame, raising up her eyes with astonishment. "Why, acushla, I myself paid him the rent these last five or six years, and always put his receipts on a file; and now I feel sure that the file is a-top of the old press in master's room; for the villains that robbed us would surely never take a file of receipts. I'll go and see now."

In less than ten minutes Jane returned into the room, with her spectacles on, and a long file of receipts covered with dust and cobwebs.

"There, my dear, she triumphantly said, "look at these; here they all are, and here's the last, dated 26th of March, 179-! that will spoil his dinner, the old sinner!"

"I think it will, Jane," returned our hero, with a smile; "and you shall take and show it him, with my compliments."

Notwithstanding this, Mr. Green actually called the following day, shook our hero by the hand with the most smiling and benevolent expression of countenance, declaring he was delighted: it made him quite miserable, the uncertainty he was in with respect to the payment: and would never have forgiven himself, had he found out his mistake afterwards.

## CHAPTER XIII.

To avoid any lengthened retrograde movements, thereby delaying the progress of our story, we will here request our readers to return with us to the good town of Liverpool, at the period of the arrival of the British Queen. The second day after her reaching port, just as it became dusk, Captain De Burgh, enveloped in his ample military mantle, left the hotel in which he was located, and proceeded to find his way to the "Crown," the hotel where he expected to find the stranger he encountered at the inn in Dungarvon. Having found his way to Spillman Street, he soon discovered the "Crown." On entering the coffee room, he called the waiter aside, and requested to know if a gentleman named Curtis resided there?

"Curtis? Oh, yes, sir; arrived this morning—is now this moment at dinner. Wish to see him, sir?"

"Yes, most particularly."

"This way, sir: the gentleman is in a private apartment."

Ascending a flight of stairs, the waiter threw open a door, and Captain De Burgh entered the room.

"Ha! so you are come," said the gentleman called Curtis, laying down his knife and fork, and holding out his hand: "Faith! I wondered what kept you; I have been here since morning, and I knew the ship had been in harbour these two days."

"Well, I scarcely thought you had had time to arrive, sir," said Captain De Burgh, throwing off his mantle, and taking a chair by the fire.

"You had a longish passage, Herbert," remarked Mr. Curtis, "but ring the bell, for the waiter to take these things away, and I'll order a couple of bottles of wine, and then we can have a comfortable evening's chat. I have heard a great deal since I saw you."

The waiter entering the room and removing the things, kept the gentleman silent for a while; but the dessert and wine being placed on the table, and the waiter done fidgeting about the room, the stranger resumed the conversation, saying:

"What kept you so long on the voyage, Herbert?—Put in anywhere?"

"No; but strong easterly winds kept us boxing about the Channel till I was sick of it; and that confounded young puppy made himself so conspicuous, by persuading the captain that he was again in danger, and pretending to get him out of it, that no one was thought of or talked to by the passengers but himself. I wanted to provoke him into a duel, but his lordship interfered, and so I gave in to his wishes, and appeared satisfied. Did you return to Dungarvon after our departure, sir?"

"That I certainly did, Herbert the very day after, and had an interview with that attorney, Mr. Green, you mentioned; and from what I picked up from him, and other enquiries, I felt perfectly satisfied that I had at last stumbled upon the very individual about whose fate I remained so many years uncertain; but a chance circumstance removed all doubt."

"Ha! How was that, sir?" interrupted Captain De Burgh, anxiously.

"Why, you see," continued the stranger, "I had important business at Athy, and so started the following morning in a car for Waterford. We stopped to feed the horse at Kilmacthomas, at a miserable inn; and as it was very cold, I stepped into a little room with a fire in it, and while looking out through the window, saw a car from Waterford drive up, with one passenger, wrapped up in a heavy mantle. The driver only stopped a moment to speak to my driver, but at that moment the passenger's head was raised, and he looked up at the house. That short glance I had was quite sufficient—I felt the blood rush to my face with a tingling sensation. It was he. The next instant he threw the folds of his mantle over his person, and the car drove on. I ran out, called my driver, and asked him if he knew the gentleman just gone on in the car? 'Be gor! I do, sir, and a kind-hearted gentleman he is; he lives in Dungarvon, your honour—his name is Mr. De Burgh.' Thus all doubt was removed from my mind."

For several minutes not a word was spoken by either gentlemen; the elder, however, kept filling his glass, and to judge by his features, he appeared much less disturbed than Captain De Burgh at the intelligence he had imparted.

At length the Captain looked into his companion's face, saying: "Startling as this intelligence is, you do not seem moved by it."

"Certainly not, Herbert, because, having discovered the evil, a remedy can be applied. Now listen to me patiently and calmly, and I will clearly explain to you how we are situated by this discovery, and the means I intend to employ to remedy this unforeseen event. Thanks to Dame Fortune, Ireland is convulsed to its centre, law and civil authority at an end in many parts of the country, and agents, able and willing, to be had for gold. Leave it all to me, you have another card to play. You must marry Miss Grey; you, perhaps, have not heard that her maternal uncle, Sir Robert Herbert, is dead. She will inherit his great wealth; in fact, by his death, she is become one of the wealthiest heiresses in England."

"How is that," said Captain De Burgh with a start, "they are not aware of Sir Robert's death?"

"No, but they will shortly. Sir Robert Herbert died the day before yesterday, in Dublin; I happened to hear of it at a clubhouse, an hour before I left. Consequently, they will not hear of his death, most probably for some days, therefore say nothing about it. Now listen to what I have to say to you."

For two hours their conversation lasted, sometimes interrupted by remarks from Captain De Burgh; but however his views might differ from those of his elder companion, he was overruled, and remained satisfied with the plan proposed to be pursued by the gentleman calling himself Mr. Curtis. It was a late hour when they separated, Captain De Burgh returning to his hotel, while Mr. Curtis the following morning left for Holyhead, thence for Dublin, where he at once commenced arranging his plans, and engaging agents to carry out his nefarious designs.

Captain De Burgh in the meantime, while our hero remained visiting Lord Delamaine and General Grey, kept almost entirely away from the hotel, stating to his uncle that he was constantly visiting an old friend, formerly in the same regiment, residing near Warrington. At length, being sufficiently rested and recovered from the fatigues of the voyage, General Grey and his daughter left for London, as did also Lord Delamaine, the latter intending to remain some weeks in the metropolis before proceeding to his estate in Hampshire.

Lord Delamaine and Captain de Burgh travelled together in a post chaise and four; his lordship appeared extremely thoughtful, and his fine features wore an expression of trouble or uneasiness.

"You do not appear well, my lord," said Captain De Burgh, breaking the long silence; "indeed, our voyage has been a series of petty disasters, easily avoided, but magnified into perils and—"

"You are really committing a great error, Herbert," returned Lord Delamaine, "in speaking as you do. You cannot mean what you say; for if you did, I should be forced to imagine envy of another's gallant and noble conduct had blinded your judgment. But let this matter rest—you ask me am I well? I am quite well, but I am sorely troubled in mind. I will speak to you seriously upon the subject that troubles me. I have brought you home from the Cape, and expressed a wish that you should retire from the army; my reason for this was, I considered you my heir to both title and fortune."

Captain De Burgh turned very pale, but he uttered not a word, while his lordship continued:

"I do not say you are not my successor, but it is quite possible that the law may find a more direct heir to both title and landed estates."

"That I should feel surprised, my lord," said Captain De Burgh, finding his lordship pause, and recovering himself in a measure, "at this communication will not appear strange, for I always thought your Lordship's family were quite extinct, and that the descendants of your lordship's sister became the next heirs in succession."

"Just so, Herbert," returned Lord Delamaine, with more vivacity of manner, "and such may be the case still; but I think, after all, I am wrong to talk of this now, when all may be surmise. Before a month expires, I shall be relieved from my anxiety and doubts; whatever may occur, I shall have still a fair fortune to bequeath to you."

"Indeed, uncle," said Captain De Burgh, with an assumed tone of affection, "the loss of title or fortune would not trouble me much, except perhaps for one reason. You must be aware that the fondest wish of my heart is to obtain the hand of Miss Grey. Her father, though a kind and generous man in disposition, is nevertheless anxious to ally his daughter with a man of rank—fortune I do not think he cares so much about. I think I have his consent to win his daughter's affections."

"And have you any idea, Herbert," said his lordship seriously, "that you have any chance of doing so?"

Captain De Burgh coloured, and bit his lips in fierce constrained passion, as he strove to reply calmly.

"I think it very possible, my lord, that, having the father's consent, I may gain the lady's hand; especially if backed by your lordship's wish for the union. You may remember, at the Cape, you expressed a wish that such a union should take place."

"True," returned his lordship, with a slight sigh; "true, I then thought you might have the good fortune to gain her esteem. and perhaps her affection; for he who wins Mary Grey, wins a pearl beyond all price."

"Then why, my lord," said Herbert De Burgh calmly, and with a steady look into his uncle's features, "then why, my lord, do you think differently now?"

"I may give my reason to you, Herbert," said Lord Delamaine seriously, "though it would not be fair or right to judge, or attempt to analyze Miss Grey's feelings to another uninterested party; but I candidly tell you, I do not think you will ever gain the young lady's consent to your proposals. Her father is touched in favour of another, and if I may presume to be a judge of that fair girl's nature and disposition, I should say, if love once enters her heart for a deserving object, that love will only cease with the beating of that priceless heart."

"You speak, my lord," said Herbert De Burgh, his voice trembling with agitation, and yet the tone was sarcastic and bitter enough, "as if there was not such another as the General's daughter to be found amongst our English fair ones."

"Not many, Herbert," returned his lordship, "not many. I do not speak of mere beauty; we have, no doubt, many as fair and beautiful, but I have taken great pleasure in studying and looking into the thoughts and sentiments of Miss Grey; and in that young heart dwell many virtues and powerful feelings."

"Pity, my lord," interrupted Herbert De Burgh bitterly, and quite unable to conceal his exasperated feelings, "that such a heart, as you describe Miss Grey's, should be won by the comely face of a mere stripling—a boy! with no other education than a home one, and whose associates have been, from childhood, rough, untaught sea bears."

Lord Delamaine raised his fine thoughtful eyes, and let them rest upon the excited features of his nephew. For a moment he made no reply, but he then said:

"Herbert, you let passion overpower your reason and judgment. If I err not, that young man's father—for I know you speak of Mr. Francis De Burgh—is one of the most accomplished gentlemen in Europe, and I think his son has nobly profited by the trouble and attention his father must have bestowed upon his education. He is as fine and gallant a young man as I ever saw, and as far as I can judge from our short interview, fully competent, when the time comes, to fulfil the duties of any station he may be called upon to occupy."

"And pray, my lord," said Captain De Burgh, passionately, "since you seem to know or surmise, who is this 'admirable Crichton's' father?"

"Time will tell," returned his lordship, calmly, as the chaise and four dashed up to the inn door, where they were to pass the night, and thus the conversation ended.

General Grey, on his arrival in London, took up his residence for a time in a handsome suite of apartments in St. James's Street. Mary Grey, from the period of leaving Liverpool to reaching London, remained in a very thoughtful serious mood. The idea of having to stay in London for several weeks gave her no pleasure: quite the contrary. Mary cared not for gaieties, or balls, assemblies, or operas. She had to submit to a number of visits from perfect strangers, though many she knew were distant connections of her mother.

The intelligence of Sir Robert Herbert's death—though she only remembered him when a child, and that he positively doated on her—pained and grieved her, for she loved the memory of her eccentric but kind-hearted maternal uncle. The aunt had been dead many years; she did not therefore remember her. The sixty thousand pounds left her by Sir Robert Herbert only caused a feeling of deep gratitude in her heart for her uncle's affectionate remembrance of her: upon the accession of wealth she did not bestow a thought. She longed for her father to make a purchase of an estate in the country, and to leave London. She dearly loved the country; its beauty, its calm retirement, and its endless variety, to a thinking and enquiring mind.

Mary Grey's young heart was no longer entirely her own. Francis De Burgh had made an impression there not to be erased by either time or absence. His high spirit, gentle unassuming manners, and noble person, joined to a highly cultivated mind,

acquired not by admixture with the busy world, but by much an(
deep reading, and the constant conversation with, and course o
instruction from one, not to be surpassed for high intellect an(
many and varied accomplishments. His very want of knowledg
of the world had a charm in it to such a disposition as Mar
Grey's.

It is a vain effort—at least we think so—to try to analyze th
human heart, especially so when that heart is swayed by th
impulses nature has planted in it. Mary Grey had passed th
period of early youth in quiet studies and in calm retirement
instructed by a highly intellectual woman, her own mother, wh
united every grace and accomplishment, with strength of mind an(
sound principles. Bright and cheerful in temper, her attainment
and pleasures confined to a limited sphere, gained strength fron
being concentrated upon few objects. Francis De Burgh was th
very person likely to gain the heart of Mary Grey, and havin;
witnessed his gallantry and noble devotion and utter disregard o
life, in the hope of saving others, added to the feeling sh(
experienced, and before the parting hour came, young love ha(
found a resting place in her heart of hearts.

During their residence in London, both Lord Delamaine an(
Captain De Burgh were constant visitors, and so was Miss Prober
and her really amiable mother. The ladies intended residin;
entirely in London, and were about to purchase a handsome hous(
near St. James's Park.

Mary Grey knew perfectly well, before quittting the Cape, tha
Captain De Burgh wished to render himself agreeable to her, an(
so long as his attentions were merely confined to the usual gallantry
of officers to the fair sex she little heeded them. For Captain D(
Burgh, though handsome, accomplished, and a brave soldier, wa:
still not at all the kind of man likely to make an impression o1
such a heart as hers.

During his visits in London his manner and attentions becam(
so marked that Mary Grey resolved to adopt a manner so repelling
and cold as would leave no doubt on his mind as to her feelings fo
him. But the departure of Lord Delamaine and his nephew fo
Hampshire, relieved her at this period from his visits, and she de
termined before they met again—for she was aware her father wa:
about purchasing a beautiful estate adjoining Lord Delamaine':
property in Hampshire, to speak to her father upon the subject
and candidly confess to him her determination of never accepting
Captain De Burgh as a partner for life, for she was aware he1
father encouraged his attentions to her.

As nothing of importance occurred in the routine of our fai
heroine's life at this period, we will leave her and the shores o
England to return to our hero in our next chapter.

## CHAPTER XV.

FRANCIS DE BURGH completely restored to health, still remained an inmate of the cottage in Dungarvon. Five weeks had elapsed, his mind and thoughts perplexed and disturbed, though restored to health, he could not forget the memory of the past, and the deep loss he had sustained in the death of his beloved father. Every effort to discover traces of the villains who had plundered the cottage had failed; Bill Mullaghan was indefatigable, but confessed he was dead beat. Even Father Flaherty was unsuccessful.

Our hero, aware of the great power of the priesthood over their flocks, whether for good or evil, and the certain means they possess of obtaining information, had great hopes of gaining some clue through that source. But week after week passed, till but a few weeks remained of his time for giving up the cottage; he therefore considered that all further attempts to elucidate the mystery of the robbery would be vain.

Father Flaherty was a simple-minded, pious, kind-hearted man, and when all around him resembled a volcano, during that terrible period he kept his little flock quiet and uncontaminated by the spirit of the times.

At last Francis De Burgh made up his mind to quit the abode where sixteen years of his young life had been spent in peace and happiness. His intention was to proceed first to Dublin and transfer his small stock of money into some banking establishment in London, and after visiting Lord Delamaine, as he promised to do, make up his mind whether he would volunteer into the navy or enter the merchant service. As to discovering anything concerning his lamented father, after the loss of all his papers, letters, and documents, he considered a hopeless task.

When he thought of fair Mary Grey a deep despondency came over him. What pretensions could he now have to gain her love, or rather her father's consent to do so, for without that he was too high-minded and honourable to seek to make an impression on her heart, when he knew insurmountable objections existed to their union. Nevertheless her image was ever before him! Sleeping or waking he beheld in imagination that fair young face, and in his dreams the touching tones of her musical voice vibrated on his ear, and frequently startled him from his slumbers.

Francis was also somewhat puzzled with respect to Bill Mullaghan. Bill was deaf to all arguments he made use of to prove to the faithful fellow that his means and his prospects were too humble to think of maintaining such a man as Bill as a follower or servant. It was placing him, our hero said, in a position of life below his situation and his means, to say nothing of his prospects, which, for a man of his class, were extremely good, as his father was very well-to-do in the world.

"Tare and ages, your honour," said Bill, after a long speech from our hero on the subject, "it's quite waste of breath talking about it. Don't you think I'm able to maintain myself, and take care of you at the same time? Haven't I nearly five hundred pounds of my own, aud didn't you say we should see the world: and, be gor, wherever you go, Bill Mullaghan must go too. So that's settled, Mister Francis, only I musn't call you by that title any longer."

Thus Francis De Burgh gave in to Bill Mullaghan's wishes; it would have been painful to him to have parted from his kind-hearted follower, therefore both were mutually pleased. Jane cried bitterly at the thoughts of her young master's departure, but our hero took care to provide for her wants, and had the satisfaction of seeing her enter the house of the worthy priest as his housekeeper.

On the fourth day of March, 1799, Francis De Burgh, with his attendant Bill, left Dungarvon for Dublin, where he arrived without any accident or adventure, and took up his residence in the same hotel at which he stayed on his previous visit, where it was his intention to remain a few days. At this period the city of Dublin was the focus of all the political parties, distracting the country, still much disturbed after the horrors of the previous year.

Walking one day up Sackville Street, our hero felt a hand laid upon his shoulder; while a good humoured voice saluted his ear with the words—

"Well, upon my honour, this is an unexpected pleasure, Mr. De Burgh. I did not expect to see you in Dublin."

Turning round, he at once recognized the good natured magistrate, Mr. McCarthy. Shaking him most cordially by the hand, he said—

"I was really going to write to you this very day."

"Then I suppose," said our hero, "that you require some further evidence about that affair at Bally——?"

"Tut! not a bit," returned Mr. McCarthy, with a laugh, "the worst is over now; we shall be all to rights in a few months. But a very curious circumstance, which concerns you, happened at Athy. However, this is no place to talk the matter over, and I am in a great hurry, so you must come and eat your mutton with me to-day. My family are all in town; there's my card—six o'clock punctually—no excuse now, for I have a couple of letters for you. There, see I have roused your curiosity—sure to have you at six o'clock," and squeezing his hand, Mr. McCarthy turned off, and taking the arm of a gentleman standing near, they both walked rapidly on, leaving our hero considerably surprised, and somewhat curious as to the letters.

Looking at the card he saw Mr. McCarthy's residence was at 24, Kildare Street.

Ruminating upon his recognition by the good natured magistrate, and wondering what two letters he could possibly have for him, Francis De Burgh returned to his hotel.

As he was setting out for Kildare Street, Bill Mullaghan said—
"Shall I come for you, sir?"

"No, William, no," returned our hero, "go to the theatre and amuse yourself, for I think of leaving Dublin to-morrow, and you said you would like to see a play."

On reaching Kildare Street, and knocking at No. 24, and giving his name to a domestic out of livery, he was ushered into the drawing-room, where he was received by Mrs. McCarthy and two very amiable girls, her daughters.

Mrs. McCarthy appeared a most befitting partner for the good humoured magistrate. She was an uncommonly sprightly, buxom dame, not more than eight or nine-and-thirty. She appeared to be greatly struck with the fine figure and prepossessing features of her visitor, and received him with great kindness, introducing him to her daughters, and apologising for her husband's absence, saying she expected him every moment from the court.

Our hero's easy pleasing manner soon wore off the first formalities of acquaintance, and induced the two young ladies to join in a lively conversation.

"I assure you, Mr. De Burgh," remarked Mrs. McCarthy, "you are not quite a stranger to us; we have talked about you many times. Eliza says you will be sure to turn out quite a hero of romance."

Eliza McCarthy, the youngest daughter, blushed as she said, laughing, "You know, mother, Mr. De Burgh's adventures amongst the rebels were certainly like a romance, and then the affair was greatly increased in interest from what occurred to papa afterwards. So you see, Mr. De Burgh, we know a great deal more about you perhaps than you are aware of."

"You raise my curiosity," Miss Eliza," said Francis De Burgh, "for the information I afforded your good father was very limited indeed."

"Oh, yes," returned the young lady, laughing, "we were told you were very cautious, but all came out afterwards, and it appears that you spent a night or two in the very haunt of the rebels, with the son-in-law of the great insurgent leader, Holt, and papa said that Sir William ———— was furious, and wanted to have you summoned to Dublin."

"I think," added Mrs. McCarthy, "you were written to on the subject. Did you receive a letter?"

"No, madam, I did not."

"However," continued Mrs. McCarthy, "my husband argued the matter over with Sir William ———, pleaded your extreme youth, and how it was impossible from many circumstances that you could have had any previous intercourse with the rebels, producing a newspaper that detailed the whole account of your gallantry and disregard of life in saving the British Queen from shipwreck, and so forth; that Sir William ——— appeared satisfied, although he declared he had received a letter—an anonymous one he acknowledged—in which the writer accused you and your lamented father (whose sudden death I assure you we were grieved to hear of) of being spies, and secretly connected with the French government for the overthrow of English rule in Ireland. Mr. McCarthy said he felt certain the letter was written by a secret enemy, and that every word in it was false."

"I really cannot," said Francis De Burgh, in an earnest tone, "sufficiently express how greatly I feel the kindness and interest Mr. McCarthy has exhibited and exerted for me. I feel anxious also for an explanation."

"Ah," said Mrs. McCarthy, laughing, "after all, you men are quite as curious as poor women are said to be; but my worthy husband likes telling a story over a bottle of port, so I must not anticipate him. But tell me, how do you like our city of Dublin?"

"Every visitor must admire Dublin, Mrs. McCarthy; its splendid situation, the lovely scenery surrounding it must charm all eyes."

At that moment Mr. McCarthy's knock announced the arrival of the worthy magistrate; a few minutes afterwards they were sitting down to an excellent dinner.

"You see, my young friend, said Mr. McCarthy, "we are quite a family party. I refrained from inviting any one to-day to meet you, as I wish to have a quiet chat by ourselves. You must not quit Dublin for a while."

"Well, in truth," remarked Mrs. McCarthy, "I cannot say much for our Dublin society at present, for what with rebellion, war, and political discussion, and bitterness of party, we women are quite forgotten."

"Oh, bless me, Eliza!" said Mr. McCarthy, laughing, "don't be alarmed, wait a while, there will be no end to festivities by-and-by. By the way, the news has just arrived of Sir Hyde Parke's victory. He has destroyed all the fortifications and batteries before Copenhagen. This will bring about a peace, then come masquerades, balls, &c."

"Well," said the eldest daughter, "there's some comfort in

that. You have no notion, Mr. De Burgh, what a winter we spent in our country residence, positively quite a state of siege. Barred windows, doors crossed with iron; guns, pistols, and blunderbusses placed upon the hall table, as if for supper. When we did contrive to fall asleep, pop goes a gun outside, and up jumps all the martially inclined portion of the household, while we females popped our heads under the quilt till we were nearly smothered with fright."

"Ha, ha, my young lady," said Mr. McCarthy, smiling, "that's your version of the affair; but you forget to tell Mr. De Burgh that, under the pretence of guarding the house, several of the smartest young gentlemen in the county visited us daily, and frequently stayed several nights; and that, notwithstanding the popping of the guns, you contrived to play the piano, and kick up a dance to smother the rattle of musketry outside, I suppose."

"Oh! Mr. De Burgh, you must not mind all papa says. We had two or three young ladies staying with us, their part of the county being the fighting ground of the rebels, so their brothers and cousins used to ride over to see them, and of course papa would not let them ride back at night through a disturbed district; and as they were very stupid young men, we played the piano, and had a dance to enliven them, and keep ourselves from imagining a thousand horrible things. Do you not think we were quite right?"

"Most certainly," said our hero, smiling, "I should think you most effectually cured the young gentlemen of their stupidity, and fortified yourselves against the imaginary foe outside."

"Oh, dear me!" exclaimed both young ladies at once, "do not say imaginary; it was far from it. One night, just as we were in the middle of a dance, pop goes a dozen guns outside; at the same moment, crash goes the shutters of the windows. You may depend on it, we all fled in divers direction; in five minutes we were all hid in every possible nook we considered safe."

"Why, Mary, my dear," said Mr. McCarthy, with a sly look, "I was away at the time you know. Did the gentlemen run with you into those nooks you speak of?"

"Well, as my mamma was present, I must confess that the gentlemen did at first consider discretion the better part of valour; but young Blake, who was undoubtedly the most valiant of the party, after locking us up, persuaded his companions and our own domestics to assemble on the top of the house, which has a flat roof and battlements—or balustrades rather—and fire a volley. Whether the rebels only wanted to frighten us or not, we cannot say; but no more shots were fired that night, and that was the only time we got a real fright."

"A pretty garrison I confided my house to," said Mr. McCarthy.

"Oh! we took capital care of it," said the eldest daughter, "but confess, Mr. De Burgh, they were terrible times, to say nothing of being eight entire months without a glance of the Paris fashions."

"This last was certainly painfully distressing," remarked our hero, laughing, as he rose to open the door, the ladies retiring to the drawing room.

## CHAPTER XVI.

"WELL, I dare say, my young friend," said Mr. McCarthy, after the ladies had retired, and the servants had placed fresh filled decanters of wine upon the table, "you are somewhat anxious to learn how I discovered your adventures in the mountains with Holt's son-in-law."

"You certainly have roused my curiosity, sir," returned our hero, "especially with respect to the letters you mentioned. I was thinking they might be some of those I was robbed of in Dungarvon, but can scarcely believe so much good fortune in store for me; for one letter I lost, written by my father, was of vast, if not vital, importance to me."

"I have no doubt," said Mr. McCarthy, "but that the two letters I hold were some of those you were robbed of; but I fear the important one you mention is not one of them, as they bear the English postmark. But to go regularly to work, I must commence at the beginning, so fill your glass—no better port in the British dominions, not a headache in a hogshead." Filling his own glass, Mr. McCarthy continued—"Just about the period of the robbery of your cottage at Dungarvon, a party of the —— Dragoons came upon a considerable body of rebels between Waterford and Dungarvon, and after a short contest they fled, leaving several prisoners in the hands of the military. Amongst the prisoners was an Englishman, but somehow he and two others contrived to effect their escape. A short time after this, two men were caught in the vicinity of Bally——s, and brought to Athy. One of them was at once recognized as one of the escaped rebels from Waterford, and also as the man who shot one of the Dragoons, after his horse had been killed. Sir William ——s, after a very short examination, ordered the rebel to be hung. I was present at his examination, and to my surprise, the fellow looked up into my face, and said boldly, "Well, Mr. McCarthy, if you will get me reprieved for three days, I will give full information concerning the shooting of a Mr. De Burgh, at Bally——s, and the robbery of his papers from his residence at Dungarvon." Sir W—— was about to order the unfortunate devil to be hung at once, when he tore open the lining of his frieze coat, and taking out two letters, handed them to me. I saw at once that they were directed to you! so my interest and curiosity were roused, and I obtained from Sir W———— a respite for three or four days. The fellow, when taken to prison, told one of the turnkeys all about your being carried up into the hills, and how Holt's son-in-law released you, or most likely you would have been shot. He then applied for papers and pens to draw up a confession, and said when that was finished he would see a priest. But, by Jove, the fellow completely outwitted us; his object was to gain time, for, on the third morning, the jailer found our friend had decamped, how or by whose connivance we could not make out; but Sir W———— accused the jailer, and dismissed him from his post, though the man swore stoutly he had neither hand nor part in it. Thus, all I obtained were the two letters the rascal gave me, no doubt to excite my curiosity, and belief in his power to give more important information. I locked them up, intending to communicate with you; but the terrible excitement of the times and my incessant occupation, drove the matter out of my head from time to time, and this very day, in opening my desk, I turned over the two letters, and intended writing to you. When we go upstairs I will give them to you; the seals are broken, and they have evidently been read; however, of course I know nothing of their contents."

"All this is very singular," remarked Francis De Burgh, as Mr. McCarthy paused, "and recalls other circumstances of that period to my recollection. Do you remember, my dear sir, the gentleman who travelled in the mail with us from Bally———s to Carlow, and who seemed so desirous of throwing some suspicion on me, and whose looks of hatred and malice I found myself forced to notice."

"Yes, my young friend, I do, and a rather important personage he has become, though well known previously in a rather notorious light."

"Is his name still a secret, Mr. McCarthy?" questioned our hero.

"Oh, by no means. I myself," continued the magistrate, "thought his conduct very strange. As he requested me then not to mention his name, I did not, but now I may do so. He is the too well known Sir Godfrey De Burgh, a namesake, at all events, of yours."

Our hero looked astonished, repeating, "Sir Godfrey De Burgh."

"I wonder if he be any relation to a Captain De Burgh I met on board the British Queen—Captain De Burgh, of the ———— Dragoons?"

"By Jove! my young friend, you have hit it; Sir Godfrey De Burgh has a son in the ———— Dragoons. But he is no longer Captain De Burgh, having very lately succeeded to the title and estates of the late Lord Delamaine."

Francis De Burgh leaned back in his chair, with an exclamation of intense surprise and sorrow, repeating the words, "The late

"Lord Delamaine! Good Heavens! then that kind-hearted nobleman is dead."

"I regret to see you so moved by this intelligence," said Mr. McCarthy; "but such is the sad fact. Lord Delamaine died from eating heartily of a poisonous mushroom in mistake; the papers stated he was extremely partial to stewed mushrooms, and most unfortunately those he ate were that very poisonous sort, so very similar to the real."

Our hero was terribly dejected and dispirited; he felt a singular interest in Lord Delamaine; his kindness and urbanity, and the real interest he seemed to feel for him, during their short intimacy, created in his mind, a strong feeling of regard, if not affection, for his Lordship. To his Lordship, he also looked for a kind friend and patron, and now he was deprived for ever of his counsel and friendship.

"Are you, then," said Mr. McCarthy, seeing his grief and distress, "any relation to his Lordship, or to Sir Godfrey De Burgh?"

"I may suspect something of the sort," said Francis; "but I have no tangible means left of ascertaining anything about myself or my lamented father."

"Will you not think me either curious or impertinent," said Mr. McCarthy, kindly, "if I request you to give me a slight sketch of all you know of yourself, and of your previous life. I feel, believe me, a great interest concerning you, and perhaps something may strike me in your recital that may have escaped your notice."

Francis De Burgh thanked the worthy magistrate, and at once gave him an outline of his and his father's life, and his meeting with Lord Delamaine and Captain De Burgh on board the British Queen.

Mr. McCarthy listened with great interest and attention. When our hero paused, he remained plunged in thought for several moments, and then looking up, said:

"All this that you have related is rather extraordinary, and I am forcibly struck with the conviction that Sir Godfrey De Burgh knows who you are, and who your father was. Your position is besides very peculiar; the robbery of your documents and papers; the words used by the Englishman when he threatened your life in the parlour of your cottage in Dungarvon, clearly prove there are persons interested in keeping you in the dark, with respect to your father's previous position in life. Whether Sir Godfrey De Burgh had anything to do with the act of depriving you of your papers, it is impossible to say. The few lines you read of your father's letter prove, that he was about to take steps to reinstate you in your rights, or resume his own station in the world. His reasons for living so many years in solitary seclusion we cannot presume to conjecture; but it is very evident, from what you relate of his kindness and liberality to all around him for years, that he possessed ample means. He must have procured his supplies from some bank, or some agent; and that agent, finding no further application to him for funds, will naturally make inquiries for the next of kin. Now, I would recommend you to go to a solicitor of high standing and well-known probity; there are a few I can mention with confidence; and if you embrace my views on this subject, we will go to-morrow to a Mr. Gardener, Rutland Square, an old friend of mine, and a man of great practice and experience. By judicious advertisements in the Irish and English newspapers, you will without fail discover your father's agent, or the place from whence he drew his supplies of money."

"I perfectly agree with you in your proposals," said Francis De Burgh; "and it surprises me I did not think of this before. Owing to my good fortune in being of service to the Liverpool ship, the British Queen, I possess a considerable sum of money at command; therefore, though not pressed for funds, my anxious wish is to obtain, if possible, some information concerning my lamented father."

"Very well, then we will go to-morrow to Mr. Gardener's. By-the-by, I suppose, from your short acquaintance with the late Lord Delamaine, you are not aware that he possessed a large estate and a very handsome mansion within a few miles of Bally——s. The late lord's only sister married Sir Godfrey De Burgh, and part of the Irish landed property was, I think, the portion of the bride, the Honourable Miss Delamaine; but being a man of most dissipated and extravagant habits, and addicted to play and associating, they say, with the very lowest society, the property he received with his wife is mortgaged to the fullest extent. Lavish, without a particle of generosity, and addicted to low vices from his youth, Sir Godfrey De Burgh was the last man a father should have bestowed his child upon. You remember you left me at the inn in Carlow with this Sir Godfrey De Burgh in the room. After your departure, he condescended to enter into conversation with me; for, though fond of low pursuits, his pride is great, as the De Burghs boast of a much higher descent than the Delamaines. I remarked to him that it was somewhat singular that you bore the same name; perhaps, as it was an aristocratic name, you might come from a branch of his family."

"'No, no,' interrupted Sir Godfrey, with a curl of his lip, and a tone of contempt, 'that young fellow is the offspring of some low adventurer; they always take high names, and in Ireland especially they frequently deceive people.'"

"'I cannot agree with you, Sir Godfrey,' I remarked."

"'Very possibly,' he returned coldly; 'whatever he is, or was, he is now most likely a united Irishman. From what I learned, while looking over the estate at Bally——s, and from what my bailiff said, I think Holt and his son-in-law have been tampering with him; and most likely, before they released him, induced him to take the oath.'"

"'I have no belief in anything of the kind,' I replied rather sharply."

"'Ah! his boy's face and specious manners have deceived you, Mr. McCarthy. If Sir William —— had hold of him he would have cut a sorry figure;' and, without another word, he walked out of the room, and I saw no more of him. I thought it strange at the time to see so much malice exhibited by a person you could know nothing of."

"His conduct was certainly most extraordinary for a mere stranger," remarked Francis, musingly: "I should very much like to know some particulars of the Delamaine family."

"When we came to Dublin," said Mr. McCarthy, "I saw Sir Godfrey De Burgh several times, both at the courts and in the streets, but we did not notice each other. I hear that his constant companion is a man whose name is notorious for his duelling propensities, and his ruffianly behaviour in all things—a most dangerous character; in fact, he must be half mad to do all the things reported of him: his name is Brian McGuire. This pleasant companion of Sir Godfrey De Burgh's boasts of snuffing a candle with a duelling pistol at twelve yards, and that his wife can do the same, each politely holding the candlestick for the other. This ruffian has killed several persons in duels—is a big, savage-looking brute, but, it is said, at heart a coward. Every gentleman avoids him, though he still gets into clubs, billiard-rooms, and gambling houses. Woe to the unfortunate man that he chooses to pick a quarrel with."

"I should never dream of meeting such a character as that of Mr. Brian McGuire," said Francis De Burgh: "such a man is a pest to society: if insulted by such a man, I would treat him as I would a highwayman."

"Ah, with your powerful frame, so you might," said Mr. McCarthy; "but the best way is to leave any place where either that man or his companion, Sir Godfrey, frequents. Now, since you will not take any more wine, let us join the ladies in the drawing-room, and then you can cast a glance over your two letters, which are locked up in a cabinet there."

The remainder of the evening passed in a most agreeable manner with the amiable family of Mr. McCarthy. Both young ladies played and sung well, and without affectation or pressing. Francis De Burgh loved music, and was himself a tolerably good musician, and promised during his stay in Dublin to make himself at home in Kildare Street.

At parting, Mr. McCarthy gave our hero the two letters; at a glance he recognized them as two of the letters stolen, but did not then look into their contents; but bidding the kind-hearted and hospitable magistrate good night, and fixing an hour to meet the next day, he departed.

A NOTE FOR YOU, SIR.

## CHAPTER XVII.

FRANCIS DE BURGH left the mansion in Kildare Street soon after eleven o'clock, his mind fully occupied with the thoughts of all he had heard from Mr. McCarthy respecting Sir Godfrey De Burgh, and with spirits greatly depressed, though he strove all in his power not to appear dejected before the kind and cheerful family he had left. Lord Delamaine's death greatly affected him, short as their acquaintance had been.

Walking slowly down Kildare Street, he was just entering Nassau Street, when a man in a long light-brown surtout and glazed hat came up to him, and touching his hat, said:

"I presume, sir, you are Mr. De Burgh?"

Our hero paused, and looked at the man by the aid of one of the very inefficient oil lamps of that day, suspended from an iron pillar. There was nothing remarkable in the man's face, figure, or manner; he therefore quietly replied:

"My name is certainly De Burgh; but there are others of that name."

"Perhaps so, sir," returned the man, in a civil tone; "but I was requested to give this note to a gentleman who would come out of No. 24, Kildare Street, and who would answer to the name of Francis De Burgh; I was told that the note contained matter of great importance to him. I was also desired to request him to read it at once."

Francis De Burgh, though much surprised, took the note, thinking, at the same time, that there was always something strange occurring to him. Stepping nearer the lamp, he opened the paper. Just then the night mounted patrol rode up the street; the officer at their head checked his horse, gazed earnestly at our hero, and then went on. Francis did not perceive that the man who had given him the note, when he saw the patrol coming up the street, dived beneath an archway, and did not come out till the guard had passed on. Our hero became intensely interested in the contents of the note, which were as follows:

"DEAR SIR,

"I have now an opportunity of doing you a most essential service, in return for the kindness you showed to my poor wife, who, you will be grieved to learn, died shortly after you left the mountain cabin. By a singular chance, all the papers and documents stolen from your cottage in Dungarvon have fallen into my hands. You may follow with confidence the bearer of this; but for God's sake be cautious, for my life hangs by a thread. You will understand who writes this without my signature. Remember Bally——s."

"Good Heavens! how fortunate this is!" exclaimed Francis to himself; and then turning to the man, he said, "I am satisfied, therefore proceed; I am ready to follow you."

"Very good, sir," returned the stranger; "I must, however, keep a good distance a-head of you; so if you perceive me plunge under an archway, or into a lane, please wait till I come out, for I must not encounter the night patrol."

Though our hero followed the stranger without hesitation, he confessed to himself that he incurred considerable risk in doing so; for though the recovery of the papers was most important, yet to be caught in any of the secret haunts of the "United Irishman"—and there existed many at that time in the City of Dublin—would be a dangerous adventure. However, keeping his guide in sight, he proceeded into College Green, passing without remark many of the useless and drowsy watchmen, and twice halting for his guide to come out of an archway or lane, as the mounted patrol paraded by them.

In this manner they proceeded the entire length of College Green, and finally got amongst the labyrinth of streets at the back of the Castle. After traversing several narrow, crooked streets, with lofty houses on each side, but singularly dilapidated, and in many streets beams being stretched across from house to house to keep them from falling, at length the guide stopped, and Francis coming up, the man said:

"Do you see that narrow entry opposite, sir?"

Our hero replied in the affirmative.

"Enter that passage, sir, and about twenty paces within you will be stopped by a door. A hard knock at that door will be answered by a woman, who will demand what you want; then you will reply 'Bally——s,' and no more. She will at once conduct you to the person who expects you. I must keep a strict look-out here, and will watch your return, so that I may conduct you out of this remote and intricate quarter of the city."

It was a dark night, but dry, with a keen wind blowing; there did not appear a human being moving in those dismal streets, whose lofty structures had witnessed better days. De Burgh, without bestowing a thought upon the danger he incurred, crossed the street, and entered within the narrow dark passage. Along this he felt his way till he came to the door spoken of by the guide; there was not a ray of light except from the doorway, and not finding any kind of knocker, he struck with his heel a strong blow against the door. After the expiration of a few seconds, a small square hole in the door was opened, and a ray of light shone out through the aperture.

"What's your business, whoever you are?" uttered a very strange kind of voice, to which our hero replied:

"Bally——s."

"Ho! ho!" muttered the voice; "all's right."

And bang went the small slide over the opening, followed by the sound of a heavy chain and strong bolts, and then the door swung open.

The visitor entered, not without casting a look at the extraordinary-looking woman by whom he had been admitted.

The individual in question was a most strange-looking hag, bent nearly double. If she had stood upright, our hero, tall as he was, would have appeared beneath her standard. To his first glance, she looked old; but having bolted and chained the door, she turned round, and raising the yellow candle she held dripping over her fingers, she took a survey of our hero, and he did the same of her.

"Ho! ho!" she exclaimed, with a grin, and a sudden and singular change of countenance, which made her actually appear not more than thirty years old, "You are avick, a well-built, tall young fellow, but I can beat you by an inch;" and she reared her huge figure bolt upright. "I dare say, acushla, you took me for me for an ould hag; but I'm neither ould nor ugly."

And this was truth, for she certainly transformed herself into a rather comely young woman, though of immense proportions, and most strangely attired, having a great belt round her waist, with a dirk and a pistol in it.

"Now follow me," said the giantess to the surprised Francis; "I dare to say you never see'd Susy Toole before."

"I can safely say I never did," returned our hero.

"Well, then," she resumed, as she snuffed her bleared candle with her fingers; "maybe you have heard my other name. I'm called the 'Moving Magazine' by the sodgers, and if ever you go to Innahinch Bridge, you'd then know, by the hokey, who I am in earnest. But come along."

With a smile at the singular-looking being who served as his guide, Francis De Burgh followed, observing:

"If you do not make haste, Susy Toole, you will burn your fingers with the candle."

"Burn my fingers!" said the 'Moving Magazine' in a tone of contempt. "Onna mon dioul! if you had burnt your fingers as often as I have mine with gunpowder, you wouldn't mind the scorch or a dirty farthing candle."

They had walked some distance, when at length they stood

before another door, which the woman opened, disclosing a flight of steps, which they descended, and then walked along another passage, which ended in a strong, iron-bound door. Against this door the "Moving Magazine" gave three distinct knocks with the butt of her pistol; when it immediately fell back, and Francis beheld standing in front of him, a stout, able-bodied man, in a grey frieze coat, buttoned to the chin, and holding in his hand a short pike.

"Bally——s," said the woman.

"Oh!" returned the man; "be gor, it's time. All right; you may go."

"Good night, acushla," said the 'Moving Magazine,' addressing our hero, "and don't forget Susy Toole."

Somewhat surprised at the proceedings, as far as they went, Francis passed through the door. The man immediately closed it, and threw two huge bars across it; and then taking up his light, said:

"This way, master."

All these precautions convinced Francis De Burgh that he was within one of the secret haunts of the Dublin insurgents, or rebel places of meeting. Passing across a vaulted stone chamber, quite void of any kind of furniture, the man paused at a door at the opposite end.

"Here you are," said the man; "the moment you see that door opened, go in."

The next instant the place was in total darkness, for the man held a dark lantern, which he had closed.

Francis De Burgh felt not the slightest sensation of fear, startling as in truth was his situation. He did not stir, but stood calmly waiting the opening of the door. Presently he heard the sound of a bell, and then the door fell back, and a strong blaze of light at the moment dazzled him. Entering without hesitation through the door, it immediately closed with a sharp noise, as if impelled by a strong spring.

Francis looked round him with some curiosity, and perhaps with a little anxiety; the chamber, he perceived, was a vaulted apartment, full forty feet long, with a strong iron-plated door at the further extremity. Along the centre of the chamber was a massive oak table, and on this table were four iron bowls of a singularly antique shape, which contained melted tallow, and had four wicks lighted in each, throwing a strong glow over the entire chamber; the walls were quite bare, and excepting two long, strong oak benches, and a high-backed carved chair at the foot of the table, no other kind of furniture was to be seen. Wondering what next was to follow, he was on the point of moving to sit down on one of the benches, when the door at the further end opened, and immediately, one after the other, two-and-twenty men entered the chamber in perfect silence;

they were all attired in the dark green uniform of the rebels, and each man, as he took his seat, placed a heavy, brass-mounted pistol before him.

As soon as they were all seated, another individual entered the apartment; he was also attired in dark green, but was masked, and instead of a pistol he placed two books and a drawn sword upon the table. Francis De Burgh was certainly astonished; the unmoved countenances of the twenty-two men, who all appeared to be in the prime of life, the solemn silence, the pistols on the table, all wore a lugubrious and somewhat imposing appearance to our hero, who waited impatiently the opening of the assembly, for he judged they were not met to maintain the solemn silence hitherto observed.

At length the masked personage at the head of the table removed his mask, and Francis De Burgh beheld a countenance not easily forgotten; it was the face of a very young man, pale and thin, but remarkable for the fine intellectual but melancholy cast of the features; the eyes were dark, and singularly penetrating; fixing them upon our hero, he said:

"Mr. Francis De Burgh, be pleased to step foward to the table."

The voice of the young gentleman—for there was no doubt in our hero's mind but that such was his rank—was singularly sweet and clear.

Willing to comply with the rules of the assembly, into which he had been so strangely brought, our hero advanced, and stood at the foot of the table, with his look fixed steadily upon the person who had addressed him.

"You are, I presume, a Protestant?" said the President of the assembly, regarding him steadily.

"Most assuredly," returned our hero, wondering what all this had to do with the restoration of his papers, and surprised that Holt's son-in-law was not amongst the assembly.

"Hand Mr. De Burgh that Testament," said the President, pushing forward one of the books.

This was done.

"Now, sir," said the speaker, "take that book, and swear to answer truly and without reservation, whatever questions I may think fit to put to you."

Francis felt his check flush as he drew his tall and striking figure to its full height, saying, in a firm but calm tone:

"Sir, I shall certainly not swear to answer any question I may think fit to refuse the answering. If you are determined to question me, I will so far comply with your request as to reply to any question that I may not have private reasons for keeping to myself."

"Sir, you are incurring the penalty of death," said the President, sternly, and his dark eyes flashed with excitement.

"Having once entered this chamber, you can only leave it by becoming one of our fraternity, or taking an oath to answer such questions as I may deem it advisable to put to you; if you persist, you will be carried out a corpse. Will you swear?"

Of a fiery and determined spirit when roused, Francis felt his chest heave with indignation; he rested his hand on the table, the eyes of all were upon him, when, in a firm, determined voice, he said:

"I have been betrayed by a cowardly artifice into this place, for what purpose I cannot exactly see; but I tell you distinctly, and once for all, I will die before I become a traitor to my country, or take the oath you demand."

As he ceased, he folded his arms upon his broad chest, and looked defiance upon his interrogator.

"Rash man! you have provoked your doom!" and raising the sword that lay before him, the President held it up; instantly the two-and-twenty men raised their cocked pistols, and took steady aim at the unshrinking form of De Burgh.

He felt his heart beat quicker, the colour might have left his cheek, but his eye flashed, and his breast heaved, as he sternly said, after breathing a prayer to Heaven, and bestowed one thought on Mary Grey:

"Cowards! fire! and learn how a loyal subject, and an innocent man, can die!"

"Hold!" exclaimed a loud and powerful voice, as if in great excitement, and a tall, strong man rushed in through the door, exclaiming, "Great God, Emmet, would you murder a brave and most innocent man?"

"You wrong me, Holt!" exclaimed the young man called Emmet, quite calmly; "I was trying our test, which this young gentleman has stood most nobly; if you examine those pistols, you will find not one loaded," and laying down his sword, every man calmly replaced his weapon on the table.

"So! this is Holt," thought Francis De Burgh, breathing hard, after the trial he had gone through, and looking at the celebrated Irish insurgent and the unfortunate Emmet with deep interest and surprise.

Holt's career is a romance in itself, but we will not touch upon it. He was then in the prime of life, to all appearance, and was of a good and gentlemanly carriage, with a pleasing, benevolent expression of countenance. Stooping down, he carried on for a few moments an animated conversation with the gentleman called Emmet, who, after musing a moment, said:

"Be it so. It shall be as you wish."

Holt then advanced, and looking, with some emotion in his features, at the excited Francis, said:

"You are a noble youth, and will, I trust, pardon this severe test of your courage and loyalty. We differ in opinion, but as brave men, we feel and think alike. Forget this, and God bless you!"

And holding out his hand, he wrung that of the surprised De Burgh, and, without another word, quitted the place.

Mr. Robert Emmet, that noble-hearted, brave, but mistaken man, then looked up, and gazed earnestly into the handsome, flushed features of our hero, and then, in his soft, musical voice, said:

"You may think, and perhaps justly, Mr. De Burgh, that I have put you to a severe and unnecessary trial. I never, however, doubted your nerve from the first moment I looked into your countenance; but I had to satisfy others as well as myself. By anonymous letters we were led to believe that you had betrayed the secret retreat of the patriots near Bally——s, and that you were now in Dublin, concocting with a well-known magistrate how to betray many of us, Holt's son-in-law amongst the number, into the hands of the Government. God knows enough blood has been spilt as it is; but traitor and spy we never spare. You were denounced, and a plan was even given us how to entrap you into our secret places of meeting. I sent a messenger to Mr. Holt, stating all this, and he sent back word to be cautious how I acted, for he was quite satisfied you were innocent; but others were not, and it was resolved to put you to the test you have stood. No traitor or spy at heart would have stood that test, and even without Mr. Holt's unexpected appearance, I was quite satisfied. Who our informant is, I cannot even surmise; but he must be your deadly enemy, and I should say we are somewhat in his power, and must be on our guard. All I have now to request is, that you give me your simple word that the events of this night remain locked in your own breast for one year at least. Before that expires, those you now see about you will have ceased to exist, or have triumphed in their righteous cause."

"Sir," exclaimed Francis De Burgh, with much emotion, "your wish shall be obeyed to the letter. On my honour, no word of what has passed this night shall escape my lips during the period you mention, perhaps never. The fear of death shall not induce me to break my word."

"Of that I am quite certain," returned Robert Emmet, visibly affected.

And waving his hand, all present rose from their seats, and with a look of considerable interest and good feeling at our hero, passed out from the chamber.

As Francis stood gazing after the departing figures, he felt a hand laid upon his shoulder, and turning round, met the comely, good-humoured countenance of the "Moving Magazine."

"Be me conscience," said the Amazon, with a pleased look at our hero, "you're a brave boy. But come along with me. Be gor, it's a mortal pity you're not one of us."

"Well, Susy Toole," said Francis, with a smile, "I am ready to follow you."

"Wait a bit, avick, till I douse the lights," and this she soon did. "Now, then, let us go; all the rest are gone by this time, but you must go out the way you came in."

She then led the way back through the same passages, closing the doors after her.

## CHAPTER XVIII.

Whilst the scene recorded in our last chapter was taking place, there sat in a quaint-looking old chamber in the old "Brazen Head" inn, Bridge Street, two individuals, widely different in rank, manner, and appearance. The "Brazen Head" inn still exists, and, excepting in its internal decorations, and a little improvement to its front, it remains nearly in the same state as it existed one hundred and fifty years ago. At the period of our story, it was a well-known and much-frequented hostelry; but as it is situated in a rather unfashionable district, though not very far from the Four Courts, and quite shut out from view, being built in a court, and hid by the row of houses forming Bridge Street, it was chiefly frequented in after years by traders and merchants from Cork, Kilkenny, and Carlow. During the period of the rebellion, it was notorious as a rendezvous for various political clubs.

Its interior consisted of endless galleries and chambers of every size and shape; rooms in places it would puzzle a stranger to find his way from, when once left to himself; and yet it was a favourite resort, for somehow or other travellers found it extremely comfortable, the fare good, the wine excellent, and the charges moderate. It retains its good name to the present day for the same commodities, with modern improvements.

Begging the reader's pardon for this short digression, we return to the two individuals sitting in a small back parlour in the "Brazen Head." Though the room was small, it contained excellent furniture, and a roaring fire, for the March wind was bitter and keen. On the table near the fire were two decanters of wine, a large jug of hot water, a bottle of whisky, with glasses, pipes, and tobacco.

Two individuals were enjoying the wine, the whisky, and the tobacco—one was Sir Godfrey De Burgh, therefore it is unnecessary to describe him; the other was a tall, athletic, well-built man, about forty years of age, with a broad, full face, coarse features, and high, broad forehead.

This last individual was mixing himself a potent tumbler of whisky punch; Sir Godfrey De Burgh drank port. Both seemed to have indulged pretty well in the different mixtures when introduced to the notice of our readers, at a late hour of the night.

"It is quite time, Captain Barlow," observed Sir Godfrey, looking at his watch, "quite time that your man Kavanagh should be here. I hope we shall not again be baffled."

"Devil a fear! Sir Godfrey," said the individual called Captain Barlow, who was an Englishman. "I wish it had been Kavanagh that you employed to follow him on the mail to Bally——s, we should not have this trouble now; the youth may stay late at the place he dines at, but at all events you could scarcely expect him to leave before eleven o'clock."

"Is Kavanagh quite sure of the haunt of those confederated United Irishmen?"

"Sure as I am of this tumbler of good whisky, which, by the way, is worth a dozen of your port, Sir Godfrey."

"It's well enough in its way," returned the Baronet; "but this wine is good. Do you know, Barlow, it strikes me as something extraordinary how this boy escapes from such apparently well-laid plans for his destruction; he got out out of the mess at Bally——s in a most singular way; that bungling ruffian, Martin, missed him with his pistol within a yard of his head; you yourself missed him again in the cottage, and then lost all the important papers and documents you incurred such a risk in getting, and which, if I had now in my possession, would put an end to all further trouble, and save us the risk we are incurring in getting rid of him."

"How the deuce could I help all that?" said Captain Barlow, lighting his pipe, and speaking at intervals. "A cursed combination of circumstances defeated me."

"You committed one grand error, however," remarked Sir Godfrey; "instead of keeping the papers and documents yourself, you let that villain Sullivan carry them, and he has baffled every search since he escaped out of Athoy Gaol."

"A devilish good reason why we can't find him," said the Englishman; "he was mortally wounded in a combat with the military, and died somewhere, but where I can't say."

Sir Godfrey De Burgh put down his glass, and stared at his companion with a look of astonishment.

"How is it, Barlow, you never told me that before?"

"I only heard it from Kavanagh three hours since, and he picked up the intelligence from a crony, one of Holt's followers. Holt, they say, is hiding in Dublin; there is such a hot search after him in the country."

"But who got the papers? By heavens! it was a cursedly ill-managed job, take it altogether," exclaimed Sir Godfrey, passionately.

"By Jove! I differ with you, Sir Godfrey," returned the other quite coolly. There was no mismanagement; there was infernal ill-luck. I considered Sullivan the most trustworthy man we had; you yourself picked him out. I gave him the papers to carry, for they were bulky, and never dreamed that such articles would tempt him to decamp, neither do I think he intended to do anything with them. We fell in with a detachment of the —— Dragoons, and were taken prisoners; we both contrived to escape, though not together, therefore I have not the slightest idea what he did with the papers. Sullivan was taken again, and was condemned to be hung by Sir William ——; a party of Holt's men contrived to manage his escape. I could never trace him afterwards, and until Kavanagh heard of his death yesterday, I knew not what had become of him."

"Most extraordinary what the fellow did with the papers," said Sir Godfrey; "surely when taken prisoner they must have been found upon him, and if so, such important documents would be noticed, and pains taken to restore them to their rightful owner by the authorities."

"I don't think they fell into the hands of the military, or the authorities who examined Sullivan; he might have pitched them into a bog-hole when attacked by the military, for we crossed a large track of bog trying to escape them at first. Hark! there's a foot along the corridor—it may be Kavanagh."

The next moment the door opened, and the very individual with the brown surtout and glazed hat, who handed Francis De Burgh the note in Kildare Street, entered the room.

The man named Kavanagh cast his hat on the floor, and throwing himself into a chair, said, in a tone of passion and vexation:

"Beat again, by ——!"

Sir Godfrey De Burgh struck the table in his passion so fiercely that he overturned a decanter and the jug of hot water, which sent its contents over the limbs of Captain Barlow, causing that worthy to spring from his chair with an oath.

Kavanagh burst into a mocking laugh; he did not seem to feel any great reverence either for the Baronet or the Captain, for rising up, he said:

"Since you have spilled the water, I must drink the whisky without it," and taking up a decanter of spirits, he half filled a tumbler and drank it off at a draught.

"How is this, Kavanagh? Have you botched this?" said Captain Barlow fiercely.

"You need not look so fiercely at me, John Barlow," said Kavanagh, quite unconcernedly; "I did not botch it; I succeeded every way we intended."

"Explain! in the devil's name, explain!" exclaimed both Sir Godfrey and Barlow impatiently. "You say that you failed and succeeded in the same breath. What do you mean?"

"By jabers, if you will give me time, I will tell you. In the first place, I intended to catch a whole gang of confederated Irishmen this night. I was to have three hundred pounds from Sir William —— if I succeeded, so I made my plot to time in with yours. I watched our quarry coming out of the house in

Kildare Street, and gave him the note, and he followed me like a spaniel. I pretended to hide under archways when the patrol came up, that he might think me a regular rebel. As soon as I saw him enter the place I knew was the secret meeting place of the "United Irishmen," though I was never inside it myself, but my spy, Murphy, put me up to the whole,—of how the door was kept by a woman, who is known by the military, and every man, woman, and child in the county of Wicklow as the 'Moving Magazine.' Well, as soon as I saw him housed, I joined the party of men Sir W.——— placed under my orders for the night, and who waited for me by appointment in Tooley Street, and led them to the spot; a strong party going round into Pill Lane, to guard the backs of the houses in case a retreat was made by the rear. After some little trouble, the doors were burst open, and in we went, intending to catch the whole party of confederates, and fully expecting to find our bird shot. By all the saints, not a living soul remained in the house or vaults! In the vaults was evidently the place of meeting, for we discovered the table, benches, and lights, but not a single article else. We could find no possible mode of getting out; the whole house was searched, but without the slightest success. The man I placed to watch the front door, while I went for the military, swears that not a living soul went out by the front, and I can trust him. The house itself was in ruins, the floors all decayed, and the beams rotten."

"It's a cursed clear case that they all escaped through some secret back outlet, though you did not discover it," said Captain Barlow.

"Who is the man Murphy," demanded Sir Godfrey, "that betrayed their proceedings to you? He must know of the outlet at the back, or you would have found him there."

"Curse the rascal!" said Kavanagh, "I think he is playing a double game. The confederates implicitly trust him, and yet, though he pockoted my money, and betrayed a certain amount of their proceedings, he never said a word about a secret outlet through the vaults."

"Most likely," remarked Barlow thoughtfully, "there was a mode of communication with one or other of the adjoining houses; many of the houses in that street are in a state of dilapidation, and uninhabited."

"It's quite possible," said Kavanagh, "that such may be the case. However, it's past remedy; but how he escaped the snare laid for him with the confederates puzzles me, for there is little mercy shown to informers, and few questions, if any, asked."

"Maybe they shot him, and buried him in some of the vaults," observed Barlow.

"No," interrupted Sir Godfrey bitterly: "he is now in his hotel, I would wager a thousand guineas. However, leave me to finish this business myself. I will have no more schemes and plots. I will try other means."

And taking out his pocket-book, he selected fifty pounds from the notes in it, and threw them on the table.

"There, Kavanagh, is the sum I promised you; you did your best, and I do not see that the fault was yours."

"Well, Sir Godfrey, you are generous," said Kavanagh, pocketing the money. I have lost three hundred pounds by my own error, or the treachery of Murphy; but this I must say, if you had allowed me to have had my own way, I would have shot him as dead as a herring as he passed one of the crooked lanes leading to Tooley Street, and without any risk to myself either."

"Well, I proposed something of that sort myself," said the ruffian Barlow, quite coolly, filling his tumbler with wine; "but you, Sir Godfrey, opposed it. You seemed to prefer crooked kind of schemes, when a straight one was quite sure."

"I do not think so," said Sir Godfrey sharply. "You missed him once, and so might Kavanagh, and ten to one but such a bungling would lead to discovery. Though we have failed, no one is the wiser; but, as I said before, leave him now to me. It is time we should separate; and I would advise you, Kavanagh, to get out of Dublin as fast as you can, or you may suffer an ugly twist of the neck."

"Not till I catch Robert Emmet, and see him hung," said the villain savagely; "he won't always escape me."

He swallowed another half a tumbler of whisky, then took up his hat, and left the chamber. After half-an-hour's further conversation, Sir Godfrey and Captain Barlow also separated, the baronet leaving the "Brazen Head," the latter remaining there for the rest of the night.

## CHAPTER XIX.

CAPTAIN BARLOW and the Irishman named Kavanagh, mentioned in our last chapter, were men common enough at the period of our story. Of his origin or his parents Barlow knew nothing, excepting that he had been a charity boy, had run away from school and enlisted, and from the ranks had risen to be a lieutenant; and being a bold, bad man, with a great deal of natural talent, for a long time he deceived those with whom he associated, but possessing a powerful frame and a brute courage, he led a forlorn hope, and at length became Captain Barlow. His real nature, however, in the end broke out, and for a succession of disgraceful acts, drunkenness, and using false dice, he got himself into such bad repute, that his savage nature conquered his prudence, and in a fit of passion he struck his superior officer, stood a court-martial, was disgraced, and dismissed the service.

We shall not pursue his life, up to the period when he and Sir Godfrey De Burgh became intimate; the latter at this time had run through a noble fortune in dissipation and every kind of low vice. Captain Barlow, as he still called himself, notwithstanding his disgrace, became his constant companion, and followed him to Ireland, joining in all his schemes.

Edward Kavanagh was a different kind of person in many respects, but quite a fit agent for any species of crime. He was the only son of a fashionable tailor, who, not content with plundering his customers by exorbitant bills, contrived to complete their final ruin by cashing their acceptances at cent. per cent.; and as Dublin was a fast city at the period of his prosperity, Kavanagh's father ruined his customers rapidly. His son received what he considered a first-rate education, dressed extravagantly, and drank, smoked, and gamed to such an extent, that his worthy father became alarmed, shut up shop, and by way of securing the property he had amassed, invested the whole in a most prosperous mining company, that engaged to pay fifty per cent. the first year, and heaven knows how much the next.

In three years the mining company, with a capital of one million, came to a stand still; the fourth year it became bankrupt, and John Kavanagh, Esq., as he then called himself, lost every fraction he had invested, and in a fit of despair hung himself by cutting a yard of good broadcloth into stripes and converting it into a halter. His son Edward, involved in debt, was cast into gaol, and when he came out became marker to a billiard table, in which occupation he continued till the year 1798; he then enrolled himself a "United Irishman," but having an idea that he could support a double character extremely well, and as there was no pay belonging to the character of a patriot, he became a secret informer, and served the Government, by which he was liberally paid, and once more he mingled in a certain class of society, frequented clubs, billiard rooms, secret societies, joining many and betraying all. In Dublin he became acquainted with Sir Godfrey, whose taste for low and vicious company led him into strange haunts. On Sir Godfrey's return from Liverpool, after his interview with his son, he at once, with his constant companion Barlow, engaged Kavanagh to aid him in his schemes. This confederation it was that pursued our hero with such bitter hostility, it being their determination to take his life by some means or other.

We left our hero with the "Moving Magazine" proceeding to leave the secret place of meeting of the "United Irishmen."—[Susy Toole, the "Moving Magazine," figured as a very important personage in the Irish Rebellion. William Colthurst, Esq., declared that all the women from Imnahinch Bridge to Roundwood, were "United Irishmen." She was the daughter of a smith; she had a mode of altering her countenance so as to appear a decrepit old hag; she deceived the military, especially the militia, and used to carry about her person a quantity of gunpowder, called Holt's Mixture. Apparently she sold cakes, fruit, and gingerbread.]—They had proceeded down the last passage to the door, when some slight noise attracted Susy Toole's notice, for she paused, and holding up her hand, concealed her light; this time she carried a dark lantern.

Her companion paused also, and being quite close to the door, he thought he heard sounds without like the murmur of men's voices. They were in profound darkness, and were standing perfectly still, when he felt Susy Toole's hand grasp his arm:

"Don't speak, avick!" she whispered; "there's some schaming devils outside the door. Come close, and I will make out who they are."

Giving Francis the dark lantern to hold, she advanced, and drawing back a small portion of the slide, looked out into the passage. All she could see was that the light from the outward door was obscured by several figures, and as she gazed earnestly out, the butts of two or three muskets were struck against the flags.

"Curse of Cromwell on them!" whispered Susy; "the sodgers are in the passage."

This was very startling news to our hero, for though perfectly innocent of doing anything against the Government, having been once suspected of confederating with the rebels, it would be awkward to be caught in their haunts a second time. He was about to request Susy Toole to turn back and get out some other way, when a man's voice outside said, loud enough to be heard:

"I say, Saunders, don't you think they have had time to get round by the back; had'nt we better knock in this door at once?"

"Oh, be gor! how easy you talk of smashing it in," said the "Moving Magazine," in a whisper; "be the immortals! if we only had a sword and musket a-piece, we'd make 'em lave that, anyhow."

"It won't do, my good girl," said our hero, in a whisper, "to resist the military."

"Bother!" said Susy, closing her slide, just as a violent push or kick was made against the door.

"Kick away, lobsters, till you kick away your shoe leather; the devil a bit of the door you'll hurt with your heels. Come along, lad," she whispered to our hero; "we must get out over the roof; it's not easy, but it's easier than swinging at the end of a rope."

Our hero, in his own mind, thought so also; but he suggested that there might be a better way of quitting the premises.

"Didn't you hear the devils say they had sent a party round to the back. I can't take you out the way the others went, for it is a secret even to me, so come along, before they knock the door in with the butts of their muskets."

"Humph!" thought our hero, as he followed Susy Toole up a crazy staircase, she having opened a small portion of her lantern, "this adventure promises anything but a pleasing termination."

He felt a great inclination, though not a very gallant one, of leaving Susy to the cat-like operation of climbing over the roofs, and stand his own ground. He could hear a tremendous hammering at the door, loud enough to awaken all the inhabitants of that quarter; but Susy only mocked their efforts. Up they went, over most ruinous staircases, and along galleries with scarcely a whole plank for supporting the foot, till they gained the garret. At length Miss Susy Toole opened her lantern, and cast its light over the dismal, dilapidated room, the ceiling a mass of dirt and cobwebs.

Our hero looked up, and beheld a trap door some ten or twelve feet above him. How to get up there puzzled him. A tremendous shock and a loud shout reached their ears, convincing him that there was little time to lose, for the assailants had nearly effected an entrance.

"You must get on my shoulders, my lad," said the "Moving Magazine" quite coolly, putting down her lantern, and taking off her belt; "when you push out that door, let down this belt, and hold tight; you are a powerful youth, and I'll be up in a shake."

This proposal of Miss Toole's staggered Francis. In the first place, the shoulders of Susy was rather a difficult place to attain, and the next he considered she was an enormous weight to lift up; let her be ever so active; so he cast his eyes round the chamber for a substitute to Susy Toole's shoulders; but there was nothing to be had.

"Oh, my darlint," said the 'Moving Magazine,' "if you're looking for a ladder, be gor, you'll have to wait till the hangman supplies you. Jump up!"

And stooping down, she offered as fine a pair of shoulders for a man to stand on as any in Ireland.

Despite his situation, and the furious noise of the final bursting in of the door, Francis De Burgh could not help laughing, as Susy Toole fairly lifted him up on her shoulders, and then rose upright with as much ease as if she had supported a boy, instead of an athletic youth of some five feet eleven inches in height.

He was now much higher than he wanted, but he pushed up the trap door and scrambled out on the leads. All this was very well; but to hoist Susy he considered no joke. However, he lowered down the belt, placed his feet against the two sides of the trap door, and prepared for a tremendous effort of strength; but Miss Toole required no such violent exertion. With surprising agility, aided by the belt and our hero's assistance, she got her hands on the ledge, and in two minutes was quite composedly sitting beside him.

"Now, avick, put down the trap; they won't think of coming up through this: we could knock a dozen of them on the head if they did; and then we'll see which side it is best to go."

The house was five stories high, and the roof very steep and broken in many places, and a very narrow ledge ran along the front to which there was no parapet, so that a passage along such a causeway was ticklish in the extreme. However, ridiculous as his situation was, there was no help for it. For a moment the idea crossed his mind, if Miss Grey could only have a notion of his situation—sitting at two o'clock in the morning, alongside a young giantess, on the top of a ruined house, her astonishment would be great indeed. He then began to consider how the deuce he was to get down from his exalted position.

His fair companion did not allow him much time for thought, for having adjusted her belt, and settled her dress after her exertions, she rose up, saying:

"Now, acushla, let us be moving. Faix! you're a fine lad, every inch of you, and I wouldn't have you hurt no how. We'll go in through the next trap door, or the one after that."

"But," said Francis De Burgh, "if the room should be inhabited?"

"So much the better, avick. They are all poor people in these old houses, and all good papists; they wouldn't hurt a hair of your head, so don't trouble about that."

By no means convinced by Miss Toole's arguments, and vowing internally that he would never again be caught in so exalted a situation, the young man followed his guide over a most perilous path; they crossed two house-tops, and at length stopped before a kind of skylight, the panes all broken, and the door shattered and rotten.

"Here we are," said the "Moving Magazine;" "this is just the one for us, avick."

And without any hesitation, she pushed the crazy door in, and out fell the remnants of glass into the room below.

Susy Toole stooped down, and threw the light of her lantern into the room below; there were neither inhabitants nor furniture, but an abundance of rubbish and broken timbers, and débris of all kinds. Into this garret she dropped down, for the old stairs to the skylight or glass door had fallen to the ground with age, damp, and neglect. Her companion followed. No sound of human voice was heard after their rather noisy descent into the garret; and listening a moment, our hero's strange guide said:

"This is an uninhabited house. The saints be praised, we're in luck; but the lamp is nearly out, so let us get down-stairs as well and as fast as we can."

The garret door was bolted, but they soon broke its crazy fastenings, and proceeded down the stairs. The house was totally deserted, but all the doors were locked; neither did it appear so dilapidated as the one they had escaped from. The lamp gave tokens of expiring as they reached the hall door, which was locked, bolted, and chained.

"By Jove, Susy," said Francis, rather startled at this formidable opposition to their exit; "if we attempt to break open this door, the watchmen will hear us, and we shall be arrested for housebreakers."

"Upon my conscience, we can't get out here, avick, that's certain; it's a strong door. Let us get into the room here, and see if we can get out of the window, the night's dark and the ould Charleys are asleep."

The parlour door, or whatever room the door led into was forced, but just then the lamp went out.

"Oh, the saints!" exclaimed Susy, "we're like rats in a hole now; but grope about for the window."

Francis stumbled over sundry objects, evidently furniture piled up in heaps, to the great detriment of his shins, forcing Miss Toole to make sundry ejaculations, not very complimentary to the owners of the house; but Francis found the window, and opening the shutters, which were well barred, a faint ray of light entered the room from an oil lamp nearly opposite.

In this street there were no areas beneath the windows, and the ground was only a few feet beneath, so lifting the window, he looked up and down the dismal street as far as he could do, and not seeing a human being of either sex in the way, he turned to his guide, saying:

"We can make our escape now," and taking four or five gold pieces from his purse he begged Susy would accept them in return for the kindness he had shown him.

"Arrah, acushla! do you mean to insult Susy Toole? is it I take gold? and for what? sure we helped one another; and God bless you, you're a real gentleman, and though you are a Protestant, the saints in glory and good luck attend you;" and putting back his hand she sprang nimbly out of the window and Francis after her; he would willingly have closed the window, but that being impossible he followed Miss Toole's nimble steps down the street. She stopped a moment, and pointing to an opposite street, said: "Keep up that street, and take the first turn to your right, and then ask your way of the first ould Charley you meet," and waving her hand and wrapping her grey coat tight about her, she dashed down a dark narrow lane, and disappeared from our hero's view.

Excessively delighted at being so well out of the awkward scrape he had got into, Francis De Burgh hurried up the street indicated, and very nearly upset a drowsy guardian of the night coming out of a gateway.

"Be my sowl, ye'r a late bird, anyhow," said the Charley, recovering his equilibrium, "where the dioul are you going to?"

"To the Castle," said Francis, satisfied if he could get there, he could find his way to his hotel.

"Oh, be the powers, that flogs all! maybe ye're going to sup with the Lady Lieutenant; make haste, my lad, or the praties will be *oould*. Ha! ha! ha!" coughed the asthmatic guardian of the night, as he tried to laugh, half-choking in the attempt.

Francis de Burgh hurried on, and turned to the right, and after divers mistakes and wrong turnings came suddenly into Castle Street. He now knew where he was, and in less than half-an-hour reached his hotel in Dawson Street; was let in by the half-sleeping night porter, to whom he gave two or three shillings, which quite enlivened him, and internally caused him to breathe a wish that our hero might return every night in the week, at the same unchristian hour.

## CHAPTER XX.

It was very late the following morning when Francis De Burgh awoke; the strange scene he had gone through, and his adventures afterwards, so occupied his thoughts that for an hour or so he found it impossible to sleep. In his dreams he was haunted with all kinds of strange visions; one in particular seemed to cling to him; he thought he was walking up Sackville Street, in broad day, arm-in-arm with Susy Toole, dressed in an old regimental coat and cocked hat, when, who should he meet but Mary Grey and the General. Both cast a look of horror at him and his companion, and turned away without further noticing him. With a feeling of despair he awoke, and was singularly relieved in finding it only a dream. It was very evident to our hero, as he reflected over the events of the past night, that, whoever it was that wrote the note enticing him to the haunts of the United Irishmen, he was well acquainted with the previous events of his life, and very probably was one of the villains who had plundered him of his father's papers. He could not exactly reconcile in his own mind the object his enemies had in placing him in such a situation, unless indeed they expected the confederates would take his life. It appeared, after all, that the young and interesting leader of the United Irishmen, named Emmet, intended only to try his nerve, as the sudden appearance of Holt was unexpected.

As he finished dressing, he, however, came to the conclusion that his life was not exactly safe in Ireland, therefore, the sooner he quitted Dublin the better. As he went down to breakfast, after having with great difficulty parried the anxious questions of Bill Mullaghan, as to his late return to the hotel, he recollected the two letters given him by Mr. McCarthy.

While eating his morning's meal, he took out the letters, and with a sigh of regret first opened the one from the late Lord Delamaine; he felt deeply his loss, as his gaze rested on the lines before him, and for several moments he could not proceed. The letter was as follows:

Milton Abbey, Hampshire.
"My dear young Friend,
"You may feel surprised at not having heard from me long before this, especially after the great and important service

you rendered to myself and others, by your courage and skill. But, on my return to this country, after an absence of sixteen years, the multiplicity of business I had to go through, both public and private, occupied every hour, and scarcely had I begun to breathe a few hours of quiet, when His Majesty sent for me, and finally requested me to become his Ambassador to the Court of Vienna. This post, though much against my will, I was constrained to accept; so that with one thing or another, I have not had a moment to myself till now. I feel an unaccountable interest in your future welfare; I have very much to say to you, and very much to inquire about. I beg you will entreat your good father to permit you to visit me at once, and ask him if the post of private secretary to me, with a salary of five hundred a year, will suit his views with respect to you."

Francis De Burgh laid down the letter on reading this noble and generous evidence of his Lordship's interest in his favour; he felt overcome with emotion, but in a few moments he resumed.

"I pray you, at all events, to come, whether the post I offer suits you or not. I now wish to say a few words on a delicate subject. I feel loth, for I fear my imagination after so many years is overpowering my reason. But I beg of you to say to your father, 'the time is come.' If he *is* your father he will understand those words; if not, they will have no effect, and the dream that deceives me will remain a dream. Farewell, but come soon and excuse this, to you most strange, ending to my letter.

"Ever your sincere friend,
"DELAMAINE."

Francis De Burgh paused, bewildered and confounded, while he repeated those strange words. "The time is come. If he *is* your father he will understand those words. "Surely, surely," and his cheek flushed at the thought, "he was my own fond and most affectionate father! who else would spend twenty long years in deep seclusion in unceasing endeavours to cultivate my mind—who could or would show that disregard of self, save a parent? Alas! how little could the noble writer have imagined that when those lines should meet my eyes I should no longer possess a father, and that he himself should so soon go to that bourne whence no traveller returns!"

For several minutes our hero remained plunged in thought, so deeply was he impressed by the contents of the letter. Even General Grey's letter, for it lay open before him, remained unread.

At length he took it up; it was a long letter, but it is not necessary to lay before our readers its details. Nothing could exceed the kindness it expressed; and the remembrances sent by fair Mary Grey soothed and pleased him. The General mentioned that he had purchased a villa residence near his old friend Lord Delamaine; and that he hoped when he (Francis) visited his

Lordship, that he would not forget those who remembered with pleasure and gratitude, the services he had rendered them.

So far, the two letters were gratifying to our hero's feelings, but he could not but sigh and feel sad as Mary Grey's position forced upon his mind how impassable was the gulf between them. Locking the letters carefully up, he resumed his breakfast, and, on the whole, his spirits were somewhat revived.

The breakfast apparatus was being removed, when Mr. McCarthy entered the room:

"What!" he exclaimed, laughing, "taking your breakfast at twelve o'clock; not infected already by the smoky atmosphere?"

"Oh, no fear of that, my dear sir; this is a mere accidental circumstance. I did not retire to rest till after two o'clock; but I am now ready to accompany you."

Accordingly the two gentlemen left the hotel, and proceeded towards Rutland Square. They found Mr. Gardener at home, and a most pleasing person in his manner and appearance; he very soon understood the particulars of the case laid before him by our hero; and after an hour's conversation on the subject, he undertook to put the matter in train.

Our hero returned with Mr. McCarthy to his hospitable mansion, to pass the remainder of the day and evening with the family. A cousin of Mrs. McCarthy's, a remarkably fine-spirited, handsome lad, about sixteen, named Carleton, was one of the party; he was a midshipman, had served three years, and was then expecting to be appointed to a frigate commanded by a cousin of his. This young gentleman took a prodigious fancy to our hero, and during the eight or ten days he remained in Dublin, was almost constantly with him, and parted from him with regret.

At the end of a fortnight our hero took leave of the worthy magistrate and his amiable family. One of the daughters, he learned, was engaged to a young Irish baronet, possessing a fine property, but he did not hear the name. As the Holyhead packet sailed at a rather late hour, Francis and his attendant, with their luggage, were stowed away in a species of caravan that left Sackville Street at seven o'clock, the mail being conveyed to Howth in a car, with a guard. Our hero perceived that there were two persons inside the caravan, and he heard one say to the other, "We arrived too late to give them a call." As they drove on, he caught a glimpse of his fellow-passengers by the light of a passing lamp; they were evidently gentlemen, and both very young men, and by their conversation he judged that the voyage from Howth to Holyhead was to be their first trial of the sea. It was blowing extremely fresh; and as soon as the vehicle cleared the streets and came out on the Clontarf Road, the gusts came strong against the sides of the carriage.

"Pray, sir," said one of the young men sitting next Bill Mullaghan, "do you know how the wind is?"

"Faix! sir," returned Bill, "the wind is mighty well, and in strong health, and seems to be in high spirits to-night."

"Ah, indeed!" exclaimed the young gentleman; "then you think it will blow hard? Pray, are you a salt-water sailor?"

"Oh, be gorra; for the matter of that, sir," said Bill, laughing, "I makes no manner of difference in respect to the water; whenever I crosses fresh water, you see, I puts a handful of salt into it to persuade myself I'm at sea, for I hates fresh water, unless half of it's whisky."

"You are quite right, my man," laughed the young voyager, good-humouredly. "I suppose when you put whisky into the water, you do not trouble about the salt?"

"Be the powers! sir, it would set the whisky outrageous; but faix! there's a gust; you're sure to have the real salt water to-night, for it's blowing right in our teeth, and these packets are mighty fine divers."

"Dear me!" exclaimed both the young men, "that's unpleasant. We have a small yacht on Lough Erin; it blows hard there, but we have no great waves, so our boats never dive. Is the sea very heavy between Howth and the Head; the distance is very short?"

"Oh, be gor! sir, you will see real mountains," said Bill, who seemed to be amused at frightening his neighbours, "real mountains, with white tops to them like—"

Bill paused, as if puzzled for a comparison.

"Like what?" demanded one of the young men.

"Faix! like cauliflowers!" said Bill, coolly.

"Cauliflowers!" repeated the young man, laughing. "I see, my man, you want to have a laugh at us."

Francis De Burgh now joined in the conversation, and rather liking the tone and good humour of the young gentlemen, soon contrived to re-assure them as to the hardships they would have to endure in the short trip across Channel.

Just then the caravan drew up to the door of the small inn that then existed in Howth for the accommodation of travellers and voyagers. [The Holyhead packets at that time sailed chiefly from the Pigeon House.] Not having the terrors of a sea voyage before them, Francis De Burgh and his attendant, with a couple of porters, proceeded at once to the packet, the two young gentlemen saying they would wait the arrival of the mail; the fact was, they wished to have as little of the packet as possible; in truth, it was what even sailors would call a dirty night, extremely dark, the wind strong and from the south-east, and inclined to rain.

The Holyhead packet lay moored to a stone pier, the gale howling and whistling through her rigging, lying under the lofty cliffs that bound the south side of the harbour; they fell at times on the cutter with startling violence. The packet was one of the smallest in the service, but commanded by a hardy and most experienced captain, a retired navy officer, who had lost one arm in the service of his country. Captain S―― was a most gentlemanly person, frank, kind, and hospitable, and every inch a sailor; he was in the cabin when Francis De Burgh entered, finishing a tumbler of punch, and buttoning a heavy pea jacket up to his throat.

"We shall have a rough night of it, Captain," observed our hero, as he requested the steward to supply him with a mixture of the same.

"Yes," returned Captain S――, looking up, and scanning the person and features of his passenger; "and it's very well if it's only a night."

"So I should imagine, if the wind remains in the south-east quarter; sixty miles to work to windward, with a Channel sea up, is no joke."

"Well, I do not think," returned Captain S――, with a laugh, throwing down his nor'-wester, or sou'-wester, for that kind of head-dress answers remarkably well for either, "that you will suffer much by it."

"No faith! Captain, excepting that having provided no prog, the fasting will be apt to disagree with me."

"Oh, you shall not fast, young gentleman, don't fear that; I always cater for those passengers who are caught, like you, with an empty hold."

Captain S―― was proverbial for his hospitality ashore and. afloat for many years. Alas! peace to his ashes! he perished crossing the same passage he had traversed for years, a heavy sea swept him from the deck of a steamer; a sailor with a boat-hook caught him by the coat, which broke, and he sank.

As Francis De Burgh was finishing his tumbler of whisky, he heard the steward say to some person in a small private cabin off the main one: "We shall have a very dirty night of it; and it's ten to one if your carriage is not washed overboard."

"Be jabers!" returned a coarse voice, "then you'll not catch me sleeping in it, my darling!"

A few minutes afterwards our hero's two travelling companions from Dublin came down into the cabin.

"Well, sir," said one of them, the elder of the two, "I fear your droll attendant's prognostics of the weather will turn out too true; it's a horrible night; it's not possible to see Ireland's Eye from the deck, though they say the island is not a mile off."

Francis was struck by the handsome, open, frank look of the young gentleman who addressed him; he appeared scarcely two-and-twenty; the other was evidently his brother, and was not more than nineteen.

"I think," remarked our hero, "as you seem rather to dread sea-sickness, the best thing you can do will be to take a hot tumbler of punch, and turn in before we leave the pier, for you will find this little craft rolling and plunging about like a porpoise in five minutes after we leave the harbour."

"I really wish we had waited a day or two," said the younger brother; "but I think your advice is good, and we will follow it."

Francis, after his fellow-travellers took their berths, went on deck; the crew were busy seeing a post-chariot hoisted aboard. Two other passengers arrived and passed our hero, proceeding to their private cabins; it was excessively dark, and all he could see of them was that they were both tall, bulky men, and so muffled and covered with coats and shawls round their necks, that their faces were completely hid; not, indeed, that he felt any curiosity on the subject. The mainsail double-reefed, and a second jib set, the packet canted round, and, skilfully handled, her sails filled, and without either noise or confusion, the warps were let go, and she glided out of the harbour. She had to make a couple of tacks to weather Ireland's Eye, bent at times to the water's edge by the powerful gusts that swept over the lofty headlands forming Howth harbour.

Our hero waited till he saw the little vessel clear the Head, and then retired below; and taking off his upper coats and boots, threw himself on one of the berths for a few hours' sleep. He could hear his fellow-passengers groaning and complaining bitterly against the uneasy motion of the vessel, as she plunged into the heavy head seas. Sundry ejaculations also were uttered against the narrowness of the berths, the detestable hardness of the mattresses, and the scanty widths of the bed clothes. At the recapitulation of all these miseries our hero smiled; he was sorry the young men suffered, but it is the lot of all who tempt the perils of the vasty deep; so he fell fast asleep, and dreamt of Mary Grey.

It was broad daylight when he awoke; he could tell by the peculiar motion of the vessel that the wind still blew very hard, and that it was still ahead. Just as he finished his toilet the steward entered the cabin, and threw a cloth over the table, saying the captain was coming down to breakfast, and hoped he would join him, to which invitation our hero willingly assented.

Captain S—— soon after made his appearance; throwing off his rough coats, he sat down with his guest to a hot beef-steak and coffee.

"I fear," observed Captain S——, "that none of our passengers are inclined to rouse from their berths; the old enemy has them fast. It was a rough night, but I have many worse during the year."

For nearly an hour our hero and the Captain continued to converse; the latter seemed greatly pleased with Francis, thought he was in the navy from his apparent knowledge of the sea, and was quite won when our hero very modestly mentioned how he came to know the little he did, and of his adventure with the British

Queen. Captain S—— had heard of her narrow escape from shipwreck from several quarters; and he congratulated our hero on the skill and seamanship he had displayed, and expressed a great desire that he would spend a few days with him at Holyhead. Francis thanked him for his kind hospitality, but politely refused the invitation, saying that he was extremely anxious to reach London. They then went on deck.

Our hero perceived his attendant, Bill, enjoying himself with the cook and steward; it was a smart bracing morning, the wind rather more southerly. The cutter had only a single reef in her mainsail, and was making good way, but plunged and rolled at times anything but agreeably to a landsman. Francis continued walking the short deck, with a steady pace, the sun shining out cheerfully, the waves dancing and sparkling under its influence, always so pleasing to a true seaman's eye.

Whilst enjoying his exercise, Captain S—— having turned in for an hour's snooze some time before, he observed a stout, burly-headed, red-whiskered man come up from the cabin; he wore a very gaudy livery, and made an effort to walk straight up to our hero, but the heavy motion of the cutter caused him to deviate considerably out of his course. However, having reached Francis De Burgh, who paused in his walk, he looked him in the face with a rather comical expression of countenance.

"Sir," began the man, taking a grasp of a backstay to steady himself, "my master sent me to say that, by the powers, you must go walk somewhere else, and not be tramping over his head like a great coach horse!"

Francis was surprised, and, looking at the man, said: "Were those the words your master desired you to make use of?"

"Oh, by the saints, there's no mistake in the words!" returned the man in a rich brogue; "be gor, I made them as polite as I could, for, says he, 'only in reason of this sickness I'd get up and make that bog-trotter take off his shoes.'"

"Your master is extremely polite, and could not have selected a fitter messenger; pray what is your worthy master's name?" demanded Francis De Burgh, more inclined to laugh than otherwise.

"Tare an' ages! an' you don't know his name," returned the Irishman, "be dad, that's queer; did you never hear of Brian Maguire, Esquire, of Ballynahinch, Ballymahon, Ballyturbot, and be gors, there's not a Bally in ould Ireland he hasn't land in."

"Brian Maguire!" repeated our hero, in a tone of surprise, "well, tell your master he must deliver his message himself; I like the exercise I am taking, and shall continue it; if he had sent a request like a gentleman, I might have complied with it."

"Be the pipers of war, do you take me for a member of parliament that can make speeches? Shall I say you won't stop walking?—that's the chat."

"Go, say what you please," returned Francis, and turning round he continued his promenade along the deck.

"Be jabers!" muttered the fellow, as he made his way to the cabin, "I wouldn't be in your skin to-morrow for one of my master's estates in Ballyturbot."

## CHAPTER XXI.

Francis De Burgh, as he paced the deck, thought how singular it was that he should cross the water with the very person he so wished to avoid while in Dublin, for he felt satisfied that the companion of the said Brian Maguire was no other than Sir Godfrey De Burgh. As the steward was passing, he stopped him, and inquired if he knew the names of the state cabin passengers?

"Faith! sir, there's no mistaking one of them; you must have heard of him in Dublin; we have had some trouble with him before, Brian Maguire is his name; the other gentleman travels by the name of Brown, but I believe he is an English Baronet."

Francis found he was right in his conjecture; from the character he had heard of Brian Maguire he strongly suspected he should hear something more of him, but he made up his mind at once how he would act in case he did. Bill Mullaghan having finished his breakfast, came to ask if his master required anything, but Francis wanted nothing.

"Do you know, Bill, who is one of our fellow passengers?"

"No, sir."

"Why, the man with the great loaded stick, and the butts of the pistols he always carries sticking out of his breast pockets, Brian Maguire; I pointed him out to you in Sackville Street."

"Be gor! sir, is he aboard?" returned Bill, with an air of vexation; "and I dare to say that big, foxy brute, with the red collar and plush breeches, is his own man;" and rubbing his hands, Bill added: "faix! sir, I'd only ask ten minutes to change the colour of his hair, anyhow."

"Keep yourself quiet, Bill; by the strange message I received from him, I suspect he knows I am on board; and the other passenger is the Mr. Brown we travelled to Carlow with after the affair of Bally——s. This Mr. Brown is Sir Godfrey De Burgh. I have reason to be on my guard with respect to him, so keep aloof from any acquaintance with their servants."

About three o'clock in the day the sea had gone down a little, and the wind was more favourable; there was now a prospect of running in before night.

Francis had just made out the Welsh coast, and laid down the glass, when he observed Brian Maguire come upon deck; he looked ghastly, having suffered terribly in the night from sea-sickness. Holding on by the hatchway, he looked all round him, at the heaving of the sea, and watching his opportunity, he prepared to advance towards our hero; still he seemed loth to let go, for though the water was smoother, it still required sea legs to walk the deck steadily; his red-whiskered servant stood behind him, ready to assist him, so making an effort, he reached within a yard of Francis De Burgh, and fixing his eyes upon him with a savage scowl, it seemed doubtful whether he was to receive the burst of his wrath or the green, sparkling sea.

"So, sir," began the bully, eyeing our hero from head to foot, who could scarcely refrain from a smile seeing such a lump of humanity reduced almost to a child's weakness, by a malady that spares neither rank, bulk, nor station, "So, sir, you wouldn't stop your d—— tramping over my head, after my sending to tell you it incommoded me. Wait till I get you ashore; if you don't make me an ample apology, by the saints! I'll shoot you like a mad dog."

"If you were not in the state you are," returned our hero, still keeping his temper, though his cheek flushed, "I would chastise you on the spot for your insolence and brutality."

Frantic with passion, Brian Maguire clenched his hand, and uttering a blasphemous malediction, made a blow at De Burgh, but a violent lurch of the cutter threw him off his legs, and pitched him headlong on his face; and in that state he became so dreadfully sick, that he looked more like a beast than a man. His servant and two of the sailors lifted him up and carried him below, cursing and uttering vows of vengeance against our hero, who continued his walk quite unconcernedly.

Captain S—— had witnessed this scene, and approaching Francis, said, in a tone of disgust:

"That man is worse than a wild beast, and it's too bad that society is to be inflicted with the penalty of his appearance; he is only fit for a mad-house. I had really to confine him the last time he came over with me for grossly insulting two English gentlemen; actually putting his pistols on the dining-table, and threatening to shoot any one who dared to remove them. I trust you do not intend to notice what such a bully says or does."

"I have not the slightest intention of doing so, Captain," returned Francis; "he is notorious as a bully, but a coward at heart. I care very little about either his rage or his vengeance."

"Do you know his companion?" asked Captain S——.

"I have met him," returned our hero, "under the name of Brown, but I know his real name is Sir Godfrey De Burgh."

"You are quite right," said Captain S——; "it is not the first time I have carried him over. He is even more dangerous than his companion as a duellist; drinks at times immoderately; and when heated by wine is a terrible character."

"A pleasant pair of travelling companions," observed our hero, with a smile; "but I shall keep clear of them both, as I intend leaving by the mail."

Shortly after sunset, the packet made the harbour of Holyhead, and our hero, after taking leave of Captain S———, proceeded to the hotel with his attendant, Bill. The mail did not start for three hours, so he ordered supper.

While waiting its appearance, a waiter entered the room, and coming up to our hero, requested to know if he was Mr. De Burgh. On replying in the affirmative, the waiter said:

"A gentleman wishes to see you, sir."

The next instant the gentleman he travelled with from Bally———s to Carlow entered the room. He paused, and looking up into Francis De Burgh's face, he said:

"'Ha! I see we have met before; I then travelled under the name of Brown, but allow me to introduce myself as Sir Godfrey De Burgh."

"I remember you quite well, sir," returned our hero, with cutting coldness, "and also the uncalled-for observations you presumed to make upon my conduct at the time."

"Well, sir," returned the Baronet, with a sneer, "you shall have satisfaction for that; but there is a small matter to settle first. You have grossly insulted a most intimate friend of mine, and he insists on a most ample apology, or a meeting to-morrow at eight o'clock, as he cannot delay his journey longer."

With a smile of scorn at Sir Godfrey, whose dark eyes never left his, Francis De Burgh said:

"I will not argue the point as to who was the aggressor in this case, but come at once to the point. Now, Sir Godfrey De Burgh, my answer is, I will not meet such a ruffian as your friend Brian Maguire."

"D—n! is this an answer to give a gentleman?" furiously exclaimed the Baronet, his cheeks livid with rage. "Do you know, sir, the consequence of this refusal to meet a challenge? First, he will horsewhip you as long as there is a piece of skin on your back, and then post you through the kingdom as a miserable coward."

"Sir," returned Francis De Burgh, with a flushed cheek, "I shall know how to manage such a bully as your friend; but I have a word to say to you, who at all events rank in society as a gentleman. In our first interview at Carlow, you endeavoured, by false insinuations, to injure my character; your present conduct is unbecoming a gentleman; so now, sir, you may act as you please."

Sir Godfrey De Burgh, a man of ungovernable passions, actually stamped with rage; his lips appeared glued together with intense vexation; for several moments he remained unable to speak.

As he stood thus, facing the tall and graceful figure of our hero, the door opened, and one of the young gentlemen with whom

Francis De Burgh travelled from Dublin entered the room, and advancing towards our hero, said, in his frank, easy manner:

"Excuse me, Mr. De Burgh, for thus intruding; I came merely to say should you want a friend during your stay here, I pray you make use of me. My name is Sir James Blake; my brother and myself remain a few days."

Sir Godfrey's face betrayed intense emotion as he gazed from one to the other of the young men, while Francis said, holding out his hand:

"This is very kind indeed of you, Sir James."

"Do not mention it," interrupted the young Baronet; "we Irishmen always assist one another if in distress; but I will bid you good-bye for the present, hoping you will permit me and my brother to join you at supper."

"Most happy," returned our hero; and then, without casting a look upon the much amazed Englishman, Sir James Blake left the room.

"Well, sir," said Francis De Burgh, fixing his eyes on Sir Godfrey, "have you anything further to say to me? I have told you my mind with respect to your friend, and I shall not alter it."

"D—n!" returned the Baronet, quivering with passion; "you have grossly insulted me, and I will not leave this till you give me satisfaction. I will insist on it."

"There is no need of insisting, sir," interrupted Francis De Burgh, calmly; "I am quite willing to meet you; but remember, sir, that Sir James Blake will only meet a gentleman in such a case as this; with such a man as Brian Maguire he will not mix himself up."

"Mark me, sir," said the Baronet, "you have in me a mortal enemy; you shelter yourself under a miserable subterfuge, but do not think you will triumph in it;" and turning round with a withering look at his young opponent, he passed from the room, slamming the door violently after him.

Half-an-hour later Francis De Burgh and the young brothers were seated at supper. After the cloth was removed, and wine and glasses placed upon the table, and the chamber free from attendants, the conversation naturally reverted to the late interview of our hero with Sir Godfrey De Burgh.

"Now, Sir James," said Francis De Burgh, "that we are by ourselves, pray tell me how you found out my name, and what induced you so generously to interfere at so critical a moment between me and Sir Godfrey De Burgh? Your name seemed to have a somewhat strange effect upon him, for I watched him closely"

Sir James laughed, replying:

"I feel sorry I cannot concoct a little romance about this affair, which will end in smoke; you will hear no more at this present time, at least, from either Sir Godfrey or that detestable fellow, Brian Maguire.

"You must, however, permit me to trouble you with a few words about myself and brother. We had the misfortune to lose both our parents when very young, and were left under the guardianship of as kind-hearted a man as any in Ireland—Mr. McCarthy, of Golden Grove. You look surprised," continued Sir James, with a smile; "well, about twelve months ago I became of age, and was put in possession of my father's property. Now, part of this property adjoins a small estate of Sir Godfrey De Burgh, enjoyed by right of his wife, near Bally——s. I took a great fancy to this estate, when I heard it was greatly embarrassed, having heavy mortgages on it, and that the owner was desirous of raising further sums on it. The best snipe and cock shooting in the county is on that property; so I employed an attorney to treat with Sir Godfrey, and to offer double its value if he would sell it.

"This I found he could not do, but I lent the sum he required on certain conditions, securing the exclusive right of shooting and sporting over the whole. I possessed a shooting-lodge near Bally——s, and when the shooting season came round, after our agreement was signed, I went there with my brother and another gentleman to spend a week. Though the country was greatly disturbed, we were so well known, and having never mingled with any political party, we felt no uneasiness in following up a sport we were particularly partial to.

"The very first day we went over Sir Godfrey's property, we were surprised to hear frequent shots in the covers. On hastening up to the spot we were rather astonished to find Sir Godfrey De Burgh and four gentlemen regularly equipped for the field, and their bags well filled with game; Sir Godfrey looked a little confused at first, but said laughing, 'You must not be angry with me, Sir James, for thus infringing on our agreement. I intended calling on you first to request this day's amusement for myself and friends —gentlemen from England—but tempted by the fineness of the day, we acted Irish fashion--shot first and intended to ask leave afterwards.'

"'Excuse me, Sir Godfrey,' I replied coldly, 'English fashion, you mean, for we do not make those blunders in Ireland so often as you English gentlemen suppose.' The Baronet laughed. 'You are quite right, Sir James, quite right: we perpetrate a lot of blunders in England which we style Irish ones; however, you must forgive me this time, and accept our apologies.' But to shorten my story, I must tell you that afterwards it was discovered that Sir Godfrey De Burgh had, with the connivance of my rascally attorney, deceived me, that my mortgage on the property was not worth a fraction, and, to complete his swindling, we found out that he had actually sold the right of exclusive shooting over his estate and that of the late Lord Delamaine, to two different parties besides myself.

"One of these gentlemen, a Mr. McMahon, called him out and received a severe wound in his side; I was so annoyed, that I do believe I should have done the same thing, but for the interference and earnest entreaties of Mr. McCarthy; by his advice I also took proceedings against him and the attorney. The case is not decided yet; so much for Sir Godfrey De Burgh's principles of honour. Last November I was spending a few days at Golden Grove, Mr. McCarthy's seat, near Athy. You have seen his two daughters, so I may as well make a confession: I am engaged to the eldest. It was at this period that Mr. McCarthy returned from Carlow. In talking over several things that occurred to him, he suddenly said, turning to me, 'By-the-bye, James, who do you think I stumbled upon at Carlow, and travelled in the mail with?' 'Who, sir?' I demanded. 'Why no less a person than Sir Godfrey De Burgh, travelling under the name of Brown; and, strange enough, in the same coach was the identical young gentleman, supposed to be murdered near Bally——s, and whose name, strange enough, was also De Burgh.' He then described you minutely, said you interested him exceedingly, and that, from some cause or other, Sir Godfrey De Burgh seemed to have imbibed a mortal dislike to you, and strove all in his power to implicate you as an abettor of the United Irishmen. In this manner it was I first heard of you. Finding our own country in so unhappy a state, my brother and I made up our minds to go and spend a few months of the fishing season in North Wales.

"My brother and I both thought when we saw you in the inn at Howth, that you were the very person described to us by Mr. McCarthy; still it was only surmise, and while on board we were too ill to think of anything; but as we left the vessel, Captain S—— said to us, 'Are you acquainted with the young gentleman you were speaking to last night in the cabin? He is a Mr. De Burgh.'

"We said we should be delighted to renew our acquaintance, for we had heard of you before. 'Well,' said Captain S——, 'I am very sure he will before morning be very glad of a friend; he was much annoyed on board here, and may, as he is very young and of high spirit, be induced to fight a duel with that notorious fellow, Brian Maguire.'

"'The deuce!' I exclaimed; 'I hope not, if I can prevent it.' 'All I can tell you,' said Captain S——, 'is, that Brian Maguire and Sir Godfrey De Burgh are both gone ashore with the determination to force him to fight, and if you can prevent it so much the better; I would if I could.' I was astounded, and my brother and I hurried ashore; you know the rest."

"I am sure," said Francis De Burgh, "I cannot sufficiently thank you for your generous interference; without it I should be in serious difficulties with these two men. I can scarcely account for the extraordinary aversion evinced against me by this English Baronet; but I trust I may not be the means of bringing you or your brother into any trouble."

"Oh, do not be uneasy about that," said Sir James, cheerfully; "in my mind, you will hear no more at this time, at all events, of either Sir Godfrey or his ruffianly friend. Brian Maguire is no hero except with a pistol, and a young inexperienced hand; the horsewhip is a sovereign remedy in so powerful a hand as yours."

Sir James Blake was quite correct in his conjecture. As they all three sat at breakfast the following morning, the waiter delivered Francis De Burgh a note, saying:

"From Sir Godfrey De Burgh, sir; he and the gentleman with him left with post-horses before you were up."

There was a curious smile on the waiter's features as he spoke that attracted our hero's attention, for he just then remembered having heard a noise under his window, which looked out into the hotel yard, and at the time he thought Bill Mullaghan's voice reached his ear.

"Was there anything the matter this morning in the yard?" demanded Francis of the waiter.

"A little bit of a row, sir, between your attendant and Mr. Maguire's servant; he has left him rather a curious figure for travelling, both eyes closed, to say nothing of three front teeth he was forced to swallow like pills."

Sir James and his brother laughed heartily, while our hero looked rather serious, inquiring, however, of the waiter how the altercation commenced.

"Why, sir, there was a little scrimmage last night, as far as words went. Certainly Mr. Maguire's servant was very aggravating, till at last your attendant, sir, told him to ease his jaw tackle, or he'd clap a stopper on it. This morning Mr. Maguire's servant came up to yours in the yard with the note you hold in your hand: 'Here,' said he, you son of a sea cook, give that to your —'; excuse me, sir, repeating the expression, 'and tell him the next time my master comes across him, he'll dust his jacket with a horsewhip.' 'Be St. Patrick!' returned your attendant, with a laugh, and clenching his fist, 'for fear you and I, you foxy-headed beauty, should never meet again, taste that, and there's more where that comes from;' and down went Mr. Maguire's man as if shot, though he stood to his guard. Three times he got up, and each time he went down like a stricken ox, till the two gentlemen came out into the yard, for the horses were to, but the postillions and ostlers were gathered about the combatants. They swore furiously at your attendant, but he very coolly told them he had plenty left for them both; and in fact, sir, he would have been a very unpleasant antagonist in the humour he was in;

so the two gentlemen had their man's head bound up with a cloth, and after a little delay and threats of prosecution, they departed. The note was given me by your attendant, sir," continued the waiter, "as he fears you will be displeased; but indeed, sir, he received great provocation."

"No, I am sure," interrupted Sir James Blake, turning to our hero, "you will not blame a brave honest fellow for punishing a rascal making use of such language in delivering a letter; he's a fine fellow, good-humoured as a child, and as full of fun."

Francis De Burgh smiled as he said.

"I hope he is not marked, waiter."

"Marked!" returned the man, "not even a scratch, sir."

The waiter having left the room, our hero opened the letter, and read its contents aloud:

"Sir,—Your unwarrantable insolence will yet meet deserved punishment; you have sheltered yourself under a cowardly pretence; knowing I was without acquaintance in this place, you presumed to question the character of the gentleman who is travelling with me. We shall meet again; you shall not then escape giving me the satisfaction I have so just a right to demand.

"Godfrey De Burgh."

"The Baronet," observed Sir James, "is wonderfully moderate and considerate in his tone and words; he will think better of this affair before he gets to town; so now you must keep your promise, Mr. De Burgh, and stay and have three or four days' fishing at Bangor with us."

An hour afterwards, with a goodly store of rods and fishing gear brought from Dublin for the purpose, the party left the Head. Near a week was delightfully spent by the three young men fishing the trout streams in the romantic and beautiful vicinity of Bangor. It was with deep regret on both sides that they parted, Francis De Burgh faithfully promising not only to correspond with Sir James Blake, but also, if ever he returned to Ireland, to spend some time with him at his residence near Athy.

In two days our hero and his attendant reached London, and as the coach stopped at the Swan-with-two-Necks, he took up his abode there, till he should make up his mind as to his future proceedings.

## CHAPTER XXII.

From the period of leaving Dublin to his arrival in London, Francis De Burgh had but little time for thought or reflection, or to turn in his mind what his future career should be. The death of Lord Delamaine was a great and unexpected blow to his future prospects; he felt, also, in his own mind, that some way or another the late Lord Delamaine was connected either by blood or acquaintance with his lamented father. What could he mean, he often asked himself, by the words, "The time is come?" If he was his father, he would understand the words. Then, again, his father, in his letter, stated that he was entitled to rank and wealth; the loss of his papers and that letter were disheartening circumstances, and created in him a restless feeling of anxiety.

The sweet face of beautiful Mary Grey was constantly before his mind's eye, and thus restless and uneasy the four first days after his arrival in London passed without any fixed purpose directing his thoughts and actions. He was not, however, of a disposition to grieve or deeply regret the loss of either wealth or station. He was young, with a strong and vigorous frame, and he felt as if he could battle with the world boldly and honestly; he little thought how soon his courage, temper, and spirit, were to be tried.

Finding his purse very low, he roused himself from the somewhat painful thoughts he had permitted himself to indulge in, and set out the sixth morning after his arrival in London for the banking establishment of Messrs. Goodwin, Grimsby, and Co. On reaching the street in which stood the bank, he stopped a ticket-porter, and requested to know where the Bank was.

"It was 54, sir," said the man; "but the Bank has stopped payment the day before yesterday."

Thus our hero learned his first lesson, with respect to procrastination, for had he taken steps to remove or inquire after his funds the day after his arrival in London, he could have saved the whole.

However, on receiving this confounding information, he stood somewhat stupified, while the porter, casting a look back, muttered:

„ Humph, another victim!" and passed on.

Shaking off the feeling of dismay that at first oppressed him, he walked on, looked at No. 54, a large and spacious mansion, but its front all closed, and no signs of life or business within its walls.

"This is a terrible blow!" thought our hero, as he pursued his way, scarcely knowing where he was going. It was a terrible fact, there he was with scarcely five pounds in the world, deprived in one moment of £2,500, his all; what was to be done was the next consideration, there was no time to lose, for the sum he possessed would not pay his hotel bill.

Though he strove and succeeded in regaining his composure before he entered the hotel, Bill Mullaghan, who came up to his room to speak of a ramble he had had to the docks, perceived that something was wrong with his young master.

"Nothing has happened to vex you, sir?" said his faithful attendant, anxiously.

"Yes, Bill, I must confess there has," returned Francis De Burgh, "and to a certain degree I am to blame myself. It seems the bank, in which I lodged the entire funds I possessed, has stopped payment."

"Stopped payment!" repeated Bill, looking somewhat confused, and taking a rub at the back of his head, which was his usual custom when perplexed. "Tare and nouns, sir! what right has any bank to stop paying people their money? What reason did they give? Be gor, we're not to be robbed so easily as they imagine?"

Our hero smiled, despite his misfortunes, at Bill's simplicity, and then explained the cause of his mishap, imputing it to bankruptcy.

"Now, you see, Bill, this unlooked-for mishap—for I inquired at a respectable shop, and I fear it's a case in which not a shilling in the pound will be paid to creditors—leaves me in a serious predicament, for I have not five pounds in the world."

"Faix, we have more than that, sir; glory be!" said Bill exultingly; "there's fifty pounds in my box, and I've a hundred and fifty pounds at home, which we can write for at once, and before that's out we shall know what to do, please God; I will just run for the fifty pounds now; and your honour can write by-and-bye;" and off ran Bill, seemingly as confident and as full of spirit as ever.

"This must not be," thought Francis, "I must not deprive this fine-hearted fellow of his little store; I must borrow part; and yet," he added bitterly, "how am I to repay it?"

In a few minutes Bill returned, put down his leather bag with the fifty pounds, saying: "That will help us, sir, to weather the gale till your honour writes to father to send on the rest."

"This will do well enough, Bill," said our hero calmly, suppressing the emotion he felt, "we shall get a ship long before this money is spent, but we must move out of this hotel to-morrow. You were at the docks to-day, were you not?"

"Yes, sir; there's a fine ship of a thousand tons and more fitting out for the West Indies; there's a first mate wanting. I did the captain a chance service to-day, and he took me aboard and gave me a glass of grog, and he wanted me to ship with him at four pounds a month."

"Well, we will talk this over to-morrow, Bill, and I will go aboard with you, and see the captain; it's early in the day. I have a letter from the Dublin attorney to a Mr. Howard, Welbeck Street; I will go and call upon him."

"Very well, sir," returned Bill, "I will go back to the dock, and have a chat with the third mate; he's an Irishman, and from our part of the world."

Francis De Burgh, though he strove to hide his uneasiness from his affectionate follower, left the hotel deeply chagrined at the misfortune that had overtaken him; the fact was his principal thoughts were centred upon Mary Grey. This second *contretemps* completely, it appeared to him, prevented him from ever seeing her again. Turning over in his brain many projects for his future proceedings, he reached Welbeck Street, and fortunately found Mr. Howard at home. On presenting Mr. Gardener's letter, the London solicitor, who was a very gentlemanly agreeable man, received him with great politeness, and reading the letter, said he understood at once his position, and also how he proposed to proceed himself in the business.

Francis, though he did not inform Mr. Howard that his entire funds had been placed in the firm of Goodwin, Grimsby, and Co., yet stated, that he had funds there, and that he understood the firm was bankrupt.

"That is unfortunate," said the solicitor, "but not quite so unfortunate an affair as was at first considered; it is now confidently ascertained that they will be able to pay ten shillings in the pound, if not more: this is better than nothing."

"Very much, so indeed," returned our hero; his spirits most considerably raised, and his face flushing with renewed hope. "I had £2,500 there, and I feel very much pleased at the prospect of recovering the half."

"Still," said Mr. Howard seriously, "you will lose a large sum; but as you made up your mind to lose all, it comes cheeringly on you to recover half, which you surely will: and I will, if you permit me, take steps for its recovery."

To this our hero, who did not understand business, willingly agreed, and accepting an invitation to dinner the following day, he left the solicitor's office considerably relieved in mind, and anxious to communicate the good news to Bill Mullaghan.

While walking up St. James's Street his attention was suddenly caught by a handsome chariot with four post horses proceeding rapidly down the street; as it passed near him a lady's hand was protruded from the side window, and waved towards him. The next minute the front window was let down, and the postillion, receiving some direction, the carriage was driven rapidly up to the flag-way.

Francis De Burgh felt his heart beat wildly; he had caught a glimpse of a female head, and before he had time to think, the beautiful flushed face of fair Mary Grey was before him, her eyes sparkling with unconcealed pleasure, and a hand, not to be surpassed for beauty, held out towards him.

So agitated did our hero feel that he could scarcely return the warm greetings of the almost equally agitated maiden, till General Grey, as the servant descended from the seat behind, and opened the door, said:

"My dear young friend, just jump in, and if you can spare the time, accompany us one stage out of town; you can return by one of the evening coaches, and I really want to have half an hour's chat with you. You seem dropped from the clouds."

The next moment Francis was seated next her who was dearer to him than all the world contained.

"Shut the door, Thomas," said the General, "and tell the postillions to go slowly over the ground."

"Mary Grey first observed that her lover—for such in truth he was, heart and soul—was in deep mourning, and she looked uneasily and seriously into his flushed features, as the General said feelingly:

"I fear you have incurred a heavy loss; you did not answer my letter."

"I have lost a beloved father," returned Francis; "a loss not to be recovered in this world. But as to your letter, General, and the late Lord Delamaine's, they were stolen from me before I was able to read them, and restored to me lately in a rather singular manner."

The General expressed his regrets with much affection in his manner, while fair Mary Grey's eyes filled with tears she in vain strove to hide, when she recollected how fondly attached Francis had been to his father; and knowing his early history, she felt in her sweet, affectionate heart that her lover stood alone, unsupported by tie of relationship or kindred in the busy and bustling, and too often selfish world.

Francis saw how Mary felt for his position; he would have sacrificed all the world contained to kiss away those tears, so precious and soothing to his mind, for it proved to him that her young heart was unchanged by time or absence.

Both father and daughter requesting a recital of events since their separation, he very briefly recapitulated the scenes and adventures he had gone through. Poor Mary felt her cheek grow pale when he spoke of the escape he had from assassination in his cottage in Dungarvon; and as he finished, the General looked very thoughtful and serious indeed, while Mary, in a few low words, expressed her surprise and sympathy at all he had gone through, though he did not mention a word about his loss in the bank.

General Grey looked up; his eyes rested upon his daughter for a moment, and then he said, as the chariot drove up to the hotel door to change horses:

"Your narration, my young friend, amazes and perplexes me. I am aware that the late Lord Delamaine was most painfully anxious to see you—Ah, here we are," interrupting himself as the chariot stopped. "Tell me, can you leave London after to-morrow, and come down to us? There shall be horses for you at the Falcon, Southampton."

Mary's eyes met his with an anxious expression; but Francis instantly said:

"You do me too much honour, General; I shall feel proud to accept your invitation."

"No, my dear boy," he returned, pressing his hand, "I do not. You saved probably all that was dear to me in the world, and now that we have met, we must not part before I do more than express my gratitude. You will come—let me see, this is Tuesday. If you leave London by the Telegraph on Thursday morning, you will reach Southampton by three o'clock, and my groom shall take horses to meet you. We are eight miles from the town."

"If living, General, I shall be there," said Francis De Burgh, as he received the hand of Mary Grey in his to bid him farewell, for fresh horses were by this time put to. The next moment, the words "All right" were heard, and waving his hand in return to the last salutation of Mary Grey, the chariot dashed on at a rapid pace, leaving our hero standing before the hotel door in a complete fit of abstraction.

## CHAPTER XXIII.

For nearly a mile after the carriage had left the post-house, not a word was spoken by either the General or his beautiful daughter. Mary Grey leaned back, her eyes half closed, and her thoughts far back in the past; far back we say, though the fair girl numbered but seventeen years ; but it was far back in her young life.

"Mary, my child," said the General, in a low, affectionate tone, laying his hand on that of his daughter's, "I see how it is."

The hand under his trembled with emotion, but the General continued :

"What I thought was a mere youthful feeling of gratitude and admiration, I now perceive is a feeling that has deeper root."

"Dear father," said Mary, the tears in her eyes, "do not speak of this now. I—"

"Nay, my heart, you mistake me. I am not going either to censure you, or to tell you this must not be."

Mary could not speak ; she could scarcely breathe, her heart palpitated so violently ; but her father continued calmly, speaking in a tone of exceeding affection :

"I feel a singular and deep interest in Francis De Burgh. As far as I have seen, he is a noble and high-spirited youth, free from the vices of the age, simple, generous, and frank. I have seen no young man that I so truly admire and esteem. So far all is well."

Mary's eyes rested with intense anxiety on her father's fine features, as he continued :

"But about this young man there is a cloud of mystery. A strange and singular idea has entered my head, which I will not now speak to you of, for I must inquire into many things first. One thing I feel satisfied of, and that is, his name is not De urgh."

"Oh, father!" exclaimed Mary, with a startled tone, and her cheeks flushing with excitement, "Francis De Burgh an impostor! Oh, father, could you for one moment think that he whose frank and honourable nature causes to lay bare every secret of his heart, would for one instant deceive you ? No, he would die first !"

L

There was a smile on the General's features, as he looked at his blushing daughter, without speaking, but then said :

"In truth, Mary, it is well the poor lad has a champion, and a fair one, for he seems to have had bitter enemies enough in his short career. But you mistake me, my love; I never dreamed of Francis deceiving me; no, far from it, for I feel satisfied he thinks his name is De Burgh, but I doubt it. There is so much mystery in the hatred Sir Godfrey De Burgh seems to feel towards him, so evident a desire to injure him, nay, his very life has been attempted—(Mary shuddered)—that I am puzzled and bewildered. But the reason I speak to you on this subject now is this :—He will visit us the day after to-morrow, and perhaps stay some short time; you expect Miss Probert also to-morrow; I am glad you will have a companion besides good Mrs. Pearson; but I have one request to make, and one promise to exact."

"Did you ever, dear father," said Mary, "find me—"

Her father interrupted her by pressing her fondly to his heart, and kissing her, as he said :

"I have ever found you, Mary, a treasure ; can you then wonder that I should be careful and watch over this treasure? All I ask is, neither make nor give rash promises; you are after all but children; let me have time to sift this matter; let me at least know the name of the man who will receive from me, when he gains your heart and hand, a prize no wealth or rank can compete with."

"Never, beloved father, never!" exclaimed Mary, with a voice tremulous with emotion, "never till you yourself pronounce the word, never shall hand of mine be bestowed upon any man living. I do not attempt to deny my affection for Francis, neither am I ignorant that he returns that affection, though not a breath of such has ever escaped his lips ; and I feel assured he is too much the soul of honour to attempt to win my consent without your approval first."

"So do I think the same myself, my love. Love is a blind tyrant, but I can trust you both."

It was late that night when the General and his daughter arrived at Southampton, where they slept, and reached home early the next day. Mary Grey passed several hours of the night in anxious thought; her father's words with respect to Francis De Burgh disturbed her. Not that she considered his observations harsh or unkind ; far, far from it. He showed the greatest solicitude for her future happiness, and she felt his kindness and affection deeply. Being herself conscious that a great deal of obscurity, if not mystery, surrounded her lover—a mystery he was himself totally unable to clear up—she therefore could not expect her father to give his only daughter to a man who knew nothing himself of his parents or kindred, and against whom such unrelenting animosity was exhibited. Till this obscurity was done away with, and her lover could speak confidently as to his name and position in society, she could not expect her father to think or act otherwise.

In the midst of these thoughts and reflections she felt an inward delight at the prospect of his visit; and with the hope that the clouds that obscured her lover's prospects might be wafted away, and leave a bright and clear horizon, she prepared to receive Miss Probert, for whom she had conceived a sincere friendship.

The villa purchased by General Grey was within nine miles of Southampton, and being seated on a very slightly wooded eminence, commanded a very beautiful view across Southampton Waters to Hurst Castle and the Isle of Wight.

Scarcely four miles from the villa was Milton Abbey, the splendid seat of Lord Delamaine, surrounded by magnificent scenery of wood and valley, hill and dale; the mansion looked out over the broad waters separating England from its garden, the Isle of Wight.

Adjoining Lord Delamaine's family seat was the fine old mansion of the Herringstone family. Lord Herringstone, the then possessor, was one of the wealthiest noblemen in England. Unfortunately, though married many years, he was without progeny. At his death the title would become extinct. Being one of the oldest friends of General Grey, he hailed his settling in Hampshire with great delight; his lady was quite captivated with Mary Grey, and became a constant visitor at the villa. The death of Lord Delamaine, however, threw a deep gloom over the social society at the villa, and at Herringstone Castle.

The Countess of Herringstone being a frequent visitor at General Grey's villa, joined the family party on the day of Miss Probert's arrival. The conversation naturally turned upon the expected visit of Francis De Burgh. Lady Herringstone was aware of the narrow escape the General and his daughter, and the rest of the passengers of the British Queen had had from shipwreck, and the courage and gallantry of Francis De Burgh was often mentioned both by the General and his daughter. Her ladyship was too keen an observer, and too well accustomed to read the inward thoughts of her sex, not to observe the emotion betrayed by Mary Grey when speaking of Francis De Burgh. His name had caused her much surprise, connected as her spouse was with the Delamaine and De Burgh family; she naturally inquired of the General whether their young friend was in any way connected with those families; but the General merely said at the time, he believed not, though the young gentleman might be descended from a branch of the Irish family of De Burgh.

Miss Probert was much pleased on hearing that Mr. De Burgh was expected, though Mary Grey did not relate any of the particulars of her lover's adventures, for she felt satisfied he would not like to be made the subject of particular conversation.

"Well," said Lady Herringstone, in taking leave, her carriage having drawn up to the front, "I shall certainly be here in a day or two; I am quite anxious to see this gallant youth. If he answers to Miss Probert's description, he would make a *preux chevalier* of the olden time. By-the-bye, Mary, when was Lord Delamaine here?"

And her Ladyship, who was still a fascinating and beautiful woman, though on the wintry side of forty, looked very archly into the sweet face of Mary Grey.

"Oh," said our heroine, quite calmly; "he was here almost every day before our departure for London. I do not know whether he is at home or not at this present moment."

"I dare say, Mary," said Lady Herringstone, as she kissed her cheek, "he will be rejoiced to renew his acquaintance with your handsome deliverer!"

"I very much doubt it," returned Mary Grey, with a serious look; "they were not very great friends when aboard the British Queen."

"I daresay not, now I think of it," returned her Ladyship, with a gay laugh, and a look that brought the colour to Mary's cheeks.

The following day the General received several letters while at breakfast. One bore an official seal; this he opened first, and after reading it through, his features became clouded.

Mary, who studied his every look with fond solicitude, observed the change, and anxiously said:

"Nothing unpleasant, dear father?"

"No, my love; but his Majesty requires my presence at my earliest convenience. I trust I shall not have to accept any official situation out of England. Indeed, I had hoped to pass the rest of my days in the peaceful happiness of my home; but his Majesty must, at this critical period, be obeyed. However, I shall not leave home just yet; I must have a few days with my young friend. I should like to know his inclination, and what pursuit he is inclined to follow. If his inclination points to the army, I will obtain him a commission in a dragoon regiment; but I fancy he prefers the sea, and he is too old to commence as a midshipman."

The following day, somehow or other, passed very slowly with our heroine; there was a degree of uneasiness about her unaccountable to herself; a vague and undefinable feeling took possession of her mind; so much so, that her affectionate friend, Miss Probert, remarked that she did not appear well.

"In truth, Helen," returned Mary, "I must confess I feel a depression of spirits scarcely to be accounted for, feeling quite well as far as bodily health is concerned."

"Those kind of sudden depressions and lowness of spirits are very strange at times, Mary," observed Miss Probert. "Do you remember how you rallied me for a feeling of the same kind that came over me a few days before we all so narrowly escaped a fearful shipwreck? The weather was then fine, the wind favourable, and all aboard were in high spirits; and yet for two or three days I suffered a terrible depression of spirits, and Heaven knows, Mary, I have a most abundant stock of them in general."

"Well, such is my case now, Helen, and yet I have no earthly reason for feeling so. Come, the day is lovely; let us put on our bonnets, and take a turn or so round the lawn and plantations."

The day wore on, and the inmates of the villa met at dinner.

"It is very odd," remarked the General, "that our young friend has not arrived. It is now six o'clock. It is very evident he did not leave London by the Telegraph, or the Umpire, for the former reaches Southampton at three, and the latter at half-past three."

Mary Grey was very serious; but in reply to her father's observation, she said:

"He may be detained by some business. Is there not another coach, for James has not returned with the horses?"

"Oh, yes, there is the Comet; that leaves London at twelve o'clock, and reaches Southampton at half-past eight o'clock. I daresay he will come by that."

But to the surprise of all parties, James returned at ten o'clock, saying that Mr. De Burgh had not come by any of the coaches from London.

Mary Grey felt more than surprised, she felt alarmed. She remembered Francis De Burgh's words, "If I am alive, I will be with you." The General himself made light of the circumstance, saying a hundred things might have prevented his leaving London that day; he would be sure to come the next day. But the next day and the next, and neither letter nor our hero arrived at the General's villa; till he himself became rather startled by the circumstance. Mary could not conceal her uneasiness. Knowing the several attempts made upon Francis De Burgh's life, she conjured up before her mind's eye a thousand strange fancies. If alive and well, she felt satisfied if he could not come, he would write; and so thought the General, who now found it necessary to proceed to London. He greatly regretted not having asked our hero where he resided in London; he thus had no way of tracing him out, or of gaining any intelligence of him. He could plainly enough see that his daughter was uneasy and unhappy, though she strove all in her power to disguise her feelings.

Lady Herringstone, who drove over the day before the General left for London, expressed much disappointment at not seeing their young friend ; and, as the General would only be absent three or four days, she insisted upon both Mary and Miss Probert returning with her to Herringstone Castle. The General thinking change of scene and society would be a relief to his daughter, pressed her to accept the invitation.

Accordingly they returned with her ladyship, while the General proceeded at once to London.

## CHAPTER XXIV.

We left Francis De Burgh, after the departure of General Grey and his fair daughter, standing at the door of the Post House. For some moments he remained in the same position gazing after the receding chariot, till it disappeared round the corner of the long street.

With his mind and thoughts fully bent upon the events of the last hour, he turned round and entered the hotel, and, ringing the bell, ordered dinner.

We trust our readers will not feel shocked at this proceeding of our hero; he ought perhaps to have dined upon his thoughts, upon love, upon anything but the very tempting sirloin of beef placed before him. But Francis lived in a very unromantic age, and though possessed of a considerable amount of romance in his disposition, he yet considered it absolutely necessary, unlike the knights of old, to eat as well as sleep, and dream of his lady love Having made a remarkably good dinner, he inquired of the waite when the next coach would pass through for London.

"The Comet, sir, at seven o'clock."

"Well, as it wants an hour of that time," said our hero, "bring me in a pint of port."

These were not teetotal times, neither was Francis De Burgh inclined to become a disciple of good Father Mathew; he would have thought it very strange that a gentleman could not enjoy his glass without making a beast of himself.

Having drank his pint of port, the horn of the Comet announced its arrival; having paid his bill he mounted the vacant box-seat, and in less than two hours he was in London.

Thinking that Bill Mullaghan would feel uneasy, or at least surprised at his long absence, he hastened on into the city: but on reaching his hotel and inquiring for his attendant, he was much surprised to hear that he had not returned since the morning; imagining he had lost his way, and would sooner or later regain the hotel, he went to bed, thinking to find his humble friend and companion in his room in the morning; but to his great surprise and uneasiness he learned from the waiter, who was an extremely civil and respectable man, that Bill had not been seen.

"I hope, sir," remarked the waiter, "that he has not gone into any of those crimping houses about the docks. I know he has been a sailor, and there's a very keen press going on by a most unscrupulous set of low villains, and the rascals that entice sailors into them get large bounty for able seamen."

This view of the case startled our hero exceedingly. The next day he had promised to leave London for the General's villa; but to desert his faithful attendant was out of the question. Knowing Bill's temper and disposition, he feared if a press-gang attempted to take him, he would make a desperate resistance.

He was at a loss what to do, what step to take; nor could the landlord, whom he consulted, advise.

"You will find it impossible, sir," remarked the latter, "to trace him if he has been pressed."

"Cannot I obtain leave to search the ships?" questioned our hero, very much depressed.

"Lord bless you! sir, who could say or tell where they take the pressed man to? Once on board a man of war, he will certainly be allowed to write; but he may be concealed for days in some out-of-the-way crimping house; let us hope after all this may not be his case."

Francis, however, determined to proceed first to the docks, and make inquiries; some of the door-keepers or porters might have observed his poor friend; after that, if he failed in hearing of him, he would consult Mr. Howard.

Just as he was about to leave his room, the waiter entered, and presenting a card, said:—

"A gentleman in the coffee-room, sir, desired me to give you this: he requests an interview."

Francis took the card and read on it, "Captain Burton requests a private interview."

"Captain Burton," repeated our hero, thoughtfully; "I do not know any such person, but show the gentleman up."

In a few moments the waiter returned, ushering into the room a tall, athletic-looking man, dressed in an undress military frock-coat, at all events, it was profusely braided and frogged, with a high fur collar. The stranger's face was almost covered with immense black whiskers and moustachios, but as far as our hero could judge, he appeared about forty years of age. The young man looked keenly into the dark, meaning eyes of the stranger, as he said:—

"Captain Burton, I presume."

"That is my name, sir, at your service; I suppose you are Mr. De Burgh."

Our hero started as the sounds of the stranger's voice vibrated on his ear; he had always a peculiar nicety of ear in remembering and retaining the sound of a voice once heard, and this man's voice touched a chord in his memory; a somewhat confused recollection at first; he, however, replied though his thoughts were elsewhere:

"Well, sir, may I request to know the purport of your visit?" requesting his visitor at the same time to be seated.

"Sir, I come on the part of Sir Godfrey De Burgh," replied Captain Burton, still standing and avoiding the scrutinizing look of his companion, "and merely call upon you to request the name of any friend of yours upon whom I can call, to arrange for an immediate meeting, for Sir Godfrey declares after the gross insult he has received, he can accept no apology."

"An apology!" repeated the young man, with a smile of scorn; and advancing a step towards Captain Burton, that gentleman at the same time making a retrograde movement, "when Sir Godfrey De Burgh," he continued, quietly, but with his gaze stedfastly fixed upon the Captain, "conceived himself to be insulted, and demanded satisfaction, I told him I was quite willing to satisfy him, provided he sent a gentleman to settle the matter with my friend Sir James Blake. Sir Godfrey then had no friend; now, you, sir, wait upon me to request I should name a friend; unfortunately it happens that I now find myself exactly in the same predicament as Sir Godfrey De Burgh, therefore Sir Godfrey must wait till I find one."

"What!" fiercely interrupted Captain Burton, with an oath, and extending his clenched hand, "do you not know that the first time he meets you in the street he will horsewhip you to within an inch of your life?"

"I would strongly advise him not to make the attempt," returned our hero, calmly, "or I will leave him in such a state that he will feel a horror of a horsewhip for the rest of his life."

"He will post you in every club-house in town as an arrant coward," exclaimed the Captain.

"Take care, Captain Burton," said Francis, with a sudden change in his tone and manner; "now that you are getting heated by passion, my memory becomes more clear, I know you." As he spoke he made a movement towards the Captain, who, uttering a savage curse, sprang towards the door, and rushing out, slammed the door after him, and locked it.

"Ha!" exclaimed Francis, "so I am right, though at first I was confused; this Captain Burton is the English robber who plundered me of my papers at Dungarvon. I wish I had seized him."

He rang the bell, and the waiter coming up was amazed at finding the door locked, but entering the room, he said:—

"Good gracious sir, how is this?—I found the door locked."

"That rascal, who calls himself Captain Burton, is an impostor; I thought to secure him, and he bolted."

"I wish I had known that, sir," said the waiter; "he passed me and James at the foot of the stairs, and we thought he looked flurried."

"It is past remedy at present," returned our hero, "though I will have him looked after. I detected in him a person who grossly injured me some time back; yet even had I secured him, I had no earthly evidence to prove he was the same individual."

"If you set the police on his track, sir, and give a description of his person," remarked the waiter, "you may catch him yet."

"I shall do so," observed Francis, and taking his hat he proceeded to call upon Mr. Howard, and request his advice with respect to Bill Mullaghan.

As he walked on, his thoughts turned upon the interview with the false Captain Burton, and felt satisfied that the robbery of his papers, and the attempt upon his life, was a conspiracy on the part of Sir Godfrey De Burgh. It was then evident there was some great object to effect in removing him out of the way. Could it be possible that he had any right or title to the Delamaine property then in possession of Sir Godfrey's son? This idea, wild and ill-supported by proofs, did not appear altogether chimerical to our hero, for what other motive could Sir Godfrey have in seeking to deprive him of life, even after the robbery of his papers.

The late Lord Delamaine's own manner and conduct and strange letter, added links to the chain, and almost confirmed him in his newly-formed idea. These thoughts and the disappearance of his faithful attendant perplexed and disturbed him, especially as he felt deeply anxious to visit General Grey on the ensuing day, trusting from him, if possible, to gain some information with respect to the Delamaine family.

Mr. Howard, unfortunately, was not at home, so writing a few lines to explain his reason for not accepting his invitation to dinner that day, he returned to his hotel to make a hasty meal and set out for the docks.

"I am glad you have returned, sir," observed the waiter as he entered his sitting-room, "there's a man below who can, I believe, give some information of your missing attendant."

"Ha, indeed," cried Francis, cheerfully, "I am rejoiced at this; what kind of man is he?"

"A sailor, sir, evidently."

"Well, show him up; I will question him."

In five minutes the man entered the room; he was a short broad-shouldered, regular built seaman, and attired as such; he had a considerable limp in his walk, and looked about fifty years of age.

"Well, my man," commenced our hero, "what information can you give me concerning my servant, William Mullaghan?"

"Why, your honour, I can tell you as how he's crimped."

"I suspected as much," replied Francis much mortified; "pray tell me how you came acquainted with Will Mullaghan, and all you know about him."

"You see, your honour, I belongs to the West India Docks, have been a sailor all my life, till the fall of a spar lamed my starboard limb; since then I does all kinds of jobs, helping to rig ships, splice blocks; all jobs a sea-faring man can do with a crippled limb. Some days ago I picked up an acquaintance with your man aboard one of the big ships, as he used to come aboard of, and we had a bit of a chat, and he used to treat me to a glass of grog, and lent me a helping hand once or twice; he told me he lived with a gentleman as good a sailor as ever trod the deck of a ship, and that you were living at the Swan, and hoped to go to sea soon.

"'The day he was crimped, your honour, I was splicing a cable aboard of the Albatross, and saw Will Mullaghan on the platform talking to a man I knew very well was one of those here chaps as seduces sailors into crimping houses, where they do be laid hold of and handcuffed, and stowed away till the press-gang goes round. Suddenly they went out of the dock together, and I threw down my work and goes after them, but in reason of my crippled state they forged a-head of me, and I just saw a glimpse of them as they went into one of those suspicious houses—gin shops to the eye. It would be more than my life would be worth for me to raise an alarm, for they would knock me in the head of a dark night, so I waited a few minutes, and then went in and asked for a glass of gin; but no sign was there of either Will Mullaghan or the crimp, so I went out and hid myself in a lane opposite, and in less than ten minutes I saw the crimp and the landlord, and two men come to the door speaking and laughing together, and then they all separated and I was then nonplussed and went home and told my wife I did not know what to do.

"'Do,' said she, 'go to the Swan and ax for the man's master, and he'll buy him out of their hands for ten pounds;' so, your honour, I came here to let you know and see if we could manage the business."

"Well," observed Francis, "the only thing to be done is to get him out, the money is of no importance; but how are we to manage? Could we not call in the assistance of the police?"

"Lord love ye, master!" exclaimed the man, "they must get secret warrants, and the Lord knows what besides, and I dare not show myself, I should lose my head. Bless me, you don't know the inhabitants of the Tower Hamlets, they sticks at nothing; they're worse nor savages, and in a shake they all rouse out like a nest of pirates."

"How do you propose to act then, my man?"

"It will be easy enough, your honour. I can take you to a house nigh the crimp shop, and I know how to bring the 'oman of the trap house to terms. They don't get half ten pounds for each seaman, and will snap at the offer, and release your man in half-an-hour."

"But will you not incur a risk in showing that you know where the man is caged?" asked Francis kindly.

"No, your honour; only I'm crippled I could not manage it. I can make 'em think I do a little business in the crimping line myself."

"Well, the sooner we leave the better," observed Francis, "it is nearly dusk now, and by the time we are there it will be dark enough.

"We can take a boat, your honour, at the next stairs to London bridge, and it will land us within a few hundred yards of the place; my crippled limb won't let me go a-head fast."

Putting twenty guineas in his purse, Francis De Burgh and the sailor left the hotel, and proceeding to the nearest stairs, took a boat for the tower. On reaching their destination it was nearly dark; having never visited that part of London, our hero was astounded at the narrow crooked streets and the abominable stench of old pork, bad rum, tar, stale biscuit, rotten fish, casks, ropes, and horrid tobacco. The low shops, and dingy cellars, lighted by flamy tallow candles, and wicks swimming in dirty grease, disclosing all kinds of wares. All smelt of the sea, and ships, and the inhabitants, an extraordinary race, half intoxicated, swearing, and laughing, and fighting, in some places dancing to the tunes of a cracked fiddle; sometimes a knot of drunken sailors passed them shouting a sea chorus at the top of their voices. Altogether such a scene and such a medley of sounds and sights he had never before witnessed.

Disgusted, and anxious to get out of such a scene, Francis De Burgh was not sorry when his limping guide turned into a rather quiet kind of narrow street, at least it was quiet by comparison. Stopping before a well-lighted gin-shop, with the front room full of persons of both sexes, all busy drinking the poison in its natural state, the guide paused, and said:—

"We had better not, your honour, go through the shop; there is a quiet back parlour we can get to by going through this entrance."

So saying he passed what appeared a private door, into a dark kind of passage.

"Stop, your honour," said the man, "till I rings for a light, it's mortal dark."

As he spoke a bell sounded as our hero thought beneath his feet, the next instant what he stood on gave way under him, and he fell with considerable violence upon a large heap of straw. Before he could attempt to rise or extricate himself from the straw, half-a-dozen men were suddenly revealed by turning back the slides of two dark lanterns; they instantly threw themselves upon him, but even in that position he was not so easily secured. The first man he struck to ground, by a violent blow in the face.

"Sarve him out, Joe; sarve him out," roared the man, "curse him, he hits like a sledge hammer."

Possessed of great power our hero made desperate efforts to cast off his assailants, when the man who had served as his guide rushed in, no longer limping, and with a loaded bludgeon struck him down nearly senseless; the next instant the fetters were forced over his wrists, attached to a chain. Francis, furious with rage, notwithstanding the effect of the blow he had received, raised the heavy chain they were about to attach to a staple, and with all his force drove it at the head of his treacherous guide, knocking him bleeding and senseless back upon the ground. Several of the men drew their knives, and were rushing upon him, when a loud voice sung out:—

"Hold hard, my darlings—hold hard; we get nothing for dead men. Keep your knives for your cheese, I'll have no murders here."

"Why curse him!" exclaimed the men to a red faced individual, who entered the vault with a lantern in his hand, "he's nearly killed Dick Mathews, and here's Jem with the loss of his front grinders; he's a devil to manage."

"Let him alone, let him alone," said the man with the lantern, "that's the best management. Come, pick up Jem, his beauty is spoiled for a while; have you cleaned him out?"

"Aigh, aigh, here's his purse, and a good haul," so taking up their lantern the villains left our unfortunate hero in total darkness, and a prey to the most bitter reflections.

## CHAPTER XXV.

IF ever Francis De Burgh felt inclined to despair or murmur at the decrees of Providence, it was during the first few moments after the departure of the gang of miscreants into whose hands he had so easily been led.

It appeared to him that every day of his life was marked out for persecution or misfortune, so rapidly did one mishap or another occur. But this despair and doubting of the mercy and goodness of Providence lasted but a brief moment, and sincerely and truly he prayed to be forgiven the momentary feeling that had crept over his heart. After a time, he rallied his thoughts, and began to turn over in his mind what might be the result of the cruel outrage inflicted upon him.

As to who the instigator of the outrage might be, he was quite satisfied it was Sir Godfrey De Burgh. The visit of the false Captain Burton was merely a species of investigation to learn if possible who his friends were in London. Bill Mullaghan had been no doubt entrapped nearly in the same way. If it was intended to carry him on board a man-of-war, he would in time be able to prove his right to be set at liberty; but he was also aware that those pressed, no matter how illegally, or what their station in life might be, there existed great difficulty in getting their case investigated. The most nefarious schemes existed at that period in London for entrapping able seamen for the navy. In the Tower Hamlets the crimping houses were numerous, and when discovered, were often attacked by parties of merchant sailors, and immense damage done to them; still they persisted in carrying on their cruel but lucrative trade in the miseries of their fellow-creatures, for government took no pains to put them down, or abolish the vile trade of the crimp.

Thus communing with his thoughts, he passed the first night of his incarceration. Our hero was of too robust and hardy a constitution to feel severely the misery of lying in the damp and dismal vault of the crimp house, though he was a little disturbed, it is true, during the night by a party of rats; not a ray of light entered the place. Often during the weary hours did the image of fair Mary Grey rise before his vision; he fancied he beheld her waiting his arrival at the villa, and wondering at his unaccountable absence. Would it be imputed to neglect? Would he be forgotten, should months, perhaps years pass over, ere again he could present himself before her? Even had he been inclined to sleep, he dreaded to do so, the rats were so very persevering; they seemed to have an especial fancy to his boots, and not knowing but that their tastes might change, he kept awake, and exercised himself in kicking away his active and determined assailants. He had no means of ascertaining when night ceased and morning began, for neither light nor sound penetrated to his abode.

After the lapse of many hours, as well as he could judge, he heard some kind of sound like heavy feet descending stone steps; the next moment bolts were drawn back, and four stout, ablebodied seamen, with drawn cutlasses in their hands, and pistols in their belts, entered the vault, one of the four carrying a large lantern; another carried a large bundle of garments, a basket, and a small black pitcher. These they put down, and one of the men said, looking at our hero, as he lay extended, bound, upon the straw:

"Now, my lad, is it to be peace or war? If you promise to be quiet, and do as you are required, we will cast you free, and do you no further hurt. If you won't, and are inclined to be obstreperous, why, you see we must even rig and unrig you some kind of fashion."

"Well," said Francis, sitting up, "what do you require me to do?"

"Well, that's all fair," said the man; "why, you see you must unrig and put on these sailor's garments; they are decent, clean ones, but on they must go. If you will promise to do that, I'll cut you free in a shake, and here's your breakfast. Before night you will be removed from this vault, and let the rats have a jollification on what you leave of your breakfast. We will give you a light; so now, my hearty, are you willing?"

Knowing how utterly useless it would be to contend against the will of his detainers, and feeling the fetters on his hands, and the strap over his ancles most painful, he agreed to the wishes of the man who had addressed him.

"Come, you're a lad of some sense," said the man, "and will make a fine seaman in a year or so. Cast off those darbies, Jack, and take off the strap. He's a gentleman, and a sensible one, and not quite fool enough to resist, and get himself sliced like a pumpkin."

"Don't know that neither," growled a surly-looking fellow, one of the number; "there's a face he's left Dick, and half Tom's grinders down his throat."

"Never mind," said the principal of the gang; "Dick was never a beauty, and Tom's wife will like him all the better, for he can't bite, an ugly custom he has when drunk."

In a few minutes Francis De Burgh was free from his bonds and stood up, much relieved.

"There's some beef and bread in that basket," said the spokes man, looking at our hero from head to foot, and muttering something to himself, and there's some beer in the jug; and putting down the lantern, he added, "In two hours we shall return, and expect to find every garment you have on changed for those in that bundle;" and turning round, they all left the vault.

For some moments our hero stood plunged in thought, but after a time, with a heavy sigh, he cast off the load of care that seemed to press upon his young heart with an overpowering sensation.

"After all, I am young," he said, half aloud, "what if I do serve my country for a year or two as a common sailor; there is no disgrace in that; I may distinguish myself, and attract notice; at all events, once on board a man-of-war, I shall be allowed to write, and represent my situation in the proper quarter."

Thus soliloquizing, he opened the basket, and took out some slices of cold beef and bread, and satisfied the cravings of hunger; in the jar he found some beer, and being very thirsty, he took a hearty drink, and then, without any hesitation, changed all his clothes, and found himself completely rigged as a sailor. As he finished, he felt a most overpowering sensation of drowsiness stealing over him; he tried to resist it, by driving away his friends the rats, who, notwithstanding the light, had commenced operations at the basket. Finding it quite impossible to resist the drowsy feeling stealing over him, he lay down upon the straw, satisfied that the beer was drugged; and with a faint recollection of seeing a legion of rats fighting for the remainder of his meal, he lost all consciousness of surrounding objects, and sunk into a deep slumber.

How long he lay in that deep sleep he could not say, but when he again opened his eyes the glare of broad day was upon the objects he then looked upon. He felt a heavy, sickening sensation, like intoxication, and a dull pain in the head; nevertheless, he raised himself up, and looked around him. One look convinced him he was in the ward-room of a receiving ship, where the pressed men were collected previously to being sent on board vessels of war. Sitting upright in his berth, he examined more particularly the place he was in.

There appeared numerous berths ranged along the sides, most of which were occupied, and several persons were moving about the ward, attending to the wants of those confined there. Suddenly a man sprung from one of the bed places opposite, with his head bandaged, and one of his arms in a sling, with an exclamation of surprise and grief, rushed across the ward, and to our hero's amazement and joy, he beheld Bill Mullaghan.

"Blessed Mary! how is this, Mister Francis; why are you here?" and catching up his master's hand, he repeatedly kissed it.

"My poor fellow," exclaimed our hero, pressing his faithful attendant's hand, "they have cruelly treated you; you look pale and ill."

Before Mullaghan could reply, several sailors came up, and laying hands on Bill, were rather profuse of their oaths at him for quitting his berth, saying:

"If you are getting obstrepulous again, you will be ironed and confined."

Bill clenched his fist, and looked as if inclined to commence a rial of strength with the men, but Francis implored him to go quietly to his sleeping place, and to say nothing aggravating, but wait patiently till he could see and speak with a person in authority.

"Come, blow me," said one of the men, with a laugh, looking at Francis with a curious expression, "that's good; who have we got here? a tip-top sawyer, or sea-lawyer, I guess. So you want a superior officer, do you, my hearty; you'll have plenty of them by-and-by; and if this here fellow doesn't keep hisself quiet, he'll taste a cat with very sharp claws." So saying, they pushed the exasperated but silent Bill Mullaghan to his berth.

Our hero felt indignant, but recollecting that he was no doubt taken for a pressed common seaman, he remained silent. Presently a gentleman, evidently a surgeon, entered the ward, and began an examination of the inmates. This proceeding was a relief to Francis De Burgh's mind, for he thought to himself, surely this gentleman will permit me to explain my situation.

After a short time he came opposite our hero's berth; he was a middle-aged man, with a harsh stern look, and casting a glance at Francis's face, called out:

"Jones!"

"Here I am, sir," returned that individual, coming forward.

"Thirty-one," said the surgeon; "when did he come here? anything the matter with him?"

"Nothing but drunk, sir, and a slight knock on the head, but not of consequence. He was brought in here dead drunk last night."

"That is false, sir," almost fiercely interrupted Francis De Burgh; "I have been cruelly——"

"Stuff! nonsense!" interrupted the surgeon; "you ought to be ashamed of yourself, at your age, and——"

"It's a false accusation, sir," interrupted our hero, curbing his passion. "I'm a gentleman——"

"Oh, yes," laughed the surgeon, "you are all gentlemen; but they'll make something better of you than that hackneyed profession," and without another word he passed on, just as our hero was springing out of bed.

"Bring a pair of handcuffs," sung out the man named Jones "this fellow is bit of that other chap opposite, and is quite in clined to be as saucy and obstrepulous." As two men came up with the irons, Jones continued: "These here big fellows are

M

never good for nothing, except filling their crows; they take as much to fill their holds as a Thames lighter."

Seeing how useless it was to contend against fate, Francis De Burgh said :

"I am neither sick, and certainly was not drunk, and am willing to do anything you please in reason, till I have an opportunity of speaking to the commanding officer of this ship."

"Then you will have to wait a d—— long time, my hearty," said the man named Jones; "this is always the way with you shore-going coves; you are all gents, and all want to speak to the Captain; howsomever, if you keeps quiet, and has a civil tongue, I won't trouble you with these ornaments; so put on your garments, and follow me out of the sick-ward, and I'll place you in a mess."

Despite his resolution to endure everything with patience, it was not without an intense feeling of bitterness in his heart that our hero finished dressing himself. He then said:

"Will you permit me, and I shall feel greatly obliged, to say a few words to the man in the berth opposite; he was in my service the night before I was illegally pressed."

The man Jones snatched his chin with a look of perplexity at our hero, whose tall and graceful figure and manner seemed to puzzle him.

"Well, upon my conscience, you're either a first-rate cove, or there's some mistake here; but I'm neither allowed to listen to or to carry messages. I can't let you communicate with the chap in forty-eight, but in two or three days he'll join your mess; so come along, you'll not find things so bad as you thinks. You're a fine looking chap anyhow, there's no denying that, so heave ahead."

It is quite unnecessary either to delay our tale or weary our readers with minute details of daily occurrence. The treatment our hero received was rough, it is true, for those were rough days in the naval service; but there was no ill-usage as long as he submitted quietly to the rules of the ship. With the petty officers he found it useless to attempt explanations. To his great satisfaction, three days after, Bill came amongst them; it was with considerable difficulty he kept Mullaghan from giving way to rage and vexation, when he saw his master performing the duties of a common seaman. Bill had been entrapped by a professed crimp, but made a desperate resistance, and received cutlass cuts in the head and arms.

"We shall soon," said Francis De Burgh, "be sent on board a man-of-war, and I have no doubt but there I shall either be able to explain our situation, or be permitted to write to persons ashore, which would put an end to our serving."

"Be gor, your honour, I don't mind a bit serving his Majesty, provided you were where your honour ought to be—on the quarter-deck!"

"Perhaps, Bill, when I can explain things, I may be permitted to serve as a volunteer."

Some eight or ten days after this conversation, some five or six and twenty seamen, our hero and Bill included, were put on board a dockyard lighter, with a party of marines, and sailed for Plymouth, which they reached in three days, and were at once put on board a man-of-war.

## CHAPTER XXVI.

THE vessel of war, into which our hero and his follower Mullaghan were transferred, was the Hannibal, 74, commanded by Captain Solomon Ferris. This ship was one of the six vessels of war commanded by Rear-Admiral Sir James Saumarez, on the point of sailing from England to maintain the blockade of Cadiz.

The ships were to sail in a few days, and the new men were put into different watches; thus, without a chance of freeing himself from the singular position he had so suddenly been entrapped into, Francis De Burgh found himself rated as an able seaman on board the Hannibal, 74.

Once placed in a position, honourable though humble, our hero set about cheerfully performing his duty. He felt no degradation in his situation, neither did he despise those with whom he was associated; far from it, for on board the Hannibal were as fine a set of men as England could boast of giving birth to. The officers also were favourites with the crew, and appeared all gentlemanly men —a few exceptions of course were to be met with—but they are met with everywhere, and in every station.

Thus, day after day passed, and as yet no chance had offered for stating his case. Bill Mullaghan was determined that nothing should stop his talking of the cruel usage his master had received, and before long the story of Francis De Burgh's ill-treatment ran through the ship. From the men our hero experienced the greatest kindness; sailors are quick observers, and the men in Francis's watch all evinced a wish to save him unnecessary labour when they could. His kindness and gentleness of manner, great strength, and hardy nature, when he exerted himself, gained him the admiration of his companions, and his perfect knowledge of a sailor's duties surprised and pleased them.

The day Captain Ferris was expected on board turned out a remarkably stormy one; the ships of war destined for Cadiz were lying in the bay with the Blue Peter hoisted at the fore. When it was made known on board the Hannibal that the Captain was coming off, every man got to his station.

Francis was standing near the gang-way looking with an admiring eye upon the striking and beautiful scene before him. Though it was blowing a gale of wind the sky was clear and bright, for the gale blew out from the shore, the waters of the bay were lashed into foam, the "short white tops" lifted off, and hurled along like snow-drifts at times, though the mimic wave curled and broke in harmless rage against the gigantic wooden walls of old England; the night rays of the sun fell upon the long-extended line of Plymouth, and to the left upon the beautiful wooded hills of Mount Edgecumbe.

While looking over the scene stretched before him, a murmur arose that the Captain's gig was coming out from the dock, and presently Francis De Burgh perceived the gig scudding before the wind under an exceedingly close-reefed lug. There appeared to be six men in the gig besides the Captain and a young midshipman, a cousin of the Captain's, who was expected on board with the commander.

Our hero thought, as he watched the light narrow boat actually flying through the foaming waters, that she was anything but a fit boat for such a gale, for the squalls swept over the bluff point of the Mount with sudden and startling violence. There were no boats down alongside the Hannibal, for the moment the Captain got on board it was intended to let go the moorings that held them and put to sea.

When within fifty yards of the ship, the boat was caught by one of the fierce squalls off the land; and though the lug was instantly let go, by some unforeseen cause, either the sheet or the halyard got foul, and the next instant she was turned over.

Almost at the same instant, divested of his jacket and shoes, Francis De Burgh slung down a rope and was overboard. The men immersed in the water were scrambling up upon the bottom of the boat, but Captain Ferris was evidently entangled under her. A bold and energetic swimmer and diver, Francis dived beneath, attracted by the cocked hat of the Captain coming suddenly up; the next instant he pulled him forcibly out, his sword-belt or some trapping having caught in a hook. Captain Ferris was a good swimmer, but greatly exhausted with his struggle beneath, still quite conscious, having retained his breath while trying to extricate himself.

By this time half a dozen men were in the water and a boat down; Bill Mullaghan was supporting the young midshipman, and two or three boats were forcing their way to the spot from other ships. When the Hannibal's boat came up Francis and Captain Ferris were helped in, while the Spencer's boat picked up the rest.

Captain Ferris, before he fell back into the boat, said, laying his hand on our hero's shoulder: "You are a gallant, fine fellow; I shall not forget you"

These few words thrilled through Francis De Burgh's heart; he felt new life, for hope, the charmer, once more laid her hand upon him.

In a few minutes they were all on board, and a signal being

hoisted that all was well, in two hours afterwards the five ships were under weigh, the Cæsar, the flag-ship, leading.

"Well, Mister Francis," said Bill Mullaghan, as he slung down a back stay, and stood beside our hero, who was busy coiling away a rope. "Be gor, all's right now; this time, anyhow, you will be listened to, and, thanks be, removed to the quarter-deck!"

Numbers of the men congratulated Francis upon his good luck and skill in diving first to the assistance of Captain Ferris, and telling him he would now be sure of receiving justice.

The next day the Hannibal was ploughing her way through the deep waves of the broad Atlantic under double reefed topsails; it was still blowing a gale from the north, but the huge ship carried along proudly, and but little disturbed by the commotion of the sea, as the gale was on her quarter. It was two o'clock in the day when Francis was summoned to the quarter-deck, the first-lieutenant desired his presence.

With a heart beating with hope, and his mind occupied with a vision of glory, and sweet Mary Grey crowning him with the gift of her fair hand, Francis stepped firmly but modestly on the quarter-deck of the Hannibal. The first-lieutenant was standing glass in hand, gazing out over the troubled waters at the Cæsar and the Spencer, some three miles ahead of them; the other two ships were double that distance astern.

Francis approached, and the first-lieutenant turned round; two other officers of the ship and a marine officer were walking on the other side of the deck, but paused and looked at the tall, powerful figure of our hero with some surprise. The first-lieutenant of the Hannibal was a very dashing officer, and a remarkably well-looking man, about five or six and thirty years of age.

The lieutenant regarded our hero from head to foot, much struck with his appearance, for though he might have noticed him before, yet, mingled with others, and performing his duty, he escaped particular attention; but now, standing erect before him, his remarkably handsome features and fine figure set off to advantage by the simple attire of the sailor, he appeared evidently surprised.

"Your name," said the lieutenant, "is, I believe, Francis Burgh?"

"Francis De Burgh, sir," returned our hero, firmly but gently.

"Pray may I ask you how you came with such a name and appearance, to be taken by a press-gang, and in such a place as the Tower Hamlets? You are also returned as having been intoxicated."

"You have been misinformed, sir," returned Francis De Burgh, "but if you will permit me to explain, which I have long sought an opportunity for so doing, but in vain."

An exclamation of joy and surprise from some person coming up from the cabin interrupted our hero; the next instant his hand was warmly grasped by a young gentleman in a midshipman's uniform, who exclaimed, regardless of either Captain Ferris's or the first-lieutenant's presence:

"Good God, Mr. De Burgh, how is this? You aboard the Hannibal, and in the attire of a sailor!"

Francis was amazed, for he beheld young Carlton, the cousin of Mr. McCarthy, whom he had met so often, and who took so great a fancy to him during his visit to that gentleman's house in Dublin.

Shaking young Carlton's hand warmly, with a flushed face, our hero turned round, and beheld Captain Ferris and the first-lieutenant conversing earnestly, with their attention fixed upon him and the young midshipman.

Captain Ferris advanced, saying:

"You are the young man to whom, under Providence, I owe my life. But here is some mystery; you are evidently out of your station. How is this, Lieutenant L———?"

"I suspected as much, sir," returned the lieutenant, "from some stories that reached my ears, and as you requested to speak to the man who so gallantly rescued you, I sent for him to question him as to the truth of those stories; but now they seem likely to be truth, since he turns out an intimate friend of Master Carlton."

"That I am proud to say he is," said the high-spirited boy; "he is a gentleman by birth and station, and well known to people of rank. Dear me——"

"Nay, nay," interrupted Captain Ferris, with a good-humoured smile, "do not be impatient, Master Carlton. Your friend, even if he had not rendered me the greatest service one man can render another, should have justice. Have the goodness, Master Carlton, to conduct your friend into the cabin; I will follow in a few minutes."

There were many lookers-on at this scene, both on the quarter-deck, and as near to that sacred precinct as many of the crew could approach.

"There, Jem, my old trump!" almost shouted Bill Mullaghan, hitting a great crony of his a slap on the back in the exuberance of his joy, which made his friend reel again, "be the immortal powers, I knew he'd get his rights some day or another. Three cheers, my hearties, for our brave captain."

That Bill would have attempted this gross breach of discipline there is scarcely a doubt, had not his friend Jem, who happened to have a signal in his hand, applied it without mercy to Bill's open mouth, saying:

"Avast there, messmate; belay your jaw tackle; you're not standing on Gosport Hard."

Francis and young Carlton having descended into the cabin of the Hannibal, the young midshipman eagerly demanded of our hero how on earth he came to be in such a situation as a sailor before the mast?

"In truth, Charles," returned Francis, "it's a long story; but you may rest satisfied it was not a situation of my own seeking But here come Captain Ferris and Mr. Holman; if an explanation is permitted, you will hear."

Captain Ferris and Lieutenant Holman entered the cabin, Francis, with considerable anxiety of mind, standing respectfully waiting till he was questioned.

"Pray take a seat, Mr. De Burgh," said the Captain kindly. "I have just had a few words with your attendant that was, William Mullaghan; he it was that saved this young gentleman," turning to the midshipman. "You may now go on deck, Master Carlton," he added, a mandate that young gentleman very unwillingly obeyed. "You have been very cruelly used, Mr. De Burgh," continued Captain Ferris, "Mr. Holman here heard about you, and made some inquiries, and intended examining into your case as soon as we were done with this gale. Will you now favour me with a full account of your impressment, and, if not exacting too much, some further particulars of your life, as, singular enough, I am connected by marriage with the Delamaine and De Burgh families."

Our hero was much surprised, at the same time highly elated, by the kindness of Captain Ferris's manner. In a brief but clear narrative, he made the commander of the Hannibal and Mr. Holman acquainted with the events of the last few months, at the same time avoiding charging Sir Godfrey De Burgh directly with the crime of his impressment: he left his hearers to come to their own conclusion.

Captain Ferris listened attentively, without once interrupting our hero; he looked much interested, and at times very serious. When his recital was ended, there was a pause of a few moments, and then Captain Ferris said:

"My dear sir, you have been most cruelly ill-used, and your case is an extremely hard one. Just as you were on the point of visiting General Grey, who might have been of great service to you, in forwarding your future projects, you were foully entrapped into a crimping house. You were then sold, no doubt, to a press-gang. At this present moment, to remedy the evil altogether is impossible: I mean, of course, your immediate return to England. However, you shall remain my guest till an opportunity occurs when you and your attached follower shall be free to leave. I shall not make any comment now upon the strange persecution you have endured. I know Sir Godfrey De Burgh well. In his youth he was the most extravagant, reckless man in England. Unscrupulous and vicious, he would dare anything to accomplish a purpose; and a purpose he must have had in acting as he has done towards you. I must now try and get you some other attire, though, by Jove, unless Lieutenant Reilly, a countryman of yours, can rig you out, we shall be at fault."

After warmly thanking Captain Ferris for his generosity and kindness, Francis De Burgh said:

"If you will permit me, and it is not contrary to the rules of the service, now that I have embarked, I should like to become a volunteer aboard this ship, as no doubt you will go into action. I experienced this wish long since, and I should be loth indeed to return to England, without endeavouring, as far as lay in my power, to serve my country."

"Your desire to become a volunteer," replied Captain Ferris in his kind tone and manner, "gives me great pleasure, and you shall at once be entered in the books as such. Depend on it, you will have opportunities enough of distinguishing yourself, which I feel satisfied you will do; and be assured I shall watch for an opening, and use my interest to promote your views."

And holding out his hand, he again congratulated our hero upon his restoration to his proper station; and summoning his own man, he sent for Lieutenant Reilly, and having introduced the two young men to each other, he consigned our hero to his care, saying at the same time:

"Remember, Mr. De Burgh, I shall consider myself your banker, till an opportunity occurs for your writing to England."

## CHAPTER XXVII.

WE pass over three months, and open our present chapter aboard the Hannibal engaged in the blockade of Cadiz with the other ships under the command of Admiral Saumarez.

During those months Francis De Burgh had become a most especial favourite with his commander, as well as with all the officers of the Hannibal, and had already distinguished himself in boat actions. Bill Mullaghan had been promoted to a captain of the fore-top, through the intercession of young Carlton, who took a prodigious liking to his preserver as did Bill to him. They were a very happy ship's company on board the Hannibal, and all went on smoothly and pleasantly without the introduction of the cat. Captain Ferris and his officers seemed to have no difficulty in governing the ship, without that odious instrument of cruelty. There was punishment, to be sure, for amidst so many it was impossible not to expect a few disorderly characters at times, but they were reclaimed without that terrible disgrace to a man—flogging!

The Hannibal was not a solitary ship in this respect at this period, there were several others; but at the same time, there were some where the cat was in perpetual requisition, on the most trifling occasion. And those ships were not patterns of either discipline or gallantry, and certainly not of fellowship, and good will and love towards their commander.

With his previous studies in navigation, and his love of the sea, and his actual knowledge, Francis De Burgh soon became capable of performing any duty required of him. His sweetness of temper and exceeding cheerfulness, endeared him to his messmates, so that there was not one man aboard the Hannibal that envied him his change of position. For Lieutenant O'Reilly he conceived a most sincere friendship; young, handsome, and high-spirited, Terence O'Reilly was just the man to gain the friendship and esteem of Francis De Burgh; their liking was mutual.

The port of Cadiz was so closely blockaded, that none of the Spanish fleet could attempt to put to sea.

One morning Francis De Burgh and Lieutenant O'Reilly were pacing the deck, when they observed a small cutter-rigged vessel working up from the eastward, and shortly after run up alongside the flag ship.

"By St. Patrick, Francis!" said Terence O'Reilly, joyfully .hat's an advice-boat from Gibraltar; depend on it, we shall get a move out of this. I'm tired blocking up the Dons, and boat actions."

"I should willingly have a pop at them, Terence, on a larger scale; ha! there go the signals."

All hands looked anxiously towards the flag-ship, the signal was for all the captains to go aboard the Cæsar. It was a glorious day, with a light wind from the westward just rippling the sparkling waters. The Hannibal was the nearest ship to the Cæsar, the Pompey was next; the Venerable and the Audacious were nearly two miles astern, but were standing in for the flag-ship.

The Thames had joined the fleet off San Juan, and a few days previously the Superb had been to the westward.

The two friends watched the six gigs under six oars each, dashing through the glistening waters towards the Cæsar, and then all became anxious for the return of their captain to hear the news, for news there certainly was.

"By Jove, O'Reilly, there's something in the wind," said Captain Colchester, an officer of Marines, coming up, ." there goes a signal —what's that?"

All were on the alert for signals; the signal midshipman at his post, Lieutenant Holman himself very anxious. "Make all sail for the Straits," was the signal, and away flew the me . aloft with sundry exclamations of pleasure. In the meantime the gigs were returning to their respective ships. In a few minutes Captain Ferris was on the quarter-deck, his officers grouped around him.

"We are to prepare for battle," said the commander of the Hannibal, "the advice-boat from Gibraltar has brought intelligence that a French squadron of three sail-of-the-line and one frigate had anchored off Algesiras, about four miles from Gibraltar."

All now became bustle, life, and activity on board the Hannibal; Jack was again in spirits, and nothing was talked of but prizes and prize-money. In fact, to listen to the conversation of the different messes, a stranger would have imagined that the enemy's fleet was already in their possession, and Jack coolly calculating its value.

The wind towards night became extremely light and baffling, but in the early dawn blew out fresh, and brought the fleet into the Straits; but then, unfortunately, it became very light. Francis felt an extraordinary excitement pervading his whole frame, he never felt so before, and actually longed for the commencement of the action, not from any love of the sanguinary strife, but as a relief from the almost painful feeling of excitement.

The signal was made for anchoring by the stern at the proper time. The Hannibal was just astern of the Venerable when she rounded Cabreta point, and made the signal "The enemy is in sight." Ten minutes after the Hannibal opened the bay, and all aboard, on the very tip-toe of expectation, at last beheld the enemy anchored before the batteries of Algesiras. Francis thought the sight he then beheld magnificent; he stood absorbed by the grandeur and beauty of the scene; right before them stood the gigantic fortress of Gibraltar, scarcely five miles distant, and distinctly to be seen in the strong glare of an unclouded sun. He could scarcely take his eyes from off the mighty bulwark of Great Britain on a foreign shore, when a gun from the flag-ship attracted all eyes.

The Cæsar signalled for the Venerable—the leading ship—to anchor between the batteries of Algesiras and an island called Green Island. The wind at this time remained with the Venerable —the Hannibal, to the intense vexation of those on board, being suddenly becalmed.

"Here's a go," said young Carlton, who was standing close beside our hero, jumping at the same time on the top of a gun to have a better look; "not as much wind as would lift a girl's curl; we shall never get in in time, Francis," he impatiently added. "Ah, there's old mother Venerable taken aback, by Jupiter!"

"Patience, you young monkey," exclaimed Lieutenant O'Reilly, pulling him down, "fire and furies, do you want to be riddled before you have a beard upon your chin."

"She is breaking off, O'Reilly," observed our hero, who was intently watching the Venerable.

"A flaw of wind, Francis," said the Lieutenant, applying his glass to the batteries, and then at the Venerable. "Ha! there goes her anchor, her commander is doubtless afraid he can get no further; and by St. Peter, she is pretty close as it is, not more than two cables' length of a large ship," which turned out to be the Indomitable, and at once the Venerable opened a tremendous fire upon her.

The Audacious being outside, the Hannibal held the wind, and passing on under the lee of the Venerable let go her anchor in a line, but ahead of her. The officers and crew of the Hannibal were all getting into a state of nervous excitement when a breeze sprung up; and Captain Ferris at once taking advantage of it, stood in, and then tacked along shore, making for an immense orange grove, thinking to lay the French admiral on board on the side next the shore.

During this gallant but dangerous attempt, the Hannibal received several shots from the French admiral's ship, which killed three men and wounded the third lieutenant slightly.

Francis De Burgh had now witnessed the real horrors of war, for shot after shot tore through the rigging and sails, and many a poor fellow lost the number of his mess. Still the Hannibal stood on, but most unfortunately, when just abreast of the battery of St.

Jago, she suddenly took the ground and then the Formidable opened a tremendous fire upon her, as did also the battery. The situation of the ship was now terribly critical, the shot from the Formidable and battery were fast mowing down the men. Just then, as Francis was eagerly attending to his duty, Lieutenant Holman came up, saying:

"Pray, Mr. De Burgh, take the command of the launch, and see if, with the other boats, you can get her off."

Amidst a tremendous fire the men sprung into the boats, and having ropes attached, worked with might and main to move her, but in vain. By this time, though the Hannibal opened fire upon both the Formidable and the battery, she was in a dreadful condition; every brace and bowline was shot away, her sails cut to pieces, her main royal mast, main top-sail yard and gaff were in splinters. The boats being re-called, after suffering great loss, they continued the action with unabated energy. Francis' courage and unceasing activity, and cheering words to the men with whom he worked, had already gained him golden opinions. As he was crossing the deck, Captain Ferris said:

"Mr. De Burgh, I fear ours is a hopeless case, will you take the gig and four men, and pull aboard the Cæsar. Say, I have more than seventy men dead upon deck, three officers severely wounded, and that unless I sacrifice the ship's company I must strike my colours; the ship, as you know, is immovable. It is a perilous service I ask of you; if you succeed, you will gain, no doubt, your lieutenancy."

As he spoke, a thirty-six pounder shot tore along the deck, a splinter knocking down poor Carlton, and ripping up the deck within a few inches of where Captain Ferris stood. Francis heard him sigh heavily, as Mullaghan ran up and raised young Carlton in his arms, placing him in the care of a couple of men to carry below.

"Go, and God bless you!" said Captain Ferris, laying his hand on our hero's shoulder; "we may never meet again."

As Francis De Burgh hurried along the deck, selecting three men, for Bill was like a leech close beside, Lieutenant Reilly came up limping, and his left arm in a sling.

"God bless you, Frank! God bless you!" wringing his hand as he spoke. "Give the ship firing on us a wide berth, it's all up with us; if we are not assisted, we must either blow up or surrender. Mind, pull in for the orange grove, or you'll be riddled by grape and canister," shouted Lieutenant O'Reilly, as Francis De Burgh swung down in the gig, with the three seamen and Bill Mullaghan.

All this time the Hannibal kept engaging the Formidable and the batteries; she looked a wreck, but still breathed defiance.

"Can you make out the Cæsar, sir?" asked the man pulling the bow oar; Bill Mullaghan pulled the stroke oar.

Francis looked round, and amidst the smoke that at times encircled the ships, he made out the flag-ship, blazing away at the enemy, and upon the batteries upon Green Island.

"We must make a sweep," said our hero, keeping the boat in for the shore, "or we shall be blown to atoms by the French Admiral's ship. Give way, my men, give way; the case is urgent."

On fled the light gig, impelled by four powerful men. The scene was sublime, and to De Burgh's eyes, one of the most exciting spectacles the imagination could conjure up.

Nine line-of-battle ships, and several formidable batteries were keeping up an incessant and tremendous fire; the sea in all directions was ploughed and tossed into the air by cannon balls, and showers of grape and canister; volumes of smoke at times obscured the ships; still the continued thunder of the cannon pealed over the waters. It amazed our hero how they escaped pulling through the storm of shot that tore the water on every side of them. But this good fortune was not to last; a loud whizzing noise was heard, and the same instant the boat was actually cut in two by a chain-shot, killing the three boatmen, and knocking Bill Mullaghan and our hero over into the water, and burying them beneath the waves.

They were, however, both unhurt, and both rose to the surface nearly at the same time, and caught hold of the half of the gig.

"The Lord be praised, Master Francis," said Bill Mullaghan, raising himself up on the keel, "that you are safe. That was a stunner, and no mistake. Poor Joe, and Collins, and his brother, all cut to smash. The Lord save us!"

"Let go, and dive," shouted Francis.

Bill did so; the next instant a heavy shot, bounding along the surface of the sea, struck the half of the gig, knocking it to splinters. As they rose to the surface, they both began casting off their jackets and shoes; both excellent swimmers, they prepared for a severe struggle to the shore, distant very little less than a mile. The water was quite smooth, and no tide of any consequence in Gibraltar Bay.

"It's lucky, Bill," remarked our hero to his follower, "that the sharks are no doubt rather startled at all this firing, or else our chance of reaching the shore would be a bad one."

"Blessed Virgin! don't mention the villains, sir; it gives me a cramp thinking of them; it's better to be prisoners to the old Dons than sarve as a dinner to those rascals."

De Burgh felt this reverse of fortune severely; all his dreams of promotion were over; how long he might remain a prisoner to the Spaniards it was impossible to say; and yet, as he swam vigorously for the shore, a thought struck him that perhaps they might be unnoticed, and by remaining concealed till night, some chance might turn up in their favour. Before they reached the shore, there was a lull in the cannonading; they were too low to distinguish objects clearly, but still our hero could perceive that some of the line-of-battle ships were under sail. Had any of the British vessels been within reach of them they would have attempted to swim to them, but the Formidable lay between them; and the Hannibal, when they were cut in two, was nearly three miles distant.

"I do not see any one on the shore," said Francis, to his companion; "we may make for those high rocks to the right, and land without attracting observation."

"Faix! sir, we may escape being made prisoners after all, and make our way to Gibraltar along shore."

"That's not possible, Bill," returned our hero, as he touched bottom, "for the Spanish lines are between us and the fortress; but here we are, at all events, thank God! The poor Hannibal is in the hands of the enemy by this time; the firing has totally ceased."

On gaining the rocks, they proceeded to hide themselves in a large cavity near the spot. Francis was extremely anxious to gain a view over the bay, but was afraid of being seen.

Having gained the cave, they both sat down, weary and dejected enough; they had not eaten a mouthful since seven o'clock; it was now past four, as well as they could judge, and they had both worked hard during the day.

"I fear poor Carlton is mortally hurt," observed our hero to Mullaghan; "he was a fine-spirited, open-hearted lad."

"No, sir, I do not think he is; he was more stunned like, and was not bleeding. Be gor! it was a bad job taking the ground; only for that, we'd a peppered that big fellow with the Admiral's flag anyhow."

Luckily it was the month of July, so that their wet garments troubled them but little, but want of food made them both rather serious; unless they surrendered themselves prisoners, it was not likely they would get any till the next day at all events.

Towards dusk it began to blow fresh out of the bay; they could perceive that the French ships were keeping as close in as possible to Algesiras, the English fleet having as they supposed, made sail for Gibraltar. It came on a close cloudy night, though here and there a bright star shone out, the wind increasing. Francis determined to move along shore towards Gibraltar, there was no use certainly in staying there; their situation in wet trousers, no jacket, hat, or shoes, was uncomfortable enough, the sharp rocks cutting their feet. It was not walking on felt certainly, still neither complained; presently they got upon the soft sand, which was an immense relief, and thus they proceeded for nearly two miles, when Bill Mullaghan drew our hero's attention to a large dark object out on a sunken reef of rocks.

"That's a boat, sir. Be the powers! there's luck for us yet;" and Bill commenced wading out to the object.

In a few minutes he returned, saying joyfully: "It's a ship's jolly boat, sir, bottom up, and not a hole in her; we can turn her over easily; there's one oar under the thwarts, I could feel it."

"By Jove! here's luck," said Francis, wading out with Bill, and after some exertion and labour they righted and floated the boat. There was one oar, but nothing else; but they could scull by turns, and the wind blew steadily out from the land.

Having bailed her out as well as they could with their hands, they got in and shoved off, the wind carrying them rapidly on. Just then a loud voice hailed them in Spanish from the beach they had quitted.

"Oh, be gor! you're late, my hearties," shouted Bill, sculling away as hard as he could. The next instant bang went three or four muskets, one of the bullets knocking a large splinter out of the boat's gunwale.

"Arrah! bad luck to ye, anyhow, but a miss is as good as a mile, ye'll not do that again," growled Bill, sculling vigorously, aided by a strong breeze, which they felt as they receded from the shore.

"By Jove! we had a squeak for it, Bill," observed Francis; "those fellows would have made us prisoners ten minutes later."

"Faix! not so easily done as said, Mister Francis; we are able for half-a-dozen of those yellow devils any day. But tare and nouns! sir, it's blowing half a gale; I can't keep the boat's head towards the rock."

"Never mind, Bill, it blows too hard for sculling; we shall be picked up by some vessel in the morning, or else be drifted ashore on the African coast: it's only fifteen miles across."

"Africa, sir! repeated Bill, sitting down and keeping the boat dead before wind. "Faix, I never dreamt of going to Africa for breakfast. What sort of chaps are they over the way, sir? Faix, maybe they'd be after making a breakfast of us. I heard tell that the niggers on the African coast often eats the missionaries for luncheon."

"Oh, we shall not, please the fates, go to that part of the African coast, Bill. But what's that, away on our larboard bow? It looks like a sail."

"It's a latine-rigged craft, be the immortal Moses!" said Bill exultingly. "She's crossing our bows."

"Take care it's not a Spanish gun-boat, though we cannot help it if it is. She will pass close to us. I see her plainly enough now. Three masts; she looks a long, low craft, and has not a single reef in her lofty sails."

The latiner was tearing through the water, her taper yards bending like a whip. When nearly abreast of them, they were perceived, for the craft shot up in the wind, and hailed them in Spanish.

There was no use in refusing to answer, so Francis De Burgh, with a sigh, seeing the fates were against them, answered the hail in French. In a moment, the stranger brailed their mainsail, and hauled their jib to windward, and then they dropped down alongside.

"Be gor, we're prisoners, Mister Francis," said Bill, dolefully; "but we'll get some supper, that's one consolation."

As soon as our hero and his follower got aboard, several men with lanterns surrounded them, and an officer in a Spanish uniform accosted them, demanding were they French?

Though a ruse in war is allowable, De Burgh thought it quite useless to pretend to be Frenchmen, as they would soon be detected when handed over to the French at Algesiras, so he replied:

"No; we are English."

"Ha, carambo, that's good," said the captain of the gun-boat, exultingly; "officers or sailors, eh?"

Francis said they were officers, trusting to get as good treatment for Bill as for himself.

"Diabolos, this will do," said the captain, ordering his men to take the boat in tow.

He again questioned our hero in bad French how they came in such a plight, without jacket, hats, or shoes?

Francis stated the simple facts; the captain then ordered each a jacket, and some biscuit and some wine, telling them they might lie down under a tarpaulin that covered the swivel gun.

"I am bound for Cadiz," said the captain. "Your ships got a mauling," he exultingly added; "I have been reconnoitring them in port. My craft sails like a witch; nothing can touch her."

"What are you going to Cadiz for?" carelessly asked our hero. "Are you not afraid of being captured by some of our cruisers?"

"Santos Dios! There's not one of your craft could get near me in this weather. I am taking orders for the San Carlos and the Hermangelde to get under weigh and join the fleet off Algesiras. Ah, carambo, if they had been here to-day, they would have annihilated all your fleet."

"What is the chap saying, sir?" questioned Bill; "he seems as full of wind as a bladder."

"He boasts enough, Bill, at all events. We have got a supper, but a deuced bad one."

Being allowed to walk about, the captain having descended to his cabin, Francis De Burgh had a survey of the gun-boat. She had four brass guns, and a swivel carrying an eight-pound ball. She appeared a very beautiful craft, of great length, and nearly one hundred and fifty tons burden, as well as he could guess.

There were ten or twelve men on deck, and he supposed as many more below; she had great beam, and carried her enormous lofty yards surprisingly.

As there was no help for their misfortune, Francis consoled himself with the thought that their lives had been spared, and therefore they ought to be thankful, after the terrible risks of the day; so getting in under the tarpaulin, they lay down, if not to sleep, at all events to rest themselves.

## CHAPTER XXVIII.

As Francis De Burgh and his follower, Bill Mullaghan, lay under the tarpaulin for shelter, for the gun-boat, carrying an immense press of sail, threw whole sheets of water over her decks, the latter, after growling at the uncivil treatment of the Spanish captain, said:
"Faix, sir, I've just been thinking if it would be possible for us to take this here craft. She's a beauty for sailing."
"What, Bill," returned our hero, laughing, "take a craft with at least four or five-and-twenty men in her, without arms!"
"Oh, be gorra, they are only Spaniards. As to that, sir, there's not more nor eight or nine on deck at a time; a good handspike is a tidy tool to work with."
"All very well if they had not firearms; but you are half mad, Bill, to entertain such an idea."
"Faix, I'm half mad and half starved," grumbled Mullaghan, "and half mad to think we may have to live, the saints know how long, upon beans and oil, and sour wine. What's the matter, now?" he added, as he began to force his way from under the tarpaulin, our hero following; for all of a sudden the vessel heeled over violently on the opposite side, and a complete Babel of voices and stamping of feet about the deck took place.
On emerging from their retreat, they at once perceived that the gun-boat had jibbed, and was going dead before the wind. Before they had time to look round, bang goes a heavy gun to windward of them, the ball knocking the caboose to atoms, and cutting away the tacks and blocks of the foresail; then our hero perceived a brig under full sail, right astern of them.
"Be the pipers of war!" exclaimed Bill, with a cheer that startled half-a-dozen Spaniards who were repairing the damage done, by making fast another tack.
"That's the little Paisley, Bill, for all the world; she that used to visit us off Cadiz, Captain S—— and that mad youngster, Master Burke, that you took such a fancy to."
"Oh, be gorra, all's right. There goes another gun."
And sure enough another ball tore away nearly the whole of the starboard bulwarks, wounding three of the men. The Spanish captain swore and stamped about the deck in a violent rage, swore no brig afloat could have caught him, only that he came upon her

round Cabrita Point too suddenly to gain a start; but if he didn't cripple him before ten minutes were over, carambo, he didn't care a fig for her. At the same time his men prepared the swivel, and blazed away bravely at the brig.

But the brig seemed to know she had no chance of outsailing her, for suddenly yawing, she poured her whole broadside into the gun-boat.

Our hero and Bill had a most narrow escape, for the last broadside settled the affair, killing the captain and five of the men. and knocking the mainmast, yard and all, over the side.

"Hurrah for the Paisley!" shouted Bill, to the infinite disgust of the crest-fallen Spaniards.

The vessel was then hove to, and so was the brig, and presently a six-oared gig was pulling alongside.

The fall of the huge latine sail nearly smothered our hero and Mullaghan; but they extricated themselves by Bill's cutting a hole in the canvas with his knife, which he carried round his neck with a string. Just as they gained the clear deck, a young middy sprung up the side, followed by his men, singing out in an extraordinary mixture of English, bad Spanish, and worse French:

"Where's the captain of this confounded craft?"

"Be gor, Master Burke," said Bill Mullaghan, coming forward while the other started back with surprise, "you're a broth of a boy, and long life to you; but as for the captain, you've knocked the life out of him, and no mistake."

Francis De Burgh then came forward, and the midshipman's astonishment was complete.

"Well, by Jove, this is curious," shaking Francis heartily and joyfully by the hand; "but how came you both here? Where's the Hannibal?"

"Surrendered, I fear, to the enemy," said our hero; and then he gave an explanation.

"This is bad news indeed," said Master Burke; "but I tell you what you can do, for Captain S—— is anxious to reach Gibraltar. You can take charge of this gun-boat; I will leave four of the men with you, and take these Spaniards aboard the brig. Captain S—— will be delighted that you have charge of her, and it will bring you into the notice of the Admiral."

To this our hero willingly agreed, highly rejoiced at the new turn fortune had given to her wheel. The Spaniards were then mustered and disarmed; they were twenty-eight in number.

"I shall have to make two trips of it to the brig," observed the midshipman.

"Oh, be Jabus, you needn't, Mister Burke!" put in Mullaghan, "just take as many as you can, never mind the rest, we'll manage them as easy as children now we have arms."

"You may do so, Charles," said our hero, "they will help us to clear away this wreck, and there's no fear of them."

Accordingly the midshipman took as many as he could, and then pulled off for the brig, which at once made sail for the rock.

They were now six hands and fourteen Spaniards on board, and at once our hero set about clearing away the wreck, having put away the dead bodies to be buried when they reached Gibraltar. The Spaniards worked very sulkily, though Bill roused them up now and then with a strange mixture of words. Having hauled in the sail and yard, he cut the wreck of the mast adrift and then made sail after the Paisley. Leaving Mullaghan at the helm and the other men with pistols and cutlasses in their belts, and the Spaniards forward, our hero went below to have a look at the cabin of the gun boat; for a vessel of one hundred and fifty tons she had a remarkably large and handsome cabin very tastefully fitted up. He could not but think of the fate of the unfortunate Captain, an hour or two back full of life and energy; but such is human life in times of war.

So extraordinarily fast did the Spanish gun-boat sail, that when the brig came to anchor off the Mole, in Gibraltar, the captured Spaniard was close up with her under her foresail and mizen only. Francis De Burgh brought his vessel to anchor alongside the Paisley. Having seen her all to rights, he proceeded in the boat turning astern to pay Captain S―― a visit before he went ashore. Having found a pair of shoes and a jacket belonging to the unfortunate captain of the gun-boat he was forced to make use of them.

Captain S―― received our hero with great kindness and cordiality; made him sit down to breakfast. After enjoying a substantial meal Captain S―― invited him to accompany him on board the Admiral's ship.

Francis remarked that his costume was rather singular for a visit to the flag ship.

"Wait a while," said Captain S――, "I'll rig you out, and if you want cash I'll take you where you will get plenty by putting your name to a simple piece of paper with a stamp on it; these are times when cash is plentiful, and eagerly offered to officers. Now to rig you out."

In a few minutes Francis De Burgh was equipped in a plain suit of Captain S――'s clothing, who fortunately was a tall, strong, well-built man. On pulling on board the Cæsar, after a little time our hero had the honour of a personal interview with Sir James Saumarez, who received him with much kindness, and requested him to state all he knew with respect to the Hannibal; and if he knew the names of the ships the late captain of the gun-boat was bearing messages to.

Having stated how he had left the Hannibal and her unfortunate situation, our hero then informed the Admiral that the two Spanish ships that were ordered to join the French fleet at Algesiras were the San Carlos and the Hermagarde."

"Both forty-two gun ships," observed Sir James Saumurez, who appeared much grieved at the disasters of the Hannibal, and stated to some of the officers present, that it was his intention to send a flag of truce to Algesiras to Admiral Lenois for an exchange of prisoners. After some kind remarks upon his conduct, De Burgh retired to wait upon deck for Captain S——. In about an hour he came up from the cabin and approaching our hero said:

"I have good news for you, my young friend; the Admiral is highly pleased with you, and desires me tell you, if it suits your views, that you may retain command of the gun-boat, with the nominal rank of lieutenant, which will most probably be confirmed in a few months. The gun-boat will be fitted up with heavier metal, and an 18-pound carronade for a swivel, with a compliment of thirty men and a midshipman; you may keep that scamp Burke, he'll be quiet by himself, and as soon as you can get ready you will have plenty of assistance for you are to sail towards Cadiz, and thence if necessary further westward till you fall in with the Superb and the Thames; you will have sealed letters for their Captains to-morrow morning. So now let us ashore till I get you some cash; I would give it you myself only my exchequer is consumptive."

Francis De Burgh felt singularly elated; here was the height of good fortune sprung out of misfortune. To have the command of the gun-boat and the nominal rank of lieutenant was beyond his most sanguine hopes. The fact was Sir James Saumarez had heard his history and his good conduct when a seaman on board the Hannibal from Captain Ferris, and that he strongly suspected he was a very near connection of the late Lord Delamaine's, and a protégé of General Grey's. Sir James was therefore prepared to receive him kindly, but his extremely prepossessing appearance and pleasing manner at once won the gallant and kind-hearted Admiral's approbation, and as officers were scarce, several being killed and others wounded in the late unfortunate affair at Algesiras, he took the opportunity of shewing his approbation and at the same time turning his services into immediate use.

Captain S——'s introduction to the banking establishment of Bright, Smith, and Co., enabled our hero to pocket £50, which he declared was quite sufficient for his outfit, and sundry comforts for the gun-boat's cabin, which he intended calling, if permitted, the Daring.

"Well, I will procure that permission; and now to get an order upon the storekeeper, so as to put to rights as soon as possible."

Parting from the good-natured Captain S——, Francis De Burgh set about purchasing an outfit for himself and Bill Mullaghan, as well as sundry stores.

At this period all the disposable hands in Gibraltar were at work night and day repairing the damages the fleet had sustained, for Sir James Saumarez was resolved again to attack the enemy, even with his crippled and inadequate force. The damages received by the Pompey placed her out of the list altogether; her crew was therefore turned over to the other ships; our hero's little craft was manned from her hands.

The flag ship, the Cæsar, was awfully mauled, but her brave captain vowed she should be ready. So rapid and expeditious were the hands in repairing damages, and so active the workmen from the shore, that the Daring had her mast in, and all her damages repaired, stores in, &c., and having received the sealed letters for the Superb and ,Thames, by twelve o'clock the following day Francis De Burgh in the uniform of a lieutenant, took the command of his little, but remarkably beautiful craft, with a feeling of intense pleasure. Once more the vision of Mary Grey rose before his mind's eye, it seemed to his buoyant spirit, as if the command of the little Daring had removed mountains from his path. Just as he was leaving the shore he encountered the captain of the Paisley brig, seemingly in great haste.

"I've a piece of news for you, my friend, but no time to tell it; there's the last two papers, you will see something about it; at all events General Grey is made a baronet and comes out here as Governor. Now, God bless you! get under way as fast as you can, and, by-the-bye, board any ship of war you may meet, and tell them to join the Admiral here,—Adieu!"

Our young lieutenant was astounded, but he hastened to get on board, waiting till clear of the bay to examine the papers.

The Paisley brig having sprung a leak was hove down, or else she would have sailed also.

Our hero found Master Burke, a fine lad of some seventeen or eighteen years of age, in a high state of glee at the prospect of a cruise in the Daring. He was in his element; pickles, jars of sardines, bottles of wine, anchovies, &c., disappeared like magic into the lockers, aided and assisted by a smart lad he had pressed into the service for a cabin boy.

Bill Mullaghan was in ecstasies; our hero made him his first mate, and calling his crew together, he looked them over, heard their names, then spliced the main brace, cast off from his moorings, and under a full sail with a spanking breeze from the northeast, ran out from the bay, making a wide reach over towards the other shore to avoid any of the enemy's heavy cruisers.

## CHAPTER XXIX.

FRANCIS DE BURGH's first care, after putting things into ship-shape on board the Daring, and settling the different watches, was to practise his men in the handling of the latine sails, as they were all new to them. The Daring was quite a new craft, and sailed remarkably fast. There was an old experienced man-of-war's man on board named Richard Roberts; he had served many years in the Mediterranean, and had often had the handling of latine rigged vessels; our hero therefore placed him and Master Burke in the same watch.

As the sun went down it looked for a breeze of wind, so much so that Francis resolved to have a trial how his crew would handle the ponderous yards in reefing. The Italian sailors reef by going barefooted up the yard, gathering in the sail as they go; in a heavy sea this is a perilous exploit, as the yard jerks like a whip. Our hero, however, lowered the yards, and reefed and re-hoisted, and this was done in a very short time. In very heavy weather, the yards are lashed upon deck, and lugs hoisted in their place.

The watch being set, and all snug for the night, the young commander descended to his cabin exceedingly anxious to examine the English papers given him by Captain S——. Thanks to Master Burke's *savoir vivre* every thing in the cabin of the Daring was in first-rate order. Our hero felt as proud of his little ship as an Admiral of a three-decker.

A handsome lamp hung suspended over the table, so sitting down he opened the two papers; one was the *Times* of recent date, the other was a *Court Journal*. He commenced with the latter paper, and running his eye rapidly over the columns, at last the article he sought met his eye. The very first lines he read made his heart beat and his face flush painfully. The article was headed "Fashionable Gossip." It ran as follows :—

"A marriage, it is said, is on the tapis between the beautiful and accomplished daughter and heiress of a distinguished general, just created a Baronet by his most gracious Majesty, for past services, and Lord Frederic Delamaine, of Milton Abbey, Hampshire. The nuptials will, it is thought, take place before the departure of General Grey for Gibraltar, the post of Governor having been conferred upon Sir Edgar Grey by his Majesty."

Francis De Burgh laid down the paper with a sickening sensation creeping over him. There was a mist before his eyes, and for several minutes he remained bewildered and confounded by the startling and overwhelming intelligence he had read.

The moment before he felt supremely happy, proud and confident in the future; but the reading of those few lines created a feeling of despair and disgust of everything and of the world.

"Oh, Mary, Mary!" he mentally and bitterly exclaimed, "I would not have believed this if an angel had whispered the words."

As he pronounced those words to himself he suddenly felt that he was doing Miss Grey great injustice, for it as suddenly occurred to him that if he would not believe an angel's whisper why on earth should he believe a gossiping newspaper.

"I am a fool and a madman to think there can be any truth in such a report! I am doing Mary great wrong in giving credit to such a lying paragraph for one single instant."

This revulsion of feeling, as is usual in one so young and sanguine, was as rapid in creating a sensation of relief, as before it had caused one of despair.

"At all events, it is very plain," thought he, "General Grey has been created a Baronet, and appointed Governor of Gibraltar."

Taking up the *Times*, which was of a much more recent date, his eye, after scanning the columns, came upon the following:—

"Sir Edgar Grey, the recently appointed Governor of Gibraltar, sailed in the 9th instant on the Thetis frigate, for the seat of his government."

As he ran his eye over the remaining columns of the paper an advertisement headed "£100 reward," attracted his attention:

"Whereas, on the 24th of April, Francis De Burgh, Esq., left the hotel of the Swan-with-two-Necks, accompanied by a man in the attire of a sailor, lame of the right leg, for the purpose of proceeding to the Tower Hamlets to search for his servant, who was supposed to be either enticed into a crimping house, or taken by a press-gang: since that period he has not been seen or heard of. Any information respecting the whereabouts of Mr. De Burgh, or intelligence that may lead to the knowledge of the locality he is in, such person or persons giving the information will receive the above reward; and should this advertisement attract the attention of Mr. De Burgh himself, he is entreated at once to communicate with Mr. Charles Howard, solicitor, Welbeck Street, London, as most important matters require his immediate attention."

"What on earth has occurred now?" thought our hero, "perhaps some information respecting deeds and papers lost by the robbery of the cottage in Dungarvon"

He regretted much not seeing this last paragraph before he left the rock, as he might have written to Mr. Howard; now he might not have it in his power to write for some time; however, as there was a probability of meeting with some homeward-bound ship, he took paper and pen, and wrote a brief account of his adventures to Mr. Howard, begging him if he had received the dividend coming to him from the late banking establishment of Messrs. ——— to remit him three or four hundred pounds to the Bank of Bright, Smith, and Co., Gibraltar.

That night was passed by our hero partly in an uneasy slumber, and partly in pacing the deck of the Daring. The next day the wind blew extremely fresh and right against them, but the Daring carried her canvas steadily, made good way, and opened the Bay of Cadiz shortly after mid-day. Strange to say not a single vessel of war was to be seen in the bay. Standing out to make a stretch to the westward, they caught sight of the topsails of a very large vessel, standing in from the westward.

Master Burke, who was as active as a monkey, went up to the lofty yards of the latine sail, as easy and expeditiously as any Spaniard or Italian could have done, commenced examining the stranger with his glass, though the yard swayed heavily with the smart sea on.

"A three-masted ship, sir; evidently a merchant vessel," sung out the midshipman, every pitch of the Daring threatening to send him some fifty yards ahead of them.

This intelligence set all the crew on the *qui vive*, calculating in their own minds whether their young skipper had not the inclination but the liberty of attacking a merchant ship should she carry an enemy's flag.

But Francis De Burgh settled that question to their infinite satisfaction. Very soon—for having made out the vessel as she rapidly rose to view, coming up with a spanking breeze in her favour—he said, speaking to Richard Roberts, who was at the helm:

"I should not be surprised but that this may be one of the Spanish treasure ships."

"Beg your pardon, sir," returned the old man-of-war's-man, "that cannot be, as the treasure ships are frigates, and this here craft, though a himposing looking ship, is no frigate; howsomėver, she may be well worth taking, if you, sir, are empowered to take her!"

"I asked that question," returned our hero, "of Captain S———, as I cannot be expected to understand all the rules of the service, and also knowing that I was carrying important instructions; his answer was, 'Take all you can get, my boy, provided the crafts carry a Spanish or French flag.' So if this fellow coming up so gallantly, standing evidently in for Cadiz, is a Spaniard, we will try our metal."

Those words were heard by several of the crew, and a hearty cheer, as discipline was not very strict in trifling cases on board the Daring, pealed over the deep. Hoisting Spanish colours, our hero tacked and stood towards the stranger, pondering over in his own mind what he would do with her should he take her, for he could ill spare half a dozen hands to take her to Gibraltar.

On a nearer approach they made her out to be a deeply laden ship of some six or seven hundred tons burden, and carrying six guns aside, and with their glasses they could perceive there were a great many hands on board her.

"She will be a tough customer, sir," said Richard Roberts, "she must be bringing home a very valuable cargo; she is carrying 12-pounders, I'm blow'd if she ain't."

"Be gor!" muttered Bill Mullaghan, as he tightened a belt round his waist, "we'll pounder her, and in style, too; she's a real Don; there goes her colours."

Down went the Spanish flag on board the Daring, and the next moment the flag of Old England flew out from the mizen yard. Crossing right under the stern of the Spaniard, who appeared astounded by the change of flags, Francis saw on her stern, in large gold letters, "The Prince of Peace." With his speaking-trumpet he very coolly told them to heave to.

This piece of impudence coming from a craft that looked like a cockle shell alongside the merchant ship, was met with a polite reply from the skipper, standing on a gun-carriage, telling them that they might go to a place unmentionable, ending with a variety of Spanish oaths all ending in O; and that if they did not shove off, he'd sink them.

This our hero thought too polite, so he resolved to show that he could bite as well as bark; so unmasking their long 18-pound carronade, and getting to a convenient distance, he commenced peppering the Don, to their infinite amazement, never imagining so small a craft could be armed with so destructive a weapon.

The very first shot from this formidable gun knocked his fore-topmast yard in two pieces. Though amazed and greatly disgusted, the Spaniard, with six 12-pounders, and a crew of fifty men, was not going to be frightened by such a little vixen as the Daring.

"Hurrah, my darlint!" chuckled Bill, as the Spaniard blazed away with his starboard guns, which passed right over them; "You must put on your spectacles, I'm afraid you can't see us!" and with as much glee as school-boys at a game of romps, Bill and his comrades, with Richard Roberts for marksman, treated the Spaniard to another shot from the swivel, which cut away his maintop-ail sheets, and splintered the main yard so badly, that running up in the wind it snapped in two.

The Spaniards were neither good marksmen nor first-rate

sailors; for though they loaded their guns with grape shot, and blazed away rapidly, so well was the Daring managed, and so beautifully did she work in the heavy sea running, that only two men were slightly wounded, the sails riddled, and some of tho planking of the bulwarks knocked into splinters. The Prince of Peace was now in an awkward position, and seemingly unmanageable, for she ran up in the wind, got in irons, and commenced rolling heavily, but still obstinately firing when she could. As yet our hero only aimed his carronade at the sails and rigging, not wishing to kill or wound any of the crew, if he could take her by crippling her. In half an hour the Don was yawing about like a rudderless ship, her sails split, and hanging about her, her fore and main yards in pieces, and her range with her guns wild and out of distance.

"Be the powers, sir," remarked Bill Mullaghan, dripping with perspiration from his exertions at the swivel, "you must give 'em a taste of grape to cool 'em; they don't seem to mind their sails and yards hanging about them, like a girl's curls in a breeze with her sweetheart."

Richard Roberts, the old quarter-master, was of the same opinion; so loading the swivel almost to the muzzle with grape and canister, the Daring tacked, and passing on, passed under the Spaniard's stern, and as the little gun-boat rose on a heavy sea, and the Spaniard presented her entire deck to her, she blazed away at him with destructive effect. This discharge settled the matter; for in two minutes down came the Spanish flag, and the Prince of Peace surrendered, while the crew of the Daring gave three hearty cheers, that pealed over the deep with a pleasing sound.

"Well done, my little beauty!" said Bill, patting the warm muzzle of the 18-pound carronade.

At that moment, while our hero was considering how he should proceed, the loud boom of a heavy gun reached their ears, and then for the first time they all perceived a vessel of war standing out towards them from Cape St. Vincent.

"That's the Superb, sir," said young Burke; "I know her well."

Our hero took the glass, and at once recognized her, for she was frequently with them during the blockade of Cadiz, and her skipper was very intimate with Captain Ferris.

Francis De Burgh immediately trimmed his sails, and leaving the prize and the Spaniards to recover from their disgust, stood on towards the Superb; when near nough he hove to, and with the trumpet, stated he had a despatch for their commander from the Admiral. The Superb then backed her topsail, and launching a boat, though the sea was pretty heavy, our hero proceeded on board. He knew Captain R——, of the Superb, extremely well, having met him two or three times at Captain Ferris's table.

"What, is that you, Mr. De Burgh?" exclaimed Captain R——, looking with extreme surprise at our hero, dressed in a lieutenant's uniform; "you have, it seems, been at hot work this morning, to judge by your sails and bulwarks. Any of your men killed or wounded? and what ship is that you have had the gallantry to attack? To judge by her size, and the noise she made, she's big enough to swallow you."

Francis laughed, but handing Captain R—— the letter, he said,

"I am afraid the intelligence I bring you, sir, will be distressing to you to hear."

Captain R—— looked serious, and hastily opened the official letter, which he read in a minute.

"Good God!" he exclaimed, the instant after, "this is sad news:—the Hannibal in possession of the enemy, the Pompey and Cæsar crippled, and many killed and wounded! Pray, Mr. De Burgh, give me the particulars; at the same time accept my congratulations at your promotion to a lieutenant's rank, for you will be sure to retain that rank from Sir James's recommendation;" and Captain R—— shook him kindly by the hand.

Francis De Burgh then gave the commander of the Superb full particulars, as well as relating to him his capture of the Prince of Peace.

"You are Fortune's favourite, Mr. De Burgh," said Captain R——. "Take some refreshment, then return on board your handsome little craft, and make sail for San Lucar; you will find the Thames off that port, and perhaps some other frigate. You can stand on, however, as far as Lisbon; you will then surely fall in with the Vulcan, or the Raymond. I will put hands on board your prize, and take her to Gibraltar, where you will hear of her when you get back; and depend upon it, you have made a good thing of your cruise."

Our hero, highly pleased, drank a glass of wine, and ate a biscuit, and with many kind wishes from Captain R——, returned on board the Daring; and repairing his damages as quickly as possible, his wounded men being very slightly hurt, and his crew in high spirits at the knowledge that their prize would be taken care of, he made sail for the land, intending to beat up along shore to San Lucar. Towards night the wind drew to the southward, and before morning they were running along the coast with a favourable breeze. On reaching San Lucar, he found the Thames, delivered his despatch, when she immediately made sail, telling our hero he would find the Thetis, thirty-six, off Lisbon.

On doubling Cape St. Vincent, our young skipper got the wind from the north-west, which soon raised a very heavy sea, so much so, that he was forced to lower the latine yards, and hoist lugs; under this rig the Daring proved a remarkably dry boat, and capable of standing almost any weather, though of course her speed was diminished. This trial satisfied our hero that she would make a splendid schooner.

For the season of the year the wind continued to blow exceedingly hard; and as they became exposed to the whole range of the Atlantic, the sea became almost more than they could bear.

Our hero, however, stood on till he made Cape Lines; and not seeing a single vessel of war, and the gale increasing, he considered it no longer prudent to proceed. He thought it very strange they had not fallen in with any of the numerous privateers of the enemy, known to be in those seas.

On the night of the twenty-seventh, he was forced to lie to, from the height of the sea; but towards morning it began to go down, and the gale to lull a little.

Two hours before dawn, Francis De Burgh was on deck, when the boom of a cannon seaward attracted his attention; it was extremely dark; and though the firing could scarcely be more than three miles off, they could not distinguish any object at half that distance. The firing, however, continued at intervals, and Francis De Burgh determining to find out the cause, stood out, just as the grey dawn was breaking, in the direction of the firing, though there was a pause in the cannonade.

Richard Roberts gave it as his opinion that some merchant ship was being chased by a privateer or enemy's cruisers. A the light increased, the gale fell to a fine working breeze, and all hands being on deck the attention of every one was directed seaward. When sufficiently light, they at once made out, about four miles to the westward of the Daring, four vessels. Taking a survey through his glass, the young skipper, to his surprise, beheld two large latine-rigged craft and a long raking schooner, and a mile a-head of them a fine handsome-rigged ship; her masts very taunt, and raking more than it is usual in merchant ships; she had very much the look of a corvette, and was lying to under her maintopsail; she had no flag, but the other three craft, as he stood towards them, had their ensigns flying, the latines under Spanish, and the schooner French; he also made out three boats full of men, pulling slowly through the heavy sea, towards the ship lying **to.**

## CHAPTER XXX.

"Those are three privateers," said our hero, "and they have captured that ship; hoist our colours, and fire a shot," he added, "it may stop the fellows from boarding the ship; for I suppose, my lads, you are willing that we try what we can do with the Dons and the Frenchmen?"

A hearty cheer, and a match applied to one of the 12-pounders was the answer, as the men eagerly prepared for action, caring not a straw for the desperate odds they were about to engage. The latined crafts were, in appearance, about the tonnage of the Daring, the French schooner about one hundred and twenty or thirty tons.

The effect of the shot from the Daring, was, as our hero expected, the signal for the privateers to recall their boats, and a considerable commotion ensued aboard them.

The crew of the Daring were busy also, the three lugs were lowered, and the latine yards hoisted, and then she went bowling along at the rate of eight knots. The swivel gun was loaded with three round shot, and two of the 12-pounders with grape, with the old quarter-master Roberts at the helm, and Bill and his gang at the swivel, and Master Burke and his party at the 12-pounders. The Daring came down upon the astonished privateers hand over hand, and wishing to try the range of his carronade, he opened fire. The gun was directed at the French schooner, who had shaken the reefs out of her main-sail, and was getting into a position to engage the Daring. The effect of this shot was to convince the Frenchmen that they had an ugly customer to deal with, and one provided with a weapon totally unthought of, to judge by her size. Down came the main-sail of the schooner; nevertheless, she returned the fire, but her metal was infinitely inferior, the ball falling short. She was only armed with brass 6's, and an 8-pound swivel.

Hauling his wind, our hero desired Roberts to put him within range of the nearest latine craft, who, as he came up, fired his two 8-pounders loaded with canister, doing very little damage, but wounding one man. Running close aboard, Master Burke with a cheer gave them the contents of his guns, loaded to the muzzle. The discharge was so well aimed and so destructively close, that the shot told fearfully upon her crowded decks. As he learned afterwards, this discharge killed seven men and wounded thirteen or fourteen, setting fire to her foresail. She cried out that she surrendered, and instantly struck her flag.

With a wild and hearty cheer, Bill and his gang, having loaded the swivel with grape, prepared for the other latine, but crowding all sail she stood in for the land. Seeing the schooner had rehoisted her mainsail, and was coming down on him, he went in stays, at the same time giving the enemy the contents of the carronade, which committed terrible havoc amongst the crew, cutting the sheets and tacks to atoms. Nevertheless, the Frenchman, who was determined to do mischief, brought his four guns on one side, and fired the whole broadside into the Daring; but the old quartermaster, keen-sighted, and singularly skilful at the helm, baffled the destructive discharge by a rapid manœuvre. The mizen-yard was, however, cut in two, and one poor fellow killed, besides a few bruises and wounds.

The schooner paid dearly for this, the next discharge of the swivel and the two 12-pounders bringing down her foremast, and killing and wounding several of her crew; still she kept up firing, but without spirit. All this time, strange to say, the ship they were fighting for lay a tranquil spectator of the fight, scarcely half a mile distant.

The schooner was now at the mercy of the crew of the Daring, who, having again loaded their guns, took up a position to rake her, just hailing her, desiring her to haul down her flag, or they would rake her. Her answer was a broadside from her two guns, which cut away the weather bulwarks of the Daring, and slightly wounding Master Burke with a splinter.

Getting vexed, Francis De Burgh again got into a favourable position, and gave them the contents of his 18-pound carronade, loaded to the muzzle. This discharge settled the affair; the crew hauled down the flag and demanded quarter, which our hero very willingly gave, although it was well known that those privateers were mere sea-robbers. Though he said nothing about it at the time, our hero was slightly hit on the right arm, and his cheek grazed by a broken piece of iron, which merely raised the skin.

Extremely curious to know what the ship lying to was, for she certainly was not a merchantman, our hero stood over towards her. He was not afraid of either of his prizes escaping him, for the schooner was nearly a wreck, and the latine was so cut up that she looked very little better.

When nearly abreast of the ship—a magnificent looking vessel of about four hundred tons—he had the boat put out, and in a few minutes was alongside. An accommodation-ladder was put over the side, and our hero, with his arm in a black silk handkerchief and a black plaister on his cheek, stepped upon deck.

No sooner did he set foot on the deck, than he was saluted with a hearty cheer from over sixty able-bodied seamen. He saw at once that the vessel was a yacht; a tall elderly gentleman, with an extremely pleasing and agreeable countenance, advanced eagerly to meet him, and holding out his hand, said:

"By Jove, you are the finest and most gallant fellow I ever saw; I watched you the whole time. Never saw a craft handled in such style," and with a hearty shake of the hand he led our hero to the quarter-deck.

Before Francis De Burgh could reply, three ladies came up from the cabin; our hero stood electrified, and for an instant bewildered, as one of the ladies started forward and then stopped, her face pale as death, and her hands clasped together. It was no mistake, strange and extraordinary as it was, there she stood like a beautiful statue, but looking even more lovely than ever— there stood Mary Grey!

The next instant she held out both her hands, saying in an agitated voice:

"Oh! Mr. De Burgh, do I owe my deliverance once again to your courage?"

"What! what!" hastily interrupted the elderly gentleman in a tone of intense surprise, as our hero, with a rapture and a feeling indescribable, kissed the fair hand he held. "What, Mary, is this Mr. Francis De Burgh? By Jupiter! this is wonderful."

"Such in truth is the case, my lord," said Mary with a happy smile, and the colour coming back to her cheeks, "allow me, Mr. De Burgh," and the fair girl trembled with agitation, "to introduce you to Lord Herringstone, and also," turning round, and presenting our hero to a still very fascinating-looking lady, not more than two or three and forty, "to my kind friend, Lady Herringstone."

The other lady was an old acquaintance, Mary Grey's attached companion, Mrs. Pearson.

"Well, upon my word, Mary," said her ladyship with a pleased smile, "this is a most agreeable surprise. I was prepared to return thanks to our gallant deliverer, but in truth never dreamed of his turning out your favourite hero, Mr. De Burgh."

Mary Grey's cheeks rivalled the peony at these words, but she felt too happy to even try to hide or disguise her feelings.

"Well, upon my honour," said Lord Herringstone, "this is a most romantic adventure. I see your arm is hurt, but if I may judge by your countenance, not seriously."

"A mere scratch, my lord," returned Francis, "but some of my men are severely hurt; and three I am sorry, deeply sorry to say, killed."

"I grieve to hear it," said Lord Herringstone, "but I have an excellent surgeon aboard, he will put himself under your orders with great pleasure."

"Then, my lord, I will take him with me at once; there are a great number killed and wounded aboard the privateers, and they may also want help. If you can spare me some of your men, as I have only twenty fit for service, you will oblige me."

"My dear sir, take as many and everything you require. Good heavens! and with such a force you ventured to attack those three privateers! Why, that schooner you dismasted has nearly eighty men on board."

"We are very heavily armed, my lord," replied De Burgh; "but it seems strange to me you do not appear to have a single gun aboard."

"Your surprise is very natural. But here is the surgeon. Mr. Martin, pray be of all the assistance you can to Mr. De Burgh. Have you your instruments and medicine chest?"

The surgeon replied in the affirmative.

"Well then, my lord," said our hero, "I will bid you farewell for the present. I suppose," turning to Mary Grey, "you are bound for Gibraltar?"

Mary Grey looked surprised, but said:

"Yes, that is our destination."

"Pray," said Lady Herringstone, "return as soon as you can, for really I am dying with anxiety, seeing you so suddenly turning up in command of a dashing little vessel of war, and all your friends and good wishers in a mortal state of anxiety about your extraordinary disappearance."

"Your ladyship may depend," said Francis, his eyes meeting those of Mary Grey, "I shall lose no time in returning. At the same time, my lord, you can be making way for Gibraltar."

"By Jove, so I would, my dear sir, but those rascals have knocked my rudder to atoms during the night, or rather this morning; but now that you have rescued us, I will set our carpenters to work. A few hours will put us in sailing trim sufficient to reach Gibraltar, at all events."

The boats were quickly lowered from the Gem yacht, and taking the surgeon and fifteen men, our hero went aboard the Daring first, and had the wounded carefully attended to. He then proceeded to the schooner, which was lying like a log upon the water; she was named the Revolution. She had her captain, first mate, and seven seamen killed, and thirteen wounded. Having a surgeon aboard, after some conversation with the second mate, he undertook to lower his boat, and send the surgeon aboard the latine-rigged privateer, which was called the Don Juan. Between the three privateers there were one hundred and seventy men, so that our hero had reason to congratulate himself upon the victory he had gained at so trifling a loss. The latine was a very smart craft, and hailed from Cadiz; she mounted one long brass 6-pounder, four 2-pound swivels on her bow, with twelve brass blunderbusses or musketoons on her sides.

Lord Herringstone's surgeon was perfectly astonished when he beheld the number of men aboard the privateers, and could not but wonder at the audacity of Francis De Burgh in attacking such a superior force.

Before sunset the rudder of Lord Herringstone's yacht was completed—at least, it was rendered effective—a jurymast got up in the schooner; and having distributed his men, with those taken from the yacht, into the two prizes, they were enabled to make sail for the Straits before dusk.

Bill Mullaghan had charge of the schooner, and Master Burke of the Don Juan, with directions to keep close up with the yacht, and to keep a careful look-out, for it was rather a dangerous run to Gibraltar, as the enemy had several cruisers on the coast, though as yet our hero had not fallen in with one. Having settled everything to his satisfaction, Francis returned with the surgeon aboard the Gem, anxious beyond measure to again behold Mary Grey, and learn how she came to be a guest of Lord and Lady Herringstone's. By this time the sea had gone completely down, as it usually does in summer gales, the wind becoming extremely light.

Lord Herringstone was watching his arrival; and on his coming on deck, conducted him into the cabin, where her ladyship, Miss Grey, and Mrs. Pearson, were seated at the tea table.

The saloon of the Gem was a very large, splendidly fitted-up cabin; no expense had been spared in its comforts and elegant arrangements. Lord Herringstone's manner and tone was kindness itself; and, indeed, her ladyship equalled her spouse n expressions of gratitude for the services rendered them. Tih conversation for some time turned upon the recent encounter with the privateers, and Lady Herringstone expressed her surprise at his most strange appearance at so critical a moment; our hero at once gave the party assembled a full account of his adventures, though he refrained from imputing his seizure in the crimping house, in the Tower Hamlets, to Sir Godfrey De Burgh.

While relating his adventures, Lord Herringstone regarded him with a most earnest and serious, if not sad look. Francis certainly did not observe it, for his eyes had too fascinating an object before them to think of turning elsewhere. Fair Mary Grey evinced the deepest interest in his recital, with difficulty hiding the emotion she felt, especially at that part where his life was so endangered.

Love may well be called a divine spark, for in truth it lighted up the hearts of those two young beings with a pure and holy flame; they loved devotedly, and needed no language but that most expressive one that emanates from the eyes, those two outlets of the soul.

"You have endured your trials, Mr. De Burgh," said Lord Herringstone, "with great patience and resignation, and, to a certain degree, you have already been requited. Now, I dare say, having satisfied our curiosity, you fairly think yourself entitled to hear how we came into the strange situation in which you found us; and no doubt, but for your gallantry, and the spirit of your brave crew—who shall most certainly be well rewarded—we should have had to endure perhaps insult, at all events a long imprisonment. It may seem somewhat rash to put to sea in a yacht in time of war; but the explanation I will now give you will, I think, shew you that our expedition was not quite so Quixotic as it appears. The presence of Miss Grey aboard also is to be accounted for; so now, though I have neither deeds of daring or wild exploits to relate, yet, such as it is, you shall have your curiosity satisfied.

"You have heard, of course, while in Gibraltar, that my old and sincere friend, General, now Sir Edgar Grey, is appointed governor of that fortress; his purchasing a villa residence so near to Herringstone Castle, gave me infinite pleasure, as we renewed our youthful intimacy. I was then meditating a voyage to the Mediterranean in my yacht, intending to spend a couple of years in Italy, when my old friend, Sir Edgar, was in a manner compelled to accept the post of Governor of Gibraltar, stipulating, however, only to hold it for three years. When preparing to leave, I also had the Gem ready for sea, intending to have the advantage of sailing as far as Gibraltar in company with the Thetis frigate. Miss Grey was on a visit with us, about or rather after the period of your sudden and extraordinary disappearance, which gave General Grey and his daughter, I need scarcely tell you, inconceivable pain and trouble. The General could gain no trace of you in London, for, unfortunately, you did not think of mentioning your abode. From General Grey I also heard many particulars of your early life, which most particularly interested me, as I will one day explain to you. Now I confine myself simply to what brought us here. I prevailed on Miss Grey's father to permit her to accompany us, with her attached friend, in the yacht to Gibraltar, which she herself wished to do, as aboard the frigate there were troops, and being almost alone, she naturally preferred being with us, as we sailed in company with the vessel that conveyed her sire to the place of his government. We therefore sailed in company; but exceeding bad weather, most unusual for the time of year, separated us, and in a succession of foggy days we lost the frigate altogether, and, losing our foretopmast, we put into the Cove of Cork. We there found the Apollo frigate, and sixty or seventy sail of merchantmen, bound for the West Indies. I forgot to mention, that on leaving England my yacht was armed like a ten-gun brig, with sixty men, and plenty of arms and ammunition. In a few days the weather moderated, and all the fleet of merchantmen, with the Apollo leading, left the harbour, and so did we; it was a very grand and beautiful spectacle, and Miss Grey and my good lady enjoyed the sight amazingly. On the twenty-fifth we were out of sight of land, with a fair breeze; but on the Sunday following, the wind suddenly shifted into the south-west, blowing extremely fresh, and before midnight blew a heavy gale, with every symptom of severe weather. My sailing master advised keeping well away to the south-east, to avoid the numerous merchant vessels, as much danger existed of running foul, or being run foul of. At this time we were not more than a league from the Apollo frigate. That night was a remarkably severe one; our main staysail split in pieces by the sheets and tacks giving way; this sent all our hands upon deck, and not a little frightened our guests. It then came on to blow a hurricane, and the night intensely dark, when suddenly, to our great amazement, and no little terror, we struck the ground; we kept thumping heavily. My master was confounded, but thought we were beating over a shoal. Overboard went our guns, and all our shot and some heavy gear, when a tremendous squall took us aback, canted our head round, and the next moment we were again afloat. We stood off near a league, and then hove to. To our carpenter's surprise, our ship made little or no water; this was most providential; the loss of our guns and shot troubled us but little. We waited anxiously for day-light, for we heard the booming of heavy cannon all through the rest of the night, and we feared some disaster had happened to the frigate or the fleet of merchant ships. At last day broke, the light struggling through the dense masses of lowering clouds, driving on with the still furious gale. We were lying to under our storm staysails, in a tremendous sea. None of our men remembered seeing such a sea at that time of year. Alas! a sad scene of desolation was before us, as we looked out over the storm-tossed sea. To our surprise and consternation, we discovered that, instead of a shoal, we had actually struck upon a projecting sand bank in Mendigo Bay; and but for the temporary shifting of the wind two or three points, we should inevitably have been wrecked. As the light increased, we were filled with horror on beholding upwards of forty merchant vessels ashore, total wrecks. A mile from them lay the Apollo frigate, with both topmasts gone in the cap. [The Apollo frigate, with her captain and sixty-three hands, was wrecked about this period.] Several dismasted merchant ships were within a mile or so of us, rolling fearfully in the hollow seas. Such a terrible scene I never hope to witness again; and what made it worse, we could do nothing, for the mountainous sea that rolled in on the beach was frightful to look at. Strange to say, after a careful survey round us, and the weather clearing a little, we made out a frigate a league to leeward of us, with her foretopmast gone, but still under manageable canvas. After a time we made her out to be the Thetis, the frigate in which Miss Grey's father sailed for Gibraltar. During the day we dropped down towards her, and communicated by signals; she was going to put into Lisbon, being leaky, and in want of spars. I was thinking of doing so also, but a dense fog came on as the gale dropped; and by the advice of my master, I stood away to the southward and westward. We had not so bad a night of it, except that we all bitterly lamented the fate of the Apollo and the unfortunate West Indian fleet."

## CHAPTER XXXI.

"'The next morning," continued Lord Herringstone (the ladies having wished them good night, being tired after the fright they had endured, and the fatigues of the day), "we discovered our rudder was damaged, or most probably I should have run back and made Lisbon, for the gale had ceased; but we stood on towards Cape St. Vincent, after a temporary repair of our rudder. Of Miss Grey I may now speak, as she has retired. She was much grieved, and fretted about her father, though assured by signals from the Thetis that he was quite well; in fact, that most amiable and beautiful girl has been out of spirits the whole voyage. As I know," and his lordship looked kindly in our hero's anxious countenance, "as I know you are deeply anxious concerning her, I will here interrupt my narration to remark a circumstance that occurred previous to our departure from England. During Miss Grey's visit to Herringstone Castle, we were often visited by the present Lord Delamaine."

Our hero felt his cheek burn; but he uttered not a word.

"You have met his lordship, for of course you know that the present Lord Delamaine was the Captain De Burgh you met aboard the British Queen."

"Yes, my lord," returned our hero, "I recollect him well; and have just cause to remember both him and his father, Sir Godfrey De Burgh."

"I know you have," said Lord Herringstone, "but we will speak of this another time, for I know all your history, and am deeply interested concerning you, more than you can possibly imagine."

Francis De Burgh was surprised; there was so much kindness, even affection, in the tone and manner of his lordship, even considering the service he had rendered him. Lord Herringstone, however, continued:

"I mentioned that Lord Delamaine visited at Herringstone Castle. Miss Grey was well aware that his lordship professed an attachment to her, which she did all in her power to discourage; but at last he made a formal proposal, which she decidedly declined. The particulars of this interview I need not mention; but

Lord Delamaine left the Castle in a towering passion. This gave very little concern to Miss Grey; but some days after this, in looking over the *Court Journal*, she beheld an announcement that agitated and annoyed her beyond measure."

"I read that article, my lord," said Francis De Burgh, with a feeling of immense relief.

"Ah, indeed!" said his lordship, with a very meaning smile. "No doubt you felt not only surprised, but indignant, at such a liberty being taken with Miss Grey's name."

Our hero coloured, though he replied, with a smile:

"In truth I was, my lord; for I felt satisfied, after a time, that this was, after all, mere gossip, and surmise."

"Not altogether, my young friend, for I wrote to the editor and indignantly contradicted the report. I received a polite letter in reply, apologizing, but assuring me he had received the report from a correspondent, and regretted having inserted it. In the next paper he apologized for his error, stating that there was not the slightest foundation for the report in the previous paper, and that Miss Grey would accompany her father to Gibraltar. Having stated this much with respect to Miss Grey, I now return to our situation off St. Vincent. I have very little more to say with respect to our cruise, for off Cape St. Vincent we were chased by those three privateers; the loss of our guns left us no choice but to make a run of it. We should have distanced them at once, when, most unfortunately, our rudder again slipped out of berth, and we could not keep out of the wind. Before we could remedy this disaster, the rascals came up with us in the night, and a random shot put a finish to our rudder; and early in the morning, sooner than be riddled by those piratical fellows, we surrendered, for the females were desperately frightened by their firing at us during the night."

"It was certainly a curious and providential circumstance that I abandoned my cruise along the coast," said our hero; "I found the sea so heavy, and the prospect of meeting any more vessels of war so remote, that I put about, and thus came within sound of the privateers' guns."

After a pause of a few moments, Lord Herringstone said:

"Pray, Mr. De Burgh, did you ever hear any history of the late Lord Delamaine's family?"

"No, my lord, I never did, but latterly have felt a great desire to learn some particulars of the late lord's early life. His melancholy and most unexpected death deprived me of a most kind and generous patron; and though I do not at this moment possess the letter he wrote to me, just previous to his death, yet from its contents, I judged he knew some particulars of my father's early history."

"I do firmly believe," said Lord Herringstone, emphatically, "that he did. I may myself suspect, but mere surmises are tantalizing; and there's no use in building castles in the air, unless you can bring them down, and put solid foundations to them. It is now getting late; when we reach Gibraltar, we will resume this conversation; then I will give you a history of the Delamaine family, with whom I am connected, my only sister having married the Honourable Francis Delamaine, the late lord's elder brother."

"Good heavens! you amaze me, my lord," exclaimed Francis De Burgh, with a start of intense surprise; "I always thought——"

"Be patient, my young friend," interrupted his lordship, rising and laying his hand kindly on the shoulder of our hero; "time unravels most mysteries; of this be assured, if you have lost one generous patron, pray count upon me, from this time forward, as a steadfast and true friend. Providence has denied me an heir; my title dies with me, and the estates go, as we now stand, to a very distant branch of the family, but my available resources are very large, and from this hour I consider your future fortune in my hands."

Francis was amazed, profoundly touched by the noble and extraordinary generosity of Lord Herringstone; he could scarcely find words to express his gratitude and his feelings for such unlooked-for kindness; but his lordship pressed his hand affectionately, saying:

"Come, let us see how the night is; the time may come when you will find my kindness is quite natural;" so saying, they ascended to the deck.

It was a remarkably fine night, bright and clear; the little fleet kept in most compact order; the Gem was leading, under her three topsails only; close aboard was the latine privateer and the French schooner; and bringing up the rear was the little Daring, with her foresail brailed.

"That beautiful little vessel of yours," observed Lord Herringstone, "must sail marvellously fast; the rest have all sail set to keep up with us, and your vessel is forced to brail her foresail to keep back."

"She sails very fast indeed, my lord; in this breeze she would, no doubt, with all sail set, try the best speed of your yacht."

"By Jove! so it appears."

Francis De Burgh then summoned his men, and bidding his lordship good night, the boat towing astern was brought alongside; and his lordship shaking him most affectionately by the hand, he descended into the boat, and full of thought and reflection, dropped down to the Daring.

The next day they were all safely anchored off the Mole in Gibraltar, having escaped the Spanish and French ships coming out of

Cadiz by a few hours. They saw them stealing out, and Francis De Burgh counted five sail of the line and three frigates. These vessels followed in their wake, and before they ran into Gibraltar he saw them round Cabrita Point, and join the fleet off Algesiras.

The intelligence brought by our hero, and communicated at once, created the greatest excitement on board the English ships, then nearly ready for sea and service. Francis was ordered to repair on board the flag-ship, and had the honour of an interview with Sir James Saumarez. Lord Herringstone had been there some time before him.

"You have executed your mission extremely well," said Sir James Saumarez, "and at the same time maintained the honour of the British flag. As Lord Herringstone said, you could not have done better had your little craft been a ten-gun brig. By-the-bye, you are also fortunate, for the ship brought in by the Superb (and which I understand you captured; how you managed it I cannot say; but Captain R——, of the Superb, says you acted very gallantly, for she might have blown you out of the water;) has a very valuable cargo, having sailed from Monte Video; she belonged to private individuals in Cadiz, and would not wait for convoy. I understand she has two hundred thousand dollars, one thousand pigs of copper, several thousand seal skins, and a lot of other valuable goods; so your cruise, Mr. De Burgh, reckoning the two privateers you have just brought in, has turned out most fortunately. I expect despatches by the next ship from England, and make no doubt, amongst other matters, your present rank will be confirmed. In a day or two I shall have something else for you to do, so any repairs or damages you have sustained, you had better see to, and be prepared at an hour's notice."

Francis De Burgh highly gratified, made some suitable reply and bowed himself out, Lord Herringstone saying:

"Do not forget, Mr. De Burgh, I shall expect you to dinner aboard the Gem, so do not be tempted away by any of your naval friends, who, no doubt, will be very anxious to congratulate you on your good fortune."

"No fear of my foregoing such a pleasure, my lord," returned our hero, and then retired, and proceeded to H——'s hotel, then the best in Gibraltar.

There he encountered Captain R——, of the Superb, and his first lieutenant, and several officers belonging to the ships in port. Captain R—— shook him warmly by the hand, introducing him to the other officers present.

"By Jove, Mr. De Burgh," said Captain R——, "you are picking up the crumbs; I assure you, your health was drunk aboard the Superb, with three times three. Do you know she was heavily armed, and had nearly eighty men aboard of her? her captain was in a most towering passion, swore had he suspected what you were at first, he would have sank you before you could have fired a shot. We all laughed, for upon my conscience you gave him a precious dusting in a short time; didn't leave him a tack or sheet whole, and her sails would do to riddle bull dogs through."

"Were there many killed, Captain R———?" inquired our hero, "for the last dose of the carronade was a heavy one, and the only one aimed to hurt his crew, for he would not strike, though his vessel was lying perfectly unmanageable."

"Well, not many, fortunately for them; there were seven in all, but a number wounded. She has an out and out valuable cargo."

"I always said," observed a Captain Parks, "that those little crafts, with a long 18-carronade, are as ugly customers to a ship armed with 12's as needs be, especially if they sail anything like that little craft of yours, Mr. De Burgh."

"At all events," observed a jolly captain of marines, with a remarkable fiery proboscis, "we poor devils of marines will expect a jolly blow out from you, Mr. De Burgh, before we get into a mixture of grape and canister again."

"That I most certainly shall be delighted to do," said our hero, "and will, if it suits you all, say to-morrow."

"Very good," said Captain R———, "so let it be; and as we Superbs intend, in honour of Mr. De Burgh's capture of the Prince of Peace, to give an entertainment on a scale 'magnifique,' I name the day after: for depend on it, Sir James will give us but little time to digest the dinners."

"Ah, well," sighed the captain of marines, "they will be far easier of digestion than the entertainment the Admiral intends to give, and to which the French and Spanish fleets are invited."

After some further conversation on various topics, De Burgh proceeded aboard the Daring, and at the hour of dinner pulled off to the yacht. Neither Lady Herringstone nor Miss Grey had as yet gone ashore, nor had his lordship returned from his visit to the Admiral; and it chanced that our hero enjoyed the society of Mary Grey alone, her ladyship being engaged writing in her private cabin, and Mrs. Pearson not very well, was lying down, the fights and storms of the last few days having overpowered her strength.

"You cannot think," said Mary Grey, after some common-place conversation had taken place, "how surprised, and indeed startled we were, at your non-arrival at the villa at the time appointed. Miss Probert was on a visit with us then, and she really felt nearly as much concerned as we did: she has a very kind and sweet disposition. Lord and Lady Herringstone did all they could to persuade her to take a trip to Naples with them, but she is not fond of the sea."

"She appeared a charming and very amiable girl," returned our hero, "and I ought to feel very proud in creating an interest in your and your fair friend's remembrance. But I assure you, I felt the loss I experienced in not being able to keep my appointment, a great deal more than the treatment I suffered at the hands of the rascals that intercepted me. However, I owe to them my present extreme good fortune, and the happiness I now enjoy; therefore I cannot complain. I was greatly surprised, Miss Grey, when I heard that your father was appointed governor of this fortress, for I knew it was not his wish to leave his native shore again."

"You are quite right, Mr. De Burgh, my father was greatly opposed to accepting this post; but what could he do, when his Majesty desired he would do so? However, it is only for three years; there will be no fear of his being disturbed again. There is one circumstance which greatly annoys me," continued Mary Grey, with some slight hesitation of manner, "and that is, that Lord Delamaine is coming out here with his regiment."

"Lord Delamaine!" exclaimed Francis De Burgh astonished, and with a look into the bright intelligent eyes of Miss Grey, "why is it possible that he is still in the army?"

"Oh yes," returned Mary, with a little increase of colour, "he never quitted the army, only exchanged into another regiment, having purchased a majority in the —— foot, and they are ordered to Gibraltar."

"Lord Herringstone," said Francis, "mentioned a circumstance last night, with which I was already acquainted, having by chance read the paragraph alluded to, in a paper given me in Gibraltar."

"I know the paragraph to which you allude," returned Miss Grey, very calmly; "it was a most infamous affair indeed, the insertion of so unfounded a piece of gossip; but of course you did not for a moment give any credence to such a report."

"It cost me a very sleepless night, Mary," returned our hero, unthinkingly, and carried away, despite his determination, into a feeling of tenderness he could not control. He felt his cheek flush, and his manner became a little agitated, as he strove to undo the personality of his words. "I felt, Miss Grey, that you would suffer great annoyance from such a paragraph." He looked up; Mary Grey's face was very pale; her eyes met his, but with no anger in them.

"Oh, far from it——"

Perhaps it was as well for Mary Grey, after her promise to her father, that Lady Herringstone just then entered the saloon, for young love will blossom and bloom, try and check it how you will.

"Ah, Mr. De Burgh," said her ladyship, holding out her hand, "I am glad to see you; I would apologize for not being here to receive you, only that I knew my absence could not be missed, with so fair a substitute as Miss Grey."

Francis made some complimentary reply, and by that time Mary Grey recovered her confidence and composure, and the conversation flowed on pleasantly and cheerfully till the arrival of his lordship; they then sat down to dinner.

## CHAPTER XXXII.

TILL the removal of the repast, and the dessert placed upon the table, the conversation of the small party assembled in the saloon of the Gem was not of any particular importance; the intention of Sir James Saumarez to attack the combined fleet was the all-engrossing subject in Gibraltar.

"And what part, Mr. De Burgh," observed Lady Herringstone, "do you think you will have to take in this expected encounter of two such unequal fleets? Surely such a fairy vessel of war as yours will not be exposed to the storm of their terrible guns."

"And yet, your ladyship, I should feel sad at being left out," returned Francis. "I can be of no service as far as fighting goes: but such small craft as I command are often serviceable as messengers between the contending ships."

"Good gracious!" remarked Miss Grey; "a worse post, I should say, than being a combatant on board the-line-of-battle ships themselves."

"You are quite right, Mary," said Lord Herringstone; "but I do not think my young friend will be put on so dangerous a service; however, whatever service Mr. De Burgh may be ordered to perform, I feel satisfied he will do his part gallantly and cheerfully."

"You are very kind, my Lord, to vouch for me; but I trust such will be the case."

Shortly after, Lady Herringstone and Miss Grey left the two gentlemen to themselves; it had evidently been so arranged by his lordship, who soon after said:—

"As the fleets sail after to-morrow, we may not, my young friend, have another evening to spend together, perhaps for some time. You expressed a wish to hear some account of the late Lord Delamaine's family; I will now give you a brief outline of the family history, you will then be able to judge—putting your own merits out of the question—why I feel so interested concerning you.

"The late Lord Delamaine's father was a nobleman of a strange, eccentric, and passionate nature; he married an heiress of the house of De Lacey; he had two sons, and one daughter; Francis the elder son, Arthur the younger; the daughter, the Honourable Miss Delamaine, was married early to Sir Godfrey De Burgh, then a young man, and very handsome. With very plausible manners, he contrived to disguise and hide a most corrupt and vicious nature. He was considered a man of very large fortune, and was a prodigious favourite with Lord Delamaine. I must now speak of my only sister. Alas! Alice Herringstone's life was a brief one, but you shall hear. At this period I was travelling over the Continent of Europe, and did not return to England till after the events I shall now record.

"There were but eighteen months' difference between Francis and Arthur Delamaine, and both brothers fell passionately in love with my sister Alice. My father was then alive; my mother had ceased to exist some years previously. Francis Delamaine was one of the handsomest men in England, singularly learned and accomplished; he excelled in everything, and yet, most unaccountably, was not his father's favourite. Arthur, though an amiable and fine youth, could in no respect compare with his brother.

"Francis Delamaine and myself were college companions; we were greatly attached, and from our boyhood we were both excessively fond of nautical pursuits. So fond of the sea, became Francis Delamaine, that after his return from college, he sailed in the Racehorse frigate, with the present Captain Ferris's father, a distant connection of the Delamaine family; was present during three severely contested actions, in which he eminently distinguished himself, and after two years returned to England, built a splendid yacht, and passed much of his time at sea. I ramble, my young friend, in my narrative, for many things and recollections crowd upon me. I said both brothers became about this time passionately enamoured of Alice Herringstone. She had just then returned to the castle, having passed the two previous years with a maiden lady of great accomplishments related to my mother. Alice was eminently lively and fascinating, yet simple and unaffected in manner and disposition.

"The brothers were not aware for some time that they were rivals. It was the wish of both Lord Delamaine and Lord Herringstone that my sister should be united to Arthur, the second son, and I believe, as far as ever I understood, my sister was willing to give her hand to him, for at that time she had not seen Francis as he was at sea in the Racehorse frigate.

"Being abroad myself, and my father dying, unfortunately, before my return I gleaned but few minute details of the unhappy occurrences that took place during that period.

"Whether she acted from persuasion or threats, or conscious that she at first consented to become the wife of Arthur Delamaine, I never knew; but there is no doubt of the fact, that Alice went to the altar with Arthur and that just as the ceremony was about to commence Francis Delamaine burst into the chapel of Milton Abbey with a dozen sailors, and carried off my sister. Furious with rage and disappointed love, Arthur Delamaine seized a cutlass, and fiercely attacked his brother before he got clear of the chapel, and might have slain him, had not he caught a cutlass from one of his men. In defending himself, so several eye-witnesses declared, Arthur, in his blind fury, rushed on his brother's sword, which passed through his body and he fell, as it was then supposed mortally wounded. In a transport of rage and agony for his favourite son, the old lord cursed his eldest born. Alice Herringstone had fainted, and in this state was borne to the water's edge, put on board a boat and rowed to Francis Delamaine's yacht, which lay off the shore, and the next moment the yacht got under weigh. It is said she reached Jersey, where they were married, but sailing from thence, from that time to this, neither ship, crew, nor Francis Delamaine, nor my unfortunate sister, have ever been heard of."

"Good heavens!" exclaimed Francis, "what a strange and fatal termination; the yacht must have foundered at sea, and all perished."

"No, I do not think so," returned Lord Herringstone; "the yacht might have suffered shipwreck, but I do firmly believe neither Francis Delamaine nor Alice Herringstone perished. I think they survived, were married, as reported, and that you Francis De Burgh, are their son."

Our hero, though he suspected or imagined something of the sort, or that his father might have been a near connection of the Delamaine's, yet never for a moment dreamt he was the elder brother of the late Lord Delamaine.

"I have no doubt," continued Lord Herringstone, seeing our hero buried in serious reflection, " that you yourself entertained some such idea; is it not so?"

"It is true, my lord," said Francis De Burgh, "that from the period I perused part of my lamented father's letters, and afterwards become so strongly persecuted by Sir Godfrey De Burgh, together with the robbery of my father's papers, I came to the conclusion in my own mind that I stood some way or other in the way of his son's succession to the Delamaine title and estates. Still, even that view of the case appeared so wild and improbable, that I should most likely have abandoned and banished such thoughts and surmises from my mind had not I discovered the actual robber of my father's papers, as a Captain Burton sent to propose a duel for an imaginary insult he said I had inflicted on Sir Godfrey De Burgh."

"I have not heard that incident in your life," eagerly interrupted Lord Herringstone, " a most convincing argument, however, that my surmises are facts; pray relate it."

"I refrained from doing so before, my lord, because knowing the connection existing between Sir Godfrey De Burgh and the Delamaine family, I felt loath to broach so glaring a statement."

Our hero then detailed that circumstance and a few others not known to his lordship.

"Ah, there is not a doubt of it, my poor boy!" said his lordship, most affectionately laying his hand on our hero's, and pressing it. "You are my nephew—poor Alice's child! The law may not prove you such, but my heart does; the first glance of your features struck me forcibly. I have no portrait here of your mother, but there are two, one as large as life in Herringstone Castle, the other a miniature."

As his lordship spoke the loud booming of cannons interrupted them both and caused them to start up.

"I should not wonder," said Lord Herringstone, "but that the guns are from the Thetis frigate, announcing the Governor's arrival. Let us go on deck, but remember, though we may not be able to renew this conversation for some time, remember I firmly believe you to be my sister's son, and as such I will acknowledge you to the world, let them think or say what they please; we may be baffled for a time to prove it, but Providence will yet unravel the mystery that shrouded the fate of Francis Delamaine."

Our hero was deeply moved by the words of Lord Herringstone; just then he recollected the advertisement he had seen in the *Times*, and at once communicated to his lordship the substance of it.

"This may, indeed, be important," said Lord Herringstone, as they gained the deck; "lose no time in writing to your solicitor, and request information may be forwarded to you here; and yet—no that will not do, for you may not return here for some time, for I think I can venture to tell you you will be ordered to Genoa. Write, however, and tell Mr. Howard to forward full information to me, and direct the letter to Genoa, for I am going there; thence I think, to Malta or Naples for the winter."

Francis was surprised, but the scene before them attracted particular attention, and caused them to pause in their conversation. It was a bright, brilliant moonlight, such a moonlight as southern climes alone can boast of; the vault above of a glorious purple blue, each star a luminary of itself, though diminished of its brilliancy by the splendour of a full moon. The giant rock was before them rising against the deep blue sky like a mighty bulwark of solid granite, while its deep dense shadows stretched far over the sleeping waters of the bay, for scarcely a breath of air floated over their surface. Around them lay at anchor the wooden walls of Old England, their towering masts tapering to the sky, and as they looked out over the waters a bright flash burst from the side of the Pompey, and then the thunder of its cannon, echoed from the rock, woke the sleeping inhabitants of the fortress from their slumbers, to let them know their new governor had arrived. Gun after gun pealed from the rock and from the shipping till the ear became stunned with the mighty uproar.

"I shall go and relieve fair Mary Grey from any further uneasiness about her father," said his lordship, "they must sleep soundly if this firing has not roused them, and, God bless you now, Francis. To-morrow I suspect will be a busy day in old Gibraltar; no doubt the Admiral will put to sea the day after."

Shaking our hero most affectionately by the hand, his lordship descended to the cabin, while Francis De Burgh, entering his boat, pushed off for the Daring. Sleep for several hours he did not, for his mind was too full of thought. Strange visions floated before his mind's eye, but they all vanished when the image of sweet Mary Grey came distinctly before him; her sunny smile banishing the wild visions that before haunted his mind, and thus getting calm and composed, her fairy fingers rested on his eyelids, and he slept.

## CHAPTER XXXIII.

Milton Abbey, the baronial residence of the Delamaine family, no doubt was built upon the spot where once stood an ancient religious house or abbey. However, at the period of our story, no remnant of the ruins of the ancient building remained.

The modern residence was spacious and commodious, and though much added to at different periods by its possessors, and each according to his taste, without exactly heeding the peculiar style of architecture he adopted, was an imposing and interesting edifice, though somewhat heterogeneous in its construction. It stood in the midst of a fine park, through which flowed a very clear, placid stream, emptying itself into the broad waters of Southampton river. From the windows of the mansion, fine views of that beautiful body of water were obtained through the vistas of the noble oaks that adorned the park. It had been magnificently furnished by the former Lord Delamaine, and contained one of the finest galleries of pictures in that county, or perhaps any county in England.

In the red drawing-room of Milton Abbey, about a week after the departure of General Grey and his daughter for Gibraltar, we request the reader to enter.

It was late in the evening; two gentlemen only occupied the apartment—Lord Delamaine and his father, Sir Godfrey De Burgh. A supper tray, with wine and glasses, covered the table, for the refreshment of Sir Godfrey De Burgh, who had only that moment arrived. The baronet, though he seemed somewhat disturbed in mind, helped himself to the delicacies before him, not forgetting copious libations of wine; Lord Delamaine, in the meantime, pacing the room backwards and forwards, seemingly in deep thought.

Having supped to his liking, Sir Godfrey looked up, and regarding his son for a moment, said:

"Of all persons, the most difficult to deal with or to convince is a man in love. Standing as you do, on the brink of a precipice of actual ruin, you yet persist, instead of putting your shoulder to the wheel, in following that will-of-the-wisp, Mary Grey. Whilst title and fortune are slipping through your fingers, you purchase a majority in a regiment of foot, in order to follow a girl to Gibraltar, who, if you had a ducal coronet to offer her, would reject it."

"We take quite a different view of this case, sir," returned Lord Delamaine, sitting down and helping himself to wine; "I think, with the father's approbation, which I feel satisfied I can have, Miss Grey will yet accept my proposals, especially now that the great stumbling-block to my hopes is effectually removed."

"Ah," said the baronet, "so you think that the cursed bungling job of Barlow has succeeded—you and he would overrule me. Pray did you read this morning's paper—I mean the *Times?*"

"No, I did not," returned Lord Delamaine, looking a little more serious. "It is over there on the table. I only returned from Winchester a couple of hours before your arrival. Our regiment leaves to-day for Portsmouth to embark for Gibraltar."

"Just give me the paper," said Sir Godfrey, "and I will read you the article that caused me to leave London in such a hurry."

Lord Delamaine handed his father the paper, and then Sir Godfrey read out the advertisement offering one hundred pounds reward for any information respecting the strange disappearance of Mr. Francis De Burgh, concluding the article where it stated that most important intelligence required Mr. De Burgh's instant attention.

"What can this mean?" said Lord Delamaine, rather startled.

"Why, what I always suspected," returned Sir Godfrey, "that the infernal bungling of Barlow has caused this. He pretends to excel in schemes, and yet, with his pistol within a foot of his victim's head, missed him; and then, having obtained all the papers and documents of importance, entrusts them to the keeping of one of his agents, instead of carrying them himself. Until now he believed the rascal that made away with them was shot, or perished in some bog-hole; but this advertisement leads me to imagine that some information concerning these papers has been given to this London solicitor, in reply to his advertisement some time back, a similar advertisement to the one in the Dublin paper. Now if these papers are found, the game is up. Francis De Burgh could have been easily put out of the way in Ireland during the rebellion, as easily as you would knock a puppy-dog on the head; but here in England it is not so easily done. I wished that he should have been handed over to one of those schooners fitting out for the slave trade; he would have been kept under the hatches till clear of the coast; thus, if the fever did not kill him on the African coast, we should at all events be clear of him for several years; instead of which, the vagabond crimper sold him to a press-gang. Do you know where he is now?"

"No," returned Lord Delamaine, "though of course if pressed, he must be on board a man-of-war."

"Just so. I have traced him to the Hannibal, 74; which sailed to join in the blockade of Cadiz."

"Well, so far," put in Lord Delamaine, "that is satisfactory; he may be shot as well as another."

"Yes," interrupted Sir Godfrey, "and escape like another, tell his story to the commander, and at once get released; and return to this country and claim his rights, if the papers are in the hands of this Mr. Howard."

"Now there is but one thing to be done," continued the baronet after a pause, "I will not commit myself any further in futile attempts on his life. My agents have all mismanaged the business, and this country is not like Ireland, convulsed to the centre by rebellion, offering a fine opportunity for getting rid of a troublesome customer. All that is passed; now we must act with extreme caution. I have got rid of that blustering coward, Brian Maguire. My plan of bringing about a duel with him was defeated by the cool determination of this almost boy, laughing at both his and my threats. To do him justice, he has a most determined spirit, and is not to be bullied by anybody; and few men, I can tell you, could contend with him in bodily strength and vigour."

"I should like to have him at twelve paces, for all that," said Lord Delamaine savagely, who prided himself on being one of the best shots in England.

"Better let him alone there, Herbert," returned the baronet, helping himself to wine enough to overturn the equilibrium of any moderate drinker; but they were drinking days, those, and Sir Godfrey had a capital head. "When I was in Dungarvon," continued the baronet, "I heard it said that Francis De Burgh was a most extraordinary shot; and he is as cool as a lettuce, so let him alone in that way, should you ever meet again."

"Well, sir, you have said a great deal on this subject," remarked his lordship, pettishly, "and as yet I have not heard how you intend to proceed. Recollect I leave England in three days at the farthest."

"Oh, yes, I am quite aware of that, Herbert," returned the father, with one of his sneering laughs, "and you think to return with the accomplished Miss Grey as a wife. You will discover your error by-and-bye, and be very thankful that your father has an eye to business, while his son has only an eye for a petticoat. Come, listen to me seriously, and I will show you what we can do to save ourselves from I may say almost destitution and ruin, should you lose the title and estates. My property in Ireland is mortgaged to the amount of twenty-three thousand pounds, its full value, if not more. My paternal estate of Parkhurst owes forty-seven thousand eight hundred pounds, and is worth about thirty-six thousand pounds, so you see that when both properties are sold, which they must be before the year is out, I shall not be worth one farthing."

"I should think, sir," exclaimed Lord Delamaine bitterly, "that you had little consideration for your son and heir, when you loaded your estates with such debts."

"Ah, Herbert, do not reproach me," said the baronet, with a very mocking, heartless laugh, " I am convinced of the error of my previous life, and am now anxious to repair that error. My present plan is for you to raise on the Delamaine estates a sum of eighty thousand pounds, for the laudable and ostensible object of freeing your worthy father from his liabilities; you will thus gain a most amiable notoriety, while, at the same time, you are putting by a handsome income, in case of the Delamaine estates being claimed."

His lordship looked very gloomily at his worthy sire, as he asked:

"And what security have I that my amiable parent may not find a way of getting involved again? Besides, though I do not pretend to know much of law, it strikes me that, should I lose the title and estates, the new claimant could seize your property."

"Ah, you are cleverer than I thought you were, and I give you credit for your foresight; but, most happily, those who framed the law, left plenty of loopholes by which to creep out of its clutches. All that I will carefully look to; I will also execute a deed, leaving myself no power to raise any further mortgage on the property, so that you may succeed to the estates as my heir, totally unencumbered."

"But supposing, after thus encumbering the Delamaine estates with a mortgage of eighty thousand pounds, that this should turn out a false alarm, or Francis De Burgh get shot?"

"Well, even supposing such a case," returned the baronet, coolly, "The rent-roll of the Delamaine estates in England and Ireland amounts to about thirty-five thousand pounds a year; there will still be a fine yearly income, besides the estates we clear of the encumbrances. After all, for a man not really entitled to a shilling, you are very fastidious, Herbert. Now look on the other side of the question. You remain a major in a foot regiment, your sole support your pay. It is my firm belief that those papers are found, and that we shall not be able now to keep this young man out of the title and property. Fortunately, he can have no manner of proof against me. Barlow has gone to America, after being paid the sum he so cursedly ill deserved; that last transaction of his with young Sir John Herbert finished him; he will show his face no more in this country."

Lord Delamaine remained silent for some time, apparently gloomy and disturbed. At length he looked into his father's face, saying:

"Let it then be as you say. Raise this money if you can; but I cannot be detained beyond to-morrow. I must sail from Portsmouth before three days are past."

"You need not be detained beyond a few hours to-morrow. Come up to town with me, and in an hour my solicitor will arrange matters so that the money can be raised without your presence being required. You may depend, Herbert, after risking body and soul for your advancement, and the attainment of the Delamaine estates and title, I will not commit an act that will not be for your future prosperity, in case we are ousted out of the estates. You are running after a false lure, while, by marrying Miss Probert, you can secure as handsome a woman as Miss Grey, and with a fortune of thirty thousand pounds just left her, as you already know, by her uncle, who died lately in Calcutta."

"How can I, sir, marry a woman," returned Lord Delamaine, "that has played so false a part as Helen Probert? She has betrayed every secret of Mary Grey's heart, professed an ardent friendship and love for her, and—"

"Bah!" interrupted Sir Godfrey, with a shrug of the shoulders and a laugh, "what will not a girl do that is in love? You tempted her to act the part she did: she betrayed Mary Grey because she desired to prove to you that you had not the slightest chance of gaining her affections; and at that time she was not mistress of thirty thousand pounds. Take my advice, throw up your commission, make Ellen Probert Lady Delamaine while you can. By this marriage, and raising the eighty thousand, you secure a brilliant destiny, despite the frowns of the fickle goddess."

"I will try my fortune with Miss Grey first," replied Lord Delamaine, in a determined tone; "I do not mind her first refusal; perseverance and her father's commands may do much; if not, why Helen Probert is not a bad spec after all."

"The fact is, Herbert," observed Sir Godfrey rising, "you pursue Mary Grey because you are haunted by the phantom of her becoming your rival's wife. Helen Probert told you that Mary Grey confessed to her that Francis De Burgh was dearer to her than all the world, and this rankles in your heart; it is not your love that urges you on, but the desire to supplant your rival in every way."

Lord Delamaine's cheek was very pale as he turned and looked his father sternly in the face.

"You have discovered my motive, sir, at last. You are right, and I will," he passionately added, "pursue it to the death! He shall never possess the hand of Mary Grey while I live, if I have to shoot him at the altar!"

"Hate is stronger than love—I always thought so," muttered Sir Godfrey, half aloud.

And without many more words, father and son separated for the night.

## CHAPTER XXXIV.

ACTING up to his declared determination, three days after the conversation related in our last chapter, Lord Delamaine sailed with a detachment of his regiment for Gibraltar, leaving his father full power to raise the eighty thousand pounds on the Delamaine estates.

Sir Godfrey had several interviews with his solicitor, Mr. Hill, a gentleman not very scrupulous in his practice, and who for years had assisted Sir Godfrey in his schemes for raising money.

Mr. Hill eagerly undertook the task of raising eighty thousand pounds on the Delamaine property, though being an extremely clever attorney, and knowing his client well, he was rather staggered at the idea of raising eighty thousand pounds on a noble, unencumbered property, to pay off mortgages on estates not really worth any thing like the sum raised on them. He observed to the Baronet that it was not a good outlay of the money; that he had better let the estates be sold, and get some one to purchase them; they would sell infinitely below the amount due.

"Very good," replied Sir Godfrey; "get the eighty thousand pounds first; we can then easily make our calculations."

"Well," returned the solicitor, "I will put a feeler in the papers, that such a sum is wanted, at four per cent., &c., and I will try my private parties at the same time. There is no doubt about getting the money; the Delamaine estate in Hampshire alone is worth double the sum; but I must have access to the title deeds, &c."

"I leave it all to you," said Sir Godfrey; "but as to the four per cent., my son would not scruple to give five to expedite the affair."

As soon as Mr. Hill was left alone, he laid down his pen, and began seriously to reflect; he was a sharp, shrewd man, and not easily deceived. Quite aware that the baronet was capable of most unscrupulous actions, he began turning over in his own mind Sir Godfrey's probable motives for raising so very large a sum, encumbering a noble estate to free one already over mortgaged.

"There is some hidden motive in this proceeding," muttered the solicitor; "I must be cautious, though, to be sure, it is nothing to me, provided I merely act as an agent in the affair."

Three or four days passed, and several persons came forward, ready to advance the money required, and Mr. Hill had already selected his man, when one morning at breakfast, which he took by himself, as his family resided some few miles out of London, an article in the *Court Journal* startled him out of his quietude, and caused him to lay down the paper with an exclamation of

"God bless my soul! can there be any truth in this rumour?"

Mr. Hill a second time took up the paper, and again read the paragraph slowly and carefully. We take the liberty of looking over his shoulder, and give our readers the extract as we read:—

"It is confidently spoken of in the higher circles, that a claimant for the title and estates of the late Lord Delamaine will shortly appear. We do not know whether our readers may remember or not the circumstance we shall now relate. Some twenty or one and twenty years ago, the Honourable Francis Delamaine, elder brother to the late lord of that name, carried off the only daughter of the late Lord Herringstone, of Herringstone Castle, Hampshire, just as she was on the point of bestowing her hand upon the late Lord Arthur Delamaine, in obedience to her father's command, although it is said she was devotedly attached to the elder brother, one of the handsomest and most accomplished gentlemen in England; embarking in the Honourable Francis Delamaine's yacht, they left the shores of England, and were never heard of from that period till the present time. Arthur Delamaine went abroad for many years, and on his return he assumed the title, his father being dead. Never having married, at his death Captain De Burgh, son of Sir Godfrey De Burgh—who married the late Lord's sister—succeeded to the title and splendid estates of the Delamaine family, as next heir; but now it appears, at least, so says rumour, that there exists a son of the Honourable Francis Delamaine, born in wedlock; that he is an extremely accomplished young man, and actually at this moment serving in the fleet under the command of the gallant Sir James Saumarez. This appears quite a romance, but nevertheless has a great appearance of truth in it. It is also said that most important documents and papers, proving the rights of this claimant to the title and property of the Delamaines, are actually in the possession of an eminent London solicitor; the truth or falsehood of this strange story will very soon be made manifest to the public; in the meantime, we refrain from any opinion on the subject."

"God bless my soul!" exclaimed Mr Hill, "this is extraordinary; there's some truth in this, I'll swear; here's the secret of raising the eighty thousand pounds; by Jove! it won't do."

Just then a loud knock at the street door was heard, and in a few minutes Sir Godfrey De Burgh entered the room.

Mr. Hill started to his feet, and although he welcomed the baronet with an attempt at cordiality, his manner, notwithstanding all his efforts, was constrained.

"Any thing wrong, Mr. Hill," inquired Sir Godfrey, looking keenly into the solicitor's face. "I thought you had fixed upon the lender, and that no obstacles were in the way, but you look disturbed."

"Well, in truth, Sir Godfrey, so I am; there is no denying it," returned the solicitor. "Pray did you cast your eyes over this morning's *Court Journal?*"

"No I did not," replied Sir Godfrey with a sudden start; "why?"

"Pray read that article," observed the solicitor, handing the baronet the paper.

Sir Godfrey took the journal, and it was very evident to the keen eyes of Mr. Hill, that he turned very pale as he read; still he continued to the end without any observation, and by the time he finished he had regained his composure.

"This is a very scandalous piece of gossip for such a paper as the *Court Journal* to permit in its columns; a most unfounded rumour. What! after twenty years, a claimant is said to be in existence to the Delamaine estates! No one will heed such trash. You do not suppose, Mr. Hill, that such a paragraph will affect our loan?"

"Upset it altogether, Sir Godfrey," replied his solicitor. "No man in his senses would lend eighty thousand pounds on the Delamaine property after reading such a paragraph."

Sir Godfrey De Burgh stood for an instant with his hands clenched, and his lips pressed hard, and then spoke:

"Do you mean to say, Mr. Hill, that because of this cursed libellous article, you will not pursue this loan further?"

"No, Sir Godfrey, no," exclaimed the solicitor, anxiously; "I do not say so; neither did I mean any such construction to be put on my words. I mean to say that if the lender has read that paragraph, he will draw back until he becomes convinced that there is no foundation in this rumour."

"Zounds!" interrupted the baronet, passionately; "how is such nonsense to be refuted? This report must have been purposely inserted."

"For what object, Sir Godfrey?" inquired the solicitor, more and more convinced that there was some truth in the article, and in such a newspaper also. "The Court paper would not take such an article from a private individual for insertion."

"I will contradict it, and defy any one to prove there is the slightest truth in such a libellous article."

"It is merely a rumour said to be afloat amongst the higher circles, Sir Godfrey, and cannot be called a libel."

The baronet paced the chamber violently agitated; a loud summons at the hall door caused him to pause.

"I expect Mr. Timmins, the solicitor for the lenders," said Mr. Hill. "I will have him shewn into the drawing-room, and if you will have the patience to wait half an hour, I will let you know the result of my interview."

"Mr. Timmins, sir," said the solicitor's clerk, entering the room.

"Very good; shew him up-stairs, William," said Mr. Hill, while Sir Godfrey threw himself into a chair, and took up the paper, and appeared to be perusing its contents, but his mind and thoughts were elsewhere. This unexpected *contre-temps* disturbed and rendered him furious; in fact, his position was critical. He had exhausted all his resources; it is true his son had paid off some thousands that pressed, and stopped important creditors, on succeeding to the title and property; but such was his fearful extravagance and debts, notes of honour, gambling debts, etcetera, that his prospects were desperate, unless he secured this eighty thousand pounds; and so utterly unpriucipled and vicious was this man, that from the very first he never contemplated paying off oue fraction of the encumbrances he spoke of to his son, but intended to appropriate the whole, and; leave England for ever he well knew his son would finally lose the title and property.

In half an hour Mr. Hill re-entered the room; Sir Godfrey De Burgh looked anxiously into his features, and at a glance perceived that nothing very agreeable had passed between Mr. Timmins and Mr. Hill.

"Well, sir," said Sir Godfrey, sharply, "what passed between you and the agent?"

"Why, the fact is, Sir Godfrey, in a loan of such a magnitude as we propose the lenders are very cautious; Mr. Timmins read the article in the *Court Journal*, and he declares he is startled by it, and uutil this matter is cleared up he would not feel justified in proceeding in the business."

"And do you tell me," passionately exclaimed the baronet, his face inflamed with rage, "that the editor of the *Court Journal* is not liable for the iusertion of an article so ruiuous to my son's prospects?"

Mr. Hill looked fidgety and perplexed, saying: "Why really it is very distressing, aud if untrue—"

"It!" repeated the baronet, with a savage curse, "and do you dare to insinuate that so d——d a falsehood has any truth in it?"

Mr. Hill started back with a very pale cheek; he was aware that Sir Godfrey was of a fiery passionate nature, but his look and manner at that moment were so truly diabolical, that he lost his nerve aud became for the instant paralyzed.

The baronet seized his hat exclaiming, still highly excited: "I will see what the editor of this cursed paper will say for himself. By Heavens! I'll horsewhip the coat off his back if he does not give me satisfaction for the libellous article he has dared to insert iu his paper."

Leaving the room, without a word of opposition from the astounded solicitor, Sir Godfrey proceeded in an exceedingly excited state of mind to the office of the *Court Journal* newspaper, and sending up his card requested to see the editor; he was shown into a sitting-room, handsomely furnished, and in a few minutes an extremely gentlemanly man about forty-five entered the room. By this time the baronet had in a measure conquered his passion, and the calm self-possessed manner and gentlemanly bearing of the editor, caused a still greater lull.

"I called upon you, sir," began Sir Godfrey De Burgh in a calm tone, "for an explanation of a paragraph in this day's edition of the *Court Journal*."

"Oh," interrupted the editor, "I can guess the paragraph to which you allude, having received your card; and, curiously enough, not half an hour ago, I had a letter from a solicitor of eminence and long-standing in this city, with respect to that paragraph."

"Well, sir, and pray what does this solicitor say about a paragraph that might have a ruinous effect upon the prospects of the present Lord Delamaine."

"The letter, which I have no objection to show you, Sir Godfrey," returned the editor coldly, "says, should any gentleman, or any inquiry be made concerning the rumour now generally talked over in the higher circles, and which appeared in to-day's paper, that he is quite ready to show convincing proofs that the rumour is no rumour, but a positive fact; that he holds documents, papers, and letters, belonging to the late Lord Delamaine's brother, the Honourable Francis Delamaine, which proves that a son of his is in existence, and, therefore, of course, the rightful heir to the title and estates."

Sir Godfrey De Burgh was annihilated, prostrated, and quite unable for a moment to reply, till the editor rising, said:

"You must excuse me, Sir Godfrey, my time is precious."

"You said the letter was from a solicitor, a Mr. Howard; may I request his adress?"

"Certainly, Sir Godfrey: No. 14, Welbeck Street."

The baronet rose from his seat, bowed stiffly to the editor, and left the chamber, crushed, his mind bewildered, and all the evil passions of his nature roused to desperation. The recovery of the papers, though he knew nothing of their contents, was a total annihilation of his son's prospects. A week or two earlier, the knowledge he had now gained might have been turned to profit; now he was lost. A terrible determination took possession of his mind; he would yet succeed or perish.

In this mood and temper of mind we must leave Sir Godfrey De Burgh, and in our next chapter return to Gibraltar.

## CHAPTER XXXV.

The 24th day of ⸺ was, in truth, a day of incessant bustle, activity, and enthusiastic ardour in old Gibraltar; for news had arrived that the combined fleets—Spanish and French—were preparing to leave the Bay of Algesiras, and Sir James Saumarez, even in the imperfect state of his fleet, perhaps to sail out of Gibraltar, and give them battle.

Francis De Burgh, during the three previous days, had been constantly employed, for the little Daring was fitted out as a schooner; and so expeditiously did all hands on shore and afloat work, aided by the materials, masts, spars, and sails being all ready, that at the expiration of the three days she was fully masted and rigged, and made a remarkably beautiful vessel,—still armed with her long 18-pound carronade ar a swivel gun, and her four 12-pounders, besides two brass swivels on her bow.

The morning of the fourth day he was summoned to the Admiral's ship, and shortly after was admitted into the presence of Sir James Saumarez.

Our hero stood several minutes in the presence of the Admiral unnoticed; Sir James was sitting at a table covered with papers. At length he looked up, and regarding the young skipper, said:

"Are you ready for sea, Mr. De Burgh?"

"In an hour, Sir James," returned our hero.

"Very good; you have been very active in changing your rig; you will find your little craft much more manageable now. To-morrow, please God, we will engage the enemy. As you can be of no use, keep out of range, but follow the fleet. Wait the result of the engagement, so as to be able to know to which side God gives the victory. Take this sealed despatch" (the Admiral's secretary handing a rather bulky one, in a sealed bag), "and make the best of your way to Genoa; there you will, no doubt, find Admiral Duckworth, with seven sail of the line. Should he not, however, be in Genoa, you will be sure to find him in Malta; give him personally these despatches, and state the result of to-morrow's battle, and remain at his orders. Now get ready for sea without a moment's delay, and attend to the signal to weigh, to-morrow;" and with a slight salutation the Admiral resumed his dictation to his secretary, and our hero, bowing, retired, rather surprised at the orders he had received, and not altogether relishing the insignificant part he had to play, and the prospect of his long separation from fair Mary Grey. But he had no time for idle lamentations over what was inevitable, he was so actively and unceasingly employed in getting in provisions, ammunition, &c.

The Admiral had hoisted his flag on board the Audacious, despairing of the Cæsar being able to complete her repairs. But her gallant commander, Captain Brereton, after a short speech to his crew, so inspired them that they vowed they would work day and night, and that she should be ready for sea by the morrow.

Francis could not leave his schooner for a single moment; but just before dusk he was able to warp her out from the mole, and let go his anchor within a very few yards of Lord Herringstone's yacht, the Gem.

About nine o'clock a boat from the yacht came alongside, with a request from Lord Herringstone that if our hero could spare half an hour, he wished to see him. Jumping into the boat, Francis, having nearly completed his work, was pulled to the yacht.

"You have been very expeditious, my dear boy," said Lord Herringstone, affectionately pressing his hand as they met. "I thought it scarcely possible you could be ready for sea tomorrow."

"Neither should I, my lord, but the masts, sails, and materials of the condemned Warspite were exactly fitted for me. An accident in launching rendered her useless unless redecked; and so, to expedite matters, I got all her materials."

"Have you heard where you are to proceed to?" demanded his lordship.

"To Genoa, my lord, or perhaps to Malta, with despatches for Admiral Duckworth, and to remain under his orders."

"Ha! so I thought. I dined yesterday with the Governor and Admiral Saumarez, and I assure you, you were highly spoken of. The Admiral said a great deal about your gallantry at that affair of the gun-boats at Cadiz. But when do you sail?"

"My orders are, my lord, to follow the fleet into action; but," added our hero, with a smile, seeing his lordship look serious, "but to keep out of range of the enemy's guns. The fact is, I am to carry the result of the contest to Admiral Duckworth."

"Yes, I have no doubt that is the purport of your following the fleet. Well, now I must tell you my arrangements. I intend sailing at once for Genoa; I am now as well armed as when I started from England; and propose proceeding to Leghorn, lay up the yacht there, and pass the autumn and winter in Florence. But I have a new arrangement to surprise and delight you with: Miss Grey and her attached friend, Mrs. Pearson, will accompany us."

Francis coloured to the very temples with surprise and delight.

A quiet smile was on the features of Lord Herringstone, as he said:

"I thought, Francis, your heart would beat the quicker on hearing this intelligence, and, moreover, I have General Sir Edgar Grey's consent to your addressing his beautiful and most amiable daughter."

The young man could make no reply, he was perfectly overpowered; he could only press the hand of his lordship with feelings of gratitude and affection.

"You see, Francis, the General is quite aware of all the circumstances of your situation, and like myself has not a shadow of doubt with respect to your birth. From several conversations he had with the late Lord Delamaine, he also felt satisfied his lordship strongly suspected, or actually knew, you were his nephew. However, though this mystery may not be cleared up for some time, you are both extremely young, and Sir Edgar Grey, for several reasons, has entrusted his daughter to my good spouse's care till his governorship ends; he does not like Gibraltar, an essentially military depot, as a residence for her, neither does he like the climate. She will therefore proceed with us, and pass the winter in Florence; in the spring we return to England.

"Now it is neither the General's wish nor mine that you should continue your naval career longer than fulfilling this mission of Sir James Saumarez; and I think I may tell you that on joining Admiral Duckworth, you will receive permission to resign the command of your little craft, when you can join us in Florence for a couple of months, and then proceed to England, and see what important matter caused Mr. Howard to insert such an advertisement. Now, does all this arrangement meet your views and wishes?"

"Oh, my Lord, how can I express to you the feeling of intense happiness your words have impressed upon my heart? My most sanguine hopes are more than fulfilled, and I only trust that a life devoted to the happiness and felicity of Miss Grey will prove that the noble generosity of her father, in consenting to my addressing her, is not unworthily bestowed."

"I will answer for you, my dear boy," replied Lord Herringstone, warmly. "When you return to England, Herringstone Castle must be your home. I have told Sir Edgar that I will settle five thousand a-year upon you at once, so that, though you may not recover your rights, you will still be enabled to appear in the world as the nephew of Lord Herringstone."

Francis was in truth overpowered; his voice trembled with emotion, as he endeavoured to express his feelings; but his noble patron would not admit that there was anything in his conduct or generosity beyond the claims he naturally had upon him, as the only child of his sister Alice.

"Now say no more on that subject, for it's settled; and I have more news for you. Captain, or rather Major De Burgh, for I will not call him Lord Delamaine, arrived yesterday, in the Bulldog transport, with part of the —nd Regiment. This, no doubt, has added to Miss Grey's desire, much as she loves and regrets to leave her father, to quit Gibraltar. What hope the Major can have of gaining Miss Grey's hand is mysterious to me; the daughter rejects him, and her father left her quite free, at that time, to accept or refuse him. Now, he would not listen an instant to his proposals. I shall be anxious to see the papers from England to-morrow; there may be something of interest in them."

"It is thought we shall put to sea to-morrow, my Lord. Captain R——— is firmly of opinion that we shall, for an advice boat brought in intelligence that the large ships had warped out from under the batteries, and there appeared every preparation made for getting under weigh."

"I trust in God the result will be favourable to the flag of Old England!" exclaimed Lord Herringstone; "but Sir James Saumarez must fight under every disadvantage. Now, if the weather continues fine, which it is reasonable to expect it will at this season of the year, I can easily wait the result of this intended engagement. Once clear of the Straits, I could lie to, and watch you pass, at night carrying light signals, such as we may fix upon."

This proposition delighted our hero amazingly; he should thus sail for Genoa in company with the Gem. His schooner, being a remarkably fast craft, would, with a little management, easily keep up with the yacht; indeed, he doubted not that she would outsail her.

"You must come ashore early, Francis," said Lord Herringstone, for the hour was getting late, and our hero rose to retire, "as the Governor expressed a most anxious wish to see you again before your departure."

"Anyhow you please, my Lord. As you pass the schooner, I shall be ready to accompany you."

And shaking his lordship's hand affectionately, Francis returned on board the Daring. He found Master Burke pacing the deck, whistling a tune to pass time, sometimes stopping to have a chat with Bill Mullaghan, who gloried in the little Daring.

"Well, Master Burke, whistling for want of thought, eh?" inquired our hero, putting his hand on the youth's shoulder.

"Faith! no, not from want of thought, sir, but from disappointment."

"You do not pretend to have fallen in love, Ned?"

"Oh, by the powers, I leave that kind of work, sir, to skippers and marine officers. A midshipman's love is like—. What is it like, you old porpoise?" added the mid, turning to Bill, who he knew was a prodigious favourite with his skipper as well as with himself.

"Be gor, Master Burke, a midshipman's love is very like his appetite—very voracious."

"Well, what disappoints you, Ned, if it is not love?"

"A love of gunpowder, sir. I'm told we're to follow the fleet, but the deuce a chance of a shot at the Don have we; we are to keep out of range; we are only to smell powder this time."

"Who the deuce told you this piece of news, Ned?" demanded our hero, a little surprised at his knowing the order given.

"Fat Captain D———, of the Marines, told me, sir. He was on board the Admiral's ship and heard it mentioned, and he said, with a sigh:

"'I envy your skipper, Master Burke; not that I dislike a bit of a scrimmage, but you see, after an affair of the kind, such as we expect to-morrow, not a mouthful of decent food is to be had for eight-and-forty hours; and I'm told you live deuced well on board that little craft of your's.'

"'Oh, don't we?' said I, in reply; 'we had a splendid dish of turtle yesterday.'

"I left the stout Captain D——— rubbing his chin with a very dismal face."

"And yet, though he is a bit of a gourmand," said De Burgh, laughing, "there's not a more gallant, high-spirited officer, I am told, in the fleet; so now I wish you a pleasant watch, Ned. Good night!" and our hero descended into the cabin.

"And so, Mister Burke," said Bill Mullaghan, "you think you'll only smell powder to-morrow. Tare and nouns! do you think our skipper is a man to snuff gunpowder like a lady's scent bottle? Be jabers! we'll be in the thick of it, somehow or other; and faix! the old girl," pointing to the swivel, "can talk French or Spanish as well as the best of them."

"Hurrah for the little Daring then?" chuckled the high-spirited lad, as he rubbed his hands in high glee.

Alas! in the thoughtlessness of youth, with as kind and affectionate a heart as ever beat, the midshipman, in his thirst for action, thought not of the widow and the orphan that to-morrow would render destitute and miserable.

## CHAPTER XXXVI.

As the enemy showed no intention of weighing anchor in the morning, Lord Herringstone called alongside the Daring in his gig, and our hero jumping in accompanied him on shore. The pier and landing-places were covered with people, and amidst a scene of indescribable bustle and apparent confusion, they proceeded through the anxious and excited crowd of men, women, children, and Jews, and in a short time reached the front of the Governor's residence, before which a portion of an infantry regiment was drawn up.

There were several officers, in a group, conversing at the entrance of Government House, and just as Lord Herringstone paused to speak to a Captain Haughton, an old acquaintance, Francis De Burgh's eyes met those of a tall officer in full regimentals. The recognition was mutual. The two candidates for Miss Grey's hand and the earldom of Delamaine had again met.

His lordship looked our hero steadily in the face, with a fierce hatred gleaming from his dark eyes; his cheek was pale from various contending emotions struggling in his breast; but his voice was perfectly composed, as, turning to a young officer by his side, he said aloud:—

"There is nothing like vulgar impudence and audacious impertinence for pushing a way in the world. There is an example," he added, directing the officer's attention directly to our hero.

This was too pointed, and too unmistakingly intended, for Francis to avoid noticing it. With a flushed cheek, he was walking up to his lordship, and no one can tell what might have occurred, when our hero's arm was grasped firmly by Lord Herringstone.

"Mr. De Burgh," said his lordship, speaking in a firm stern tone, "I pray you pay no heed to the intemperate and absurd words you have just heard. No man calling himself a gentleman would use such language; therefore the utterer is beneath your notice. Your duty at this moment belongs to your country. Come with me; you need not fear any one doubting your courage."

The tall and dignified figure of Lord Herringstone, well known to the officers present, and the words he made use of, struck all who heard them forcibly. Francis De Burgh felt the greatest difficulty in mastering his vexation; but Lord Delamaine walked close up to Lord Herringstone, and, with a face pale as death, said:—

"The words I made use of, my lord, I will repeat and will maintain. The name of De Burgh has been assumed by this person, under your lordship's protection, and I say publicly he has no title to any such assumption."

Francis would, in the heat of passion, probably have felled the speaker to the ground; but Lord Herringstone stepped before him, saying in a cold, haughty tone:—

"You are quite right, Major De Burgh; his proper name, when he assumes it, will be Francis Lord Delamaine, and you know it!"

Lord Delamaine fell back utterly confounded, while the group of officers stood perfectly bewildered by the strange and incomprehensible scene they had witnessed, and which they could not understand.

Lord Herringstone then, putting his arm within that of our hero, passed on without another word into the house.

"This is too bad!" exclaimed his lordship, as they proceeded towards the reception-room; "I did not think it possible that he would thus publicly give way to the evident hatred he experiences for you. Did you observe the start of intense pain, fear, and astonishment he gave on hearing my words? Nevertheless, Francis, great as the provocation is, it would not do for you to notice it. Your country's honour first—your private feelings after."

Before the young man could reply, for he was extremely agitated, the doors of the saloon were thrown open, admitting them into the great reception-room. Just then Lord Herringstone said in a low voice:—

"Nothing of this before the Governor."

Sir Edgar Grey was alone, and looking out of one of the windows that overlooked the bay. Turning round, he welcomed his lordship and our hero with great cordiality.

"I have not had a single opportunity, my young friend," said the governor, addressing Francis, "to thank you for the signal service you rendered to us all, by preventing the capture of his lordship's yacht. It would have been a sad business but for your strange but most opportune appearance; but as we shall have little time for conversation, I wish to ask you a question. Pray have you seen any of the last-arrived papers from England?"

"I was just going to ask your excellency if you had any near at hand?" replied Lord Herringstone.

"Here," said the governor, taking one from a case lying on the table, "the *Court Journal* of a tolerably late date, came last evening in the government despatch boat, along with letters and other papers."

Taking it up, he turned to the very paragraph which had caused the indignation of Sir Godfrey De Burgh, and handed it to Lord Herringstone.

"By Jove! this looks as if things were coming to a crisis," remarked his lordship. "I suspect, Francis," he added, handing our hero the paper, "that your solicitor, Mr. Howard, set this rumour afloat, to prevent, very likely, any fraudulent attempts upon the Delamaine estates. I conjecture the lost papers are found."

Just then the door from the governor's private apartment opened, and Mary Grey entered the room, looking lovelier than ever, for there was a bright smile on her beautiful lips, as she frankly placed her hand in that of the delighted Francis, saying:—

"So we are to have the pleasure of your company as convoy to Genoa. We shall now be a match for any piratical craft, if we should meet one."

"I trust, Miss Grey, that we shall not encounter any of those rovers. Your voyage to Genoa, however, proves that you are not afraid of again venturing on the great deep."

"Oh, there's no fear in Mary," replied the governor. "I do believe, if she had the command of the Gem, she would insist on taking her into action. You accompany the fleet, Mr. De Burgh?"

"I do, your excellency, but I regret only as a spectator."

"Why, I understood," said Mary, with a slight change in her tone and look, "that you were to escort us to Genoa, your mission being to that city; at least, Lady Herringstone said so this morning."

"Oh, so he will," said Lord Herringstone, with a smile, as he looked into the sweet features before him, the glow upon which rather increased; but the whole party were interrupted by the loud boom of a heavy gun. All started and hastened to the window; by accident or design, the two young people stood together, the sole occupants of one window, while Lord Herringstone and the governor sought another.

"The signal of 'prepare to weigh,'" said Francis De Burgh, in a low voice to Mary; "I must go." He gazed, his heart in his eyes, into Mary's face; she looked sad, but her eyes met his with so much confidence and love, that he impulsively took her fairy hand in his, whispering, as he felt it trembling in his grasp, "dear Mary, I have heard words this day from Lord Herringstone that have made me the happiest of human beings; you have long known my feelings, but I would have died ere a word should pass my lips, until permission was given. Do I pain you, Mary?"

"Oh, no, Francis," she uttered, in a trembling voice; "but promise me," and she tried to smile through her tears, "promise me you will not push that little Daring into a conflict you can surely have no part in."

"Then its commander may hope for Mary's prayers," said the delighted Francis, as he kissed the fair hand he still held.

Another gun startled them from their first dream of love, and Lord Herringstone called out:

"Now, Francis, you must be moving. The Admiral's flag is hoisted, and, after all, on board the Cæsar."

"Her gallant captain vowed it should," answered Francis, "and he has kept his word."

The governor held out his hand, and pressing that of our hero, said, with much affection:—

"My dear Francis, do not let your enthusiasm carry you into unnecessary peril; recollect you have some one now to care for you, therefore obey orders, but do not go beyond them."

One look at Mary's face, then pale enough with all her resolution, and our hero, with Lord Herringstone, left the Government House.

"We have little time for words, Francis," observed his lordship, as they hurried to the Mole: "perform strictly your orders, and remember, two bright lights at the mast-head, and two blue lights over the bow will be the signal, should you not make us before night-fall; you must not run back here to seek me; I will keep a careful watch; and now God bless you!"

The young sailor wrung his lordship's hand with much emotion, and then sprung into the boat that awaited him, and in a few minutes was again on the deck of the Daring.

There was no time for thought, for the scene before him absorbed all other feelings, dear as they were to his heart. It was certainly a glorious and inspiriting spectacle, such as he could scarcely have imagined. It was a bright, unclouded sky, the breeze blowing strong from the eastward; the enemy had moved out from Argesiras Bay, and had taken up, as it was reported, their position off Cabrita Point. The whole population of the rock swarmed out to behold the imposing scene; the Mole, the line wall, the batteries, and all the sides of the hill were covered with a dense crowd; to the ragged staff every inch seemed occupied. The Cæsar was warping out from the Mole, with her band playing, "'Tis to glory we steer," while the military band of the garrison answered with, "Britons, strike home." The vessel with the Admiral's flag hoisted, passed under the stern of the Audacious, and then up went the signal for the squadron to prepare for battle, and there was not a heart amid all those assembled that did not respond to the signal.

The crew of the Daring had their anchor up and stowed, and under her mainsail and jib alone, stood out into the bay.

"Oh, wouldn't I give five years of my life," exclaimed Ned Burke, "to stand on the deck of the Cæsar this day."

"Be gor, Mister Burke," replied Bill Mullaghan, who was performing some duty close at hand, "keep up your spirits, the day's not over yet."

"Hoisting more canvas, the Daring stretched in for the Spanish snore, keeping clear of the noble bulwarks of old England, as they majestically, under a cloud of canvas, swept on through the sparkling waters of the bay. He could hear the loud cheers from the shore, and see the hundred flags waving from the batteries and walls, and even from the house tops, as they quickly receded from the stern old rock, that so often had thundered forth defiance against the foes of Great Britain.

It was nearly three o'clock, p.m., and keeping according to orders at a certain distance, yet still quite near enough to distinguish every movement and signal flying, Francis De Burgh kept his attention almost exclusively fixed upon the Cæsar, which brought to off Europa Point, and each vessel, as she came up, closed round her. It became quite evident to our hero and his anxious crew that the battle could not commence before night, for at five o'clock the signal was made from the Cæsar for the other ships to closely observe the Admiral's motions after dark, and keep in close order of sailing. Master Burke, who had served as signal midshipman on board a seventy-four, and was a remarkably quick, intelligent youth, full of life and spirit, was now of great use.

"It will be a dark night, sir," he remarked, "before they close with those two huge Spanish ships. They said in Gibraltar that there were many of the young Spanish nobility on board them, being proud of their conquest, as they termed it, of the poor Hannibal."

"They may pay dearly, Ned, before morning for that little triumph. What ship is that closing with the Cæsar?"

"That is the Superb, sir, Captain R——, the fastest ship of the lot."

"I thought so," replied our hero. "Keep us away a little," he added, turning to the quarter-master, who stood by the helm; "it is getting rapidly dark."

Notwithstanding the darkness, they could see huge ships looming through the gloom, and the land still quite visible. An hour afterwards they observed a blue light from the Admiral's ship, and then they could perceive that she was running right alongside one of the great Spanish ships; the next instant a sheet of flame burst from her broadside; she had fired into the Spanish three-decker.

To the surprise of all on board, the Daring—for our hero could not conquer the intense desire he had to witness the engagement close—to their surprise, the Spanish ship wore round as her foremast fell over the side, and immediately ran foul of her consort, the Hermangelde. Almost simultaneously a vast sheet of fire burst out between the two Spanish three-deckers, who were evidently entangled; and in an incredible short time the two monster ships were enveloped in a fearful sheet of flame. The cause of this terrible and horrible catastrophe Francis did not learn till long afterwards; we, however, explain the cause here. Thrown into confusion by the broadside of the Cæsar, and her fore top-sail falling over the guns as she by a most extraordinary oversight, actually mistaking the vessel she ran foul of, opened fire upon the Real Carlo; the flames spread with awful rapidity, so much so that the

Cæsar with great difficulty got clear of them, as they flew with lightning speed to the mast-head of each vessel; the sight, terrible in its grandeur, lighting up the whole sea around them with a crimson glare. Francis De Burgh beheld, with a nameless horror, two ships one-hundred-and-twelve-guns each, with above two thousand men in them, become entirely surrounded by the devouring element. He could almost see to pick up a pin where he stood upon the deck of the Daring. The waves rippling under a strong breeze, appearing like a sea of gold, the masts, sails, and spars of the different ships looking like pillars of the same metal, or rods of glowing iron. Our hero could not but shudder at the thought of so horrible a catastrophe, for the very shouts and screams of the devoted Spaniards, left to their fearful doom, pealed through the air. So near did the Daring stand towards them, keeping to windward, that several of her shots went over them, and they could even feel the heat of the flames. Hundreds were throwing themselves frantically into the glowing waters, and perished alongside. Down came masts and yards, crushing and slaughtering the wretched crowd, for not a single ship attempted to help the sufferers. Much as our hero wished to succour the doomed crews, he dared not go to leeward of them, and soon after his attention was called to the battle between the other ships, then going on furiously, and with a firm determination to retrieve the failure of the previous fight, the British Admiral dashed at the San Antonia, which afterwards struck to the Superb. De Burgh, by going in stays, with some difficulty avoided being run down by the Thames, and just then one of the one-hundred-and-twelve gun ships blew up with a terrible explosion, scattering human bodies, spars, and all kinds of materials far over the troubled sea, and in ten minutes after the other also exploded, with a terrific shock; a huge piece of spar, as the Daring tacked in their direction, fell across the deck with great violence, carrying away the back-stays, and smashing several yards of the bulwarks, but fortunately not injuring any one.

At this period the wind rose, and it began to blow extremely hard, forcing our hero to take in a couple of reefs, his large mainsail, and stand in shore; he could just make out several vessels, blazing away into each other with incredible rapidity and animosity. Before morning, however, the wind fell, and when daylight came, all on board the Daring anxiously looked around them after the terrible night they had passed. To the dismay of our hero, he beheld the Venerable, seventy-four, Captain Hood, ashore upon the Pedro Shoals. The Daring was then close up with the Cæsar when a signal was hoisted for him to come alongside, which he immediately did. His orders were to run in close to the Venerable, his light draught of water allowing him to do so with impunity, and say that the Admiral's orders are, if Captain Hood thinks fit, to withdraw his men from the ship, and destroy her. The Cæsar then made all sail, five of the enemies' ships being visible, coming up from the westward; she was followed by the Audacious, while the Thames lay to, to render assistance to the Venerable, if necessary.

The young commander of the Daring at once stood in for the Venerable, but in doing so was attacked by a Spanish brig of war of ten guns, that evidently had come out from Algesiras in the night to watch proceedings.

This was a formidable antagonist, for the little vessel, full of men, and apparently sailing remarkably fast, was carrying an immense press of canvas. The brig thought to pour a broadside into the Daring, but in this attempt she signally failed owing to the cool judgment of our hero, and the great skill with which the old quarter-master handled the craft, for excepting a few splinters, one man slightly wounded, and a few sheets and tacks cut, the broadside was abortive.

"Oh, be J——! you'll catch it for that, my darlings!" exclaimed Bill Mullaghan with a cry, swinging round the swivel, while Master Burke, with the two twelve-pounders previously crammed with grape, brought them to bear just as the Daring crossed the forefoot of the Spanish brig as she hove in stays.

"Now, my lads," cried Francis De Burgh in an excited tone, "give it them!"

Bang went the three guns, the swivel loaded with three balls. Down came the foremast of the brig, with all her heavy hamper of sails, rigging, &c., and the next instant she struck her flag and surrendered.

Three cheers pealed over the deep from the crew of the Daring, but she still stood on for the Venerable, and as she passed close under the stern of the Thames, her crew gave a hearty cheer as she passed, while an officer on the quarter-deck, with a speaking trumpet, sung out—

"Well done, Daring! we'll send your prize into Gibraltar for you."

This officer was Lieutenant Gould, who had been seated next our hero at the dinner given by Captain R——, of the Superb, and a mutual liking sprung up between them.

Francis waved his hat in reply, and then stood steadily for the Venerable. As they approached they became exposed to the guns of the Formidable, but the Thames coming up drove that vessel after her consorts, whilst the Daring got quite close in with the Venerable, who thumped very hard, and then delivered his message.

Captain Hood declared he would get her off, but at all events," he added, "the enemy will never get her."

The Daring stood by, and was of infinite service towing the heavy boats out, with cables and anchors, and long before sunset, the Venerable, under a cheer that shook her old sides, was once

more afloat, and before the sun went down was going round Cape Trafalgar under jury masts.

This, indeed, is one of the most spirited actions on record, the enemy having lost three sail of the line; the two Spanish three-deckers, and all on board save about seventy souls, who escaped in the launch.

Having the next day ascertained the full particulars of the action, and repaired the damages he had sustained, De Burgh made sail for the Straits, and though the wind was right ahead, he made good way, owing to the set of the current to the eastward, which always runs rapidly into the Mediterranean.

then made all-sail, five of the enemies' ships being visible, coming up from the westward; she was followed by the Audacious, while the Thames lay to, to render assistance to the Venerable, if necessary.

The young commander of the Daring at once stood in for the Venerable, but in doing so was attacked by a Spanish brig of war of ten guns, that evidently had come out from Algesiras in the night to watch proceedings.

This was a formidable antagonist, for the little vessel, full of men, and apparently sailing remarkably fast, was carrying an immense press of canvas. The brig thought to pour a broadside into the Daring, but in this attempt she signally failed owing to the cool judgment of our hero, and the great skill with which the old quarter-master handled the craft, for excepting a few splinters, one man slightly wounded, and a few sheets and tacks cut, the broadside was abortive.

"Oh, be J——! you'll catch it for that, my darlings!" exclaimed Bill Mullaghan with a cry, swinging round the swivel, while Master Burke, with the two twelve-pounders previously crammed with grape, brought them to bear just as the Daring crossed the forefoot of the Spanish brig as she hove in stays.

"Now, my lads," cried Francis De Burgh in an excited tone, "give it them!"

Bang went the three guns, the swivel loaded with three balls. Down came the foremast of the brig, with all her heavy hamper of sails, rigging, &c., and the next instant she struck her flag and surrendered.

Three cheers pealed over the deep from the crew of the Daring, but she still stood on for the Venerable, and as she passed close under the stern of the Thames, her crew gave a hearty cheer as she passed, while an officer on the quarter-deck, with a speaking trumpet, sung out—

"Well done, Daring! we'll send your prize into Gibraltar for you."

This officer was Lieutenant Gould, who had been seated next our hero at the dinner given by Captain R——, of the Superb, and a mutual liking sprung up between them.

Francis waved his hat in reply, and then stood steadily for the Venerable. As they approached they became exposed to the guns of the Formidable, but the Thames coming up drove that vessel after her consorts, whilst the Daring got quite close in with the Venerable, who thumped very hard, and then delivered his message.

Captain Hood declared he would get her off, but at all events," he added, "the enemy will never get her."

The Daring stood by, and was of infinite service towing the heavy boats out, with cables and anchors, and long before sunset, the Venerable, under a cheer that shook her old sides, was once

more afloat, and before the sun went down was going round Cape Trafalgar under jury masts.

This, indeed, is one of the most spirited actions on record, the enemy having lost three sail of the line; the two Spanish three-deckers, and all on board save about seventy souls, who escaped in the launch.

Having the next day ascertained the full particulars of the action, and repaired the damages he had sustained, De Burgh made sail for the Straits, and though the wind was right ahead, he made good way, owing to the set of the current to the eastward, which always runs rapidly into the Mediterranean.

"'Sir,' replied the young woman, with a voice trembling with emotion and agitation, 'I am; but I require no compensation, and would not receive any other reward than Mr. Francis De Burgh's thanks for worlds. All I can say to you, sir, is this: they fell into my hands honestly, but in a strange and singular manner. In this letter,' and she drew a sealed one from her bosom, 'all is explained; it is directed to Mr. De Burgh, and I trust in God you will, before long, be able to give it him, and that he will be in safety and in health. Now, sir, if you will send your clerk with me, I will deliver to him the papers and documents, fourteen in number. In two hours I quit London for Gravesend, where the ship that is to carry me to America lies.'

"I was surprised, my lord, fascinated, and no little annoyed, that I could not, by any persuasion, induce 'the lady to take the reward. With a calm, sweet smile, she bade me adieu. I sent my confidential clerk with her; when he returned, he stated that she was evidently a married woman, had two lovely children, mere infants; was in extremely comfortable private apartments, and had a comely Irish girl for an attendant. As I strictly desired my clerk, a most respectable, kind-hearted man of middle age, he asked no questions about her, but received the fourteen papers, and, calling a hackney coach, returned to me with them. You may be sure, my lord, I was fidgety and anxious to examine them. It will be quite sufficient to say here that they fully prove Mr. Francis De Burgh to be the only son of the then Honourable Francis Delamaine, whose wife was the Honourable Alice Herringstone; they were married in Jersey, and immediately afterwards sailed from thence. I have not read over the private memorandum of Lord Delamaine's life, because I consider it would not be correct; I have sealed this up for the special perusal of the son. Amongst the papers is the marriage certificate; and now all that is wanting is that of the birth of the son, the time and place, and witnesses. All this, no doubt, is explained in Lord Francis Delamaine's memoirs; but, having ascertained sufficient to convince me that Mr. Francis De Burgh is the real Lord Delamaine, I managed to spread a rumour to that effect, and which was noticed in the papers. Since that, finding out that Sir Godfrey De Burgh was attempting to raise a sum of eighty thousand pounds on the Delamaine estates, I took effectual steps to stop any human being having anything to do with the matter. Now, my lord, you may perceive the necessity of your nephew returning at once to England, and asserting his claims; as little time as possible should be lost in such cases. Trusting that the importance of the matter will excuse this long letter, I await your lordship's communication anxiously. I also inclose the letter left by the unknown female, for your lordship's nephew, as I dare say you

are not far asunder. Hoping your lordship will enjoy your excursion, but will soon return to old England,
"I have the honour to remain,
"Your lordship's obedient servant,
"C. L. HOWARD."

"By Jove! this looks as if things were coming to a crisis," remarked his lordship. "I suspect, Francis," he added, handing our hero the paper, "that your solicitor, Mr. Howard, set this rumour afloat, to prevent, very likely, any fraudulent attempts upon the Delamaine estates. I conjecture the lost papers are found."

Just then the door from the governor's private apartment opened, and Mary Grey entered the room, looking lovelier than ever, for there was a bright smile on her beautiful lips, as she frankly placed her hand in that of the delighted Francis, saying:—

"So we are to have the pleasure of your company as convoy to Genoa. We shall now be a match for any piratical craft, if we should meet one."

"I trust, Miss Grey, that we shall not encounter any of those rovers. Your voyage to Genoa, however, proves that you are not afraid of again venturing on the great deep."

"Oh, there's no fear in Mary," replied the governor. "I do believe, if she had the command of the Gem, she would insist on taking her into action. You accompany the fleet, Mr. De Burgh?"

"I do, your excellency, but I regret only as a spectator."

"Why, I understood," said Mary, with a slight change in her tone and look, "that you were to escort us to Genoa, your mission being to that city; at least, Lady Herringstone said so this morning."

"Oh, so he will," said Lord Herringstone, with a smile, as he looked into the sweet features before him, the glow upon which rather increased; but the whole party were interrupted by the loud boom of a heavy gun. All started and hastened to the window; by accident or design, the two young people stood together, the sole occupants of one window, while Lord Herringstone and the governor sought another.

"The signal of 'prepare to weigh,'" said Francis De Burgh, in a low voice to Mary; "I must go." He gazed, his heart in his eyes, into Mary's face; she looked sad, but her eyes met his with so much confidence and love, that he impulsively took her fairy hand in his, whispering, as he felt it trembling in his grasp, "dear Mary, I have heard words this day from Lord Herringstone that have made me the happiest of human beings; you have long known my feelings, but I would have died ere a word should pass my lips, until permission was given. Do I pain you, Mary?"

"Oh, no, Francis," she uttered, in a trembling voice; "but promise me," and she tried to smile through her tears, "promise me you will not push that little Daring into a conflict you can surely have no part in."

"Then its commander may hope for Mary's prayers," said the delighted Francis, as he kissed the fair hand he still held.

Another gun startled them from their first dream of love, and Lord Herringstone called out:

"Now, Francis, you must be moving. The Admiral's flag is hoisted, and, after all, on board the Cæsar."

"Her gallant captain vowed it should," answered Francis, "and he has kept his word."

The governor held out his hand, and pressing that of our hero, said, with much affection:—

"My dear Francis, do not let your enthusiasm carry you into unnecessary peril; recollect you have some one now to care for you, therefore obey orders, but do not go beyond them."

One look at Mary's face, then pale enough with all her resolution, and our hero, with Lord Herringstone, left the Government House.

"We have little time for words, Francis," observed his lordship, as they hurried to the Mole: "perform strictly your orders, and remember, two bright lights at the mast-head, and two blue lights over the bow will be the signal, should you not make us before night-fall; you must not run back here to seek me; I will keep a careful watch; and now God bless you!"

The young sailor wrung his lordship's hand with much emotion, and then sprung into the boat that awaited him, and in a few minutes was again on the deck of the Daring.

There was no time for thought, for the scene before him absorbed all other feelings, dear as they were to his heart. It was certainly a glorious and inspiriting spectacle, such as he could scarcely have imagined. It was a bright, unclouded sky, the breeze blowing strong from the eastward; the enemy had moved out from Argesiras Bay, and had taken up, as it was reported, their position off Cabrita Point. The whole population of the rock swarmed out to behold the imposing scene; the Mole, the line wall, the batteries, and all the sides of the hill were covered with a dense crowd; to the ragged staff every inch seemed occupied. The Cæsar was warping out from the Mole, with her band playing, "'Tis to glory we steer," while the military band of the garrison answered with, "Britons, strike home." The vessel with the Admiral's flag hoisted, passed under the stern of the Audacious, and then up went the signal for the squadron to prepare for battle, and there was not a heart amid all those assembled that did not respond to the signal.

The crew of the Daring had their anchor up and stowed, and under her mainsail and jib alone, stood out into the bay.

"Oh, wouldn't I give five years of my life," exclaimed Ned Burke, "to stand on the deck of the Cæsar this day."

"Be gor, Mister Burke," replied Bill Mullaghan, who was performing some duty close at hand, "keep up your spirits, the day's not over yet."

Hoisting more canvas, the Daring stretched in for the Spanish snore, keeping clear of the noble bulwarks of old England, as they majestically, under a cloud of canvas, swept on through the sparkling waters of the bay. He could hear the loud cheers from the shore, and see the hundred flags waving from the batteries and walls, and even from the house tops, as they quickly receded from the stern old rock, that so often had thundered forth defiance against the foes of Great Britain.

It was nearly three o'clock, p.m., and keeping according to orders at a certain distance, yet still quite near enough to distinguish every movement and signal flying, Francis De Burgh kept his attention almost exclusively fixed upon the Cæsar, which brought to off Europa Point, and each vessel, as she came up, closed round her. It became quite evident to our hero and his anxious crew that the battle could not commence before night, for at five o'clock the signal was made from the Cæsar for the other ships to closely observe the Admiral's motions after dark, and keep in close order of sailing. Master Burke, who had served as signal midshipman on board a seventy-four, and was a remarkably quick, intelligent youth, full of life and spirit, was now of great use.

"It will be a dark night, sir," he remarked, "before they close with those two huge Spanish ships. They said in Gibraltar that there were many of the young Spanish nobility on board them, being proud of their conquest, as they termed it, of the poor Hannibal."

"They may pay dearly, Ned, before morning for that little triumph. What ship is that closing with the Cæsar?"

"That is the Superb, sir, Captain R——, the fastest ship of the lot."

"I thought so," replied our hero. "Keep us away a little," he added, turning to the quarter-master, who stood by the helm; "it is getting rapidly dark."

Notwithstanding the darkness, they could see huge ships looming through the gloom, and the land still quite visible. An hour afterwards they observed a blue light from the Admiral's ship, and then they could perceive that she was running right alongside one of the great Spanish ships; the next instant a sheet of flame burst from her broadside; she had fired into the Spanish three-decker.

To the surprise of all on board, the Daring—for our hero could not conquer the intense desire he had to witness the engagement close—to their surprise, the Spanish ship wore round as her foremast fell over the side, and immediately ran foul of her consort, the Hermangelde. Almost simultaneously a vast sheet of fire burst out between the two Spanish three-deckers, who were evidently entangled; and in an incredible short time the two monster ships were enveloped in a fearful sheet of flame. The cause of this terrible and horrible catastrophe Francis did not learn till long afterwards; we, however, explain the cause here. Thrown into confusion by the broadside of the Cæsar, and her fore top-sail falling over the guns as she by a most extraordinary oversight, actually mistaking the vessel she ran foul of, opened fire upon the Real Carlo; the flames spread with awful rapidity, so much so that the

Cæsar with great difficulty got clear of them, as they flew with lightning speed to the mast-head of each vessel; the sight, terrible in its grandeur, lighting up the whole sea around them with a crimson glare. Francis De Burgh beheld, with a nameless horror, two ships one-hundred-and-twelve-guns each, with above two thousand men in them, become entirely surrounded by the devouring element. He could almost see to pick up a pin where he stood upon the deck of the Daring. The waves rippling under a strong breeze, appearing like a sea of gold, the masts, sails, and spars of the different ships looking like pillars of the same metal, or rods of glowing iron. Our hero could not but shudder at the thought of so horrible a catastrophe, for the very shouts and screams of the devoted Spaniards, left to their fearful doom, pealed through the air. So near did the Daring stand towards them, keeping to windward, that several of her shots went over them, and they could even feel the heat of the flames. Hundreds were throwing themselves frantically into the glowing waters, and perished alongside. Down came masts and yards, crushing and slaughtering the wretched crowd, for not a single ship attempted to help the sufferers. Much as our hero wished to succour the doomed crews, he dared not go to leeward of them, and soon after his attention was called to the battle between the other ships, then going on furiously, and with a firm determination to retrieve the failure of the previous fight, the British Admiral dashed at the San Antonia, which afterwards struck to the Superb. De Burgh, by going in stays, with some difficulty avoided being run down by the Thames, and just then one of the one-hundred-and-twelve gun ships blew up with a terrible explosion, scattering human bodies, spars, and all kinds of materials far over the troubled sea, and in ten minutes after the other also exploded, with a terrific shock; a huge piece of spar, as the Daring tacked in their direction, fell across the deck with great violence, carrying away the back-stays, and smashing several yards of the bulwarks, but fortunately not injuring any one.

At this period the wind rose, and it began to blow extremely hard, forcing our hero to take in a couple of reefs, his large mainsail, and stand in shore; he could just make out several vessels, blazing away into each other with incredible rapidity and animosity. Before morning, however, the wind fell, and when daylight came, all on board the Daring anxiously looked around them after the terrible night they had passed. To the dismay of our hero, he beheld the Venerable, seventy-four, Captain Hood, ashore upon the Pedro Shoals. The Daring was then close up with the Cæsar when a signal was hoisted for him to come alongside, which he immediately did. His orders were to run in close to the Venerable, his light draught of water allowing him to do so with impunity, and say that the Admiral's orders are, if Captain Hood thinks fit, to withdraw his men from the ship, and destroy her. The Cæsar then made all sail, five of the enemies' ships being visible, coming up from the westward; she was followed by the Audacious, while the Thames lay to, to render assistance to the Venerable, if necessary.

The young commander of the Daring at once stood in for the Venerable, but in doing so was attacked by a Spanish brig of war of ten guns, that evidently had come out from Algesiras in the night to watch proceedings.

This was a formidable antagonist, for the little vessel, full of men, and apparently sailing remarkably fast, was carrying an immense press of canvas. The brig thought to pour a broadside into the Daring, but in this attempt she signally failed owing to the cool judgment of our hero, and the great skill with which the old quarter-master handled the craft, for excepting a few splinters, one man slightly wounded, and a few sheets and tacks cut, the broadside was abortive.

"Oh, be J——! you'll catch it for that, my darlings!" exclaimed Bill Mullaghan with a cry, swinging round the swivel, while Master Burke, with the two twelve-pounders previously crammed with grape, brought them to bear just as the Daring crossed the forefoot of the Spanish brig as she hove in stays.

"Now, my lads," cried Francis De Burgh in an excited tone, "give it them!"

Bang went the three guns, the swivel loaded with three balls. Down came the foremast of the brig, with all her heavy hamper of sails, rigging, &c., and the next instant she struck her flag and surrendered.

Three cheers pealed over the deep from the crew of the Daring, but she still stood on for the Venerable, and as she passed close under the stern of the Thames, her crew gave a hearty cheer as she passed, while an officer on the quarter-deck, with a speaking trumpet, sung out—

"Well done, Daring! we'll send your prize into Gibraltar for you."

This officer was Lieutenant Gould, who had been seated next our hero at the dinner given by Captain R——, of the Superb, and a mutual liking sprung up between them.

Francis waved his hat in reply, and then stood steadily for the Venerable. As they approached they became exposed to the guns of the Formidable, but the Thames coming up drove that vessel after her consorts, whilst the Daring got quite close in with the Venerable, who thumped very hard, and then delivered his message.

"Captain Hood declared he would get her off, but at all events," he added, "the enemy will never get her."

The Daring stood by, and was of infinite service towing the heavy boats out, with cables and anchors, and long before sunset, the Venerable, under a cheer that shook her old sides, was once

more afloat, and before the sun went down was going round Cape Trafalgar under jury masts.

This, indeed, is one of the most spirited actions on record, the enemy having lost three sail of the line; the two Spanish three-deckers, and all on board save about seventy souls, who escaped in the launch.

Having the next day ascertained the full particulars of the action, and repaired the damages he had sustained, De Burgh made sail for the Straits, and though the wind was right ahead, he made good way, owing to the set of the current to the eastward, which always runs rapidly into the Mediterranean.

## CHAPTER XXXVII.

As the little Daring beat to windward through the Straits, the weather being fine and clear, all hands were remarkably busy repairing the damages to sails and rigging, and the carpenter new planking the shattered bulwarks. The crew pulled remarkably well together; the spirit, kindness, and good fortune of their commander, made him greatly beloved. They were a remarkably happy set of fellows, worked willingly and well. They had their frolics at times, for we must confess the discipline was not of the strictest kind, but every rope and spar, every pin and brace, were in their places; she was scrupulously neat, and her decks, to use a common expression, fit to eat a meal upon.

Beside Ned Burke there was another midshipman on board named Thomas Thomas, a native from the land of leeks, and these two lads kept all alive with their pranks and humour. The Welsh lad vowed he could trace his ancestors back to one Ap-Thomas, in the reign of Shem, one of Noah's sons, and that at a wedding of one of his grandfathers, there were three hundred cooks employed.

"Oh, that's easily accounted for, Tommy, my boy!" laughed Master Burke, "for all the guests toasted their own cheese! But my grandfather's great grandfather's mother was a first cousin of St. Patrick, and for killing with the heel of her shoe the last toad on the green island, she was raised to the peerage; there's ancestors for you, Master Tommy!"

"Oh, be gor, gentlemen!" said Bill Mullaghan, as he sat near the middies splicing a block, "if you are talking of your posterities, be the pipers of war! I can beat you to smithereens!"

"Out with it, Bill," said the old quartermaster, who was fond of a yarn, "who was your grandfather's mother?"

"Oh, faix, be easy! the devil! The Lord save us, I didn't mean to call him neither; but the dickens a mother my grandfather ever had!"

"How do you make that out, Bill?" cried the Welsh lad with a laugh.

"Faix! he was born at sea, old ocean was his father, and, be gor! neither you nor I ever heard of his having a wife; but, oh, you may laugh, my darlings, but my real ancestor was a broth of a boy; he came to Ireland on a millstone!"

"On a mill-stone," shouted both the mids, "go it, my man; by the powers! you are improving; did he carry sail on it, Bill?"

"He did, be gor! so they say; I don't remember it myself, for, glory be, it was about two thousand years ago!"

"Oh, well; that was before the deluge," interposed the Welsh lad.

"Faix! to be sure it was, Master Thomas; how else could I get to windward of that ancestor of yours, Ap-Thomas, who lived under King Shem?"

"Well, let that be," interrupted the quartermaster, "but where did your ancestor come from? and what brought him on a mill-stone? the worst species of craft I ever heard of for the purpose of navigation?"

"Where he came from," continued Bill, "I can't tell you, for he spoke a queer lingo; but when he landed he had a huge skin under each arm which contained a white fine smelling liquor, which he gave the people to taste; this was whisky. The people were astonished, tasted it again, and before the two skins were finished, be gor! they made him King of Ireland, on his promising to teach them how to make whisky, and faix, thus my ancestor became the first King of Ireland, and the inventor of the best liquor in the wide world!"

"But, Bill, how do you account for a mill-stone floating?"

"Oh, faix, Master Thomas! those were queer times: there were no mill-stones in Ireland at that period, and my ancestor knew they must crush the corn to make whisky, so by some means or other he floated this mill-stone and brought it with him; there's a piece of the old stone still to be seen near our place, for we likes to keep in our remembrance the grandeur of our posterity. Now, Master Thomas, be gor! my ancestor flogs your Ap-Thomas to chalks!"

Francis De Burgh's thoughts, now that the excitement of the battle and its attendant circumstances were over, all centred upon Mary Grey, and the unexpected and unlooked-for prospect before him of gaining her hand. He felt intense anxiety, fearing he might run past the Gem yacht, and thus make the voyage to Genoa without falling in with his friends.

Determined that it should be no fault of his, he paced the deck during the whole night; in the day time he had no fear, as the weather was clear and bright. As soon therefore as they had passed through the Straits, he ordered a strict watch to be kept day and night for the Gem; the wind was still dead on end. Their progress, though assisted by the current, was very slow, though the Daring went rapidly through the water. Having gained the open waters of the Mediterranean during the night, and no lights to be seen during the remainder of the hours of darkness, our hero retired to rest just at daybreak, leaving Bill Mullaghan to keep a good look out.

The following day the weather was clear and beautiful, with a steady working breeze to the eastward. About mid-day they made out the top sails of a large ship. Young Burke ran up to the main cross-trees with his glass, and in a few minutes declared that he could swear it was the Gem yacht lying too; and in half an hour they made her out, and setting more canvas and hoisting their distinguishing flag, they stood towards her close hauled as she lay in shore of them.

In an hour's time they were observed by those on board the Gem, and the yacht immediately hoisted her own colours, and setting top gallant sails and a large jib, stood in for the Spanish coast.

"His lordship is going to try us on a wind, sir," said the old quarter-master at the helm, "but he will be beat in such weather I am sure; we sails like a witch."

The Spanish coast was quite visible, the high blue hills above Malaga dwindling away to a point, in the direction of Cape De Gatte. It soon became evident that the Daring gained upon the Gem, the sea being exceedingly smooth, the wind drawing off the coast as they approached. By three o'clock they were within gun shot, when the yacht went in stays, and having filled upon the other tack, backed her foretop sail to lay to, hoisting a signal at the mast-head.

"Run down, Ned," said the young commander, "and bring up the yacht code of signals his lordship gave us."

Down went the middy, and returning, our hero said, as he laid the book upon the companion:

"Turn to page nine."

"Here it is sir; blue, chequer, and red."

"What's that, master Ned?"

"Here it is sir, one of the best signals in the yacht code, 'Expect you to dinner.'"

"I agree with you, master Ned, so get yourself ready and I will take you with me."

In half an hour the Daring was within hailing distance of the yacht, the gig was lowered, and four hands put our hero and his midshipman alongside the Gem. In a minute more they were on the deck, and warmly welcomed by all the party.

The smile of gratified pleasure with which Mary Grey received our hero, made his heart beat with rapture, as he gazed with love and admiration into her beautiful and animated features.

"You have beat us in a surprising manner," remarked Lord Herringstone, "but the news—let us hear the news first of all, for I can see by your craft, notwithstanding fresh paint and new ropes, and a sail or two, that you have put your oar in amongst the big ones."

"We have gained a most glorious victory, my lord, this time; the banner of old England was signally triumphant."

He then gave his auditors a rapid but distinct account of the action, which delighted his lordship, and made her ladyship and Mary Grey shudder, as they heard his account of the burning of the two Spanish three-deckers. Shortly after they sat down to dinner, and a most agreeable three hours was spent in cheerful conversation; and then having settled with his lordship the course he intended to pusue, Francis De Burgh and Master Burke, who had become a great favourite with Lady Herringstone, returned to the Daring.

We shall not pursue the daily events of a voyage of seven days. The two vessels by skilful manœuvring kept each other in sight, and the eighth day, having had throughout the transit a fine favourable breeze, they made the harbour of Genoa, and before sunset were at anchor under the shelter of the west Mole. But to the exceeding regret of our hero not a single vessel of war lay in the harbour, saving and excepting a small ten gun brig, called the Vampire.

To this vessel De Burgh at once proceeded, and from her commander he learned that Admiral Duckworth had sailed three days previously for Malta, where he intended to remain till he received despatches from England. Our hero much chagrined, then pulled towards the Gem, for it was his intention, without an hour's delay again to put to sea, and follow Admiral Duckworth to Malta.

This determination was highly approved of by Lord Herringstone. It was his duty to lose no time, and though Mary Grey looked a little disappointed, still her high sense and feeling for her lover's honour, made even her voice second his lordship's.

"On reaching Malta, then," said his lordship, after much friendly advice and affectionate regulations as to his future prospects, "you will surrender your vessel and command into Admiral Duckworth's hands."

"Such is my intention," replied Francis, "but should Admiral Duckworth not be at Malta, I must follow his course till I come up with him."

"Yes," said Lord Herringstone, "such I believe is your duty. There were rumours you know in Gibraltar that England and Russia, being allies, England had an intention of sending a fleet to force the Turks to accede to the terms proposed by Russia. I trust you may not have to follow the Admiral with your little craft to the Bosphorus."

"I should not be at all surprised," said our hero with a gay smile, looking into the serious face of Mary Grey, and making light of the matter purposely; "I remember my factotum Bill Mullaghan used to say that he and I would like to see the world, he was tired of jolly Dungarvon. It seems we have contrived to see a portion of it, and likely to see more."

After some further conversation, the hour getting late, our hero with a most affectionate leave of Lord and Lady Herringstone, and whispering a few words that told all the feelings of his heart into the ear of poor Mary Grey, who did not at all like the thoughts of her lover's voyage in search of Admiral Duckworth, he with devoted affection kissed her hand and departed. The next morning he was under weigh for Malta, with a fine steady breeze off Tramontana.

The same day Lord Herringstone and family landed, his lordship having determined to pass a month in Genoa, having previously hired for that period one of the superb mansions in Strade Balbé, and which on his arrival he found in perfect readiness.

Genoa, at this period, was no longer the famous Republic; the French Revolution had swept away in its torrent Doge and Coenseller, and all its ancient usages. But it was still a great commercial city, and afforded to Lady Herringstone and her fair charge infinite pleasure in the inspection of the ancient and magnificent palaces, which had gained for it an unperishable name, "The city for kings."

Lord Herringstone was extremely anxious for letters from England, amongst which he hoped to receive one from Mr. Howard, Francis De Burgh's solicitor; but three weeks passed over before they arrived, when a rather ample supply of both letters and papers was placed in his hands. Anxious to learn what Mr. Howard had to say, he read that gentleman's letter first; it was rather a long one, but most satisfactory.

As it is necessary to the elucidation of some previous matters, we must trouble our readers with its contents:

"London, Welbeck St., —— 14th, 18—.

"MY LORD,—

"According to Mr. Francis De Burgh's instructions, I address this letter to you in Genoa. It gave me much gratification receiving his letter; for though I discovered that he had been pressed and sent on board the Hannibal, I remained ignorant of his future situation till the reception of his letter. I have now to inform your lordship of some proceedings I took in consequence of the restoration of most important papers, stated by Mr. De Burgh to have been stolen from his cottage in Dungarvon. The seals and fastenings of the letters and documents were all broken, and had evidently been several times perused, and that by persons not very particular in the handling. I have done the same as directed by Mr. De Burgh, when first we communicated, he having then authorized me to examine and read any documents that might fall into my hands, which was thought necessary in consequence of my having put advertisements in several papers, from which something might turn up of importance.

"I must now, my lord, briefly state how these important papers came into my possession.

"One morning, very shortly after the disappearance of Mr. Francis De Burgh, I was told a young lady wished to see me strictly in private; she was shown into my library. On entering, I perceived a most interesting looking female, simply but neatly attired; though pale, somewhat thin, and with an expression of sadness on her features, which, however, did not detract from her beauty. She hesitated a little in speaking at first, but her voice gained strength and firmness as she proceeded.

"'I have waited on you, Mr. Howard, in consequence of an advertisement I only this morning saw in a London paper. Had I not seen it, it was my intention to call upon some gentleman connected with the law, and whose character was unimpeachable; for what I have to say is most important with respect to the future prospects of a gentleman you know by the name of De Burgh—Francis De Burgh——'

"'Good heavens!' I interrupted eagerly, 'then you know something of his strange and unaccountable disappearance?'

"'In truth, sir, I do not; I regret to say.'

"I looked blank, my lord, at this reply. She immediately continued:

"'But the matter that now induces me to call upon you, sir, is to place in your hands a bundle of most important papers, stolen from Mr. De Burgh's cottage in the year '98.'

"'God bless my soul!' I exclaimed, starting to my feet, 'this is a discovery. Pray, madam, where are those papers?'

"'They are much too bulky, sir,' returned this very interesting young woman, 'for me to carry through the streets; they are at my residence, and, if you will send a confidential clerk of yours with me, I will deliver them at once to him. I sail to-morrow for America.'

"'Would to goodness, madam,' I replied, 'that Mr. De Burgh was here himself to thank you. Are you aware that five hundred pounds is offered for their restoration, and that you are entitled to that sum without a single question being asked concerning them?'

"'Sir,' replied the young woman, with a voice trembling with emotion and agitation, 'I am; but I require no compensation, and would not receive any other reward than Mr. Francis De Burgh's thanks for worlds. All I can say to you, sir, is this: they fell into my hands honestly, but in a strange and singular manner. In this letter,' and she drew a sealed one from her bosom, 'all is explained; it is directed to Mr. De Burgh, and I trust in God you will, before long, be able to give it him, and that he will be in safety and in health. Now, sir, if you will send your clerk with me, I will deliver to him the papers and documents, fourteen in number. In two hours I quit London for Gravesend, where the ship that is to carry me to America lies.'

"I was surprised, my lord, fascinated, and no little annoyed, that I could not, by any persuasion, induce the lady to take the reward. With a calm, sweet smile, she bade me adieu. I sent my confidential clerk with her; when he returned, he stated that she was evidently a married woman, had two lovely children, mere infants; was in extremely comfortable private apartments, and had a comely Irish girl for an attendant. As I strictly desired my clerk, a most respectable, kind-hearted man of middle age, he asked no questions about her, but received the fourteen papers, and, calling a hackney coach, returned to me with them. You may be sure, my lord, I was fidgety and anxious to examine them. It will be quite sufficient to say here that they fully prove Mr. Francis De Burgh to be the only son of the then Honourable Francis Delamaine, whose wife was the Honourable Alice Herringstone; they were married in Jersey, and immediately afterwards sailed from thence. I have not read over the private memorandum of Lord Delamaine's life, because I consider it would not be correct; I have sealed this up for the special perusal of the son. Amongst the papers is the marriage certificate; and now all that is wanting is that of the birth of the son, the time and place, and witnesses. All this, no doubt, is explained in Lord Francis Delamaine's memoirs; but, having ascertained sufficient to convince me that Mr. Francis De Burgh is the real Lord Delamaine, I managed to spread a rumour to that effect, and which was noticed in the papers. Since that, finding out that Sir Godfrey De Burgh was attempting to raise a sum of eighty thousand pounds on the Delamaine estates, I took effectual steps to stop any human being having anything to do with the matter. Now, my lord, you may perceive the necessity of your nephew returning at once to England, and asserting his claims; as little time as possible should be lost in such cases. Trusting that the importance of the matter will excuse this long letter, I await your lordship's communication anxiously. I also inclose the letter left by the unknown female, for your lordship's nephew, as I dare say you

are not far asunder. Hoping your lordship will enjoy your excursion, but will soon return to old England,
"I have the honour to remain,
"Your lordship's obedient servant,
"C. L. HOWARD."

## CHAPTER XXXVII.

As Lord Herringstone sat, after the reading of Mr. Howard's letter, greatly surprised and astonished, though at the same time highly gratified, Lady Herringstone and Miss Grey entered the room; they had just returned from visiting the gorgeous saloons of the Brinoletti Palace.

"You are just in time," said his lordship, "to hear most important intelligence; this is Mr. Howard's letter we so anxiously wished for. I wish Francis was here, instead of running after the flying Dutchman, Duckworth."

Mary Grey looked anxious, and her cheek flushed as Lady Herringstone said:

"Are the tidings satisfactory?"

"Most satisfactory," returned his lordship; "but judge for yourselves," and he read aloud Mr. Howard's letter.

"Ah!" exclaimed Mary, with the tears in her eyes, as she listened to the part concerning the unknown female, "I know who she is."

"Who?" inquired Lord Herringstone in evident surprise, for his lordship did not know the minor adventures of our hero as well as Miss Grey did.

She, however, with a slight tremor in her voice, replied: "That female must have been the daughter of the great Irish insurgent leader, Holt; she married a Dublin barrister, who afterwards joined the United Irishmen, under his father-in-law."

She then proceeded to explain how her lover became acquainted with her, the slight service his humanity prompted him to perform for her, and her consequent gratitude.

"Well, upon my word!" said Lady Herringstone, "this nephew of our's is quite a hero of romance. What became of the Irish leader, Holt? I remember seeing some account of him in some magazine not very long ago."

"Oh, Holt was a most remarkable man," replied his lordship; "he had some extraordinary escapes, but I believe he managed through the medium of Mrs. Latouch to surrender, and was finally dismissed to Botany Bay."

"I trust his daughter's husband managed to escape," said

Mary, "for Mr. de Burgh spoke highly of him. By his young wife going with her children to America, I strongly suspect and hope he has taken refuge there."

"This letter to Francis, would doubtless explain all," remarked his lordship. "But I do not feel justified in opening it."

"Oh, not for worlds!" exclaimed Mary, with a heightened colour; "poor thing, she intended it for him, and him only."

Lord Herringstone looked affectionately into the fair girl's excited features, saying, as he handed her the letter: "Then, Mary, I give it into your charge; some time or other, no doubt, you will surrender your liberty into his hands, you can then give him the letter."

Mary's till then pale cheeks rivalled the peony as she received the letter, and then his lordship took up some of the others, and the ladies, leaving him to their perusal, withdrew to talk over the interesting intelligence they had just received.

In the evening, his lordship remarked, as he handed a paper to Mary Grey: "You will be surprised, Mary, to see amongst the departures from England, for a winter's residence in Italy, your fair friend, Helen Probert."

"Indeed! how strange; it is quite possible then that we may meet in Florence, as the Florentine States are in perfect tranquillity," remarked Mary Grey, reading the announcement. "The mother and younger sister accompany her, I see; her sister was rather delicate, and it is to restore her health, I suppose, they leave England."

"Well, it is a wonder," said Lord Herringstone, "that Helen Probert, with her beauty and now fine fortune, has not yet changed her single state of blessedness; she is no longer in her *premiere jeunesse;* is it fair, Mary, to inquire the lady's age?"

"Oh, she is quite young still, replied Mary, "Helen is not more than six and twenty."

"Well, really," remarked Lady Herringstone, "I shall be glad to renew our acquaintance with the fair Helen; she is very lively, very handsome, and very witty."

"Then more is the wonder," laughed Lord Herringstone, "with all these accomplishments in one scale, and thirty thousand pounds in the other, that she still keeps her liberty. I thought I heard that Major De Burgh, before he saw your sweet face, Mary, was one of the fair Helen's most devoted admirers, I mean at the Cape."

Mary blushed as she answered: "You heard that report, my lord, from my dear father."

"No, indeed," returned his lordship, "Mrs. Pearson, whom, I am sorry to tell you, has not recovered the effects of our voyage, told me that he really was attached to her, and she to him."

"How very strange," said Mary; "Helen always appeared to

me to amazingly dislike Major De Burgh, and I never myself, during our long voyage home from the Cape, ever saw him pay her any marked attention."

"Certainly not, Mary, with you in the ship; it was long before your arrival at the Cape. At that time I do not believe it was surmised that he was next heir to the title and the Delamaine estates, for it was generally believed that the late Lord Delamaine had married an officer's widow in Ceylon, and had two sons living. How this false rumour reached England, I cannot say, but for several years it was believed; indeed, I myself thought it was true. There is a great deal of mystery in the life of the late Lord Delamaine's brother Francis; what became of the yacht, and all on board her, how he himself and my sister escaped, where his son was born, and where my poor sister died, is all a mystery to us; but I suppose a perusal of his life so strangely recovered will clear up all that is dark and mysterious."

"I have no doubt," observed Lady Herringstone, to her lord, "that the strange and terrible scene that took place when Francis Delamaine carried off your sister, made a powerful impression on a sensitive mind like his. Then, again, the loss of the yacht with its crew, for they must have perished; and then the death of your sister, all preyed, no doubt, on his spirits, and caused him to resign his title and live secluded from the world."

"It puzzles me to think," observed Lord Herringstone, "from whence he drew his resources for so many years, for Francis declares he had always a command of money, was generous, liberal, and charitable to all the poor in his vicinity. Ireland at that period was little visited by English visitors, and in the remote district he resided, his seclusion was complete."

"It was a melancholy, and much to be regretted event," said Mary Grey, with a serious expression of countenance, "the affections of both brothers centring on the same lady; no doubt the after life of both was entirely influenced by the unhappy results that followed that circumstance."

Ten days after this conversation, the Gem yacht, with Lord Herringstone and party, sailed from Genoa, and a few days afterwards the family were most delightfully located in the ———— Palace, in Florence; the views from the back windows of which embraced a most beautiful and varied prospect across the waters of the classic Arno, over a country rich in cultivation, and blooming in every species of aromatic and odoriferous plants.

A month passed pleasantly enough. The society of Florence consisted of many families of rank and wealth from England, while the Florentine nobility, and the Grand Duke himself, not only mingled in the aristocratic circles of England, but vied in rendering their city agreeable to the wealthy foreigners visiting it. The Grand Duke gave at times sumptuous entertainments; and, as the winter advanced, great hunting parties to the immense range of forest between Pisa and Florence, and which formerly was abundantly stocked with wild boars, for the especial amusement of the Duke and his court.

At the expiration of the month, Miss Grey began to feel a little anxious. No tidings had reached them direct from her lover; but intelligence had been received by Lord Herringstone from England, that Admiral Duckworth had sailed with a fleet, to bombard Constantinople, if the Turks did not accede to the Russian proposals. An English paper also announced the retirement of Lord Delamaine from the army, and his lordship's return to England.

"I greatly fear," remarked Lord Herringstone to the thoughtful Mary, "that Francis again missed Admiral Duckworth's squadron at Malta, and has followed him to the Dardanelles; but excepting that the delay is vexatious, there is nothing alarming in that supposition, Mary. There will be no fighting; the Turks will not expose their city of Constantinople to a cannonade."

The beauty, grace, and accomplishments of the English girl, created quite a sensation in Florence, whilst the rank and wealth of Lord Herringstone rendered him an object of attraction to the English residents, who felt honoured by an invitation to his palace, as he entertained in a magnificent style. His lordship and family also visited, and were invited often to the private suppers of the Grand Duke.

One morning, they were all surprised by the arrival of the Proberts in Florence, from Milan. The meeting of Mary Grey and Helen Probert, was exceedingly agreeable to both; Mary was really attached to Miss Probert, and apparently the attachment was mutual.

Mary felt rejoiced at her arrival; she had now a friend, who was aware of her attachment to Francis De Burgh, and now that they were lovers with the consent and approbation of her father, she had no reserve in her communications with Helen.

Mrs. Probert rented handsome apartments in one of the large mansions in the Corso. The beauty of her daughter, and the knowledge that the lady possessed thirty thousand pounds fortune, created another sensation amongst the English cavaliers residing there.

One evening, the two friends sat in Mary's private apartment; it was the first time they had had a couple of hours absolutely to themselves. Lord and Lady Herringstone were at the ducal palace, where Mary had declined going, and Mrs. Pearson was writing in her own room; so that the friends were completely left to a comfortable chat with each other.

"I have a great deal to say to you, Mary," began Helen; "I know the state of your little heart, and, indeed, I feel so rejoiced that the difficulties that were in your way when we parted in England, are removed. What a noble, generous heart your father must have, to bestow his only and cherished child upon a man without fortune; and, indeed, you may say, without a name. Handsome, noble, brave, and accomplished as he is, still Mary Grey had a right to look for a match amongst the magnates of the land."

Mary changed colour several times, during Helen's rather strange address; but she very calmly replied:

"Whether Francis De Burgh possessed a name or not, that circumstance could make no manner of difference with me as regards my affection, Helen, and that you know. But such is not the case; he has a name, an honourable and a high name, and I trust he will assert his right to it shortly. At all events, since he left England, he has earned a name amongst the gallant and the brave, if he possessed no other!"

"Now you are half offended with me, Mary," returned Helen playfully, and putting her arm round her friend's neck, she kissed her affectionately, continuing, "but you misunderstand me. You know when we parted at Herringstone Castle, I knew but little of Mr. De Burgh's private history; I knew you loved him, and that he idolized you in return. You acknowledged there was a mystery about him; but you did not like speaking on that subject. Now, a most strange rumour has spread amongst the higher circles in England. It states that the present Lord Delamaine has no right to the title and estates he holds, and that a son of the late Lord Delamaine's elder brother is in existence. Now, in turning over many thoughts in my mind, and recollecting the mystery about Francis De Burgh, his bearing that name, and some other observations I made, I came, Mary, to the conclusion that Francis De Burgh is the expected claimant to the Delamaine estates. Now am I right, Mary love?"

"Yes, you certainly are, Helen," returned Mary; "on this subject I can have no reserve with you. Indeed, on the return of Francis De Burgh from his present expedition, he will proceed at once to England, and assert his claims to the title and estates of his father, who was the elder brother of the late Lord Delamaine."

"Was Major De Burgh, or rather the present Lord Delamaine, for of course till he is proved not to be the heir, he remains so, —was he aware of this when you saw him in Gibraltar?"

"I think he has been aware of it for some time; indeed, I fancy from the very first meeting with Francis, on board the British Queen."

"It is very strange," mused Helen; "his lordship has, I see, resigned his commission, left Gibraltar, and returned to England; this will be a great blow to him, but more especially to his father, Sir Godfrey De Burgh."

For a couple of hours the two friends continued to converse upon a subject deeply interesting to both; but when Helen bade adieu for the night, Mary, as she sat thinking over the conversation that had passed between them, reflected very seriously upon some of Helen's observations, and for several hours she could not rest, puzzled by a feeling of distrust that, despite of her reasoning to the contrary, came across her mind, with respect to Helen's feelings towards herself and towards Major De Burgh.

The winter, nevertheless, rolled on, and still no tidings of Francis, further than a letter which reached them, dated from Malta, and which, though it explained the cause of his long absence, was still unsatisfactory. He stated that he reached Malta thirty-six hours after the departure of Admiral Duckworth, that he felt obliged to follow him, and should accordingly sail for the Dardanelles and Constantinople; but he fully expected to come up with the Admiral before his arrival there.

There were no steamers in those days, and news travelled slowly in comparison; therefore, whether the Turks would accede to the terms proposed by England or not, would not be known for some time in Florence, and Lord Herringstone was resolved to sail for England the first week in April. Mary Grey had received several letters from her father, and she was rejoiced to hear that he was not only well, but he stated that owing to certain political reasons, he would be able to resign his governorship before the following June, and return to England. This was delightful intelligence to our heroine, and greatly raised her spirits. A letter also from Mr. Howard to Lord Herringstone, informed them that he had effectually prevented Sir Godfrey or his son raising money on the Delamaine estates, but he pressed for the return of Francis De Burgh to England. Sir Godfrey and his son were in Ireland. Thus all parties, about the beginning of March, were intensely anxious for some intelligence from the east, and from our hero.

Mary and Helen still continued great friends; the latter, in a great measure, had done away with the impression she had made upon our heroine's mind. The weather was, for March, exceedingly beautiful, and the greatest pleasure to both seemed talking together, and taking evening excursions on the Arno. With two boatmen in the gaily decorated barges kept for the purpose of water excursions, the two girls were sometimes accompanied by Lady Herringstone and Mrs. Pearson. They usually allowed the boat to drop down the stream, drifting only with the current, while they enjoyed the delicious scenery of its banks, and the infinite and beautiful variety every turn of the river presented.

Lord Herringstone was at Leghorn, getting his own yacht prepared for sea, intending an excursion to Naples previous to sailing for Gibraltar, *en route* for England.

"This is a lovely evening," said Helen to Mary, as they walked together towards the Bridge of the Trinity, the handsomest of the bridges that span the Arno. "Suppose we take a sail down the stream to Little Lastrá, and back through the beautiful gardens of Count Ambrograna, now thrown open to the public."

"I should like it very much," said Mary; "but we have come out without Mrs. Pearson, or a single attendant."

"Oh," returned Helen, "we are able to take care of ourselves for a distance of two miles, and this is not a part of the world where any risk is incurred by being alone. We will take old Jerome's boat; he can land us at Lastrá, and the walk back will be delightful through the Count's gardens."

Mary allowed herself to be persuaded, and descending the steps to the river, they found the old boatman dozing under his awning. In a few minutes they were gliding down the placid stream towards Lastrá.

The stream of the Arno at that period of the year is extremely gentle, and the two girls, chatting and regarding the beauties of the landscape, were wafted gently onward. It was not their intention to go so far as Lastrá, which is about four miles from Florence, but to disembark at a landing place called Little Lastrá, about two miles down the river; from thence it was scarcely a mile back to Florence, through a continued pleasure-ground, open to the public, and remarkable for its beauty of arrangement.

Just as the little barge turned an abrupt angle in the stream, a four-oared boat shot suddenly out from the bank, and before old Jerome could avoid the shock, ran foul of the barge. A faint exclamation of alarm escaped Mary Grey's lips, as two men sitting in the stern of the strange boat leaped into the barge.

"What is the meaning of this rude treatment?" exclaimed Helen, indignantly.

The men were attired as common boatmen, but without a word of reply, they suddenly threw a boat cloak over the person of the amazed Mary, and lifting her up, despite her struggles and stifled cries, bore her into the boat, and the four men applying themselves to their oars, shot down the river with amazing rapidity.

## CHAPTER XXXVIII.

Though half suffocated, and painfully distressed by the manner in which she was held, Mary Grey yet remained perfectly sensible, and quite alive to the strange and terrible position in which she was placed. In less than half an hour, she was conscious the boat stopped, and then she felt herself lifted out and carried a short distance, and placed in a vehicle of some sort, which was instantly set in motion, and moved with great rapidity; and then a voice said in Italian:

"If you will remain quiet, Signora, I will relax this mantle and leave you to sit upright, though you must still keep the mantle over your face."

The poor girl felt the oppressive tightness of the mantle relax, as she replied:

"I have no desire to be otherwise than quiet, though such cruelty is shameful."

"I have no desire to treat you cruelly, Signora," said the same strange voice, "you will meet with no further rough usage."

Mary made no reply; she felt the tears of bitter vexation running down her cheeks, and she trembled to think of her situation; neither could she imagine or conjecture the cause of her abduction, or guess at who could be the instigator. The carriage continued at a very rapid rate over a very rough road for quite an hour, without a word being spoken by the person beside her; the vehicle then stopped, she imagined to change horses, and then it proceeded as rapidly as before.

Good God! thought the miserable and terrified maiden, where can they be taking me? Another hour as well as she could guess passed, and then the carriage again paused. She felt the mantle gently lifted from off her person, and she perceived that it was night, and that more time had passed on the road than she had calculated. She could only perceive that there was a man beside her, and that he threw open the door of the carriage and jumped out. The vehicle was a kind of berlin, with leather curtains at the sides, rendering it quite dark within, and in trembling anxiety she drew back one of the curtains and looked out. She perceived three figures earnestly conversing close by, and about fifty yards off she could see a broad glistening of water, which she thought must be the river. There were no houses or signs of habitation as far as she could see; but presently one of the figures came away from the others, and approaching the berlin, threw open the door.

"You must please to alight, Signora," said this man in Italian; he wore a large dark cloak, and appeared a tall strong man.

To dream of resisting the will of those in whose power she was, the poor girl did not for a moment think of doing; and as to asking questions, or imploring pity to be restored to her friends, she knew would be equally futile. She therefore summoned all her firmness and spirit to support her in whatever trials were before her, and wrapping the mantle over her person, she descended from the vehicle.

"We must cross the water, Signora," observed her conductor, pointing to the river, "there will be a carriage on the other side by that time; in an hour more we shall reach our destination."

Mary did not reply, but looked round her with intense bitterness of heart, to see if any help was near; but through the gloom that surrounded her she could only perceive the three men, the berlin, and horses. One of the three was a postillion, for as soon as she descended from the carriage he separated from the other two, mounted into his seat, and drove off at a rapid pace. The other two then moved on towards the river, requesting our heroine civilly enough to proceed with them.

It was but a very few yards to the water's edge; and as she mechanically obeyed, she observed through the gloom a boat pulling across from the opposite side.

"Ah! here is the boat," observed one of her conductors to his companion; "I was beginning to be uneasy."

As Mary reached the side of the river, the boat pulled by two men also reached the bank.

"Is the carriage at the other side?" demanded one of the men of the boatmen.

"It has just come down to the bank," was the only reply.

The man turned and civilly offered to assist Mary into the boat, but with a sign of bitter disdain she refused his aid, stepped into the boat and sat down. Only one man, the one who appeared to have the chief care of our heroine, stepped in after her; and in a few minutes, without a word being spoken, they reached the other side. It was a fine bright starlight night by this time, and Mary could perceive a close berlin with two horses and a postillion, drawn up near the river's bank; though there was not the slightest appearance of road, it looked like a common or waste ground, skirted in the distance by a thick belt of trees or a forest.

The man opened the door of the berlin, and without a word she got in. He then closed the door, drew the curtains, and mounted up into the seat in front, and the postillion drove on. Our heroine leaned back and burst into a flood of tears; left to herself, having no one to witness her grief, she gave way to all the anguish she felt at thus being torn from her protectors. She thought of her lover far away, perhaps in the midst of a sanguinary contest with the Turks, herself a captive to an unknown enemy; for not the slightest idea or surmise could she entertain as to who was the cause of the outrage committed upon her, or for what purpose. For the first two or three hours she felt a secret hope that Helen would spread an alarm, and that she should be pursued and overtaken, but now that they had crossed the river she despaired; the whole affair seemed to be so systematically planned, that hope fled as the time ran on.

At first the carriage proceeded but very slowly, the ground they went over appeared uneven though smooth, but at length they reached a road, and at once the horses quickened their pace. As well as she could judge, they continued at a rapid pace for more than an hour and a half, and then it suddenly went at a very slow pace, and finally stopped. The poor captive's heart beat violently, the light of a torch or a lantern flashed in through the curtains of the berlin; and then they were drawn aside, and she perceived her abductor holding a large glass lantern.

"Will you please to alight, Signora?" said this man, speaking in a language and with a manner far above what his dress denoted.

Trembling, but still collected and firm in resolution, Miss Grey descended the steps of the vehicle, and then perceived they were in a large court-yard, and close beside a building seemingly of great extent. She next became conscious of the presence of an elderly female standing a little behind the man, but who, as soon as our heroine left the carriage came forward, and giving the unfortunate girl an inquiring look, said:

"Please come with me, Signora; your journey is over for tonight, and I dare say you are tired and require refreshment."

"Refreshment," repeated Mary in Italian, in a tone of bitter reproach, as she followed the woman; "a day of reckoning may come, when all concerned in this cruel outrage wil' assuredly suffer."

"So you may think, Signora," returned the woman calmly, "but you may be wrong; I am simply performing my duty."

As she spoke they entered through what appeared a back entrance to the building, and were met by a young girl dressed in the short boddice, and short petticoat of the peasantry. She was a pretty looking girl, not more than sixteen; she had a candle in her hand, and looked with exceeding wonder into the pale but very lovely features of the captive. They had reached a lofty hall, which they traversed till they came to a long flight of stone steps which they ascended, crossed one or two corridors, and mounting another flight of stairs, the woman threw open a door, and requested our heroine to enter.

The room was a large handsome saloon, furnished in the heavy though rich cumbrous furniture of the preceding century. Lighting a very large handsome lamp that stood upon the table, she said:

"Your bed-room, Signora, is there," pointing to an open door at the further end of the room, "I will bring you some coffee, or tea if you prefer it."

The woman's manner and tone were respectful and even kind; her age appeared about fifty, and there was a strong likeness in her features to those of the young girl, whose large dark eyes were intently fixed upon poor Mary, who replied:

"I will thank you for a cup of tea, for my lips are parched, but I require nothing else."

"You shall have it directly, Signora," returned the woman; you will find a fire in your bedroom, for the old house not being occupied, gets damp and dreary. There are many articles belonging to a lady's toilet that you may want, and anything you may desire to have I will endeavour to procure for you."

Mary Grey, in her sweet musical voice, thanked the woman, saying she desired nothing but liberty, and that of course she could not restore her to.

"No, Signora, that I cannot; but this restraint imposed upon you may be only for a short time." So saying she retired, followed by the young girl.

With a heavy sigh the young girl when left alone threw herself into an immense cumbrous easy chair.

"What the meaning of all this can be surprises me," she murmured; "whose mansion am I now in?" and she gazed with an inquiring eye round the lofty chamber. The paper on the wall was much defaced, it had once been very handsome, and so were the huge gilt frames that hung against the wall, containing some old portraits and one or two very dingy landscapes. The marble mantel-piece supported an extremely-antique clock, resting on two bronze figures of gladiators; on each side stood a huge blue and gold porcelain vase. There were three very lofty windows to the room, the curtains of which had lost their original colour from age and damp; altogether the saloon presented a cheerless and sombre appearance.

Taking up a wax-taper that stood upon the table, she lighted it at the lamp, and proceeded with aching heart to inspect her sleeping chamber.

This room, from having a bright cheering log fire burning in the wide grate, had a much more cheerful aspect. The walls were dark oak panelled, there was an immense cumbrous bed, with heavy draped curtains, and a flight of steps to mount to it. There were neither pictures nor ornament on the walls or mantel-piece, but on the toilet table was a large mirror, and a variety of articles useful to ladies.

As she sat down by the fire, for the air in the old uninhabited chambers was chill and damp, the woman who had received her, entered with a tray containing tea, cold fowl, and some bread and butter, and placing them on a small table near the fire, said:

"You will be more comfortable here, Signora, than in that dismal old room. I will put a fire in it to-morrow, but to-night I thought you would not want it; there has been one several days in this room."

"Then you expected me, dame? inquired Mary, looking inquisitively into the Italian's face.

"Oh, yes," returned the woman, quite quietly; "we expected you several days ago; indeed, day after day."

"Do you know who I am, my good dame?" questioned Mary Grey, more and more surprised.

"Oh yes," she replied, with a smile, as she poured out a cup of tea for her.

"And whose mansion is this?" hazarded our heroine, as she drank the tea, which refreshed her exceedingly.

"Oh, this house," observed the dame, sitting down quite composedly, "once belonged to a very old and noble family, the Count De Sarto; but it does not belong to them now. It and the adjoining land came into the hands of a distant connection, but he ran through it all, and went out of the country, so deeply in debt that he has never come back. He went to England, I think."

"And does he hold the house now?" again questioned Mary.

Dame Margarita smiled good-humouredly, as she said:

"Why, he does and he doesn't. You see, they put a kind of receiver over the property, but I don't think the creditors claim the estate."

"And, pray, what may his name be?" still questioned our heroine.

"Ah, you know nothing of him, Signora; never saw him, neither heard his name, I am sure, nor he yours."

"Then I do not owe my present cruel treatment to him?" said Mary Grey, still more anxious to discover who the person was that had caused her to be torn from her protectors.

"I see you have no idea," said dame Margarita, "who it was that ordered you to be brought here. Now, you will think it strange, but I am ignorant also."

"But, good heavens! dame," said Mary, greatly astonished, "you must be aware that you have placed yourself in a dangerous position, aiding and abetting the wicked persons that have carried me forcibly off. Lord Herringstone, my guardian and protector, is personally acquainted with the Grand Duke, and when it is known to his highness that I have been forcibly abducted and imprisoned, he will send armed sbirri all over the country to find me out."

"Well," returned Dame Margarita, quite placidly, "I trust they may find you, and take the responsibility off my hands in having the care of you, for you appear to me very reasonable, and as yet I have seen no cause to justify such proceedings against you."

Mary Grey's large lustrous eyes opened to their widest extent, as Dame Margarita's strange words sounded in her ears.

"What can you mean, my good dame?" she exclaimed, her eyes flashing, and her cheeks flushing with excitement; "surely you are not insane enough to have been misled into the belief that you have the charge of a lunatic."

"Ah," said Dame Margarita, "how your eyes sparkle, and the blood flies to your temples. My poor child, take some rest; you will be better to-morrow, and then we will talk this over quietly;" and with a kind glance at her astonished charge, who for the moment was actually unable to open her lips, she sailed out of the room, closed the door, and a sound always hateful to hear—the turning the key in the lock—proclaimed to our heroine that she was locked in for the night.

## CHAPTER XXXIX.

For several moments after the abduction of Mary Grey, Helen Probert stood bewildered and terrified, while the old boatman kept wringing his hands, and uttering incessant lamentations, and calling on all the saints in the calendar to come to their assistance. Helen was the first to recover her presence of mind, and desired the old man to put her ashore, as she could walk back faster than he could row against the stream; and thus she should be enabled to spread the alarm, and send the Florentine mounted sbirri in pursuit.

Old Jerome, trembling with fright, pulled the boat ashore.
"How far can a boat go down the stream?" demanded Miss Probert of the boatman.
"About this time of the year, signora, about two miles below Lastrá; the shallows then extend nearly two miles, and no boat can pass till the floods come."

On landing, Miss Probert proceeded at a quick pace through a beautiful park towards Florence, her thoughts and mind completely absorbed; she did not proceed to Lord Herringstone's mansion, but to her own; and going at once to her chamber, took pen, ink, and paper, and wrote a hurried note, folded, and directed it to Lady Herringstone, and calling her own maid, desired her to take it at once and give it into her ladyship's own hands, or into Mrs. Pearson's. She then changed her dress for a very simple costume, packed a few things in a bundle, put a considerable sum in her purse, and in five minutes after left the house privately, leaving a note for her mother on her dressing-table.

Helen's maid in the meantime was much struck with her mistress's strange manner and highly flushed face, hurried to Lord Herringstone's abode, and, on entering the hall, encountered Mrs. Pearson; this lady recognizing her, said:
"Did you meet your mistress and Miss Grey? I have been looking for them for some time."
"My mistress," answered the maid, "has returned home in great agitation, and wrote this note, desiring me to take it without delay to Lady Herringstone."
"Your mistress returned!" exclaimed Mrs. Pearson, with a

startled look. "How is it that Miss Grey has not returned also; she must be at your house."

"No, madam," replied the maid, beginning to think there was something wrong; "she did not come into our house. My mistress was alone; she wrote this note, which, perhaps, will explain!"

"Good God! what can there be to explain?" interrupted Mrs. Pearson; "but give me the note, I will take it to her ladyship."

The servant gave the note, and Mrs. Pearson hurried into the saloon, where her ladyship was sitting reading.

"Where is Mary all this time?" said Lady Herringstone, looking up; "they have stayed unusually long."

"I really am uneasy," said Mrs. Pearson; "though why I should be so appears absurd. Here is a note from Miss Probert, and her maid says that Mary was not with her mistress at their residence."

"Where on earth can she have gone, then?" said her ladyship, opening the note, and letting her glance fall upon the writing inside.

"Heavens!" exclaimed Lady Herringstone, letting the note drop, and turning exceedingly pale; "some villains have carried her off. Good God! what is to be done? At all events, send off James this instant to Leghorn to his lordship. Get me paper, and read that note while I write a few lines; I am so agitated, I neither know what I am saying or doing."

Mrs. Pearson picked up the note, and, although greatly agitated, her presence of mind was greater than her ladyship's, as with something approaching to calmness, she read aloud:

"I am so distracted that I have no power to give your ladyship full particulars of an event that will fill your mind with grief and dismay. Mary was carried off by some ruffians in a boat as we sailed down the stream in old Jerome's barge. I leave my home at once, and will not return till I gain tidings of her.

"HELEN PROBERT."

"Your ladyship must send for the officer of the mounted sbirri, and let him, after examining old Jerome, instantly follow the track of the villains," said Mrs. Pearson, now quite collected.

In a few minutes the whole household of Lord Herringstone were in a state of exceeding excitement. Mary Grey was greatly beloved, and all the domestics, male and female, were eager to assist and be of service. One of his lordship's grooms left with a letter at once for Leghorn, another proceeded to the chief of the sbirri, who, after an interview with Lady Herringstone, proceeded at once to examine old Jerome. Half an hour afterwards four mounted sbirri were spurring along the high road to Lastrá, with a subordinate officer, to investigate the affair to the utmost of hi power.

The officer was well aware that no boat could push on past Lastrá. It was night when he and his men reached the post-house; nevertheless, he commenced inquiries immediately about the four-oared boat. After some slight difficulty he discovered the owner; he was brought up to the inn by two of the police belonging to the place in great trepidation.

"You are the owner of a four-oared boat, the only one, I'm told, in the village."

"I am, signor," returned the man regaining his courage, conscious he was innocent of crime."

"Where is that boat now?" demanded the sbirri.

"She was brought back to me two or three hours ago," replied the fisherman, "by the two men that hired her this morning for a pull up the river; they had used her several days before this, and always brought her back, and paid for the hire."

"What kind of men were they?" questioned the officer.

"They were dressed like sailors or boatmen, but they did not appear to be such. I took them for gentlemen disguised for a frolic, or else practising for a rowing match. Indeed, I did not mind them much, so they brought back the boat safe, and paid for her."

The officer paused; he felt satisfied the man was speaking the truth, for he knew him to be an honest industrious fisherman, with a wife and several children.

"Have you any idea what became of these two men, after bringing back your boat?"

"No, Signor Sbirri, I have not; my cottage is on the river bank, and they walked up towards the village, after leaving the boat."

"What aged men might they be? You speak only of two men; now there were four men in the boat when the outrage which I explained to you was committed; did you at any time see more than those two men in the boat?"

"No, Signor, never; if you look at the river from my cottage you will see there are two very sudden bends in the stream, both thickly wooded. I cannot see fifty yards from my cottage up the stream. The men were both about forty and thirty, perhaps; tall lusty men, one very good looking, and speaking quite different from seamen or boatmen."

The landlord was then examined, and also several other persons in the village. One or two had noticed the men going down the river; but on a strict examination, it did not appear that they had entered any house or inn in the village.

"It is a very clear case," said the sub-lieutenant to his sergeant, "that it will be next to impossible to make any progress to-night. They have landed with the unfortunate young lady, that's certain;

s

but which side of the river is the question. Three or four hours are lost, and in three or four hours many miles might be got over. However, get torches, and we will examine this side of the river for traces of landing; you can mount the owner of the boat behind one of the men."

This was done, and then an examination of the banks of the river by torch-light commenced. About a mile and a half above Lastrá they came upon the track of a carriage with a pair of horses, leading to within fifty yards of the river.

"Ha, by St. Peter! here's some mark that has no right to be here," said the lieutenant, throwing himself from his horse.

The fisherman also dismounted, and on investigating the soft bank of the river, he called out: "Here, Signor Captain, here is the mark of a boat's keel in the bank, and the trampling of many feet."

"Come, we are on the right track," said the lieutenant, as one of his men held a torch close to the sod; "but there is no mark of a female's foot, they carried her." Then tracking the feet, they came to the spot where the berlin had been stationed. "Now, my men, we must track this steadily; this will be easy to do, till we reach the main road."

He was a keen observing man was the Lieutenant of Sbirri, and he walked along the track of the wheels over the green sod till they reached the road. Here he paused puzzled, for the road was as hard as flint, and a strong wind swept along it.

"This is very odd, sergeant," he remarked, "the track of the wheels turning off this waste piece of sod turns towards Florence, but there are no traces whatever on the road, this wind has swept it as clean as the palm of your hand."

"They never went towards Florence, sir," said the sergeant, "they may have turned the carriage that way just to get up the bank easily; but they are sure to have gone on towards Lastrá."

"But the post-master declared no vehicle except the Veturino to Leghorn, and the one to Pisa from Lienne passed this way this evening, up to the time we arrived."

"Then there must be some by-road, sergeant."

"There is a road," remarked one of the sbirri, "within half a mile of Lastrá, which avoids the village, and comes out again a league below the post-house; I rode through it a week back when in pursuit of that rascal that got out of Manzini's grasp, and caught him there too."

"Benissimo!" said the lieutenant, "let us move on then; on a by-road we may find tracks of wheels."

"You will be sure to know if a carriage went that road, lieutenant," said the sbirri, "for a rivulet crosses it and divides it from the main road."

Pursuing their way, they soon came to the road mentioned by the sbirri, and using their torches they discovered that the man was right; a stream a few yards broad and three or four inches deep ran across the road, and running under an arch, found its way to the river.

On the opposite side of this rivulet, where the ground was soft, they readily made out the track of four wheels and two horses, and measuring the space between the wheels the sergeant declared that the track was evidently made by the same carriage, whose marks to the Arno's bank they had traced.

The road was extremely narrow the whole way, so much so that it was quite impossible the carriage could turn till it came out at the other end upon the main road. Here, the route being sheltered and the ground moist from over-hanging trees, they readily made out the recent traces of the same carriage, and this they continued till they reached the post-house at Ambrogiano. There the master of the inn was summoned, rather startled at perceiving five mounted sbirris with torches.

"Pray," questioned the lieutenant of the host, "did a carriage stop here to change horses some two, three, or four hours back?"

"Si, Signor Lieutenant!" replied the landlord and post-master, "a berlin stopped here about three or fours hours ago, and had a pair of horses put on."

"Ha, Corpo De Baccho!" exclaimed the lieutenant, "we are tracing them; what became of the horses taken out of the berlin and the postillion?" he demanded of the landlord, "for the horses were not from Lastrá!"

"Not from Lastrá!" said the post-master, "that's odd; they must have been private horses then, for while mine were getting ready, the postillion took his off, and mounting rode back, as I thought to Lastrá."

"Did you see who occupied the berlin?" demanded the lieutenant.

"I saw only one signor in a brown mantle, lieutenant," said the post-master, "and that only at a distance, for the berlin did not, as usual with private carriages, drive into the yard by one gate and go out by the other; it stopped a short distance from the house."

"Where were your horses taken for?" demanded the officer.

"The next post-house, La Scala; they were going on to Leghorn."

"La Scala," repeated the lieutenant, "that's about three leagues."

Ordering some refreshment for his men and horses, in twenty minutes he remounted, and with steady perseverance pursued his way to La Scala, expecting to meet the returning postillion on the road. Such was the case.

On questioning the man he stated that he had left the berlin at La Scala, getting fresh horses on for Leghorn.

"Who was in the berlin, my man?" demanded the lieutenant.

"One gentleman," returned the postillion, "I saw no other; there might have been a female inside, for the curtains were kept closed, and the signor in a dark mantle merely paid the post-horses and my fee, which he doubled as he desired me at starting to drive fast."

"This looks serious," said the lieutenant to the sergeant, "they may find time to put this young lady on board ship and baffle us."

On reaching La Scala they found they had gained considerably on the fugitives, who were now only an hour in advance, but the horses of the sbirri after a fast ride of more than twenty miles required rest; still the lieutenant was anxious to overtake the berlin, so merely refreshing the horses with a mouthful of meal and water, they pushed on for Leghorn; he had inquired of the post-master the name of the hotel where his postillions generally drove travellers to, and pressing on his horses in an hour's time he rode into the inn-yard of the hotel of the Aquila Nero, and there before his eyes stood a travelling berlin with leather curtains. There was no one up in the hotel but the night porter, and the ostler and stable boys.

Throwing himself from his horse the lieutenant began questioning the surprised and startled ostler.

"When did this carriage arrive?"

"Half an hour ago, Signor Captain."

"Who was in the berlin?"

"Not a soul, signor; it was empty. The postillion from La Scala, who came in with it, is even now doing up his horses, as he will not go back till morning."

The officer of the sbirri was astounded.

"Call out the postillion."

The man came out of the stable with a wisp of straw in his hand, looking amazed at the dismounted sbirri.

"Who did you bring in that berlin from La Scala?" questioned the officer.

"A signor, a stranger to me, lieutenant," said the man.

"Pray what did you do with him then?" for the ostler here says you brought the berlin in empty.

"Signor, si," said the postillion, "when inside the town the signor in the carriage called to me to stop. 'What hotel are you taking me to?' he demanded. 'The Aquila Nero, signor,' says I. 'Ha,' said he, 'I know the inn, but I have a friend to see to-night, late as it is; here is your master's money, and a double fee for yourself; take the carriage to the Aquila Nero, and have it carefully put up, I will be there in the morning.' So he jumps out after giving me the money, and walked rapidly up the street. I thought nothing of the circumstance,' continued the postillion; 'when I came in here the ostler and I examined the inside of the carriage thinking there might be luggage, but there was not a single thing.'"

The lieutenant of the sbirris bit his lip with vexation, and looked at his sergeant, who rubbed his nose in great perplexity.

"Put up your horses, sergeant," said the lieutenant of the sbirri, "I will order beds and refreshments for us; it's very clear nothing more can be done to-night," and turning to the ostler, he ordered him on no account to allow the berlin to leave the hotel yard.

Thus ended the first night's pursuit.

## CHAPTER XL.

Francis De Burgh we left pursuing his way with the little Daring to Malta, in quest of Admiral Duckworth and his fleet. Notwithstanding his love for the sea, the excitement of his command, and the enterprise he was pursuing, his love for Mary Grey so much overpowered every other feeling, that he heartily wished Admiral Duckworth had remained quietly at anchor in the port of Genoa; at least until he had delivered his despatches. But once more at sea, the natural buoyancy of his disposition, his love of adventure and his brilliant prospects for the future, took possession of his mind; and secure in the love of his beautiful Mary, he shook off the feeling of vexation caused by so suddenly parting from her, and became himself again, that is, eager for some adventure or exploit, such as a brush with any enemy of equal size, or, for the matter of that, double their size.

The wind was favourable, and carrying on as much canvas as the craft could stagger under, he made rapid way towards Malta, not a little curious to behold that island stronghold of Great Britain. Early on the sixth day his little vessel came within sight of Malta, and before mid-day was at anchor in the harbour of Valetta.

Here another disappointment awaited him; Admiral Duckworth had received important despatches which compelled him, after calling at Malta, to make sail for the Archipelago. He left just thirty-six hours previous to the arrival of our hero in the Daring.

"Well, be gor, Mister Burke," said Bill Mullaghan to the young midshipman, who had just returned on board, having left his skipper with the governor, and who brought the intelligence that they were to get under weigh that night and follow Admiral Duckworth. "Be gor, we shall see the world in earnest this time. So we're going amongst the Turkeys; faix, may be Mister Burke, we may get spliced to some of them Turkey girls. I hear the Grand Turk himself has a lot of 'em always on hand, and makes presents of 'em to his officers, who sell 'em off on the sly."

"Who the deuce told you such nonsense, Bill? if you are caught admiring the Turkey women, as you call them, and admiring their ancles as you did the Spanish girls, you'll have your head on the seraglio gate, and your carcase in the Bosphorus."

"Faix, Mr. Burke, they'll not get my head so easily as all that, it looks better where it is than stuck upon a gilt spike."

That night the little Daring was again under weigh, steering for the Archipelago, where it was sure to come up with Admiral Duckworth, who was to rendezvous there till the ——— frigate joined his squadron; and until ministers finally made up their minds whether Constantinople was to be bombarded or not.

Hitherto the weather had been remarkably fine and favourable, but the second day after leaving Malta a violent thunder-storm broke up the weather, and a succession of heavy gales from north and north-east, forced the Daring rather close in with the Barbary coast near Toloreta. The Daring had her foretopsail split to ribbons, and a tremendous sea striking her in her stays, carried away not only her gib-boom, but the bowsprit to the very stem.

The commander of the Daring as the gale moderated, and he became aware that he was close in on the Barbary shore, began as rapidly as possible to repair his disasters, in case any of the numerous pirates that belonged at this period to the Barbary coast, should come from their harbours and attack him.

Though the gale lessened, the sea running in on the bluff headland of Toloreta was tremendous, the wind blowing right on shore. Towards sunset, as he replaced his topsail with a new one, and rigged out a temporary bowsprit, one of the men aloft reported two zebecs and a brigantine coming out from Toloreta, under close reefed canvas. Master Burke was up on the fore-topmast crosstrees in a moment with his glass, and in a very short time made them out to be two armed zebecs, and a long smart-looking brigantine full of men.

"We must prepare for action," said De Burgh to the old quarter-master, "if we cannot work off this shore, the sea is going down fast; a point or more to the westward, and we should look up for the island of Candia."

"Yes, sir," returned the quarter-master, "but it doesn't look for a shift in that quarter, that brigantine will stretch right across our bows, sir; she looks a lively craft. But these robbers will not trouble us if we give them a taste of our swivel, take us very likely for a merchant craft, as we have no colours flying."

The two zebees our hero remarked had tacked and stood along shore, while the brigantine, as the quarter-master observed, was stretching across their course.

The Daring stood on under a single reefed topsail and double reefed mainsail, her guns loaded with round shot, and the swivel with grape. Bill Mullaghan was watching anxiously the brigantine's movements, and longing to give the Barbary pirates, for there was no mistake as to their occupation, a taste of his pet's powers.

In this manner the brigantine and Daring had approached each other, both close hauled and within range of the Daring's swivel; but the brigantine showed no intention of commencing a contest, but stood on without any flags flying. In the meantime the two zebecs having tacked in shore, and gained an advantage by doing so, stood out in the track of the Daring. Our hero strongly suspected that they had arranged their plan of attack, so at once hoisting the British pennant and flag he put the Daring about, and stood direct for the brigantine.

This manœuvre at once decided the corsairs, for the brigantine instantly hoisted the well-known and detested flag of the Barbary Rovers, and running up her ports, suddenly opened fire from her four starboard guns, eight-pounders.

"Hurrah, my darlings!" chuckled Bill Mullaghan, as his crew swung round the swivel, and waiting for the word, and the rise of a sea, poured its deadly contents within musket range into the brigantine, whose decks were crowded with men.

This discharge evidently confounded the crew of the rover, for considerable confusion ensued; the vessel shot up in the wind, and remained with her fore-top-sails aback, and in this state the Daring gave them, within pistol-shot, the contents of her two twelve-pounders, and the large bell-mouthed brass-swivels on her bow.

A loud cheer from the crew of the Daring declared the result of this discharge, which sent the brigantine's fore-mast yards, topmasts and all, over the side.

Just then the foremost of the two zebecs, as the Daring again tacked, without firing a single shot, eased off her sheets, put her helm up, and ran right on board the schooner, crashing in the starboard bulwarks, and entangling her long latine yards in the Daring's rigging and spars. With the yells of a parcel of fiends, the pirates, a swarthy-looking and ferocious set of men, with pistols and cutlasses, prepared to board; but Bill Mullaghan and his gang, and Master Burke with his, short as the time was, were prepared to give them a deadly dose; the four twelve-pounders, brought to one side, and being loaded almost to the muzzle with round shot, were discharged into the hull of the pirate, just between wind and water.

The zebec heeled over with the terrible shock, and the next moment, or, rather, the same instant, blew up with a terrible explosion. The guns had set fire to her powder magazine, and having a quantity of powder on board, taking to some fort on the coast, she was shattered to atoms, scattering her crew into the air, torn asunder, and pitched over the heavy billows in disjointed fragments. The little Daring reeled over on the opposite side, till her deck was under water; the bulwarks next the zebec were shattered to pieces, her fore-top-mast, sails, spars, and rigging, blown clean out of her, several of her crew knocked prostrate, and our hero himself, standing near the helm, pitched violently against the starboard bulwarks, and for a moment buried in a flood of water that poured in over her deck, while those of the crew who escaped unhurt thought she was going down head foremost.

In this state the other zebec, which, fortunately for them, sailed but indifferently, got within musket shot, and instantly opened fire from four guns she carried. Bill Mullaghan with his face begrimed with blood, and blackened by the explosion, and yet, strange to say, but little injured, first recovered himself. Two men lay dead upon the deck, besides several fearfully disfigured bodies of the enemy, blown on board by the explosion. Seven or eight of the men were wounded and cut by splinters, but neither dispirited nor disheartened. As soon as Francis De Burgh recovered his feet, and his recollection, at first a little bewildered by the shock, he ran to the helm; the old quarter-master lay stunned against the lee bulwarks. Fortunately the jib remained uninjured, and filling on the opposite tack to that the pirate zebec was on, and the main-peak haul-yard being let go, the Daring wore round, and stood on dead before the wind, instantly followed by the corsair.

But by this time the crew of the Daring had quite recovered themselves; the carpenter reported her as sound as a bell, and each man, with a fierce vow of revenge, prepared for a contest with the zebec, the largest of the three piratical craft. The intention of the corsair was evidently to run them on board; she had not only the advantage of the wind, but all her sails were bent and uninjured, while the Daring had lost all her top-sails and yards, and was only under her main-sail, fore-sail, and second jib.

The crew of the little vessel had thrown off their jackets, tightened a handkerchief round their waists, and armed with pistol and cutlass, vowed a terrible resistance to the pirates, should they attempt to board them. The swivel was loaded to the muzzle with a murderous charge, to pour into the corsair the moment our hero gave the word.

On came the zebec, with her monstrous latine sails extended like wings, her swarthy crew yelling in anticipated triumph, and brandishing their scimitars. They were within pistol shot, when Bill Mullaghan and some of the men, by their commander's orders, dragged one of the twelve-pounders aft, and getting a good aim, poured its contents into the pirate, smashing in her bows, and cutting away the whole of her head-gear, and killing several of her crew. But still she came on, with a wild yell from the crew pealing over the deep, when Francis De Burgh suddenly ordered the helm to be put down, and the main-sheet hauled in, and thus the pirate ran alongside, but as she did so the eighteen-pound carronade swept the deck with fearful effect, and before the astounded pirates, aghast at the frightful slaughter it caused, could recover, Francis, cutlass in hand, and closely followed by Bill Mullaghan, with a loud cheer, leaped upon the zebec's deck, the whole crew of the Daring, with the gallant young midshipman, followed, and a furious hand-to-hand fight took place. It lasted but a few moments, many of the corsairs leaped over the side, the rest were driven along the decks by the gallant crew of the Daring, and their commander being shot through the head by Francis De Burgh on first leaping on board, the remainder of the pirates threw down their arms and demanded quarter.

This was granted by our hero though the crew of the Daring seemed rather inclined to exterminate them, but Francis De Burgh called their attention to the perilous situation of the two vessels, entangled as they were, the sea grinding them against each other.

Just then Bill Mullaghan and Master Burke, who were engaged in fastening the pirates down below, perceived that the piratical brigantine had cut away the wreck of her foremast and yards, and using long sweeps contrived to get her before the wind, and when they observed her she was bearing down on them under all the sail she could carry on her mainmast, evidently with the intention of running them down if they could, or renewing the contest by boarding.

Both Bill and his favourite, Master Burke, left their employment and ran to their commander, who was intent with a party of his crew in trying to separate the two vessels, but the lofty latine sails of the zebec were so entangled in the rigging and spars of the Daring that the work was neither easily nor expeditiously performed.

"By the powers, sir! here's the brigantine coming down dead before the wind," exclaimed Bill in a high state of excitement, "there's no time to free ourselves from the zebec; we must load the swivel to the muzzle."

The commander turned, and at a glance saw the dangerous position he was in.

"We must try and sink her as she comes up," he exclaimed, addressing the old quarter-master. "Get the guns on this side, load them all with round shot, watch the moment when she rises on a sea and shows her side clear of the water, and then pitch it into her."

"Yes, sir, that's the ticket! we'll give her a dose; she'll have cause to remember her sauciness. She can only attack us as she runs before the wind, and a broadside well aimed may settle her log."

And away went the crew to the guns, leaving a few to help to separate the vessels, which was only to be done by cutting away their own rigging.

In the meantime on came the brigantine under her after canvas, yawing at times so exceedingly that their long sweeps were required to keep her in her course.

When within musket shot she opened fire from her two foremost guns, but the shot merely cut away some of the running rigging, and slightly splintered the main top-mast. With great exertion and considerable skill, Francis, hampered as he was by the zebec, was enabled to bring his broadside to play upon the advancing brigantine, but to avoid her boarding him if he failed in sinking her was out of the question, with the grinding of the two vessels alongside; the whole of his starboard bulwarks were in splinters, and his rigging injured, the fore latine yard had broken off under the main cross-trees of the Daring, and become so entangled that some of the crew were cutting everything away to free themselves.

Watching with intense anxiety for a favourable moment, our hero stood by the guns ready to give the word. When just within pistol shot the brigantine yawed so much on a heavy sea that she exposed several planks of her bottom clear of the water; that moment the word was given, and instantaneously the swivel and the twelve-pounders poured their deadly contents into the exposed side of the brigantine; they were aimed with deadly precision and with consummate skill, and that single discharge sealed the fate of the pirate vessel. Its planks were fearfully shattered, and as it fell back in the sea, it began to fill rapidly and became ungovernable, shooting up into the wind and then getting stern way upon her.

Just then the Daring got free from the zebec, and dropped to leeward, leaving the zebec with her crew fastened under hatches rolling in the troughs of the seas.

On board the sinking brigantine a scene of indescribable confusion prevailed; she was rapidly going down, and the crew were crowding into her three boats which they had lowered at once when they perceived that the vessel was sinking from the effect of the Daring's broadside.

There appeared, as well as our hero could judge, upwards of one hundred men on board the brigantine; he immediately guessed their object would be to board the zebec, but the moment he was able to make sail on the Daring he stood on between the zebec and the sinking brigantine. The latter rolled fearfully, and in a few minutes—even before her crew got into the boats—she plunged forward, rolled heavily, and then went down stern foremost, striking one of her boats with her main-yard and turning her over, while a fearful yell pealed over the water from her doomed crew.

The English sailors could not bear to fire upon the despairing wretches in the boats, cruel and ferocious as they always were to those that fell into their hands.

Finding they had no chance of getting on board the zebec they pulled away from the Daring, making for the coast.

"Shall we pepper the villains, sir?" said Bill Mullaghan, running his eye along the eighteen pound carronade with a marvellous inclination to apply the match to the gun, as he asked the question.

"No, no," replied our hero, "let the rascals make the land if they can; enough lives have been sacrificed between fire and water. Get out our boats and board the zebec; she appears to me to be in deep water, and may be a valuable prize. Put the wretches now on board into her boats, and let them follow their comrades ashore; half a dozen men with Master Burke will do to take the prize on with us; she is above a hundred and fifty tons, and a fine looking craft.

## CHAPTER XLI.

THE piratical zebec turned out a most valuable prize. She had a very large amount of specie on board, which she was taking from Toloreta to Tripoli, besides the valuable cargo of a Smyrna brig she had plundered the week before, and carried into Toloreta, consigning her crew to slavery.

Before the sun went down, the Daring and the zebec, under the charge of Master Burke, the old quarter-master, and eight hands, were shaping their course for Candia, where our hero was determined to stay a few days to repair the serious damage the little Daring had received. She made a good deal of water, was without a single topsail, and had not another spare spar on board; her starboard bulwarks and chain plates were all carried away, besides her bowsprit; and her main topmast so injured as to be incapable of carrying sail. Two of his crew had been killed in the action; one died of his wounds afterwards; and as many as sixteen were variously hurt, five or six seriously.

Fortunately the weather moderated, and the wind shifting, they made the island of Candia the evening of the third day; but an old man-of-war's man on board advised our hero, as the wind was fair, to make for Scio, the best seaport in the Archipelago, and where, most likely, he would come up with Admiral Duckworth's squadron.

This advice turned out very fortunately, for after rounding the island of ———, he caught sight of Admiral Duckworth's fleet lying at anchor off the Island of Scio.

Our hero counted seven sail of the line, and as soon as he came within sight of the Admiral's ship he prepared to let go his anchor, getting, however, much nearer the shore.

While preparing to go on board the Admiral's vessel, the signal was made from the flag-ship that his presence was required.

So taking his despatches he pulled alongside, and in a few minutes was ushered into the presence of Admiral Duckworth; but not before his appearance had attracted the curiosity of all the officers of the ship, to whom he was quite strange, as was also the Daring.

There were three elderly officers in the cabin when Francis De

Burgh entered, and Admiral Duckworth, who was pacing the cabin with his hands behind his back, carrying on an animated conversation with his guests, captains of the other ships, turned round, and examined our hero from head to foot, seemingly with some interest, and evidently with considerable surprise.

The Admiral was a stout, hale old man, with rather a stern, severe expression of countenance.

"You are a stranger to me, sir," said the Admiral, with his hands still behind his back, and looking keenly into our hero's face. "Pray what is the name of your craft, and what's your business in these waters?"

"The name of the schooner, sir, is the Daring. I was sent by Admiral Sir James Saumarez from Gibraltar to Genoa, to deliver these despatches. Not finding you, sir, in Genoa, I followed you to Malta, and thence here," laying on the table as he ceased speaking the bag he held in his hand.

"Upon my word," said the Admiral, turning round with a laugh to one of the officers, "this gentleman appears of a very persevering disposition. What craft is that you have brought in with you? As far as I can judge, you both appear in rather a crippled condition."

"I was attacked, sir," returned our hero, "off Toloreta, by three piratical craft, this zebec and another, and a large brigantine."

"Ah, the deuce you were!" cried Admiral Duckworth, who was a great admirer of a bold and spirited action. "What became of the other two, and how did you contrive to capture this zebec, which looks quite large enough to match you by herself?"

"One zebec blew up alongside, trying to board us, sir," returned De Burgh, with the eyes of all present fixed upon him, "and the brigantine we sunk; the zebec we captured contains a large amount of specie, and a valuable cargo."

Admiral Duckworth stepped forward, and in his bluff, straightforward manner, held out his hand.

"Give me your hand, my lad. By Jove, you're a fine fellow, whoever you are; I love a bold action, and yours must have been a very dashing affair. Take a chair; I shall find out who you are as I examine the contents of this bag."

But no sooner had the Admiral read a portion of the letters, than he laid them down, and turning to the officers assembled, said:

"This gentleman, Lieutenant De Burgh, has in truth brought us important intelligence, and Sir James Saumarez speaks highly of Lieutenant De Burgh's conduct and gallantry. Admiral Saumarez suffered severe loss, it seems, off Algesiras, and the Hannibal has been captured by the enemy. There has been a battle since, I am led to expect by this letter, and Lieutenant De Burgh was expected to be able to give me the result. Now, sir," continued the Admiral, turning to our hero, "let us hear your account of the engagement, such as you witnessed it."

Francis thus called on, gave a minute and accurate account of the splendid action he had witnessed, and its results. His narrative and his manner of relating it, highly pleased the Admiral and the other officers present; they seemed to consider the engagement he recorded as one of vast importance to the glory of England, and one that raised the fame of Sir James Saumarez as a gallant and high-spirited officer, and a commander of consummate skill, to gain so glorious a victory against such extraordinary odds.

Admiral Duckworth then resumed the reading of the letters; some of their contents seemed to surprise him, for turning round, he remarked to one of the captains present:

"I see we cannot advance further in this expedition till the arrival of the —— frigate from England. I find, Mr. De Burgh," turning to our hero, "it is your intention, from certain reasons, family ones, it is stated, to retire from the service. I deeply regret that such is your intention; short as your career has been, you have singularly distinguished yourself, and been fortunate to a degree, and your good fortune seems to follow you. If it would not materially interfere with your future prospects, for I see Sir James Saumarez states that you are the undoubted heir to the Delamaine estates and title; but as I was saying, if you could delay so long as to accompany this expedition against Constantinople, you and your fine little craft could be of great use and importance in an expedition of the kind. I have often wished for a vessel like yours, and such an enterprizing, gallant officer to command her; can I therefore prevail on you to join the expedition with the Daring?"

After so flattering a reception it was quite impossible, much as our hero wished to resign and proceed to Florence, to refuse the Admiral's request; he therefore at once acquiesced in his desire, stating he felt highly honoured by the Admiral's request, and was at his command as long as he considered he could be of service to his country, whose interests he considered it was his duty to attend to, whatever might be the injury to his private affairs.

"You are a very gallant fellow," said Admiral Duckworth, "by Jove! and I feel gratified by your acceding to my wishes. I shall expect you to dinner; in the meantime you had better get the Daring into port, and your prize also, and every assistance shall be rendered you in re-fitting her; we shall have plenty of time, as I do not expect the —— frigate can be here for a week, or longer."

Our hero left the cabin, after a very cordial shake of the hand from the Admiral and officers present, and proceeded upon deck; here he was surrounded by several of the officers of the ship, the first lieutenant amongst the number, and half an hour passed very pleasantly, all being extremely anxious to know who he was, what the two crafts were, and what brought him into the Archipelago. Having satisfied their curiosity, and received a very warm and cordial shake of the hand from all, and many an invitation, he returned to the Daring, and before the Admiral's dinner hour, the little schooner and her prize were at anchor within the Mole of the harbour of Scio.

Drawing to the close of our third volume, and finding our space limited, we are forced to be extremely brief in the future naval career of our hero. This expedition to bombard Constantinople, so as to force the Turks to concede to the wishes of Russia, was quite as unfortunate in its results as the late expedition to the Crimea to compel Russia to let the Turks alone; then we were allies of Russia; but, nevertheless, through the incapacity of those in office at home, and the insane neglect of providing the squadron with troops, the expedition against Constantinople totally failed.

Admiral Duckworth's squadron sailed for the Dardanelles; but when it arrived in the narrow channel between Sestos and Abydos, the fire from the castles which defended the passage, became fearfully destructive, the ships being forced to sail within point blank shot of the enemy's guns. The leading ships suffered most; they, however, returned the fire so gallantly, that the castles were silenced, and the rest of the squadron passed with comparatively little damage. The little Daring had, however, a most extraordinary escape from a granite shot, of more than two hundred weight, which struck the water within five yards of her stern.

Our hero was afterwards sent to Sir Sidney Smith with orders to attack a Turkish squadron which was lying at anchor to the north-east of the Castles; into this action he accompanied the gallant Sir Sidney, and highly distinguished himself by engaging a large Turkish brig, forcing her ashore, and finally making her a wreck, with the loss of but one man and five wounded. He was then employed in various expeditions during the time the fleet remained at anchor. It unfortunately happened that the British Ambassador, Mr. Arbuthnot, then on board one of the ships in the fleet, was taken seriously ill, and all negociations for peace became suspended. In the meantime, the Turks, doing exactly what the Russians are doing now, prepared formidable means of defence during the inactivity of the fleet, for the weather became so bad, that Admiral Duckworth could not get his ships into a proper situation for commencing offensive operations.

The Daring had just returned to the fleet, from a cruise of inspection of the enemies' operations. Francis De Burgh had won golden opinions from all quarters, and had become a most especial favourite with Admiral Duckworth; and from his generous, affable, and pleasing manners, highly esteemed by many of the officers of the fleet, especially with Captain ——, of the Windsor Castle, and Mr. Grantham, first lieutenant of the —— frigate.

Both these officers had accompanied him on a cruise of inspection up to the very batteries of Constantinople. The whole coast was lined with a chain of batteries; in the harbour were twelve line of battle ships getting ready for sea, and all filled with troops, besides several fire ships. So audacious was the little Daring in her desire to ascertain all the means of defence possessed by the enemy, that she became exposed to the fire of one of the batteries, and was chased for two hours by a sloop of war; but escaped by her superior sailing on a wind.

Admiral Duckworth became aware of the critical situation in which he was placed; there appeared but little chance of the weather becoming favourable, and the immense force against which he would have to contend, should he attempt the bombardment of Constantinople, unless he completely succeeded, would so cripple and disable his ships, that he feared the passage of the Dardanelles would be rendered doubly dangerous, especially as the enemy had repaired the damages they had sustained, and rendered their defences even more formidable. Then it was that the error of the ministers who planned this ill-starred expedition became singularly apparent. Had the Admiral been supplied with troops they could have landed and destroyed completely the defences of the Dardanelles, and thus have left themselves a secure retreat in case of failure; and they might also have been employed by land while the fleet bombarded Constantinople by sea. At length Admiral Duckworth made up his mind to repass the Dardanelles, and proceed into the Mediterranean.

Harassed and deeply chagrined at the situation in which he was placed, the Admiral made the signal to weigh, and having a strong and favourable wind, the fleet bore away for the Dardanelles, which they passed suffering a terribly destructive loss. The Windsor Castle was struck by a granite ball weighing 800 pounds; nearly three hundred officers and men were killed in this unfortunate and ill-planned expedition.

Amidst the hurricane of shot from both sides of the channel, the Daring had a marvellous escape, her diminutive size no doubt allowing her to sail through the straits almost unnoticed. A stray shot or two caught the topmast and sails, but she had not a man on board wounded.

The fleet came to in the Archipelago, and there Francis had an interview with Admiral Duckworth, who, after thanking him for services he had rendered him, informed him he was at liberty to return to England in the Daring. He would furnish him with letters and despatches, and as he had stated his first intention was to proceed to Leghorn and thence to Florence, he could put in there on his way; and as no doubt he would meet there with some British ships of war, he would provide him with letters accordingly. So that he might delay there for a few weeks if necessary, and also touch at Gibraltar.

This kind and considerate conduct of the Admiral elicited warm expressions of gratitude from our hero, to whom this permission of returning to England in the Daring was most gratifying. After taking a most friendly leave of all the officers whose friendship he had enjoyed during the time they had been together, and the damages the Daring had received being repaired, he bade adieu to the fleet, and left the delightful waters of the Grecian Archipelago for the broader waters of the Mediterranean, and without meeting with any occurrence worthy of notice, made the port of Leghorn after a most prosperous and rapid passage. To our hero's intense delight, on entering the harbour he beheld the Gem yacht at anchor, and getting ready for sea. A loud cheer from the crew of the yacht testified the pleasure they all felt when they recognized the Daring, and to add to his happiness after his long absence, our hero beheld on board Lord Herringstone, whose pleasure at the sight of Francis De Burgh was in truth as great as his own.

We shall in our next chapter, having finished the nautical career of Francis De Burgh, return to our fair heroine; merely stating that it was on the day of her abduction that her lover arrived in Leghorn, consequently his pleasure at meeting Lord Herringstone was not damped by anxiety.

## CHAPTER XLII.

THE first night of Mary Grey's bondage was passed almost without sleep, so troubled and disturbed were her thoughts. Judging from Dame Margarita's words, she conjectured that the old dame considered her not in the actual possession of her reason. What could be the motive of such a proceeding on the part of those who had so daringly carried her off puzzled her; but she was infinitely more puzzled in conjecturing who were her abductors, and what their object could be.

With such thoughts flitting through her brain, mingled with visions of her long absent lover, about whose personal safety she felt greatly disturbed, the night wore slowly and sleeplessly away. Towards morning she fell into a slumber, from which she was roused by the entrance of the young girl she had seen the previous evening with Dame Margarita.

The maiden entered the room with a timidity of air and manner that struck the captive at once, and speaking, as she did, the Italian language fluently, and which sounded so well in her sweet musical voice, she addressed her as she entered, saying:

"I suppose, my good girl, that I have overslept myself; but in truth I did not sleep at all till I beheld the dawn through the windows. Is it late?"

"It is near midday, signora," said the girl, "and my aunt was afraid you were not well, as she looked in once or twice, and you did not awake. Will you have breakfast in bed, signora?"

"Oh, no, my dear," replied Mary; "I am quite well enough in health to get up and take my breakfast in the other room. I have nothing to complain of, but being made a prisoner against my will and torn from my home, leaving those behind to grieve and distract themselves at my strange disappearance."

The girl, who appeared an innocent and simple creature, looked surprised; but her first timidity evidently wore off as she assisted Mary to dress.

"Pray, my good girl, what is your name?" questioned our heroine, finishing her simple toilet.

"Maria, signora."

"Are you and your aunt the only inhabitants of this large mansion?"

"Oh, no, signora."

Just then Dame Margarita entered the room, and after a keen look at Mary, which subsided into a pleased smile, she said:

"I am glad to see you looking so well, signora. Your breakfast is quite ready in the next room. I have had a fire lighted for you.

"Thank you, dame," replied Mary, with a pensive smile; "I am sure I may safely say I grieve to give you this trouble, and for the life of me I cannot imagine how so respectable a person, and one so apparently kind-hearted, could lend herself to so cruel an outrage as the forcibly tearing me from the protection of my friends. My guardian, Lord Herringstone, will have all the assistance the Grand Duke can afford him, to discover my place of captivity, and punish those who have no doubt imposed on you, and induced you to lend your aid in so iniquitous a transaction."

Dame Margarita's pale cheek had an increase of colour, as she replied very calmly, though somewhat struck by the tone and address of Mary, and her quiet, self-possessed manner:

"In truth, signora, I have no design or intention of hiding you from your friends, and trust you may be restored to them. The persons who have placed you here will no doubt arrive this evening, and they will, I dare say, arrange matters to your satisfaction. I have undertaken the care of you till their arrival, and will do so. I now really believe that I am in a manner imposed upon; but please to come and eat your breakfast, and we will talk this strange business over quietly."

More and more surprised, yet pleased, at the moderate and even kind tone of Dame Margarita, Mary followed her into the next room. A cheerful fire made the old chamber and its cumbrous, antique furniture look less dismal than it had done the preceding evening. There was a breakfast of tea, and coffee, and fowl, and preserves on the table; altogether, though she was a prisoner, she could not complain of harsh or unkind treatment.

As she sat down, Mary entreated Margarita to do so likewise, for though she felt her situation exceedingly, she endeavoured to appear in a measure resigned.

Dame Margarita remained for some time with her gaze fixed upon the fire, seemingly in deep thought, while the poor prisoner made but a very slender repast.

"You must make a better breakfast than you have this morning, my dear," observed the dame, looking up, and gazing into the beautiful features of her captive with a good-natured smile, "or you will not do credit to my care."

"A caged bird always languishes in its prison at first, let the wires be of gold," replied Mary, "but tell me, dame, how came you to undertake the office of gaoler to a free-born English girl connected in no way with Italy or its inhabitants?"

"Well, I see no harm in telling you, cara," said Dame Margarita; "you are much too pretty to be hid from the world, and I feel satisfied that there is some mistake in this matter somewhere; but I will inform you how I came to be engaged in the business.

"You must know, my dear, that this extensive and tolerably ancient building, and the surrounding land to some distance, belonged to the Counts Del Sarto; but by marriage and various other causes, all the property but this mansion, and about five hundred acres of the adjoining land, by degrees passed away into other families; and on the death of the last Count Del Sarto, there being no direct heir of that noble family, this mansion and land went to a very distant branch, and a Signor Luigo Castricci became the possessor.

"Now it is not right of me to say anything of the Signor Castricci, for he is my master; but I may say this much, that he was obliged to fly this country from political causes, and I believe went to England. Before his departure, he made over this house and land to my son, to save it from confiscation. My son was his foster brother, and so he came to live here and farm the land; not, indeed, that my son understands or superintends it, but he employs people to do so, and I look over the concern as well as I can, for my son is not often here; he has been to England with the Signor Castricci, and is with him now, I believe.

"About a month ago, perhaps less, I received a letter from my son—(I forgot to tell you my husband has been dead these many years). Well, in this letter was enclosed one from the Signor Castricci, desiring me to prepare two apartments in the best wing of the mansion, for the reception of a young English girl, the daughter of a great friend of his, who was travelling on the continent for the recovery of her health—a disease of the mind more than the body, caused, however, by a fall from her horse, inflicting an injury on the head; that at certain periods—sometimes at long intervals, perhaps a month—a terrible derangement of mind ensued, which happily lasted only two, three, or four days.

"The Signor Castricci also gave me particular instructions to pay this young lady every attention during the fits of derangement, which fits, so far from being painful to behold, were merely a delusion of the mind, and whilst they continued, he stated that the young girl appeared more rational than ever; but the delusion was, she fancied herself quite a different person, would give quite a clear and particular account of herself, fancy herself to be a prisoner to some unknown enemy, and that she had been carried off in some strange and cruel manner, &c. The Signor Castricc ended by saying that I should only be troubled with the care o this young English girl for the few days the fit lasted; but of all things to take care and not let her get beyond the two rooms prepared for her. When the paroxysm was over, her father would come for her.

"Now, my dear child," continued the dame, regarding the placid, unmoved countenance of our heroine, "this is all I know of the business. I prepared the two rooms and waited till your arrival, bestowing very little thought upon the matter, till I saw and looked earnestly into your beautiful and innocent face, and then my first thought was, what a sad pity it was that such an accident should have happened to so young and so fair a creature."

Mary, with her sweet, affectionate manner, so artless and so natural, rose up, and putting her arms round the old Dame's neck, kissed her cheek, saying:

"How grateful I am, that those who have so cruelly treated me should have placed me under the care of so kind a person as Dame Margarita. So they wished to persuade you that I am subject to a strange delusion, believing myself to be in fact, not myself. I never in my life ever heard of this Signor Castricci. My father, General Grey, who is now Governor of Gibraltar, never mentioned such a name to me during my life. Who is it that has carried me off, and for what purpose, baffles all my conjectures; I can see no object in it. But you, my dear dame, can easily undo this mischief, and repair the evil that has been inflicted on me. We can not be more than six hours' distance from Florence; a messenger could be sent to the D—— Palace, where my protector, Lord Herringstone, resides, and who must be as well as his wife, in a state of distraction. Only let him know where I am, and in a few hours he will be here, and you will then see how disgracefully you have been imposed upon."

"That, cara, I will assuredly do, and as soon as possible, for though I am merely a housekeeper and kind of superintendent of the Signor Castricci, still I will not be made a party to any bad projects of his or my son's, whom it grieves me to say, leads a very wild and reckless life."

Whilst the old lady was speaking, they heard the trampling of horses' feet beneath the window, and jumping up, she walked over and looked down into the wide court beneath.

"Two or three signors have just dismounted, and gone into the house," she said; "I did not see their faces, so I will go and learn who they are. Be of good heart, carissima; I now know what to do. Be not afraid; I will see that no one disturbs or molests you."

And turning round, she quitted the room.

Mary remained for some time buried in thought, bewildered with the difficulties of her abduction; as to the Signor Castricci, she knew nothing of him; he must therefore be only an agent in the transaction; perhaps the arrival of the two persons Dame Margaret spoke of, would enlighten her on the subject, and, anxious for the elucidation of the mystery, she rose from her chair and proceeded to look out from the window, but was disappointed in the view she obtained. She gazed down in a very spacious courtyard, surrounded apparently by farm buildings and outhouses, but the doors did not open into the court-yard, which was paved with an immense tank in the middle full of water, with two narrow stone conduits carrying it off in different directions; where it was supplied from she could not see, but it ran off very rapidly without its contents diminishing. Looking over the buildings across some few acres of arable land, her view was bounded on all sides by an immense extent of forest, and behind that again rose the summit of some high hills, the sides of which were covered with timber. She could not see much of the house, but she judged it to be very extensive; it had nothing of a castellated form in it, and the great iron gates of the court were supported upon immense solid square stone pillars. There was not a soul to be seen stirring about the court or along the small space of road visible through the gates.

Turning away from the window, she began surveying the saloon itself, but there was nothing in or about it worthy of observation; the pictures were evidently old, but of no great beauty, and what with neglect and time, not very attractive. An antique bookcase contained a few books, and finding time hang heavy on her hands, she opened several, and at last found a very old edition of Dante; before sitting down to peruse its pages, she went to the door and tried it, but found she was still a prisoner; it was locked.

The day wore on, and the poor girl wondered she did not see either Dame Margaret, or her niece, the pretty Maria.

It was rather late in the afternoon, when she heard the door unlock, and looking round she perceived a middle-aged woman, with a remarkably stupid, if not forbidding expression of countenance, enter the room carrying a tray covered with a cloth; the tray contained a roast fowl and some other trifles, and a decanter of wine. This she placed on the table, and Mary asked:

"Pray where is Dame Margaret?"

"Que sa, signora," returned the woman bluntly, and putting some logs on the fire, without another word she retired, carefully locking the door after her.

"This does not augur well," thought Mary, a little startled. "I hope my persecutors do not suspect that Dame Margaret is inclined to befriend me."

These and other thoughts rendered Mary too uneasy to bestow much attention to the food. Her repast was soon finished, and in half an hour after, the same woman came and removed the tray, brought some wood, and placed candles on the table. Her aspect was so disagreeable that our heroine did not address a word to her, but in a very sad frame of mind took up her book to avoid thought.

From this she was, however, roused by hearing the key turn in the lock. The door opened, and a gentleman in a riding dress entered the room. Mary uttered an exclamation of intense surprise and alarm, for on raising her eyes to the stranger's face, she beheld standing before her Lord Delamaine; she felt her cheeks glow and her whole frame tremble from agitation, and a feeling of indignation as the conviction flashed into her mind, that he was the author of the cruel outrage she had endured, and the detention she was suffering.

Lord Delamaine, for such he is certainly still entitled to be called, advanced coolly into the saloon, with his dark eyes steadily fixed upon the prisoner; his face was pale, and he looked thinner than when last she saw him; but there was an expression on his features, cold, stern, and repelling, that threw a chill over our heroine, and very soon banished the flush raised by indignation on her cheeks.

Lord Delamaine took a chair and sat down, saying: "You are no doubt surprised, Miss Grey, at my appearance here."

"I am, indeed, surprised," said Mary Grey firmly, and recovering her spirit, "to see a man calling himself a gentleman degrade himself so much as to commit so wanton and cowardly an act as you have committed, my lord. For what purpose am I torn from the protection of Lord Herringstone?"

"I am very glad, madam," returned his lordship with a sneering smile on his lip, "that you have the spirit to question me, as it will save time. I will answer you at once; I brought you here to become my wife."

Though at first appalled by the cool reply of Lord Delamaine, Mary did not let it appear by her tone or manner that she was frightened, but at once calmly replied:

"You dare not attempt an act of such daring villany. Your wife I shall never be, death would be far preferable."

"So all young ladies say," replied his lordship, with a loud laugh, "when they are deeply in love with a beardless boy, and another lover proposes; but do not mistake me, madam, there is no love in this business," and in a bitter almost exasperated tone he added: "No, madam, my motive for the act I have committed is revenge!"

Mary felt sick, her heart beat more wildly as she began to feel and to know the dark motives and passions that swayed the mind and actions of Lord Delamaine.

"Yes, madam," he continued, seeing Mary leaning back in her chair pale as death, and unable for the moment to speak, "revenge is my aim and sole motive. I did love you, and you knew it; and you did not scorn my love, till the beardless face of a mere boy captivated your fancy, and——"

The maiden rose to her feet, her fine graceful figure became erect, and her eyes flashed with indignation and passion, as she with a wave of her hand interrupted Lord Delamaine.

"When you add a base falsehood, my lord, to your cowardly conduct, I will no longer remain to be so grievously insulted. Your own heart tells you that what you have said is false—utterly false and unfounded. I did not know that you persisted in pursuing a line of conduct with respect to me that was folly to persevere in, and was repugnant to me; before you saw me, it was well known at the Cape that you had declared an attachment to Miss Helen Probert."

"Has Helen Probert dared to utter such a falsehood!" exclaimed Lord Delamaine passionately, and rising from his chair; "but no matter, madam, for a first interview this has lasted long enough; you now know your position and my determination. One thing is certain, the wife of him you now know as Francis De Burgh you shall never be, while I live," and turning round, without a look at the indignant maiden, he left the room, closed the door and locked it, leaving Mary thankful he was gone, though she sank back in her chair, covered her face with her hands, and burst into a passionate flood of tears. And thus we must leave her, and in our next chapter see what became of Helen Probert.

## CHAPTER XLIII.

HELEN PROBERT, her mind and thoughts fully occupied, and closely wrapped in her mantle, under which she carried a small bundle, left her residence, and crossing the Corso directly facing the church styled Or San Michelo, with its handsome bronze statue, turned down a narrow side street forming a pathway into an intricate maze or labyrinth of poor mean-looking houses. The gloomy dilapidated appearance of this quarter of the city, offers a strange contrast to the airy, handsome, modern buildings of the Corso, and the imposing feudal palaces of old Florence.

As Helen passed down this narrow street, she paused one instant to gaze up at one of the meanest dwellings; it had but two windows in front, and was three stories high. So narrow was this gloomy street, that a sunbeam rarely visited its gloomy length, even in the height of summer. Helen looked up at the house and over the door, till she perceived a large sandstone, on which was perceptible a much-defaced escutcheon; beneath this, on a marble tablet, she read the following words: "In questa casa degli Alighieri nacque il divino Poeta."

What an abode, thought the gazer as she walked on, counting the houses, till she came to the fourth from that in which the great poet was born. She glanced up at the house, it was one of the best in that narrow gloomy street, and entering through the open door, she looked around for some person to speak to. A side door attracted her, and against this she knocked; in a few seconds it was opened by a young woman well attired, with a very young child in her arms.

"Pray does Pietro Sanzi dwell here?" demanded Miss Probert.

"Si, Signora," replied the woman civilly, "he is my husband, but he is not at this moment in the house."

"I am very anxious to see him," said Miss Probert; "do you think he could be found?"

"Oh, yes, signora; please walk into the room, and I will see and find some one in the house to go for him; I think he went to the Palazzo Uffizzii."

Helen entered the room, and sat down on a chair the young woman placed for her; the room was clean and tidy, decently furnished, and had sundry scriptural pictures hung against the walls, and a tolerably large image of the Madonna in a niche in the wall. There was a little girl about three years old, with eyes as dark as sloes, playing on the floor with a diminutive Italian greyhound. The child ceased its sport, and so did the dog; and both looked eagerly into the fine and then flushed features of the visitor.

Pietro Sanzi's wife placed her sleeping baby in an adjoining apartment on the bed, and then going out of the room, she called from the foot of the stairs:

"Bembo, Bembo, are you above?"

She had scarcely uttered the words when Helen heard a noise, just like a ball bounding down the stairs, and the next moment something like a bundle of rags rolled into the room, the young woman trying to stop it, though she was laughing heartily all the time.

The bundle of rags all of a sudden unfolded itself with a spring of three or four feet from the floor, and came down again upon two legs; and then became visible to the eyes of the English girl, one of the strangest looking urchins, about twelve years old, she ever beheld. Of the boy's figure it was impossible to judge, for it was so strangely invested and covered with various coloured rags and strips of cloth, that no part of the form was visible; but the face made up for the want of shape. It possessed an indescribable expression, intense intelligence beamed from a pair of large lustrous jet black eyes, and when the lips parted and the boy laughed, he disclosed teeth that rivalled ivory in whiteness. Such was the boy's expression when you could catch his face in repose, but he made such frequent and singularly droll contortions of features, that not one moment did they retain the same expression.

"You maladita boy!" exclaimed the young woman, catching him by the shoulder; "are you not ashamed to go on with such gambols before the signora?" giving him as she spoke a good shake. "Listen, boy; run to the Palazzo Uffizii; you know where to find Pietro Lanzi, and tell him to come here as quickly as possible, that a lady wants him."

"Here, my good boy," said Helen, taking a silver coin from her purse, "take this for yourself, and be sure to bring the Signor Lanzi back with you."

The urchin got the coin in his possession some kind of way—how, it was impossible to say—and the next instant he rolled out of the room in the same manner as he had entered.

"What a strange child!" remarked Helen to the young woman, "can you trust him?"

"Oh, yes, signora," replied the woman with a smile; "he is my husband's right hand; he could not do without him. He picked him up when an infant on the steps of a house, without a rag to his little body. We were not married then; but as nobody owned the child, or would own it, my husband took compassion on it, and placed him under the care of an old woman, and he grew up quite wild-like about the streets, but devotedly attached to my husband. He appeared to be gifted with a strange knowledge, and before he became eight years old, he somehow picked up intelligence of everything going on in the city. Nothing escaped the boy; he even knew what took place in the Ducal Palace. If anything was lost or stolen, Bembo knew where to find the lost article, or he knew who stole it.

"When we took this house, Bembo established himself above stairs, and has his own room. You must not think, signora, that he is always covered with rags; he puts them on to follow his pursuits. Sometimes he stays away days and nights; but where he goes, or how he employs himself, he does not even tell my husband. Through his means, my husband has detected several notorious robbers and assassins, and gained large rewards. Ha! here is my husband; I know his step."

The next instant the door opened, and the well-known thief-taker and detective, Pietro Lanzi, entered the room. He was a man of middle size, strongly built, with a very dark complexion, but rather pleasing expression of countenance. He did not appear to be more than six-and-thirty; he was well dressed, like a substantial Florentine citizen. He showed no surprise at being summoned into the presence of a young English lady; but after saluting her respectfully, requested to know in what way he could be of service to her; whilst his wife, thinking there might be something to confide to her husband not intended for her ears, very prudently withdrew, thus shewing that she had not the bump of curiosity, or else satisfied that her husband would impart the matter to her afterwards.

Helen meanwhile distinctly detailed to the Florentine detective the minute particulars of the abduction of her friend.

Pietro Lanzi listened attentively; then begging Helen to excuse his absence for a moment, he went to the door, and whistled in a peculiar manner. In a moment the boy Bembo was at his side; he whispered some words into his ear, after which the boy, without any preparation, dashed out of the d r a l disappeared.

"Now, signora," observed Pietro Lanzi, as he re-entered the room, and closed the door, "I suppose you wish me to track the ruffians that carried off this English lady?"

"Just so," returned Helen; and taking ut he purse, she placed twenty gold ducats on the table. "I will double that, Signor Lanzi, if you discover for me the place—mind you, the place to which they have carried Miss Grey. Leave the rest to me; but all this must be kept secret."

"You are liberal, signora, very liberal, and you shall be well served; before two days are out, you shall know all you require.

May I ask you a question or two? Your answers may assist me."

"Certainly," answered Helen.

"Do you suspect any particular person to have committed this outrage?"

"I am positive as to the person," replied Miss Probert; "but though the instigator, he could not have committed this act without a superior agent in the affair."

"Then the lady is carried off by some English lover, no doubt Is the gentleman—or, rather, has the signor shown himself in Florentine society this winter?"

"No; he has not appeared in Florence."

"Well, signora, that will do. Pray where shall I see you at the expiration of two days?"

"At the Hotel della Posta, in Lastrá. I shall remain there for three days."

"Then the sooner I am off the better," said Pietro Lanzi shortly.

Helen rose, and seeing a sheet of paper and a pencil, observed she would write down her name.

"There is no occasion, signora," replied the Italian detective, with a smile; "my trade requires me to know everyone's face, foreign as well as native, in Florence. You dwell in the Goro Mansion, on the Corso."

"You are correct, Signor Lanzi," said Helen with a serious smile, and wrapping herself in her mantle, after a few more trifling observations she left the detective's house, and proceeding to a venturino's procured at once a carriage to Lastrá. In the evening her own favourite and special attendant arrived at the hotel, bringing with her a small trunk and a letter from Mrs. Probert.

Two days passed over tediously enough to the anxious Helen at the inn at Lastrá, for she did not stir out. She heard of the search that the Florentine police were making for Miss Grey, and that as yet they were completely baffled. It was three hours after sunset of the second day, when Pietro Lanzi requested permission to see her.

When he entered the room she knew by his countenance that he was the harbinger of good news.

"You have succeeded, Pietro Lanzi," she exclaimed.

"Si, signora, not only succeeded in discovering where the young lady is, but have discovered the chief agent in the affair; a notorious political offender, for whose apprehension a large reward is to be obtained; he is even at this moment engaged in a conspiracy against the Duke and ministers, a conspiracy that has hitherto baffled me to find out the head."

"You are generally very successful in your undertakings, Signor Lanzi," said Helen, "but now for particulars."

"This time, like many another, I owe my chief success to

Bembo. The first day I was baffled; I followed on their track to Leghorn, and was there, like the Florentine police, thrown out; but I learnt that Lord Herringstone and an English officer—captain of an armed schooner—had gone in pursuit towards Piombino, having somehow or other been induced to believe that Miss Grey had been carried off in that direction. The English nobleman had good reasons for his belief, but which belief I did not share, so I retraced my steps to Ambrogiano, where I parted from Bembo, disguised as a peasant boy. He laughed at my disappointment, saying:

"'Ah, papa Lanzi, you must resign your post to me, I have found them out.'

"'The devil you have, Bembo.'

"'Evero, they went across the river two miles from this, and the postillion that drove them from this was heavily bribed; do you know where the girl is?'

"'No,' said I, 'but where is she, boy?'

"'In the old mansion of the Counts Del Salto, now belonging to the Signor Castricci.'

"'How did you find this out, Bembo?' I questioned, greatly rejoiced, for I began to think the affair cleverly managed.

"'While you went on to Leghorn,' said Bembo, 'I set out, having an idea in my own head, to examine the roads well, though they were not very easy to make out; still I here and there caught the track till I came to a little common leading down to the river. Here some curious marks on the road attracted me, and induced me to go down towards the stream; the banks are muddy here, and you know, Pietro Lanzi, that the water every day is getting lower in the river, and sure enough I found tracks of feet, and a small tiny foot—a signora's foot—as I will show you; and in the mud under the bank was the mark of a boat's keel; the water had left the mud, and the mark was plain enough.'

But not to weary you, signora, the boy crossed the river below where there is a very shallow ford, and with incredible patience and ingenuity, and questioning people while asking for work as a farm boy, he got on till he came to the Castricci Mansion, and had an interview with Dame Margarita Musone, who is my wife's aunt. He told Dame Margarita that I would recommend him if she would take him into her service. She was very kind to him, but said he was too young, and looked too delicate for the drudgery of farm service, and told him he had better stay with me for a year or two more; he remained several hours in the house, talking and joking and playing all manner of tricks to please the young niece of Dame Margarita, and so cunningly did the boy manage matters as to discover that there was a beautiful English girl in the house, not quite right in her head, and her friends had sent her there for change of air. Finally Bembo departed with a present from the dame, and a message to her niece, my wife."

"He is a clever boy and shall be well rewarded," remarked Helen; "and now, Signor Lanzi, I will explain my plans to you; they will benefit all parties, and restore the young lady to her home without risking lives, or making the public acquainted with family matters, better kept secret. I will double the sum I proposed, and when you hear me, romantic as you may think my projects to be, you will yet see they are the best that can be adopted under existing circumstances."

What passed between Miss Probert and the Florentine detective we must leave our story to disclose.

## CHAPTER XLIV.

Two days had passed since the fair captive's interview with Lord Delamaine, and she began to feel to the heart's core the full bitterness and desolation of her situation. In the power of a man, whose worst passions were roused by disappointed love and ambition, in a country also where agents for the commission of crime were so easily obtained, she trembled to think, if not rescued from her persecutor, what might be the result of his daring and reckless desire of revenge upon the man, who had not only supplanted him in his love, but would deprive him in the end of rank, station, and fortune.

Knowing that Francis De Burgh was beyond his reach, and fully conscious that his whole heart and hopes were centred in a union with her, Lord Delamaine's hate would be fully gratified by placing for ever a bar between her and his rival. Though resolved to perish, sooner than pronounce words that would bind her destiny to that of Lord Delamaine, she still felt she had no power to resist being dragged to the altar; and though her lips pronounced no assent, Lord Delamaine's object would be gained to a certain extent. Miserable, dejected in heart and mind, hopeless and desponding, she retired to the inner chamber, fastened her door, and was proceeding to throw herself on the bed when a folded slip of paper lying on the table attracted her attention ; it had certainly not been there in the morning.

How slight a cause sometimes revives hope in the human breast; in truth we scarcely ever entirely lose sight of that divine feeling, even under the most despairing situation. The feeling for a moment may be crushed, but it springs into being like a meteor's flash, from some unlooked for, unthought of circumstance.

That folded piece of paper, evidently placed in a conspicuous situation so as to attract her, caused Mary Grey's heart to beat with renewed hope. Her pale cheek flushed as she eagerly grasped and unfolded it, and read with transport the few words it contained She knew the handwriting well. Filled with wonder and joy, she read half aloud:

"Have no fear, dear Mary, to-night I will see you; therefore courage and hope.

"HELEN PROBERT."

With tears running down her cheeks, Mary Grey pressed the precious paper to her bosom, and to her lips. No lover's avowal of affection could have given such an ecstasy of feeling as at that moment filled the heart of our heroine.

For several minutes she remained clasping the paper to her breast, quite incapable of even thought, so sanguine did she feel of deliverance now that her friends knew where she was. But after some time she began to collect her scattered thoughts, and then wonder and surprise pervaded her mind, and she asked herself, why, if Helen were acquainted with her place of imprisonment, a moment should be lost in releasing her; for surely if Helen knew where she was, Lord Herringstone would also be made acquainted with it. And if so, by applying to the authorities, why any need of mystery or artifice in her release? The next thought that struck her was how the paper came upon her table, no one had passed through the rooms after the new attendant had arranged them. Could she have placed the paper there? To judge by her manner and countenance, Mary answered "decidedly not." Another question she mentally asked, "how was Helen to visit her that night?"—but determined to abide the issue patiently, she gave up perplexing her mind with vain conjectures.

It was late when her new and silent attendant brought her tea and coffee, and on the tray was a letter addressed to her. The woman having asked her if she required anything further for the night, and receiving the answer "no," departed, carefully locking the door after her.

Mary Grey looked at the letter, well aware it came from Lord Delamaine, and her first impulse was to put it on the fire, her second determined her to open it, and she read as follows:—

"MADAM,

"In order to avoid interviews that only lead to useless reproaches and recriminations, I now submit to you a proposition, which, if you accede to, will restore you in twenty-four hours to your friends. If you will consent to become my wife quietly, and without opposition in word or deed, the moment the ceremony is over a carriage shall be in readiness to convey you back to Florence. At the same time, I will take the most solemn oath before the clergyman who is here to perform the ceremony, never to claim you as my wife: unless, regardless of the vows you will pronounce, you attempt to evade them by permitting another to aspire to your hand. If you refuse this you must be mine by force, and an hour afterwards we shall leave this country so as to defy pursuit; if you are wise you will accept this proposal. A simple 'yes' or 'no;' tomorrow will decide your fate and mine.

"DELAMAINE."

"Never!" exclaimed our heroine, with a flush of intense indignation; "never shall lips of mine pronounce vows abhorrent to my soul."

Helen had not stated at what hour she would visit her, neither could she imagine, when she gazed round her chamber, how she would obtain access, unless through the walls, which were of dark oak panelling. And that idea inspired hope, for she was aware that in almost all old Italian houses and palaces, there existed passages and modes of communication with various chambers. Having carefully fastened her door, she sat down by the fire to wait patiently for Helen's appearance. The silence of all around, the heat of the fire, and the last night passed without sleep, overpowered her, and she fell into a slumber. How long she dozed she knew not, but when she awoke up with a start, she beheld her expected friend sitting opposite her reading Lord Delamaine's letter. She sprang to her feet with an exclamation of pure joy, and throwing her arms round her visitor's neck wept passionately, with her head upon her shoulder.

Helen seemed much affected; she kissed Mary's cheeks repeatedly, and soothed her. Having, in a few minutes, conquered the hysterical feeling that had oppressed her, Mary Grey sat down and gazed into the pale but anxious features of her friend.

"How is this, Helen," she inquired, "that you can come and go in this mansion as you please, and I still a prisoner? Why does not Lord Herringstone come and deliver me from this villain and coward, who has so cruelly outraged my feelings, and who has dared to threaten that he would force me to become his wife? You know what I mean, Helen, for you have read his letter."

Helen's pale cheek became crimson, and her voice and manner betrayed great agitation, as she replied in a low voice:

"There is no longer any need of concealment, Mary, between you and me. Hitherto I have deceived you in some respects; but never, so help me Heaven! never with the intention of injuring you in any way."

"I can partly understand you," replied Mary, more calmly; "but answer me one question. Does he know that you are at this moment in this house?"

"No; God forbid, Mary, that he did!" returned Miss Probert; "that knowledge would be fatal to our designs."

"Then, since that is the case, Helen!" exclaimed Mary eagerly, "why not, as you have contrived to enter this mansion without his knowledge, why not let us both quit it this instant? Once clear of this detested place, surely we can easily obtain the means of returning to Florence?"

Helen Probert bent down her head, and did not meet the earnest gaze of her friend with a confident look; but after a moment she raised her eyes, saying:—

"Will you listen patiently to me, Mary, for a few minutes. Believe me," she almost passionately added, "that I have your true interest at heart, and that there is no more fear of Herbert De Burgh—for he never was, and it is not probable that he ever will be, Lord Delamaine,—succeeding in his daring and mad project, than there is of your consenting to be his wife."

"I will listen to you, Helen, patiently; and, despite of many vague and bygone reminiscences, I will trust you."

"You are a dear, true-hearted, loving soul, Mary!" cried Miss Probert, with great emotion, "and Heaven forbid I should ever again deceive you!

"I need scarcely tell you that I am devotedly attached to the very man you despise and abhor; the great object of my life was to become his wife. When at the Cape, he professed to be passionately attached to me; but at that time he was not aware that he was next heir to the Delamane title and property, for it was confidently believed that the late Lord Delamaine was married to an officer's widow in India, and had two sons. We were both, therefore, but moderately gifted with fortune, and he stated that he would offer me his hand the moment he obtained a step in rank, so as to enable us to live in comfort. Some little time after your arrival in the Cape, I perceived a change in Captain De Burgh's manner, and it soon became very evident that, attracted by your beauty, and perhaps, also, your reputed wealth, he was forgetting his vows to me. The arrival of Lord Delamaine at the Cape, on his return to Europe, settled the wavering mind of Captain De Burgh. He then learned that his uncle had never married, and that if he did not marry, which was not at all likely at his age, that he was next heir to the title and estates.

"It is needless to dwell on these scenes. My mother had long wished to return to England, so that when General Grey, and Lord Delamaine, and Captain De Burgh, embarked in the British Queen for England, we did so likewise.

"All this time I kept my feelings to myself; I neither upbraided my fickle lover, nor made you the confidante of my hopes and wishes. I saw from the first that Herbert De Burgh's attentions to you were anything but pleasing, and, therefore, I felt quite satisfied his suit would fail.

"You may wonder, Mary, that I should continue to love a man who so little deserved a true affection. Alas! when once you love, truly and devotedly, it is hard to wean the heart from the object of its first choice, unworthy though he may be; but I still thought that when quite satisfied you would never consent to become his wife, he would return to his first vows. Alas! we women are very weak in judgment when love once gains dominion over us.

"I pass over the events that followed, and our narrow escape from shipwreck. Before Francis De Burgh left the British Queen, in Liverpool, I perceived that he would become your lover; and, pardon me, Mary, that you would not look as coldly upon him as upon his namesake, Herbert De Burgh.

"When we reached London, we still continued our intimacy, and, strange enough Herbert, also continued to visit and keep up a rather more than friendly intercourse with us. He became Lord Delamaine, though I fancy, from many circumstances, that he strongly suspected he was not the true heir to the title. On the death of an uncle, I became possessed of a fortune of thirty thousand pounds.

"Your father was appointed Governor of Gibraltar, and you sailed from England in Lord Herringstone's yacht. I had heard you had steadily refused to become the wife of Lord Delamaine, and I hoped and believed he would have abandoned all thoughts of you, when, to my infinite surprise, I learned he had sailed with his regiment for Gibraltar.

"However, in a very short time he resigned his commission, and returned to England. I need not tell you by what means I was informed that he intended going on the Continent; I knew you were passing the winter in Florence, and therefore felt convinced he would go there also, and in a country like Italy, might accomplish his project against you, either through love or revenge. I prevailed on my mother to spend the winter in Florence, and thus we mét again; but to my surprise, Herbert De Burgh had not visited Florence, though I suspected he was not very distant. You may remember, about a month ago, Lady Hasard was robbed of a case of jewels in rather a mysterious manner; there was a miniature in the case she valued highly; she offered a great reward for its recovery; she received a note from an unknown hand, stating that the miniature would be returned, if no questions were asked, for half the reward offered.

"It happened at that time that Lady Hasard had consulted a Florentine detective famous for his singular good fortune in tracing thieves, and recovering stolen property. She showed him the note; he looked at it, examined it critically, and then said, 'Benissimo, you must not, my Lady, accept this proposal; in three days you shall have both case and miniature.' He was true to his word, and the detective, whose name was Pietro Lanzi, gained, besides a large reward, great credit.

"When you were carried off in the boat I surmised at once that Herbert De Burgh was the instigator, if not the perpetrator, of the outrage. I recollected at once the name of Pietro Lanzi, returned home, wrote a note to my mother, telling her not to be uneasy, to send my maid Laura to me at Lastrá, and to say nothing about my absence to anyone.

"I had an interview with Lanzi, and then went and took up my abode at the hotel at Lastrá. At the expiration of two days, through the cleverness of a very strange boy, Pietro Lanzi discovered that you were detained a prisoner in this place, and in the vaults of this very house a dangerous party of conspirators were in the habit of meeting, for the express purpose of raising a revolution in the Grand Duke's dominions."

"I learned that Herbert De Burgh, whom Lanzi knew as Lord Delamaine, had for agent in this affair, an Italian named Castricci, a man of the most profligate habits, and imbued with the most dangerous schemes of aggrandisement. Castricci is the owner of this mansion; but for years the farm has been managed by his foster-brother, a man of notoriously bad habits, and his mother, Dame Margarita, as kind-hearted a being as ever breathed, lived in this house. Pietro Lanzi's wife was Dame Magarita's niece."

Helen paused a moment, and looked almost timidly in the face of her attentive and surprised listener; then she continued:

"You naturally will ask why, having discovered your abode, I did not at once make it known to Lord Herringstone, and thus instantly obtain your release?

"You shall hear my reason for not doing so. I wished to avoid bloodshed, and certain disgrace and exposure to Herbert De Burgh. I resolved instead to get into the house, disguised as you see me, like a Florentine peasant girl. The young boy who first made the discovery of where you had been carried, managed to introduce me to Dame Margarita, and in a few minutes I gained her over to assist in my projects. We had formed our plans, when the arrival of Herbert, accompanied by Castricci, and a stranger, frustrated all. Dame Margarita concealed me in this wing of the house; but it seems she was at once suspected of being inclined to aid you in escaping, and they have shut her and her niece up in this wing also, and sent for another person to attend on you. I was in despair, but Dame Margarita only laughed, saying, 'We can baffle them now when we like. I know more of the secrets of this old place than they do, or probably anyone else now alive. I can go out of the house when I please; and I know also a secret passage to the young signora's chamber.' Thus, Mary, I gave you notice of my being here, and you were asleep when I entered or you would have seen me pass through a secret door in the oak panelling. De Burgh's writing struck me, I took the liberty of of reading it; and now if you will assist me, I will, in twenty-four hours, get you away from this imprisonment, and send you to Florence, without either contention, disgrace, or public exposure to any person."

Mary sat thoughtfully silent for a moment, and then said:

"What do you wish me to do? for it appears to me, even from

what you say, that nothing is easier than for us both to quit this house this very night, as Dame Margarita knows the way to leave it, unknown to our jailors."

Helen Probert coloured slightly, as she replied:

"We might attempt it certainly, but there would be a greater risk than you imagine; besides, you would be still exposed to the machinations of your enemy, infinitely more exasperated by failure and disappointment."

"Once more under the protection of Lord Herringstone, and on my guard, I should feel but little apprehension of Lord Delamaine's schemes," replied Mary, calmly: "but how do you propose to act, Helen?"

Miss Probert seemed much agitated, and paused as if to gain composure ere she replied:

"The reading of that letter has suggested to me a plan that will for ever prevent De Burgh molesting you in any way."

Again she hesitated, but mastering her nervousness, she took from her vest a letter, and opening it, ran her eyes over the contents, and then handing it to Mary, and pointing to the last few lines, requested her to read them.

Mary did so, and thought Helen's character did not shine in a more exalted light from the perusal.

The words Mary read were as follows:—

"In fact, Helen, I am not actuated by love, but—revenge! I am aware I shall lose rank, station, and fortune, for there can be no doubt of Francis De Burgh's birth; but if I could but poison the cup of felicity that seems already in the grasp of that man I abhor, I would throw myself at your feet, implore forgiveness for the past, and quit with you this country for ever. I am miserable. Hatred is gnawing at my heart, and impelling me to acts I really detest. Would I had never seen Mary Grey, or ever succeeded to a title and wealth I had no right to. I read your letter a dozen times over. You are right; but revenge is sweet.

"Yours devotedly evermore,
"DELAMAINE."

Mary laid down the letter with a painful feeling at her heart, and raised her eyes towards those of Helen who was weeping bitterly, as, burying her face in her hand, she sobbed out:

"Do not despise me, Mary—oh! do not think contemptuously of me because I still love a man who could express such sentiments as those you have read."

"My poor Helen!" cried Mary, conquering the feeling the perusal of that letter had excited, and rising up, she threw her arms round her friend's neck, and kissing her, continued:

"And do you think, Helen, supposing you were united to this—to Lord Delamaine—do you think your happiness would be ensured?"

"I do," returned Helen, looking up, and speaking solemnly. "At one time he was a most devoted and affectionate lover, and though of a rather passionate nature, I never heard that his passions or disposition led him to commit any act unbecoming a gentleman, till his succession to that unfortunate title. His father, Sir Godfrey De Burgh, all know is a bad and terribly vicious man; but he was never till lately even on friendly terms with his son, whose fortune he dissipated in a shameful manner."

"Then tell me, Helen, plainly, and without fear, what your project is, and how I can consistently assist you."

"May you, dear Mary, be as truly happy as your kind and noble heart entitles you to be; and I feel sure you will, for your love is bestowed on as pure and generous a heart as your own. My plan may appear wild; but I feel positive, now I have read that letter, that it will succeed. Simply, then, answer that letter, consent to —nay, start not, hear me to the end—consent to become the wife of De Burgh, provided that the moment the ceremony is over, you enter a carriage and return to Florence."

"Good God, Helen!" interrupted Mary, with a startled tone and pale cheek, "actually let a sacred ceremony——"

"Dear girl, you are impatient," mildly interrupted Helen, "no such ceremony will be performed with you. I will take your place, while you, under the guidance of the boy Bembo, and in this dress, proceed to Spinello, where there will be a berlin ready to convey you to Florence. This must be done at once, for Pietro Lanzi has determined to arrest the Signor Castricci and one-and-twenty other conspirators who will meet here on Thursday night; this is Tuesday."

"But, good gracious, Helen! how can you possibly expect to pass for me?" asked Mary.

"Quite easily; we are the same height and figure. You must insist on the ceremony being in the evening, and that you will be merely required to repeat the few words necessary. With this immense thick long veil thrown over my head, my features will be perfectly concealed, and the trembling voice that such a ceremony naturally and often causes will prevent the difference of tone being noticed. At all events, let me incur the risk. Leave it all to me, for I intend you to quit this place long before the hour you will fix for the ceremony; and if discovered before the ceremony is completed, I will abide the issue. You will be safe, for Lanzi has a careful watch over these premises."

We cannot delay our story by detailing all the arguments used by Helen to conquer the repugnance Mary felt to the deception proposed; but Helen's tears and her own ardent desire to escape from the power of a man she feared and abhorred, caused her at last to consent.

The letter was written under Helen's dictation; she also requested that no one should be present but the clergyman, as she was determined not to expose herself to the gaze of any stranger, and hoped Dame Margarita might attend during the ceremony.

In great agitation, the task of writing the letter was completed; and after some further conversation, as the night was far advanced, the two fair girls separated. Mary saw Helen go through the secret panel, into a dark, narrow passage between the walls, with an intense desire to follow; but Helen quickly closed the panel, and our heroine remained alone, not exactly satisfied with herself, and yet not well seeing how she could act otherwise, for Helen seemed so determined to carry out her own projects, cost what it would.

## CHAPTER XLV.

It was near the hour of twelve the day following the scene described in our last chapter, that three individuals were seated at breakfast in a remote chamber in the Castricci mansion. A most substantial breakfast was spread upon the table, supplied with wines of various kinds to slake thirst, should coffee not satisfy the guests.

We will briefly describe the appearance of two of the party who were evidently not content with the coffee; the third person, who appeared extremely thoughtful and silent, requires no description, our readers being well acquainted with the appearance of Lord Delamaine.

Sitting opposite to his lordship was the Signor Luigi Castricci; he was a tall full-bodied man between thirty and forty years of age, with features which might have been good in early youth, but which now told of a life of reckless intemperance, of perpetual scheming, of restless political ambition, and vice; dark overhanging eyebrows; a perpetual sneering smile on his short upper lip, disclosing a row of large, but well-formed and well-coloured teeth, added to long masses of straight dark hair and long beard, formed altogether a somewhat remarkable countenance. The stranger was a thin, almost emaciated young man, certainly not thirty, habited in black; his dark eyes were sunk in his head, and his cheeks sallow and hollow from intemperance. Sorry are we to record it, he was a clergyman, and an Englishman, and was drinking brandy and water, and in truth could scarcely be said to be sober when thus introduced to the notice of our readers.

"You had better take more water and less brandy, at all events until our business is over," observed Lord Delamaine looking over, and with evident disgust, at the thin young man.

"Oh, Santa Madonna!" said the Signor Castricci laughing, "let Signor Wilkins sober himself with the same medicine that put him under the table last night; it will give him courage to get through his task, a rather unusual one for him of late years."

This was said in Italian, not one word of which the said Mr. Wilkins understood, but he filled his glass again and replied to Lord Delamaine's observation, in a ghastly grin, saying :—

"I am only steadying my hand, my lord; a hair of the dog that bit me is a good cure."

"You do not seem to be in particular good spirits this morning, my lord," observed the Signor Castricci, pushing away his plate and filling a goblet with wine, "how is that, and after receiving so favourable a reply from your fair intended? though, upon my soul, I cannot understand your projects; she consents to marry you, on a certain condition; but surely you do not mean to comply with her terms. Per Baccho! a splendid girl and a noble fortune to let slip through your fingers, even after the knot is tied, appears ridiculous."

"I told you before, Castricci," said his lordship rather haughtily, "that I seek revenge, not a wife."

"Yes, yes, Cospetto! I understand you well enough," returned the Italian; "revenge is a very fine thing in its way; we Italians understand that passion thoroughly, but I cannot comprehend why you should place a bar against yourself. In gratifying your revenge by preventing this girl from marrying, you also prevent yourself; you mar your own fortune. Knowing, as I do, your situation with respect to the Delamaine estates, your worthy father has deprived you of your natural rights, having kindly spent your inheritance, pardon me if I ask you a question; when you lose the Delamaine property, what do you intend to do?"

"I will tell you, Signor Luigi," said Lord Delamaine, with perfect calmness, "when that time comes; always provided the Grand Duke leaves your head upon your shoulders till then."

"Ha! ha! if you think head and shoulders will part company so soon," returned the Italian with a careless laugh, "you are mistaken. My plans are too well laid this time to fail; before a month is out, this country will be revolutionized. The French have already overrun the Milanese; the tri-colour is everywhere triumphant; Venice and its tyrants extinguished for ever!"

"Well, as I am not at all revolutionarily inclined," interrupted Lord Delamaine, "I will not argue the matter with you; I have fulfilled my part of our contract before leaving England, and you as yet have faithfully performed yours, but as I do not want to get mixed up in your political schemes, I shall bid you adieu directly this marriage is performed; I wish to get back to England as soon as possible. All is not lost yet; the claimant to the title I hold may be shot by this time, especially as he is a fire-eater, by all accounts, everlastingly putting himself in the way of being blown up or sunk."

"Corpo De Baccho!" cried the Signor Castricci, "I wish I had him here in Tuscany, I would secure you your title and estates for a thousand ducats!"

Lord Delamaine made no remark to this kind observation of his friend, but said:—

"Pray, have you inquired for one of those white veils, like those worn by the Genoese maidens?"

"You are very considerate, my lord, and I see wish to spare the bride from blushing; they are easily procured, Dame Margarita will supply one; they wear them here in all religious pageants. Will you have the ceremony performed in the old family chapel?"

"No," replied Lord Delamaine, "I see no occasion to proceed further than the saloon the lady occupies."

"Benissimo!" returned the Signor Castricci rising, "you will excuse me for a few hours. I have arrangements to make for Thursday." So saying, he rose up and retired, leaving Lord Delamaine and the Rev. Frederick Wilkins together.

This disgrace to the church had by this time satisfied his thirst, at least for the hour; he had steadied his nerves, his hand no longer shook, he could last now till his thirst came on again in the evening. He was running a race with death, but it was not a fair race, the grim enemy was certain of victory, and a speedy one.

Mr. Wilkins was the type of a class common enough in his time, but thank God! getting rare in the British dominions. He was a fast man in college, and a much faster man after he was ordained; of a good family but of small means, his mode of life soon brought him into debt; and finally his intemperate habits into disgrace, and he lost his vicarage. It is quite needless to follow his career; he sunk into debauchery, picked up a livelihood by acts disgraceful but at that time countenanced by the law; thus Lord Delamaine found no difficulty in engaging him to second him in his schemes. He was to have a large sum for his services, but what those services were, so he was provided with the quantity of brandy he required, he little cared.

"Let the ceremony be as short as possible, Wilkins," said Lord Delamaine rising from the table; "and I insist on your not taking any more brandy till this affair is over, and then take my advice, get out of this country as fast as you can."

"Cannot I travel with you, my lord?" said the miserable young man, gazing anxiously at his employer.

"Yes, if you will swear to drink water for ten days. I shall travel night and day, and you know you could not do that"

"No," returned the infatuated drinker, "I could not," looking even then inclined to return to the table.

But Lord Delamaine, who knew his man well, took him by the arm and led him from the room, locking the door and putting the key in his pocket.

"Now go and lie down, it will revive you, I will call you when it is time."

The day wore on, till the shades of evening threw a gloom over the lofty and wide apartments of the Castricci mansion. In the saloon adjoining Mary Grey's sleeping chamber, were assembled the same three individuals we introduced to our readers at the commencement of this chapter. The Rev. Frederick Wilkins was sober and dressed in canonicals, on the table was a large open bible and prayer book, Lord Delamaine looking exceedingly pale and agitated; and the Signor Castricci, who stood carelessly leaning on a high-backed chair with a sneer upon his lips, as his eyes rested upon his lordship. There were no lights in the room, and the shades of fast advancing night rendered objects in the dark wainscoted saloon not very distinct.

Stepping up to the door of the sleeping chamber, Lord Delamaine knocked gently. In a few minutes it was opened, and then Dame Margarita came forth supporting on her arm the supposed Mary Grey, her whole figure enveloped in the long thick white veil so common throughout Italy.

Dame Margarita looked extremely serious, and the intended bride evidently for a moment trembled. Grasping the thick folds of the veil, which, aided by the dusk and gloom of the chamber, completely concealed the outline of her features, Helen, in the attire of Mary Grey, advanced close to the table with her back to the light; Mr. Wilkins motioning to Lord Delamaine to stand by her side, the Signor Castricci also moved forward and stood a few paces distant from the veiled lady.

The ceremony began; the young clergyman was a clear and distinct reader, and read well. He proceeded calmly, requiring the usual responses from the man and the woman, the latter replying in a trembling agitated voice—I will! Low as the sound of the voice was, it somehow caused Lord Delamaine to cast his eyes upon the shrinking figure beside him, but nothing more. When the minister pronounced the words, " Who giveth this woman to be married to this man ?" the Signor Castricci stepped forward and performed his part, with his usual sinister smile on his lip. When Lord Delamaine took the hand of the bride it glowed like fire. The remainder of the ceremony was very much shortened, the final blessing pronounced, and thus Helen Probert and Herbert De Burgh became one ! There was a momentary pause, all, even the Signor Castricci seemed struck by the solemnity of the scene, heightened by the rapidly increasing gloom of the evening.

Lord Delamaine was exceedingly pale, he was about to address his bride, when Helen suddenly threw back the folds of her veil, and turning with pale cheek but a firm clear voice, said to the paralyzed Lord Delamaine, who drew back with a fearful exclamation on his lips:—

" You have now, my lord, fulfilled the pledge you so solemnly made three years ago, to Helen Probert. *You* have sought revenge upon the innocent, *I* revenge upon the guilty."

Lord Delamaine trembled with intense passion but could not speak, while the Signor Castricci, who understood English perfectly, burst into a most fiendish laugh, which caused the blood to fly like a torrent into the face and temples of Lord Delamaine. Turning round with a fierce gesture upon the Italian, he said:—

"Take care, sir, how you mock or laugh at me; you must have been an abettor in this accursed piece of treachery, and this d—— woman," turning to Dame Margarita, "was your agent."

"Come, come, my lord, or no lord, as the case is likely to be," said Signor Castricci, with as fierce a tone as his lordship, "you speak falsely! I never saw this bride of yours in my life. I know she is not Miss Grey, but who the diavolo she is, is best known to your lordship."

Before the exasperated Lord Delamaine could reply, there was a violent trampling of feet heard on the stairs, the door was burst open, and a man rushed in with an alarmed look. It was Dame Margarita's son.

"Quick, for your life! Signor Castricci; a dozen mounted troopers of the Ducal Guard, and two signors, are spurring up the road towards the house. I have barred the great gates to gain time; but be quick!"

All present looked astounded; Signor Castricci's face grew livid with rage; with his clenched hand, he advanced close to Lord Delamaine, exclaiming:

"Curse you and your schemes! This comes from joining in a fool's project; but I will have my revenge!" and he rushed from the room, just as a body of troopers, in the uniform of the Grand Duke's Guards, galloped up to the iron gates, and leaping from their horses, strove to gain admittance.

"Oh, Signor!" exclaimed Dame Margarita, turning deadly pale, "get out of the house as fast as you can. Castrieci is a terrible man. Holy Virgin! he has fifty barrels of gunpowder in the vaults; he will blow us all up!" and without another word, the old dame hurried out of the saloon, instantly followed by the panic-struck Mr. Wilkins, still in his canonicals.

"Oh, Herbert, save your life!" implored Helen, laying her hand on the statue-like figure of Lord Delamaine. "Forgive one who loves you dearer than life! Nay, if you will not stir, I can still die by your side!"

Lord Delamaine's chest heaved with excess of emotion; he struck his hand violently against his forehead, but still stood unmoved. Helen, in a passionate flood of tears, threw her arms round his neck, she laid her beautiful head upon his breast, and her eyes rested upon his with an expression of love and devotion. The conflict of passion had passed; he looked down into that loving face, and a tear fell upon her cheek. He said not a word, but placing her arm within his, he was passing from the room, when a loud shout was heard from without, as the great gates gave way; at that same instant an appalling explosion took place; Lord Delamaine felt the floor heave beneath his feet; with a frenzied prayer to Heaven, he clasped Helen to his breast, as they were hurled from their feet, and clouds of dust, timbers, walls, and rafters were tossed in wild confusion around and about them.

The moment before the explosion, old Dame Margarita had reached the iron gates, and was drawing back the bolts, crying out at the same time:

"Go back, men! for the love of the Madonna go back! The Signor Castricci is going to blow up the building!"

The men fell back appalled, but a young man in a naval uniform, with an exclamation of "Great God, my Mary!" rushed madly on towards the house. At that moment the west wing was, as it were, lifted from the ground, and scattered wildly and fearfully through the air. The trained horses of the troopers burst from the equally horror-struck men, and galloped furiously over the country. The men were in a measure protected from the falling beams by the high walls and farm buildings round the great court. The naval officer, as he rushed across the court, felt the ground heave beneath him, and then he was thrown violently forward. Still he rose to his feet, amidst a shower of broken timbers, tiles, and stones; except a few slight bruises, he had miraculously escaped serious injury; the remainder of the mansion was in flames, which raged fiercely in the strong wind blowing. The young man, in a wild fever of excitement, rushed into the house through the crushed walls. The west wing was entirely demolished, but the middle of the building was still partly entire, though in flames. Ascending the broken stairs, he perceived a human form clad in white, with a beam of timber lying across his chest. Stooping down he looked at the individual; he was dead; he was in the dress of a clergyman: in his hand he grasped an empty bottle.

Francis heard his name shouted from below, but he still went on leaping over gaps in the floors, till again something white attracted him beneath a great heap of fallen plaister and a pile of broken rafters, forming a kind of shed. Scarcely able to draw his breath, for the smoke was driving rapidly towards him, and the roar of the flames, as they seemed to glory in their destructive power, warned him that there was no time to lose, rushing to the spot, he beheld a female struggling amidst the flames.

"God of Heaven! is this Mary?" and dashing aside the obstructions in his way, he extricated the female. She was quite sensible, being only slightly stunned; he looked into her face, and beheld Helen Probert. "My God! where is Mary?" exclaimed the distracted lover.

Helen's eyes met his, and then in a low voice she said:

"Quite safe, and in Florence by this time. Save him!" and she pointed to a man, lying on his back, with a rafter across his body, and his eyes closed, but still breathing; then he recognized

Lord Delamaine. Putting Helen aside, who was fast recovering the shock, he lifted the beam off the prostrate figure, whilst the roar of the flames, as they first burst into the spot where they were, caused Helen to shriek out, "Oh, God, we are lost!"

Francis De Burgh lifted the senseless body of his enemy in his powerful arms, saying:

"Can you walk, Helen?"

"Yes; God bless you!" was the emphatic answer.

Francis advanced with his burden, followed by Helen, and the next minute several of the troopers had entered the house, headed by Lord Herringstone, to seek him; a loud cheer testified their joy, and putting beams across the gaps in the flooring, they reached his side.

"Good God, Francis!" said Lord Herringstone, "who have you got? We called out to you that Mary was quite safe: but you rushed on like a madman. Heavens!" he continued, "this is Lord Delamaine and Helen Probert. Thank God they are saved! I feared they had perished."

"He is alive, my good lord," answered Francis, laying his burden down, "but what injuries he may have received I know not; happily, Miss Probert seems to have miraculously escaped."

Two of the troopers had also brought out the lifeless body of Mr. Wilkins. Dame Margarita had declared that there were no more persons in the mansion, as her niece had accompanied Miss Grey in her flight, and the farm servants all slept in the out-buildings. Many of the troopers were dispersed over the land to catch the runaway horses.

In the meantime the still senseless body of Lord Delamaine was carried into an out-building, and all the care and attention his devoted wife could bestow, to restore him to consciousness, was done, assisted by Dame Margarita and two other women belonging to the farm.

One of the troopers, by the orders of his officer, rode off to bring a surgeon. In the interim a strict search was made amongst the ruins over the vaults for the bodies of Luigo Castricci and Dame Margarita's son, but without success.

"This is a most strange and incomprehensible affair altogether, Francis," observed Lord Herringstone. "As well as I could understand the old dame, she says that Helen was married to Lord Delamaine instead of Mary, who left this house last evening, accompanied by the old woman's niece and a boy called Bembo, to proceed to the next town, where she would procure a berlin for Florence. Had you not better mount your horse and ride to that town, and see if she reached it, and follow her to Florence? I will stay till the surgeon arrives, and a carriage to convey Helen and her husband to the next village, where there is an excellent inn."

Lord Delamaine. Putting Helen aside, who was fast recovering the shock, he lifted the beam off the prostrate figure, whilst the roar of the flames, as they first burst into the spot where they were, caused Helen to shriek out, "Oh, God, we are lost!"

Francis De Burgh lifted the senseless body of his enemy in his powerful arms, saying:

"Can you walk, Helen?"

"Yes; God bless you!" was the emphatic answer.

Francis advanced with his burden, followed by Helen, and the next minute several of the troopers had entered the house, headed by Lord Herringstone, to seek him; a loud cheer testified their joy, and putting beams across the gaps in the flooring, they reached his side.

"Good God, Francis!" said Lord Herringstone, "who have you got? We called out to you that Mary was quite safe: but you rushed on like a madman. Heavens!" he continued, "this is Lord Delamaine and Helen Probert. Thank God they are saved! I feared they had perished."

"He is alive, my good lord," answered Francis, laying his burden down, "but what injuries he may have received I know not; happily, Miss Probert seems to have miraculously escaped."

Two of the troopers had also brought out the lifeless body of Mr. Wilkins. Dame Margarita had declared that there were no more persons in the mansion, as her niece had accompanied Miss Grey in her flight, and the farm servants all slept in the out-buildings. Many of the troopers were dispersed over the land to catch the runaway horses.

In the meantime the still senseless body of Lord Delamaine was carried into an out-building, and all the care and attention his devoted wife could bestow, to restore him to consciousness, was done, assisted by Dame Margarita and two other women belonging to the farm.

One of the troopers, by the orders of his officer, rode off to bring a surgeon. In the interim a strict search was made amongst the ruins over the vaults for the bodies of Luigo Castricci and Dame Margarita's son, but without success.

"This is a most strange and incomprehensible affair altogether, Francis," observed Lord Herringstone. "As well as I could understand the old dame, she says that Helen was married to Lord Delamaine instead of Mary, who left this house last evening, accompanied by the old woman's niece and a boy called Bembo, to proceed to the next town, where she would procure a berlin for Florence. Had you not better mount your horse and ride to that town, and see if she reached it, and follow her to Florence? I will stay till the surgeon arrives, and a carriage to convey Helen and her husband to the next village, where there is an excellent inn."

"Such was my wish, my lord," said our hero, proceeding to look for his horse, which, fortunately, one of the troopers had contrived to catch.

The next moment he was mounted, and spurring along the road towards the town.

## CHAPTER XLVI.

THREE months have passed since the event recorded in our last chapter took place; and now the Gem and the Daring are ploughing their way through the broad Atlantic, on their way to their island home. We must, as our allotted space draws to a close, very briefly state the few simple events that occurred previous to the departure of Lord Herringstone and family and our hero in the Daring for England.

Under the unceasing care and attention of his fond and devoted wife, Lord Delamaine slowly recovered from the severe injuries he had received. When sufficiently strong to sit up, he requested interview with Lord Herringstone, which was granted. During this interview, little was said of the past; he simply requested his lordship to express his regret that his conduct had caused Miss Grey so much suffering, and he sincerely begged her forgiveness. He acknowledged his wife, and thanked God that she was his wife. He also said he had no intention of disputing the succession of Francis De Burgh to the title and estates of the late Lord Delamaine, as he felt perfectly satisfied that he was the rightful heir; and ended by saying it was not his intention to return to England for many years, and that as soon as he was able he had determined on going with his affectionate wife to Naples.

Lord Herringstone easily enough perceived that there was still much bitterness in the heart of Lord Delamaine; he could not yet forget the past, neither could he conquer the feeling he had so long nourished so unjustly against Francis De Burgh; he, however, expressed his gratitude to him for his generous risk of life in saving him and his wife from the burning mansion. He also explained to Lord Herringstone his connection and great intimacy with Luigo Castricci, who, in truth, urged him to worse acts than he felt inclined to commit. He first met the Italian in London, having fled to England to avoid the punishment of treason, in conspiring against the Grand Duke of Tuscany. On his return to England from Gibraltar, he again met the Signor Castricci, who was preparing to return to Italy, having been invited by a band of conspirators, who wished to create revolutionary feelings in Tuscany, and who declared there were over twenty thousand men ready to rise in Florence alone, and overturn the government. On telling Castricci that he intended himself to proceed to Florence, and how he was situated with respect to Miss Grey, and his feeling of resentment against Francis De Burgh, Luigo Castricci offered, if he would supply him with a certain sum to purchase arms and ammunition, that he would ensure him the possession of Miss Grey without the slightest risk. Lord Delamaine agreed to do so. They left England together, and reached Leghorn, and then proceeded in disguise to Salino, where Castricci planned the whole affair; but not intending the same results as Lord Delamaine himself intended, and about which they had some words. He then requested to know how Lord Herringstone and Francis De Burgh came to arrive at the Castricci mansion with the Duke's troopers at the time they did.

Lord Herringstone stated, that while preparing his yacht for her return to England, the Daring arrived from the Bosphorus on the very night Mary Grey was carried off by the emissaries of Luigo Castricci. The next morning as they were preparing to set out for Florence, Lord Herringstone's groom arrived with the letter from her ladyship. Astonished at the intelligence, they were setting out for Florence to beg the assistance of the authorities to track the abductors, when they encountered the officer of the police and his five men, who had picked up intelligence that a berlin, with four post-horses, with a lady and gentleman inside, had gone towards Piombino, to embark for Elba. Hiring horses, they followed on the track of the fugitives, and on reaching Piombino found out their mistake: there was a lady and gentleman, it was true, but not Mary Grey and her abductor. Thus two days were lost. Baffled and chagrined, they set out for Florence, and on the way were accosted by Pietro Lanzi, who was on his return to procure an armed force to take the conspirators at the Casa Castricci. Lord Herringstone at once had an audience of the Duke, who ordered an officer and twenty men instantly to follow Lord Herringstone to the Castricci mansion; thus they arrived at a critical moment, as they thought, for they did not of course know that Mary Grey, under the guidance of Dame Margarita's niece, and the boy Bembo, had reached the village, and thence Florence, to the infinite joy and delight of Lady Herringstone.

The Signor Castricci had no intention of blowing himself up with his mansion. Short as was the time he had, he knocked in the head of a barrel of gunpowder, laid a train to the trap-door leading out of the vaults, and then fired the train with a pistol, he and his associate, Musono, getting to a sufficient distance before it exploded. Nevertheless, though they escaped destruction by a miracle, the indefatigable Pietro Lanzi and Bembo were lying in ambush for them, and, with the assistance of two of the police, captured Luigo Castricci; Musono escaped out of the country.

Castricci was tried, and condemned to be imprisoned for life; while Pietro Lanzi reaped the reward offered by the government, besides a munificent gift from Lord Herringstone for himself and little Bembo. Dame Margarita and her niece were, through the intercession of Lord Herringstone with the Grand Duke, reinstated in the farm of the Castricci mansion, and Lord Herringstone left them the means of furnishing a neat cottage for themselves.

Mary Grey parted with Helen with much emotion; they spoke no word of the past, but each, as they embraced for the last time, fervently prayed for the other's happiness through life.

On the twenty-fourth of May the Gem and the Daring sailed for England, our hero and his beautiful Mary the happiest of the happy. They touched at Gibraltar, and spent a delightful week with General Grey, who was to resign his post and return to England in July; thus all parties looked forward to a speedy re-union.

While in Florence, Mary Grey presented our hero with the letter received from Mr. Howard, his London solicitor, and left by the female who restored the papers. On opening it, he saw it was from the insurgent Holt's daughter. The letter was written in the most friendly and kind style, and the writer fully explained the way the papers came into her possession. The man who robbed the cottage at Dungarvon with Captain Burton was one of Holt's followers. When separated from the Captain in their flight, he secured them in a safe place, knowing they were of great importance, and determined to use them for his own interest hereafter; but rejoining Holt, and going with a party to conduct the insurgent's daughter to a place of safety, they were attacked, several killed, and he himself escaped to the hills, mortally wounded, though he did not think so at the time. But he quickly found that his wound would cause his death. He was kindly attended by Holt's daughter, who did all she could to alleviate his sufferings. Finding his hour was come, and no priest to be had, he made a confession to her of the robbery at Dungarvon, and his having concealed most valuable documents belonging to Francis De Burgh, describing minutely the place in which he had buried them.

Holt's daughter, after the man's death, sent a person she could trust, and who knew the country well, to search for the papers, which he was at last successful in finding, and brought them to Mrs. M——. During the whole of the trying scenes she went through, she preserved the documents, till her husband finally made his escape to America, and she with her two children quitted Ireland and got to England. Shortly before his escape, her husband was left a large sum by a distant relative, which he contrived to get, through a mercantile house in London, secured to his wife.

On reaching London Mrs. M—— was preparing to advertise in the papers for intelligence of Francis De Burgh, when Mr. Howard's advertisement attracted her notice; thus the papers were restored.

Mrs. M——, after transferring her property to America, followed her husband there.

Deeply grateful for this singular act of gratitude for a trifling service, our hero sincerely hoped the kind-hearted Mrs. M—— might pass the remainder of her days in peace and happiness, undisturbed by further trials.

A splendid run from Gibraltar, brought the Gem and the Daring within sight of the English coast the evening of the fifth day, and before the sun set they beheld the tall pinnacles of the Needles rise before them. The Gem made for Southampton, the Daring made for Portsmouth. To the deep regret of Master Burke, and the intense sorrow of her crew, the little Daring was paid off; but through the great interest of Lord Herringstone, after Master Burke had passed his examination, he was made a lieutenant and appointed to a first-class frigate, and in after years distinguished himself and rose rapidly in the service.

Francis De Burgh purchased the Daring from the government, and had her fitted out as a yacht, constituting his faithful follower Bill Mullaghan her skipper. And as many of the men were paid off, having acquired very large sums from their share of the valuable prizes taken, they eventually, after spending a few weeks ashore, reshipped aboard the Daring yacht which then lay at Southampton. This is, however, anticipating events, for several months passed over before this took place.

As soon as possible our hero went to London, where he met Lord Herringstone by appointment, and both proceeded to a conference with Mr. Howard, the solicitor, to examine the papers in his possession, before asserting his claim to the estates of the late Lord Delamaine. Nothing could be more satisfactory than the papers and documents in the solicitor's hands, there was the marriage certificate, birth, christening, &c., all clear and easily vouched for, as Mr. Howard had ascertained that several witnesses to the documents were still living. Anxious to become acquainted with the causes and reasons of his father's renouncing the title, and living so many years in such retirement, our hero in the evening sat down to reveal the record of his father's life to Lord Herringstone, which **our readers will find in our next and last chapter.**

## CHAPTER XLVII.

WE shall pass over that part of Francis De Burgh's father's narrative already known to our readers, and take up the thread of his story at the period he carried off the Honourable Miss Herringstone, and quitted England in his yacht.

"Horrorstruck by the fall of my unfortunate brother," continues the narrator, "I felt a deep remorse thrill through my frame; and made a solemn vow in my own heart, that if my brother recovered I would never claim the title or estates as long as he existed, unless I should myself live to see him without a child of his own to succeed him: then if I should happen to have a son myself, and I found a remote kinsman succeeding, I would put forward the claims of my son.

"We sailed for Jersey. There, in the presence of competent witnesses I became united to the woman I adored, who was herself most anxious I should keep the vow I had made, for she felt deeply the consequences that had followed one rash act. From Jersey I wrote a long letter to my brother, for I received intelligence from a stranger who arrived there, and who had been in Southampton at the period, that my brother did not and was not likely to die of his wound. In my letter I mentioned my determination of never taking the title or estates whilst he lived, but that a *time might come* that I should do so."

"Ah!" said our hero, pausing in the perusal, and looking at the attentive Lord Herringstone, "this account for the late Lord Delamaine's expression of '*The time is come.*' He must have received his brother's letter, but believing him and all on board to have perished, he in the lapse of years gave them up."

"I have no doubt such was the case, Francis," observed his lordship, "but I feel satisfied, after his meeting with you he became convinced his brother had lived. But go on."

"Some months previous to my intention of carrying off your mother," continued the narrative of Francis's father, "I sold a property I possessed in Dorsetshire, and which I inherited from a near relation, for a sum of £33,000; this sum I placed out at interest in the name of De Burgh, which name I determined to take. The money was placed in the trust of an opulent Scotch house, who only knew me by the name of De Burgh. After our marriage in Jersey, I resolved as my wife wished it, her health suffering from the severe shock her mind and body had received, to proceed and pass the winter at Madeira. The weather became extremely unsettled, and two days after leaving Jersey, a tremendous gale with thick fog from the south-east overtook us. As night came on we ran before the gale under our double-reefed topsails alone, and steering as we supposed a good course, so as to avoid the coast of Ireland, which owing to the dense fog we had not made the previous day. I did not retire to my cabin till near midnight, the storm howled through the rigging, and the sea tremendously heavy, broke at times over our stern. It was a fearful night, still the yacht was a noble boat, and having reduced our sail to a mere wing of the forecourse, she went along without appearing to suffer.

"When I went below I found your mother lying dressed on the sofa, she could not conquer the dread that was over her. I tried to sooth her and calm her apprehensions, and persuaded her to retire to rest, when—oh, God! I shall never forget it—the ship struck with a fearful shock, and instantly heeled over; a wild cry that pierced to my heart, burst from your mother's lips as we were both thrown upon the floor of the cabin. I caught her up in my arms, and strapping a belt containing a large amount of gold round my waist, rushed upon deck. Merciful God! what a scene of horror! the wild sea swept with fearful fury over the doomed craft; you could not see ten yards ahead, the tempest howled in its might, and as we gained the after-part of the vessel, the main and foremast went over the side, carrying with them to eternity five of my ill-fated crew. Just then she beat over the reef, we could not see whether we were on a reef or the mainland, but I judged it was a reef or a large rock. We had two fine life-boats on board, and with incredible exertion one was got into the water, and aided by my gallant and generous fellows, I got your mother wrapped in a mantle, into her; I sprung in and expected the few men left to follow, when a violent surge threw the vessel, rapidly filling, over on her beam ends; the warp broke, and away we drifted from the doomed ship. I saw her sink for a moment, rise upon a giant sea, and the next instant she disappeared for ever. Heavens! the agony of that moment! your mother was insensible, the boat, half full of water, drove broadside before the wind till, leaving your mother down on the stern sheets, I got out an oar and steered her before the sea. Suddenly a huge black object rose before me; I heard the terrible sound of the sea lashing the rocks in wild fury. I let go the oar, for to avert our course was impossible, and catching your mother in my arms, prepared to make an effort to gain land or die together.

"Up, up, we rose on a mighty billow; the next moment the boat was crushed against the black mass before us, and yet the Almighty' han d was there, for the shock threw us on the rock, and before the next sea came I exerted all the power left me, and grasping my adored wife in my arms, I gained some paces in advance. Again the surge came rolling up as if eager for its prey, but I had a fast hold, and for an instant we were submerged; but as it receded I again made an effort, and gaining a kind of level covered with a short scrubby species of plant, I lay down exhausted, pressing your mother, then recovering her senses, to my heart, and fervently returning thanks to Providence for our wonderful preservation.

"Your mother rapidly recovered consciousness; she was shivering with cold, for though the weather was not cold, still her drenched garments struck a chill through her frame. My ill-fated crew had all perished, no doubt, for the yacht went down evidently in deep water. I could come to no conclusion as to exactly where I was, but from my own personal reckoning I judged we might have either struck upon some reef off Valentia Island, or some of the numerous rocks and islands forming Blasque Sound. The storm continued unabated through the remainder of the night, and we anxiously waited for the break of day. It came at last, the light struggling through the dense masses of clouds fell upon a dreary and wild scene indeed. From my knowledge of the chart as soon as it was clear enough I at once saw that the yacht had first struck upon the most eastern of the five islands lying off Pentre Head, forming the Blasque Sound; we had drifted on to the largest, off which appeared several large rocks with their heads just above water. This island had several huts and cabins, to one of these I helped your mother to walk. The first we came to contained a man and his wife and three children; they were miserably poor, ignorant, and totally unable to speak a word of English; they looked at us stupefied. I had some silver in my pocket besides upwards of two hundred pounds in gold, which I had thrust into my belt, and strapped round my waist before leaving the cabin of the yacht. The man looked savage and wild enough; nevertheless nature and the wretched life the man led on that miserable island made him look as he did, for his heart was far from a bad one. I showed him some silver and put it in his hand, and by signs requested a fire might be made, and dry garments of some kind procured till your mother's were dried.

The woman eagerly complied with my wishes, and the man, putting back the silver shook his head, muttered something in Irish, and left the cabin. Our situation was not free from danger, I at first thought, but I was wrong, very wrong; poor, miserable, hard-working creatures, they were, living by what they could fish from the sea, for they had two boats; cultivating the potato on various patches on the island, and on the eggs of the numerous wild fowl and plovers, that frequented the shores of the various islands.

"In a few minutes the man returned with a well-looking young woman dressed in a man's coat, and short canvas petticoats, carrying a heap of dry garments in her arms. The poor people did their best, but unfortunately, not one word of English could any one of them speak. However, not to weary you, my dear boy, with these simple details, we managed the best we could; we had a good fire from wrecked timber; some potatoes and a few hen's eggs were all we had to eat during the two days we stayed there. The third day your dear mother had greatly recovered, though suffering from a severe cold and pains in all her limbs. The gale having gone down, and the sea much calmer, I made the men understand I wished to be conveyed to the main land.

"The man pointed across the sound to a deep kind of inlet on the main, saying: 'Dunvarlings harbour;' and then adding in Irish something about 'Dingle.' I caught the word Dingle, which I knew to be a very good town in the county of Kerry, so I was satisfied to go to Dunvarlings, which could not be far from Dingle. The previous day I had traversed all round the island, thinking some of the bodies of my unfortunate crew might have been washed on shore; but not a vestige of them or the doomed yacht could we discover, the strong tide of the Atlantic had swept them —God knows where!

"It was a very crazy boat that we embarked in. I distributed all the silver I had, and a couple of guineas in gold amongst the grateful creatures, who humbly kissed your mother's hand, and blessed her in their simple way as we parted. I did not like to show much gold —for alas! human nature is weak; for the very sight of the two gold pieces made the men's eyes glisten with delight, but I determined when upon the main to reward them well.

"It took us two hours to reach the main land, and even then, owing to a strong breeze that sprung up and a strong spring flood against us, we could not make the harbour, but landed about a mile to the eastward of it. I gave the astonished crew of the boat five guineas, which they received with a round of blessings in Irish: and then we proceeded to a village where we procured a common cart to Dingle, and putting up at a good inn, we enjoyed what were then a great luxury, a good meal and a good bed.

"We did not wish to create any remarks; our arrival in a common car was not a very uncommon circumstance in that part of the world, and as they could know nothing of our unhappy shipwreck, I resolved to be henceforth dead to the world as Francis Delamaine, and live in the future as Francis De Burgh. Being extremely anxious to hear intelligence of my family, I daily read the English papers; but for some time nothing of any import met my attention. After resting some few days, and purchasing several necessaries, we moved on into the county of Cork, and there I rented a very pretty cottage on the banks of the Miros river. Here, my son, you were born, and to the worthy and kind-hearted pastor, the Rev. Richard Beamish, I confided my story; and my reasons for never again mingling in the world under my own name while my brother lived. Long before this I had learned that he had quite recovered, and that my family considered that the yacht with all aboard had perished at sea.

"Mr. Beamish endeavoured by sound reasoning to prove to me I was wrong; for the sake of my child I was wrong; but the vow I had so solemnly made I would not break, unless under the circumstances already stated. Alas! misfortune still followed my steps; I was struck by a blow from which I never wholly rallied. Your beloved mother never thoroughly recovered the terrible effects of our shipwreck, and a slight cold caught after your birth, consigned her in three weeks to the grave. I cannot dwell upon this sad event, even now, after seventeen years have passed away, my reason for a time wavered; and to that excellent man, the Pastor of Miros, I owe the feeling of resignation I afterwards acquired, in the decrees of Providence. He advised me to travel for awhile through Ireland; I did so, and chancing to see the cottage at Dungarvon, I resolved to reside there for a time; for the very sight of the little church of Miros recalled all the memory of the past so vividly, that my mind gave way under its influence.

"You were nearly four years old when I moved to Dungarvon, having furnished the cottage to my taste, sending the furniture from Cork. Before removing there I made a journey into Scotland, and established a correspondence with the wealthy firm of McGregor, Ivan, and Stuart, and settled the interest I should draw for the use of the £33,000 left in their hands; they had no reason to suppose me any other person than Mr. De Burgh. As you grew up you became my delight, my sole treasure: to instruct you myself in everything was a constant source of exquisite pleasure. I drew my income—much more than I required—from a banking establishment in Waterford. I contrived to hear at times about my family. After my father's death my brother Arthur, still unmarried, went abroad, and inspired with a passion for visiting distant parts of the world went to India. Years passed over, and you grew up all a fond father could wish. Then came a gnawing at my heart, and I felt the gross injustice I was doing to you—my beloved son!

"The wild and ruinous career of Sir Godfrey De Burgh had, after my poor sister's death, dissipated a fine property; his son entered the army, and after some years went to the Cape. Years rolled on and you had reached your sixteenth year, when intelligence reached Eagland that my brother, then Lord Delamaine, had married an officer's widow in Ceylon, by whom he had two sons. This intelligence smote me to the heart, and increased a malady that had attacked me some years before, a kind of disease of the heart; for according to my solemn vow, you were thus for ever cut off from your rightful inheritance. It was not till a few months before the event that introduced you to the notice of your uncle aboard the British Queen, that I learned by paragraphs in the Court paper, that Lord Delamaine had never married; an unfortunate connection with an officer's widow, whom he met in Ceylon, led to this report. They travelled through various parts of Hindostan, when this unfortunate lady and her two children lost their lives by a contagious fever, raging fearfully in Delhi. Thus, again your chance of the inheritance of your ancestors opened before you. You were in your twentieth year when the British Queen was rescued from destruction by your courage and skill.

"Imagine my astonishment and dismay when I learned from a fisherman who came up early in the morning to tell me of your adventure, that amongst the passengers of the British Queen there was a Lord Delamaine and his nephew, a Captain De Burgh, and that they were all coming up to visit Dungarvon. I immediately, as you know, departed for Waterford, where I stayed till the departure of the British Queen. When I returned I found your letter, stating that you intended going on in the Queen to Liverpool. I shall here close my narrative for the present; the fact of Captain De Burgh succeeding to the title of Delamaine absolved me of my vow, and I shall commence proceedings so as to secure you the succession after my brother's death, should you survive."

Here ended the narrative of our hero's father.

"It appears to me," said Lord Herringstone, after some conversation on the subject of the narrative, "it appears to me very singular, that that Scotch house of McGregor, Iver, and Stuart, never took any steps to discover the heir to the property in their hands. They must have seen the advertisements in the various papers."

"Well, it does appear strange," said our hero, "perhaps they may be bankrupt."

"Indeed, such may be the case," said his lordship, "though I scarcely think so; we will get Howard to make inquiries to-morrow."

On questioning the solicitor the next day, he at once said the firm was still the wealthiest in Scotland, but he believed he had heard that they were winding up accounts, and dissolving partnership, but he would write at once.

In a few days an answer was returned, saying they had not

seen the advertisements, that the winding up of their immense business, after so many years, prevented their attending to the circumstance, but that they were ready to pay up interest and capital at any moment when called upon.

As no opposition was put in against the claims of Francis Delamaine to the title and estates of his late uncle, or rather father; and as all the documents were most satisfactory, and the witnesses all ready to come forward, including the Rev. Richard Beamish, of Miros, things rapidly progressed, and a month had scarcely passed before our hero was duly declared to be the rightful heir, and in all due form was installed in his rights.

We have little more to add, except that on the return of General Grey, Lord Delamaine received the hand of beautiful Mary Grey, on which occasion great rejoicings took place at Milton Abbey and Herringstone Castle. Bill Mullaghan, as commander of the Daring, which lay at anchor off Milton Abbey, kept up a most incessant cannonade, the yacht being dressed in flags from the main-mast to the deck. Shortly after Bill proceeded to Ireland to visit his old father, and seeing the happiness of his lord so much increased by his marriage, determined to try if he could bring back a wife with him. In this speculation Bill succeeded admirably, returning in triumph with an extremely pretty young woman from Jolly Dungarvon, his journey, courtship, and marriage, occupying only the short space of seventeen days. Lord Delamaine established his faithful follower in a very neat cottage, near the water, from whence he had a full view of the Daring, of whose beauty he was quite as proud as he was of his wife's.

Whatever were the intentions of Sir Godfrey De Burgh in his secret threats of vengeance against Lord Delamaine they were frustrated in the most summary fashion: quarrelling at a billiard table with a French gentleman, in his passion he struck him a violent blow, and the next day paid the penalty of his rash act, being shot through the heart in the duel that ensued.

THE END.